BASIC
TAILORING

THE ART OF SEWING

BASIC TAILORING

BY THE EDITORS OF TIME-LIFE BOOKS

TIME-LIFE BOOKS, NEW YORK

TIME-LIFE BOOKS

FOUNDER: Henry R. Luce 1898-1967

Editor-in-Chief: Hedley Donovan
Chairman of the Board: Andrew Heiskell
President: James R. Shepley
Group Vice President: Rhett Austell

Vice Chairman: Roy E. Larsen

MANAGING EDITOR: Jerry Korn
Assistant Managing Editors: Ezra Bowen,
David Maness, Martin Mann, A. B. C. Whipple
Planning Director: Oliver E. Allen
Art Director: Sheldon Cotler
Chief of Research: Beatrice T. Dobie
Director of Photography: Melvin L. Scott
Senior Text Editor: Diana Hirsh
Assistant Art Director: Arnold C. Holeywell

PUBLISHER: Joan D. Manley
General Manager: John D. McSweeney
Business Manager: John Steven Maxwell
Sales Director: Carl G. Jaeger
Promotion Director: Paul R. Stewart
Public Relations Director: Nicholas Benton

THE ART OF SEWING
SERIES EDITOR: Carlotta Kerwin
EDITORIAL STAFF FOR
BASIC TAILORING:
Assistant Editor: David L. Harrison
Designer: Virginia Gianakos
Assistant Designer: Robert McKee
Text Editors: Gerry Schremp, Bryce S. Walker
Chief Researchers: Wendy A. Rieder,
Gabrielle Smith (planning)
Staff Writers: Sondra R. Albert, Carol I. Clingan,
Michael T. Drons, Marian Gordon Goldman,
Angela D. Goodman, Frank Kappler,
Marilyn Kendig, Wendy Murphy, Joan S. Reiter,
Sandra Streepey
Research Staff: Cinda Siler, Nancy Jacobsen,
Ginger Seippel, Vivian Stephens, Jean Stratton
Art Staff: Sanae Yamazaki (art coordinator),
Angela Alleyne, Penny Burnham,
Patricia Byrne, Catherine Caufield,
Jean Held, Jill Losson
Editorial Assistant: Kathleen Beakley

EDITORIAL PRODUCTION
Production Editor: Douglas B. Graham
Assistant Production Editor: Gennaro C. Esposito
Quality Director: Robert L. Young
Assistant Quality Director: James J. Cox
Copy Staff: Rosalind Stubenberg (chief),
Mary Orlando, Ricki Tarlow, Florence Keith
Picture Department: Dolores A. Littles,
Jessy S. Faubert
Traffic: Feliciano Madrid

THE CONSULTANTS
Salvatore Bertolone has been teaching the craft
of tailoring for more than 25 years. He has also
served as production manager for an apparel
manufacturing firm. At present, his teaching time
is divided between The High School of Fashion
Industries and the Fashion Institute of Technology in New York.

Gretel Courtney taught for many years at the
French Fashion Academy in New York City. She
has studied patternmaking and design at the
Fashion Institute of Technology in New York and
haute couture at the French Fashion Academy.

Tracy Kendall has worked in many capacities for
various fashion firms in New York. She is pres-
ently a freelance costumer and set designer for
television commercials and print advertising.

Julian Tomchin is a textile designer who has been
awarded the Vogue Fabric Award and a Coty
Award of the American Fashion Critics. A grad-
uate of Syracuse University's Fine Arts College,
he has been chairman of the Textile Design Department at the Shenkar College of Fashion and
Textile Technology in Tel Aviv and now teaches
at the Parsons School of Design in New York.

Portions of this book were written by Don
Earnest and Henry Moscow.
Valuable assistance was provided by these
departments and individuals of Time Inc.:
Editorial Production, Norman Airey; Library,
Benjamin Lightman; Picture Collection, Doris
O'Neil; Photographic Laboratory, George Karas;
TIME-LIFE News Service, Murray J. Gart;
Correspondents Margot Hapgood and Dorothy
Bacon (London), Ann Natanson (Rome), Maria
Vincenza Aloisi (Paris).

CONTENTS

1   THE TRIM, TAILORED LOOK   6

2   FABRICS TO SUIT YOURSELF   20

3   FIRST STEP TO A PERFECT FIT   48

4   MASTERWORKS OF TAILORING   80

5   TAILORED TROUSERS   168

APPENDIX

GLOSSARY   200
BASIC STITCHES   202
CREDITS, ACKNOWLEDGMENTS   204
INDEX   205

6

1

THE TRIM, TAILORED LOOK

ashions in clothes are notoriously fickle; today's chic is tomorrow's cliché. But behind the endless whirl of fashion lie two basic and unchanging methods of adorning the human figure—dressmaking and tailoring. Dressmaking begins with a piece of relatively supple material, such as silk or cotton, that is simply draped or wrapped around the body. The resulting garment may be called a toga, a sari or an evening gown. But by any name

THE LEGACY OF BEAU BRUMMELL

it adjusts itself to the wearer and takes its shape chiefly from the contours of the body.

The second basic method of making clothes begins with relatively stiff fabrics, such as tweeds, worsteds and heavy silks, which are cut into precise patterns. The pieces are then sewed together with form-giving seams and darts and reinforced with a firm structure of padding and interfacing. These are the techniques of tailoring.

In essence, the difference between dressmaking and tailoring is a little like the difference between a painter's soft brush stroke and the ring of a sculptor's chisel. The painter's dab of color adorns the surface to which it is applied, without giving structural shape. But the sculptor's stone has shape and structure of its own. Thus, the tailor becomes a sculptor of fabric. The very name of his craft comes from the French *tailleur,* one who cuts—a term that applies equally well to a cutter of stone or a cutter of cloth.

The art of tailoring began somewhere in Europe during the Middle Ages, practiced exclusively by men for the nobility. Upper-class gentlemen took their appearance seriously, for in a hierarchical society like feudal England or France, clothes proclaimed a man's rank. The length of the train on his robe or of his pointed shoes denoted his station. High noblemen wore toes that stretched out 24 inches beyond the end of the foot; mere gentlemen had to be content with only 12 inches.

When fashions changed with the whim of the king or other ranking tastemaker, the tailor interpreted these whims—always keeping the emphasis on the shape of the garment rather than the shape of the man inside it. For example, Elizabethan nobles wore doublets with puffed-up shoulders and heavily padded bellies, and they sported breeches with still more padding. Amid this fashion pageant, the one thing nobody thought worth doing was to use tailoring techniques to achieve the trim and subtly shaped fit we know today as the tailored look.

In fact the few suits surviving from the 18th Century show clearly that men's clothes of that time did not fit at all in a modern sense. They simply enveloped the figure; any freedom of movement or relative comfort came from the often inelegant fact of being too large. Moreover, the changes in men's fashions were almost entirely superficial—distorting the silhouette here and adding some ornament there.

However, the 18th Century was a time of change all through Western civilization, and the genteel realm of men's attire was due for its own revolution. The *provocateur* turned out to be the English gentleman of leisure. Unlike his French confrere, he had never been forced into long attendance at court, dawdling about throne rooms, as ornamental and useless as a hothouse flower. The English lord spent a great deal of time riding, racing and hunting on his country estate. There he lived in sportsman's clothes—simpler and more practical than a courtier's finery. Instead of a silk dress coat, he went about in a frock coat of sturdy wool cloth, and breeches of buckskin extending into his riding boots. For greater ease in the saddle, he cut away the front of his frock coat. Instead of the three-cornered hat that perched precariously over the powdered wig of the courtier, he developed the topper, which was easier to keep on his head at full gallop and which served as a kind of crash helmet should he be unhorsed.

So popular was this sporting gear that by the late 1700s it had migrated into town and won admission to even the finest London clubs. This acceptance of informality by London gentry was part of a Continent-wide turning away from the ornate past that occurred not only in clothes but in architecture and the other creative arts. The new taste for simplicity did not necessarily mean an end to elegance. Quite the contrary. The clean lines of avant-garde painters like France's Jacques-Louis David were the epitome of elegance, as were the Classical proportions of the porticoed buildings designed in England by men such as John Nash—and by Thomas Jefferson in America.

The fashion counterpart of these trendsetters was a young man about London named George Bryan Brummell, who became known to his contemporaries and to posterity as Beau Brummell.

A fellow Londoner, the poet Byron, once remarked that his era could boast three great men: himself, Napoleon and Brummell. Among the gentlemen of Regency England for whom style was everything, Byron's remark was by no means facetious. To these career dandies and boulevardiers, Beau Brummell was a genuine revolutionary and high achiever, who led them out of the wilderness of outmoded puffery into the elegance of perfect fit. In so doing, he codified the principles of modern tailoring.

It was Brummell's genius to recognize what could be done with structural elements skillfully laid in beneath the surface of men's tailored clothes. Keenly conscious

Clad in well-cut prototypes of today's tailored suits, these Frenchmen of 1826 display the sculptured style set a few years earlier by the modish Beau Brummell in London. The first three models on the left wear pantaloons

anchored under the instep, a Brummell innovation; the fourth shows the still-newer fashion of loose-cuffed trousers. All the garments are turned out in conservative fabrics and colors, with the emphasis on immaculate fit.

of his lean, well-proportioned body, he demanded clothes that were subtly shaped to accentuate his physique. His goal was a kind of idealized natural figure, like those in the newly unearthed Roman sculpture.

Starting with the unadorned lines of the country gentleman's sporting gear, he literally reshaped men's fashion from the inside out. Not that Brummell, whose father had been private secretary to Lord North and later High Sheriff to Berkshire, ever soiled his own hands with a tailor's shears or needle. Rather, he shopped around London until he found two tailors who would cut his clothes exactly as he wanted.

What Beau Brummell wanted, to begin with, was fit. And in the end he wanted to look the exact opposite of the ostentatious fop. His standard outfit was a streamlined version of the hunting costume. For morning, he wore a blue cutaway coat with a buff waistcoat and buff buckskin pantaloons tucked into his knee-length black Hessian boots. His cravat was always crisp, snowy and perfectly tied—even if it took his valet all morning to achieve the effect. His evening clothes were much the same, except that the waistcoat was white, and in place of buckskins and boots he wore long black pantaloons that buttoned at the ankles, striped silk stockings and black pumps.

Any rigors that Brummell's tailors suf-

These early-20th Century belles wear decorously feminine adaptions of the man-tailored look. Though the 1902 American suits *(center)* retain a ladylike flare in their skirts, the jackets have taken on trimmer lines and notched lapels—supplemented with high-collared shirts and knotted ties. In the English walking costumes of 1909 on either side, strictly tailored silhouettes are softened by a shawl collar or puffed sleeves.

fered in pleasing him—and there must have been many—were amply repaid when the cream of the cream of London society followed Brummell to their doors, demanding to be outfitted in clothes of the same cut and proportions. "Yes, his tailor makes him," Brummell remarked of one expensively turned-out fellow—and added with immodest accuracy, "Now I—I make my tailor."

In his prime, roughly the years from 1800 to 1816, Beau Brummell was the supreme stylesetter and tastemaker of Regency London, the original best-dressed man. Even his close friend the Prince Regent—first gentleman of the realm, future George IV, and himself an assiduous student of fashion—deferred to Brummell. On one occasion, according to the poet Thomas Moore, an eyewitness, the Prince "began to blubber when told that Brummell did not like the cut of his coat."

As single-mindedly as he had pioneered good fit, Brummell set about removing any remaining aspects of the stables from the drawing rooms of the aristocracy. The dandies of the day had either become indifferent to their horsy aromas or tried to mask them ineffectively with perfume. The fastidious Beau insisted on absolute cleanliness, spending hours on his bath and toilette, and changing his linen three times a day.

Brummell's attention to detail also served to set him apart from the admiring throng. His boots, for example, had to be polished to a high shine, not only on the tops but also on the soles—an unheard-of refinement that, like everything else he did, provoked endless comment. Upon being asked what he used for polish, Brummell replied, "champagne—the froth of champagne."

Alas, his extravagant life style (and a penchant for gambling) eventually exhausted the £30,000 he had inherited from his father; in 1816 he fled to Calais to escape his creditors. Hopelessly in debt, he was never able to live again in England. By the time of his death in 1840 he had apparently lost not only his fortune but all interest in clothes, and had grown slovenly in his personal habits. What later generations remembered, however, was not the broken old man but the dashing young Beau, the Emperor of Fashion, who had dictated even to royalty.

Nor was it just the men who eventually became Beau Brummell's disciples, for any breakthrough in male fashion so successful and pervasive was bound to arouse the women of society, first to envy and then to emulation. By the latter part of the 17th Century, women had already begun donning a duplicate of the man's riding coat when they joined the hunt. They also found the riding coat a useful garment when traveling in the uncomfortable coaches of the period. A lady typically had such a coat made by her father's or husband's tailor—if need be, sending her measurements by post to London. But as travel became easier and the Brummell revolution took hold in the 19th Century, a lady often paid a personal visit to one of the London tailoring establishments.

In subsequent decades, as Victorian women took part in more and more outdoor activities, increasing numbers of tailors came forward to outfit them. Tailored costumes of great ingenuity were devised for yachting, for walking, for fishing, for shooting, for driving (in a hackney coach) and even for mountain climbing. Their chic, however, was not always matched by practicality. A tartan "Costume for the moors" of 1887, from the top-drawer women's tailor Redfern, was a model of trim fit above the waist. From the waist down, however, the tartan was spread over the then-fashionable bustle (that "monstrous monkey behind," as one victim of the appendage called it) so that the long skirt degenerated into a billowing extravaganza. Nevertheless, the ladies adored what they called "tailor-mades." In fact, the demand for such clothes was so great that many ladies' dressmakers found they had to learn to imitate the tailored look in order to survive. By the 1890s, they had modified their dressmaking techniques to turn out coats and jackets with firm, clean-cut, uncluttered lines. The tailored look— whether created by tailor or seamstress —was firmly entrenched in Paris, London, New York and Boston. And the trinity of coat or jacket with skirt and blouse became a staple of everyday wear—the modern suit, which has never since been absent from ladies' closets.

The pantsuit, delight of today's liberated woman, did not win acceptance so easily. Western man was loath to let his wife and daughter wear trousers. When Amelia Bloomer and her sister feminists, around 1850, displayed 12 inches or less of demure ankle below the pantaloons of their "Bloomer Costume," society was outraged. And the pioneer women's righters discreetly pulled back from radical modes of dress to press their attack on other fronts.

However, the great bicycling craze of the '90s gave women a legitimate excuse to wear a type of primordial pants in public —knee-length knickers at this time, with stockings or gaiters below. True tailored trousers, however—the full-length type virtually indistinguishable from a man's—did not make their way into the wardrobe of the average woman until the 1930s. Then, almost overnight, the glamorous Marlene Dietrich swept away the last hesitancy by posing for photographers with her famous legs sheathed in custom-made trousers.

Unfortunately, every woman was not blessed with Dietrich's shape. Nor were the tailors of the '30s and '40s entirely adept at modifying so mannish a garment as trousers to the subtleties of the female anatomy. The disastrous results of some of the more primitive efforts were summed up by one wit in a famous couplet:

"Ladies in slacks
Should not turn their backs."

Today's designers and manufacturers of clothes for women have obviously learned their lesson. Just as the tailors of Regency London discovered techniques for catering to both a trim Beau Brummell and a pudgy Prince Regent, women's tailors now know how to cut, trim, pad or reinforce a pair of pants—or any other garment—so that it will flatter almost any woman's shape. As a result, tailored clothes have become chic and appropriate for women as well as men, no matter where they are—at work, at home, at the opera or cantering through the countryside on horseback. Indeed, the basic tailoring methods of today can produce for a woman the kind of trim-fitting, finely detailed, man-tailored pantsuit of which even Beau Brummell might have approved.

A stylish cut for business

The two-piece suit is the staple of any tailored wardrobe, especially that of a business person whose workaday contacts do not allow for informal sportswear. The double-breasted charcoal pinstripe at center left has been a stockbroker's and lawyer's favorite for decades, while the wider-lapelled two-button gray, offset with a large bow tie, gives a more contemporary look to the sales executive. Long considered the special preserve of the professional custom tailor, garments such as these are well within the competence of the home tailor.

The same smartly tailored look is just as right (and just as workable) for women's wear, whether in the office, at luncheons or for shopping downtown. The glen-plaid suit in the foreground, for example, with its crisply cut jacket and trousers, proves as flattering to a woman's figure as its masculine counterparts have always been to a man's.

Casual grace for day wear

The easygoing lines of the tailored daytime outfits on these pages bespeak leisure. The wrapped coatdress of pale wool gabardine in the foreground would be just right for tea at Claridge's or for a 10th reunion. And its simple lines make it a good beginner's tailoring project.

The sportier and more complex camel coat and pants ensemble of wool melton *(center)* can be tailored to take in a day at the racetrack —nicely accompanied by the Shetland wool sport jacket and twill gabardine slacks at far right.

Elegance for evening

Tailored evening clothes achieve their bravura presence by simple means, such as uncluttered styling and exquisite fabrics that are a special pleasure for the home needlecrafter to handle.

The woman's waist-nipped evening suit at right, for example, is an understated design executed in a smart imported wool gabardine that invites such immaculate detailing as bound buttonholes and inverted pocket pleats. With similar restraint, the man's dinner jacket and silk-lined wool crepe cape depend for drama mainly on the silhouette they create—and the cape is perhaps the simplest of all tailoring projects.

2
FABRICS
TO SUIT
YOURSELF

Britain's highest judicial officer, the Lord Chancellor, presides over the House of Lords while seated atop a large square cushion of red wool. At first glance, this seat —with neither arms nor back—seems a rather humble perch for so lofty a peer. But for centuries the woolsack has been a symbolic seat of honor, a tacit recognition by England's government that a significant portion of the country's original wealth and

THE EXALTED ORDER OF ENGLISH WOOLS

livelihood sprang from the production and marketing of woolen textiles. Today, it also serves as a reminder that English woolens are still the best in the world (and the *sine qua non* of fine custom tailoring).

Wool cloth has always been the classic fabric for tailoring. Other textiles—linen, silk, cotton and many synthetics—lend themselves to attractive tailored clothes. But none possess the versatility, durability and body of fabric made from wool. The tough, resilient woolen fibers can be spun and woven into the lightest of tropical weights, or made into heavy tweeds and worsteds that will stave off the cold of Northern winters.

Moreover, these high-quality woolens are easy to stitch and will hold their shape through years of arduous wear. And while many countries besides England produce woolens, the British consistently have made the finest woolens for more than 800 years. From the 12th to the 19th centuries, wool manufacture was the country's single most important and lucrative industry.

But it started much earlier than that. When Caesar's legions landed in Britain in 55 B.C., they found that the natives kept large flocks of domesticated sheep and were already weaving cloth. With their passion for organization, the Romans soon set up factories at Venta Belgarum (later renamed Winchester) for spinning, weaving and finishing cloth. By the Third Century a geographer named Dionysius Periegetes was touting the cloth woven in Britain for the emperors as the product of a "wool so fine it is comparable to a spider's web."

As the Roman Empire declined, so did England's wool business. Not until after the arrival of the Normans did the industry regain its former eminence. Within 60 years of the Conquest, large numbers of French monks came to Britain to found abbeys in the remote marshes and valleys. They started raising sheep, and quickly became the largest producers of raw wool in Britain. When Richard the Lionhearted fell into the hands of the Holy Roman Emperor on his way home from the Third Crusade, the good monks donated an entire year's clip to help pay the King's ransom.

Though they were canny sheep raisers, the monks were not clothmakers. The spinning and weaving were accomplished in centralized towns, such as London, Lincoln, Oxford, Huntingdon and—once again—Winchester. The weavers sold cloth to the Crown—Henry II sent the Sheriff of Lincolnshire to buy several lengths in 1182—and started up a brisk export trade. By the 13th Century, cities as far away as Venice were importing English woolens.

Despite the growing popularity of the English fabric abroad, many Englishmen still preferred the fancier cloths imported from Flanders: silks, linens and some woolens as well. To protect and encourage the domestic industry, Edward II decreed in 1326 that no imported cloth could be bought except by the nobility, "their children born in wedlock," clerics and those seculars who paid £40 a year for their rent. This meant that most of the middle class, all of the lower classes—and not a few illegitimate aristocrats—had no choice but to learn to love English woolens.

Subsequent monarchs continued Edward's protective policies, and added some crafty devices of their own. In 1331, Edward III initiated a devastating talent drain in Flanders. With letters of protection and promises of very liberal franchises, he lured hundreds of skilled Flemish weavers to England. This clever maneuver all but destroyed the Flemish wool industry. Within a century, for example, the population of Ypres, a major weaving town, fell from a flourishing

80,000 to fewer than 6,000 inhabitants.

By the time of Elizabeth I, woolen goods provided 80 per cent of England's exports. And still the protective laws continued. In 1571 the Queen ruled that on Sundays and holy days every man, woman and child over the age of six had to wear a woolen cap out of doors. The fine for being caught bareheaded was three shillings and fourpence. Charles II went a macabre step further in 1665 by pushing through Parliament a bill that required every dead Englishman to be buried in a fine woolen shroud.

These measures paid off. In the 17th Century more Englishmen earned their living at cloth manufacturing than in all other industries put together.

Much of the popularity of English fabrics was focused on a special kind of woolen cloth called worsted. In the 12th Century the little village of Worstead in East Anglia had pioneered the making of a smooth, durable cloth woven from tightly spun yarn. Thus, some 700 years before England's custom clothiers created the tailored look in men's and women's fashions, such contemporary tailoring favorites as serge and gabardine worsteds constituted the top of the line of English fabrics.

Eventually Scotland also contributed to the industry. The brightly colored, cross-checked Scottish tartans had for hundreds of years been the ordinary dress of the Highland people, often reflecting their regional and clan loyalties. But after English forces crushed a rebellion of the Highland Scots at the Battle of Culloden in 1746, Parliament outlawed tartans as odious symbols of the late resistance.

By 1822, however, anti-Scottish feelings had cooled, and King George IV decided to show up in Edinburgh for a state visit wearing a red tartan kilt. Though his intent was politic, and the result gratifying in diplomatic terms, the actual execution was a bit embarrassing. The Hanoverian monarch had decked himself out in a tartan whose design belonged to the deposed Scottish royal line—the Stewarts.

Despite His Majesty's gaffe, in the wake of his visit tartans came into such vogue in England that society wits complained of "Highland Fever" or "Tartanitis." Fashionable folk sported tartans in their kilts, in tight-fitting trousers (trews), in tailored jackets and even as decorations for houses. Queen Victoria raised tartanitis to epidemic proportions when she decorated her second home in Balmoral, Scotland, in 1853. The Queen used tartans for rugs, chairs, sofas, curtains. Even the ceilings were bedecked with bright tartans.

While the tartan fad swept England and even France, another family of ancient Scottish fabric, called tweed, was gaining an even more permanent popularity. Villages near the English border, such as Galashiels and Hawick, and Peebles, nestled on the banks of the River Tweed itself, produced the nubby herringbone and hound's-tooth checks. But the sturdiest, warmest and perhaps most durable of the tweeds was the local cloth from the Outer Hebrides islands, off the Scottish coast. This thick, rough-surfaced woolen was called Harris tweed after the name of the main island's Southern district, and every yard of it was—and is —completely hand woven.

In the making of a typical bolt of Harris, a small farmer, or crofter, would clip the fleece from his sheep and wash it in rain water. His wife and daughters would dye the wool with wild plants they had picked from the moors and rocky shores, then card and spin it by hand. Next, the farmer—sometimes aided by his family—stood for hours on end, weaving the cloth on a hand loom in his living room. When a long web had been woven, a call would go out to the neighbors to help with the last step in processing: a softening and shrinking procedure known as waulking.

With an eat-drink-and-be-merry spirit (below) akin to an American barn-raising party, the local women would soak the tweed in ammonia and soapsuds. Then they would knead the cloth against a long scrubboard, using their feet when their arms and hands gave out. Finally the cloth was strung up to dry in the wind.

When Harris tweed began appearing in London shops in the mid-19th Century, it met with instant success. Soon Americans too were clamoring for bolts of the rugged tweed that carried a romantic aura of mist and heather, and even a lingering scent of peat smoke from the weavers' small cottages. Ultimately it became the most popular tailoring tweed in all the 20 centuries of England's wool-making history.

Ten women of the Scottish Hebrides use their feet to work a bolt of soaked and treated tweed against a communal washboard in the ancient softening and shrinking process called waulking. Two others grind grain in a hand mill for dinner. The scene appeared in a 1772 travel book by naturalist Thomas Pennant, who reported that the women—who sang while they waulked —sounded like a "troop of female daemonics."

Classic clothes for tailoring

Fine tailoring rests on a base of certain classic fabrics—primarily the woolens and worsteds shown on these pages. Besides having a stylishly dignified look, these materials possess a rare degree of body and strength that enables them to hold a tailored shape.

The source of their strength and substance is the weave, which is dense and compact, and produces a relatively hard, smooth finish. In the case of the worsteds, the yarns have been tightly twisted for extra toughness. The navy serge at far left, the glen plaid below it, and the beige gabardine at bottom are all worsteds. The Saxony plaid and houndstooth check at far right—both hard woolens—have the same body and are almost as tough. Any of these fabrics would be perfect for a business suit. And the bolder plaid woolen *(third from left)* is right for a tailored jacket, or for a striking pair of party trousers.

A sporty look from soft weaves

Some fabrics seem to belong out of doors—the rough country tweeds, the sporty knits, the comfortable flannels that bring an air of relaxation to the most fastidiously tailored costume. Woven more loosely than the hard-faced worsteds and woolens, they have a built-in suppleness.

Thus the heavy novelty plaid below, the green-and-blue Harris tweed next to it, and the olive-speckled tweed at far right will all work up into garments with soft, easy lines that tend to shape themselves naturally to the person who wears them. So too, will the light-blue double knit, with its extra degree of stretchability. The Kelly-green flannel is a cheerful compromise, soft to the touch, but with body enough for crisp tailoring.

All such soft fabrics require extra care in cutting and stitching so that they do not stretch out of alignment. In addition they may require underlinings to provide the substance, or body, needed for shaping.

Warm weather lightweights

The multicolored silks, cottons and linens of summertime bring a special brightness to tailored clothes. They should be chosen with caution, however, to be certain they are neither too thin nor too loosely woven to hold a tailored shape.

Shown here are six such lightweight fabrics. They are, left to right, a novelty cotton, raw silk, a cotton blend reminiscent of homespun, Thai silk, Indian cotton and linen. All will make up into cool and crisp clothes for warm weather.

Choosing the right materials

The chart at right gives brief descriptions of the most frequently used tailoring materials, and tells what you need to know in order to select the best one for your own tailoring project. For example, the first category on the chart, Makeup, deals with the various fabrics' weave, texture and finish—characteristics that affect the way the materials behave during tailoring and subsequent wear.

Though each fabric has distinctive makeup, appearance, etc.—as the chart shows—certain general rules are applicable to most of them. Linings for all wool and linen women's garments can be made from China silk, silk taffeta, acrylic crepe, rayon or polyester blends; for men's garments, the heavier silk surah, polyester blends or rayon are preferable. To line cotton garments, cotton blends or polyester blends are best. For silk, line with silk or polyester blends. Underlinings, used only for women's garments, can be made from special rayons with trademark names such as SiBonne and Siri.

When choosing interfacing material for a wool garment for men, you will need wool interfacing, haircloth and protective cover cloth. For a woman's garment, interfacing is made entirely of wool. For women's linen, cotton and silk garments, substitute lightweight wool interfacing.

FABRIC NAMES	MAKEUP
WOOL cavalry twill	Hard-finished twill weave worsted of medium weight, characterized by a pronounced and steeply angled diagonal rib.
WOOL Donegal tweed	A soft-finished and thickly napped twill weave available in both medium and heavy weights.
WOOL double knit	A hard-finished firm knit available in light to heavy weights. The fabric is constructed of two layers, interlocked back to back, leaving both sides thinly nubbed.
WOOL flannel	A soft-finished plain or twill weave available in light to medium weights. The twisted yarns used for the weft, or crosswise threads, are full of air pockets; as a result, flannel serves as excellent insulation for the body in cold weather.
WOOL gabardine	A hard-finished twill worsted of light to heavy weight and exceptional durability; characterized by diagonal ribbing.
WOOL Harris tweed	A soft-finished twill weave of medium to heavy weight. Authentic handwoven Harris (there are many mass-produced imitations) carries the certification of the Harris Tweed Association: a globe surmounted by a cross, stamped on the selvage of the fabric at three-yard intervals.
WOOL novelty tweed	A soft-finished plain weave of varying weights with an uneven texture produced by the combination of two or more novelty, or irregularly spun, yarns of varying thickness.
WOOL saxony	A soft-finished plain weave of medium weight made from closely twisted, fine yarn developed in the German province of Saxony. The name has since become a synonym for a range of lightly napped woolens and worsteds.
WOOL serge	A hard-finished twill weave of medium weight, woven with diagonal wales or ridges that run at a 45° angle from the lower left to the upper right selvages of the fabric. Serge is noted for holding a crease well, but it tends to become shiny with wear.
WOOL tropical worsted	A hard-finished plain or novelty weave of light weight. Tropical worsted holds a crease well, and the porous weave and tightly twisted yarns make it a comfortable fabric for hot-weather garments.
WOOL unfinished worsted	A hard-finished plain worsted of heavy weight. Despite the term unfinished, it is woven smooth and the slight nap that characterizes the fabric is applied to its surface during the finishing process.
COTTON novelty weave	A hard-finished plain or twill cotton of varying weights, with an uneven texture produced by yarns that are spun with deliberate irregularities.
COTTON seersucker	A hard-finished plain-weave washable cotton of light weight, distinguished by alternating crinkled and flat lengthwise stripes.
LINEN suit weight	A hard-finished plain-weave linen of medium weight. Linen is notable for the clean, crisp shape it takes. The smooth fibers resist soiling and also conduct heat—away from the wearer, thus making this a comfortable fabric for hot-weather garments.
SILK linen textured	A hard-finished plain-weave silk of mediumweight yarns that are subtly graded in thickness—a characteristic of linen yarns.

APPEARANCE	SPECIAL HANDLING	USES
mooth-surfaced solid colors, especially military tans.	None.	Men's and women's coats, jackets and sport slacks. Women's skirts.
Multicolored and rough-surfaced. Donegal tweed is woven with a single color for the warp yarn and a blend of colors n the weft—a technique developed in County Donegal, Ireand.	Should be lined.	Men's and women's suits, coats, jackets and trousers. Women's A-line and gored skirts.
ightly nubbed surface, in solid colors and patterns.	Ball-point pins and needles and polyester thread should be used. For machine stitching, the thread should be kept under loose, balanced tension. When the fabric is laid out, it should be kept flat to prevent stretching.	Primarily for women's garments—all types of sportswear, jackets and coats, trousers and skirts.
ightly napped, in solid colors, most notably grays.	All garments should be lined. A minimum number of pins should be used in working on the fabric; otherwise the wool nap will wear and show the marks of pin holes.	Men's and women's suits, jackets and trousers. Women's A-line and pleated skirts.
mooth-surfaced solid colors; the selection is usually widst in late winter, when spring pastels are introduced.	Because of its clear, hard finish, machine stitching permanently marks the fabric. Thus, precision sewing is essential.	Men's and women's sportswear, suits, coats and trousers. Women's A-line and pleated skirts.
ubbed surface; multicolor—especially peaty brown nd beige combinations derived from the traditional colors otained with native dyes.	In men's garments, trouser knees need additional reinforcement with underlining. All cut edges should be overcast to keep them from raveling.	Men's sport jackets and coats. Women's jackets, coats, gored and A-line skirts.
ariegated surfaces and multicolored effects in which ach yarn is a different hue.	Women's garments should be fully underlined. All cut edges should be overcast.	Men's and women's coats and jackets.
ightly napped; solid colors, mottled multicolors, and mall-scaled plaids, including glen plaids.	None.	Men's jackets, vests and sport slacks. Women's skirts, slim-styled coats and jackets.
mooth-surfaced solid colors, notably navy blue.	None.	Men's and women's suits, coats, jackets and trousers. Women's A-line and pleated skirts.
mooth-surfaced light colors; suitable for summer.	Stress areas should be lined.	Men's and women's suits, jackets and trousers. Women's skirts.
ightly napped; solid colors, plaids and checks.	None.	Men's and women's suits, jackets and trousers. Women's skirts.
ariegated surfaces and multicolored effects produced ith yarns of one or more colors.	Soft woven fabrics should be fully underlined. Because of the irregularity of the yarn and weave, novelty cottons should not be cut with pinking shears.	Women's suits with simple lines; A-line and gored skirts; jackets.
pple-surfaced two-color combinations that follow the alrnating stripes of its weave, in solid colors, and in checks, aids and other patterns.	Stress areas such as the seats of skirts should be lined.	Men's suits, jackets and trousers. Women's A-line skirts, tailored jackets and pants.
mooth-surfaced; solid colors and patterns.	None.	Men's and women's suits, jackets and trousers. Women's A-line, gored and pleated skirts.
mooth-surfaced; lustrous, solid colors and prints.	Women's garments should be fully underlined.	Men's and women's suits, jackets and trousers. Women's A-line skirts.

Preparing the fabrics

The technique of tailoring combines more kinds of fabrics in a single garment than does any other sewing method. Most of these fabrics require preparation—straightening of the grain or preshrinking—if they are to work together perfectly.

Knit fabrics and lining materials are the easiest to prepare. Both can be sufficiently straightened with an L square as shown at right. And because knits are flexible and linings are attached rather loosely, neither requires preshrinking.

For woven fabrics the more time-consuming but also more accurate method of straightening by pulling threads should be used. To be certain the sizes remain constant, these outer fabrics must then be preshrunk as described opposite (even when the label says this has been done). Wool interfacing and twill tape do not require straightening but should be shrunk by being immersed in water, air dried and steam pressed. Other interfacings, underlining and pocketing materials need only be steam pressed.

Once the fabric is ready for cutting it should be folded in such a way that the edges align, the grains run straight and the designs match. If the fabric has a discernible nap, mark its direction before pinning the folded fabric. Stroke the material with the palm of your hand, back and forth, parallel to the selvages; the direction that feels smoother is the one in which the nap runs.

PREPARING KNIT GARMENT FABRIC AND LINING FABRIC

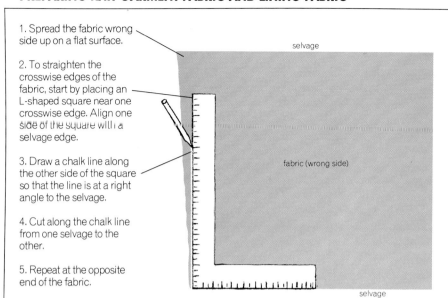

1. Spread the fabric wrong side up on a flat surface.

2. To straighten the crosswise edges of the fabric, start by placing an L-shaped square near one crosswise edge. Align one side of the square with a selvage edge.

3. Draw a chalk line along the other side of the square so that the line is at a right angle to the selvage.

4. Cut along the chalk line from one selvage to the other.

5. Repeat at the opposite end of the fabric.

selvage

fabric (wrong side)

selvage

PREPARING WOVEN FABRIC

A STRAIGHTENING THE CROSSWISE EDGES

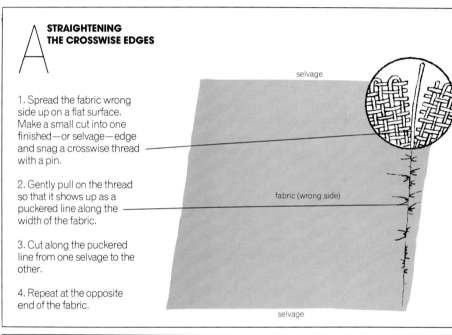

1. Spread the fabric wrong side up on a flat surface. Make a small cut into one finished—or selvage—edge and snag a crosswise thread with a pin.

2. Gently pull on the thread so that it shows up as a puckered line along the width of the fabric.

3. Cut along the puckered line from one selvage to the other.

4. Repeat at the opposite end of the fabric.

selvage

fabric (wrong side)

selvage

B CHECKING THE ALIGNMENT OF THE EDGES

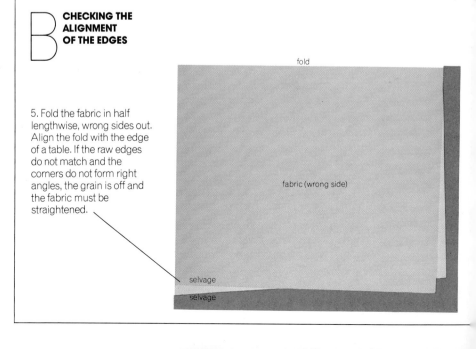

5. Fold the fabric in half lengthwise, wrong sides out. Align the fold with the edge of a table. If the raw edges do not match and the corners do not form right angles, the grain is off and the fabric must be straightened.

fold

fabric (wrong side)

selvage

selvage

PRESHRINKING AND STRAIGHTENING THE FABRIC

6. If the fabric is not washable, send it to a dry cleaner to be preshrunk by steam pressing. Then recheck the alignment of the edges (Step 5). If the fabric still needs straightening, skip to Step 9.

7. If the fabric is washable, preshrink it by folding it in deep folds and immersing it in cold water for about an hour. Then gently squeeze out the water, but do not wring. Lay the fabric on a flat surface until it is only slightly damp.

8. To straighten the damp fabric, begin by grasping one corner and a point as far along the diagonally opposite selvage edge as you can reach. Pull hard. Move both hands down along the selvage edges and repeat. Continue to pull diagonally at intervals until you have stretched the entire piece of fabric.

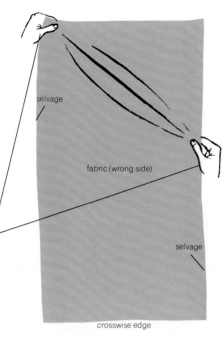

selvage

fabric (wrong side)

selvage

crosswise edge

9. Fold the fabric in half lengthwise wrong side out, and pin it together along the selvage and crosswise edges at 5-inch intervals, using rustproof pins. As you pin, smooth the fabric toward the fold with your hands.

10. Using a steam iron, start ironing at the pinned selvage edges and move toward the fold. Continue moving in parallel paths until you have ironed the entire length of the fabric.

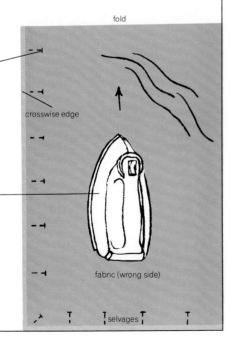

fold

crosswise edge

fabric (wrong side)

selvages

FOLDING SOLID FABRIC

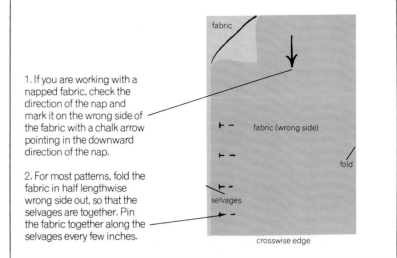

fabric

fabric (wrong side)

fold

selvages

crosswise edge

1. If you are working with a napped fabric, check the direction of the nap and mark it on the wrong side of the fabric with a chalk arrow pointing in the downward direction of the nap.

2. For most patterns, fold the fabric in half lengthwise wrong side out, so that the selvages are together. Pin the fabric together along the selvages every few inches.

FOLDING PLAID OR STRIPED FABRIC

1. If you are working with a napped fabric, check the direction of the nap, and mark it on the wrong side of the fabric with a chalk arrow pointing in the downward direction of the nap.

2. If the fabric is a stripe or plaid with an evenly balanced design, fold it lengthwise wrong sides out, so that the fold line falls exactly in the center of a plaid design or midway through a stripe.

3. Starting near the fold and working to the selvages, insert pins through the top layer of fabric at points where plaid lines intersect, or at intervals along the edge of stripe lines.

4. Fold back the top layer and make sure that the pins bring together the two layers at points where the pattern matches exactly. If the pattern does not match, adjust the fabric.

5. To hold the fabric layers together, push the point of each pin up through both layers. Continue to insert pins in this manner at a number of points. Then pin the fabric at the edges.

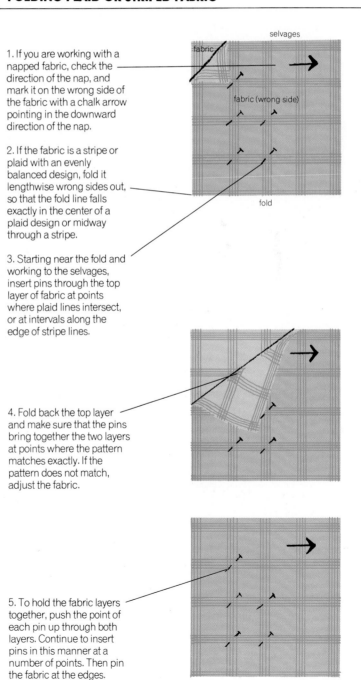

selvages

fabric

fabric (wrong side)

fold

Modifying the pattern

No matter how carefully you choose your pattern, the one you pick may lack certain crucial tailoring details, or may include some standard sewing features you should eliminate, as shown at right.

For example, the back of a well-tailored jacket never has shoulder darts. If your pattern includes darts, ignore them and use the material allotted to them for easing. If your pattern has neither darts nor ease allowance, add compensating width to the jacket back pattern. Similarly, the pattern for the sleeves and the back lining of the jacket may need adjustments that will enable you to use the best tailoring techniques when you sew these parts.

Trouser patterns sometimes include front waistline darts or an attached fly. For men's tailored trousers, both must be removed. For women's pants, if you want a man-tailored effect, remove the fly piece; but keep the darts for a closer fit.

In addition, there are two modifications you may want to make for style. If your pattern has a slightly curved collar and you are using a plaid or striped fabric, the collar should be straightened to allow the designs to match. If your pants pattern has no cuffs, these can easily be added as shown opposite.

Finally, before you lay out and cut the fabrics, make all fitting adjustments on the pattern pieces as shown on pages 56-73.

MODIFYING THE JACKET PATTERN PIECES

A ADDING EASE ALONG THE BACK SHOULDER SEAM

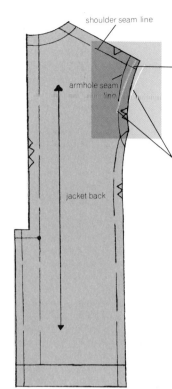

1. To determine if you need to ease the shoulder seam line of the jacket-back pattern piece, begin by checking to see if the pattern piece has a shoulder dart.

2. If it has a shoulder dart, simply cross out the markings for the dart—and the material that would have been taken up in the dart will provide the needed ease. Then skip to Box B.

3. If the pattern piece does not have a dart, compare the shoulder seam line on the jacket-front pattern piece with the one on the back pattern piece. If the seam line on the back piece is longer, the needed ease has already been added in the pattern. Skip to Box B.

4. If the seam lines are the same length, tape a piece of paper along the armhole edge of the back pattern piece. Then measure out along the shoulder seam line 1/2 inch beyond the point where it intersects the armhole seam line, and make a mark.

5. Starting at the mark, draw a new armhole seam line, curving it so that it meets the original seam line slightly below the armhole notch. Then draw a new armhole cutting line 5/8 inch outside the new seam line.

6. Repeat Steps 4 and 5 on the back lining piece.

B CORRECTING THE VENT OF THE BACK-LINING PATTERN PIECE

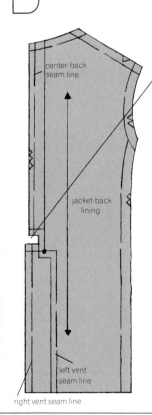
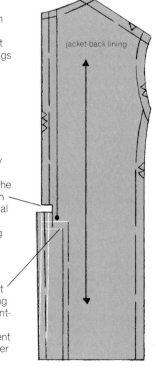

7. If the back-lining pattern piece is designed with a cutout area above the vent as shown, the vent markings should be changed to eliminate the cutout area —which would otherwise weaken the lining.

8. To do this, first re-mark the right vent seam line by drawing a straight line to connect the lower end of the center-back seam line with the lower end of the original right vent seam line. Re-mark the right vent cutting line in the same manner.

9. Now correct the left vent pattern markings by tracing over and extending the vent-top cutting line so that it intersects the new right vent cutting line. Then trace over the vent-top seam line.

C CORRECTING THE VENT CORNER ON THE UPPER-SLEEVE PATTERN

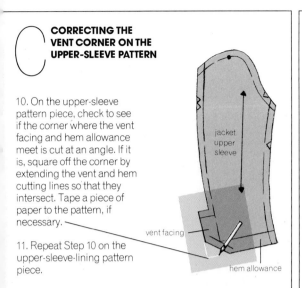

jacket upper sleeve

vent facing

hem allowance

10. On the upper-sleeve pattern piece, check to see if the corner where the vent facing and hem allowance meet is cut at an angle. If it is, square off the corner by extending the vent and hem cutting lines so that they intersect. Tape a piece of paper to the pattern, if necessary.

11. Repeat Step 10 on the upper-sleeve-lining pattern piece.

D MODIFYING THE UPPER-COLLAR PATTERN PIECE FOR PLAID FABRICS

12. If your fabric is a plaid, check to see whether the outer edge of the upper-collar pattern piece is straight so that it can be properly aligned on the design of the fabric. If the curve of the edge is slight, as shown in this example, it can be straightened. To do this, you will need to mark new outer seam and cutting lines. If the curve of the edge is pronounced, do not try to align it completely.

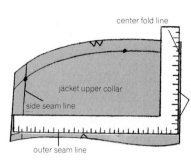

center fold line

jacket upper collar

side seam line

outer seam line

13. If the pattern piece is for the whole collar, cut the pattern in half along the center fold line.

14. Mark a new outer seam line on your half pattern piece by placing an L-square on the piece so that one side aligns with the center fold line. Align the other side with the intersection of the side and outer seam lines and draw a line along it. Then draw a new cutting line 5/8 inch outside the seam line.

MODIFYING PANTS PATTERNS

A MAKING THE BASIC MODIFICATIONS

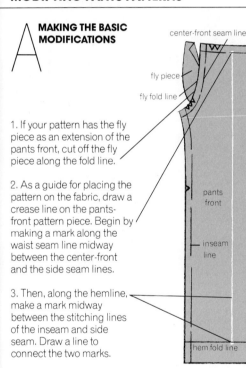

center-front seam line

fly piece

fly fold line

side seam line

pants front

inseam line

hem fold line

1. If your pattern has the fly piece as an extension of the pants front, cut off the fly piece along the fold line.

2. As a guide for placing the pattern on the fabric, draw a crease line on the pants-front pattern piece. Begin by making a mark along the waist seam line midway between the center-front and the side seam lines.

3. Then, along the hemline, make a mark midway between the stitching lines of the inseam and side seam. Draw a line to connect the two marks.

4. Check the position of the side pockets on both the front and back pattern pieces. Begin by measuring down 2 inches along the side seam lines from the waist cutting line. If the markings for the top of the pocket openings are not located at this point, re-mark them so that they are.

5. Then check the markings for the bottom of the pocket openings. If the pants are to have a waistline 24 inches or less, measure down 5 inches from the top pocket marking. For a larger waistline, add 1/8 inch for each inch of waistline measurement over 24 inches. For example, if the pants will have a 31-inch waistline, measure down 5 7/8 inches. Re-mark if necessary.

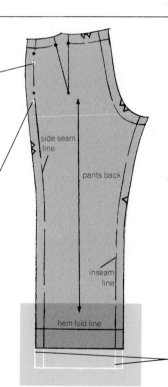

side seam line

pants back

inseam line

hem fold line

6. If your pattern has allowance for cuffs, or if you are making pants without cuffs, skip to Step 9.

7. To add cuffs to a pattern, decide how wide you want the cuffs to be; 1 3/4 inches is a customary minimum. Then, to determine the hem allowance needed, double the cuff width you decided on and add 1 1/2 inches.

8. On both front and back pieces, lengthen the seam and cutting lines for the side and inseams so that they extend beyond the hem fold line the distance determined in Step 7. Then, draw new hem cutting lines by connecting the ends of the extended cutting lines.

B REMOVING THE FRONT WAISTLINE DART ON MEN'S PANTS

9. If you are making men's pants and there are markings for a waistline dart on the pants-front pattern piece, cross them out.

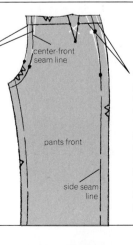

center-front seam line

pants front

side seam line

10. Then, to reduce the waist seam line by the width of the dart, begin by measuring in from the center-front seam line a distance equal to half the width of the dart. Starting at this point, redraw the center-front seam line down to the marking for the bottom of the fly. Then, draw a new cutting line 3/4 inch outside the new seam line.

11. Measure in along the waist seam line from the side seam line a distance equal to half the width of the dart. Starting at this point, redraw the side seam line, curving it to meet the original seam line at the bottom pocket mark. Make sure to re-mark the top pocket mark. Then, draw a new cutting line 5/8 inch outside the new seam line.

Laying out, cutting and marking

When you are ready to construct your garment, lay out and cut only the outer fabric, lining and underlining from your paper pattern pieces. Everything else will be cut later.

The first rule for laying out the pattern on the fabric is to arrange all pieces in one direction—from top to bottom as shown here. Standard cutting guides call this a nap layout, because it follows the direction of the fabric nap. Such layouts should be used not only for fabrics having an obvious nap, but also for those with a smooth surface. This is because some tailoring fabrics, even those that look smooth, have a subtle nap and others have a visible directional weave. In the finished garment, light will be reflected from each section at a different angle, emphasizing color variations that would arise if the nap directions varied.

In laying out the pattern on striped or plaid fabrics, there are additional considerations: besides the nap, attention must be given to the way the design will meet when the garment is assembled (pages 41-43).

After cutting the pieces, transfer pattern markings to the outer fabrics, using tailor tacks (overleaf). Linings and underlinings can be marked with a tracing wheel and dressmaker's carbon.

1. Fold the fabric, following the instructions for folding solid-colored fabric (page 35).

2. Loosely arrange the pattern pieces for the pants front and back on the fabric so that the waist-to-hem direction on both is the same. If the fabric has a nap, be sure that the nap runs downward from the waist to the hem. For the other pants pieces—which will be cut out during the actual process of constructing the garment —reserve as much fabric as you can along the lengthwise grain. At least half this fabric should be along the selvages. If your fabric is wide enough, this can be done by arranging the pattern pieces so that one is close to the fold and the other is close to the selvage edges, as shown. If the fabric is narrow, place the two pieces end to end near the fold.

3. Align the grain-line arrow of the back piece so that it is parallel to the selvages. Pin at each end of the arrow.

4. Align the crease line you drew on the front piece (page 37) so that the line is parallel to the selvages. Pin at each end of the line.

5. Pin the pieces diagonally at the corners. Then pin them parallel to—and just inside—the cutting lines.

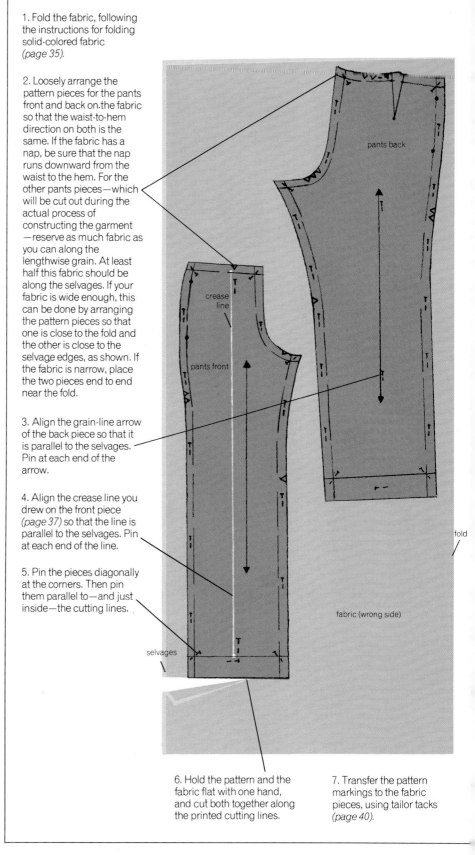

pants back

crease line

pants front

fold

fabric (wrong side)

selvages

6. Hold the pattern and the fabric flat with one hand, and cut both together along the printed cutting lines.

7. Transfer the pattern markings to the fabric pieces, using tailor tacks (page 40).

1. Fold the fabric, following the instructions for folding solid-colored fabric on page 35.

2. Separate all pattern pieces to be laid out on the garment fabric. Set aside any pieces for double-piped, double-piped flap, or welt pockets; these pieces will be cut when the jacket is constructed. However, include any pattern piece for patch pockets. For a woman's jacket, include the pieces for the back neck facing and undercollar.

3. If you are making a man's jacket, lay out the undercollar pattern piece on wool melton or other flannel cloth (page 93) according to the cutting guide supplied with your pattern.

4. Following the pattern cutting guide, loosely arrange the pattern pieces on the fabric so that the top-to-bottom direction of all pieces is the same. If necessary for fitting in all the pieces, place them with the pattern markings face down. If the fabric has a nap, be sure the nap runs downward from the top of the garment. Place the pattern piece for the collar —and back neck facing, if any—so that the line marked "center fold" or "place on fold" is on the fold of the fabric.

5. For a man's jacket, check the arrangement to be sure you have enough room between the pieces to increase the seam allowances to 1 inch at these places: along the shoulder, back neck, side-back and center-back seam lines of the front, front-facing, side and back pieces and along the seam line of the sleeve cap on the upper-sleeve piece. Rearrange the pieces if necessary.

6. If you are going to make welt, double-piped or double-piped flap pockets, be sure the arrangement reserves enough fabric to construct these pockets (for welt pockets, page 114; for double-piped and for double-piped flap, pages 118-119). Rearrange the pieces if necessary.

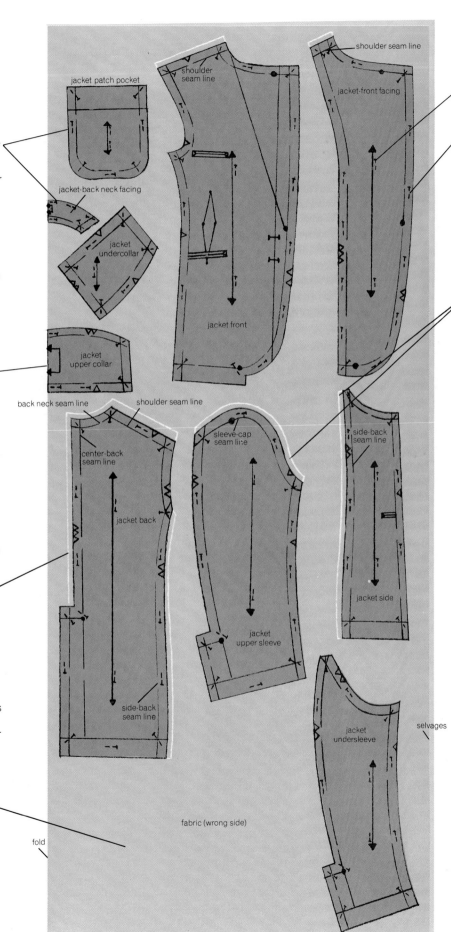

jacket patch pocket

shoulder seam line

shoulder seam line

jacket-front facing

jacket-back neck facing

jacket undercollar

jacket upper collar

jacket front

back neck seam line

shoulder seam line

center-back seam line

sleeve-cap seam line

side-back seam line

jacket back

jacket side

jacket upper sleeve

side-back seam line

jacket underersleeve

selvages

fabric (wrong side)

fold

7. Align the grain-line arrows so that they are parallel to the selvages. Pin at the ends of the grain-line arrows.

8. Pin each pattern piece diagonally at the corners; then pin parallel to—and just inside—the cutting lines.

9. If you are making a man's jacket, redraw the sleeve cap, shoulder, back neck, side-back, and center-back cutting lines on the upper-sleeves, front, front-facing, side and back pieces, so that they are 1 inch outside the seam lines. Using chalk, mark these cutting lines on the fabric.

10. Hold the pattern and the fabric flat with one hand, and cut both together along the printed or chalk-marked cutting lines. Do not cut out the notches. For pieces that are awkward to reach, cut loosely around the entire piece, remove it, and then trim along the cutting lines.

11. If your fabric will require underlining (pages 32-33), remove the back, front and any side pattern pieces —without transferring pattern markings to the fabric. Then, follow the directions for making and attaching underlining (page 41).

12. Using tailor tacks (page 40), transfer the pattern markings to the fabric pieces.

13. To cut out the jacket lining, fold the fabric, following the instructions for folding solid fabric (page 35). Arrange the pattern pieces for the front, back, upper-sleeve, undersleeve and any side and patch-pocket lining pieces according to the pattern cutting guide. But do not include any pieces for welt, double-piped or double-piped flap pockets. Then, follow Steps 5-10.

14. Transfer the pattern markings to the lining pieces using a tracing wheel and dressmaker's carbon paper (page 40).

USING TAILOR TACKS TO TRANSFER PATTERN MARKINGS

1. Mark all notches by making 1/8 inch clips into the seam allowances at the center of each pattern notch. Be sure to clip through both layers of fabric.

2. By making rows of tailor tacks (*page 97*), transfer all seam lines—except for dart seam lines, which will be drawn in chalk at the time of construction. Space the stitches at 1/2-inch intervals around curves; on long straight seam lines, they can be farther apart.

3. Transfer all pattern dots or circles—including those along the dart seam lines—by making a single tailor tack (*page 97, Step 3*) on each one. If the marking is along a seam line, make the tack at right angles to the row of tacks—or use thread of another color.

4. Mark the position of each buttonhole by making a single tailor tack at the intersection of the center and the outer placement lines. If you are making pants, skip to Step 8.

5. If you are making a jacket, transfer the collar and lapel roll lines, the vent fold line and the placement lines for patch pockets—if any—by making a row of tailor tacks along each. Transfer the center-front line from the bottom edge to a point just below the lapel roll line.

6. Mark the position of welt pockets by making a single tailor tack at each end of the long bottom line.

7. Mark the position of double-piped pockets by making a single tailor tack at each end of the long middle line.

8. Cut the loops of the tailor tacks, and carefully remove the paper pattern.

9. Mark an "X" with chalk on the wrong side of each layer of fabric.

10. Separate the layers of fabric, clipping the tailor tacks between the layers as you do.

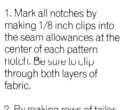

lapel roll line

pattern piece

garment fabric (wrong side)

garment fabric

TRANSFERRING PATTERN MARKINGS WITH A TRACING WHEEL AND DRESSMAKER'S CARBON PAPER

1. If you are marking two layers of fabric, remove just enough pins from one area at a time so you can slip dressmaker's carbon paper, carbon side up, under the bottom layer of fabric. Then place another piece of carbon paper, carbon side down, over the top layer of fabric.

2. Run a tracing wheel along all stitching, placement and fold lines. Use a straight-edged ruler as a guide for straight lines; trace curves freehand.

3. Using a dull pencil, trace the notches and draw an "X" through the center of all dots and circles.

4. Remove the pattern from the fabric and make a line of basting stitches or tailor tacks (*page 97*) along any markings that must show on both sides of the fabric (for example, the placement lines for pockets).

carbon paper

fabric

carbon paper

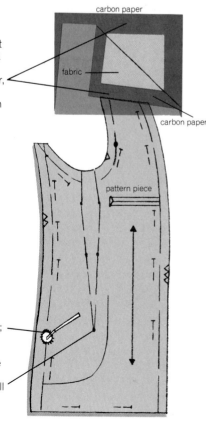

pattern piece

fabric (wrong side)

MAKING AND ATTACHING JACKET UNDERLINING

1. Using the jacket-front, back and any side pattern pieces, cut underlining pieces from underlining fabric (page 32). For a man's jacket, be sure to increase the shoulder, back neck, side-back and center-back seam allowances to 1 inch —as you did on the pieces cut from garment fabric.

2. Using a tracing wheel and dressmaker's carbon paper (page 40), transfer all pattern markings to the underlining pieces.

3. Working on one section of the jacket at a time (a jacket front in this example), lay the underlining piece marked side down, and place the corresponding garment piece wrong side down over it. Align the edges all around, and pin the two pieces together at the upper corners.

4. Starting at the upper edge, run two parallel rows of basting several inches apart down the length of the pieces. To eliminate puckers and wrinkles as you go, smooth the upper layer of fabric toward the hem and side edges.

5. Turn the basted pieces so that the underlining faces up. Baste just outside all seam lines—except for the top and front lapel seam lines on the jacket-front pieces. As you sew, smooth the layers of fabric outward from the bastings made in Step 4, so that both layers lie flat.

6. On each jacket-front piece, also baste along the lapel roll line and along the center-front line from the roll line to the hem edge.

7. Make a single tailor tack (page 97, Step 3) through each pattern marking for a large dot or circle. Remove the pins.

8. Check to be sure that both the underlining and garment fabric are smooth. If either layer wrinkles, clip the nearby bastings and rebaste.

LAYING OUT A PANTS PATTERN ON PLAID OR STRIPED FABRIC

1. Fold the fabric, following the instructions for folding plaid or striped fabric (page 35).

2. Then follow the instructions for laying out a pants pattern on solid-colored fabric (page 38, Step 2).

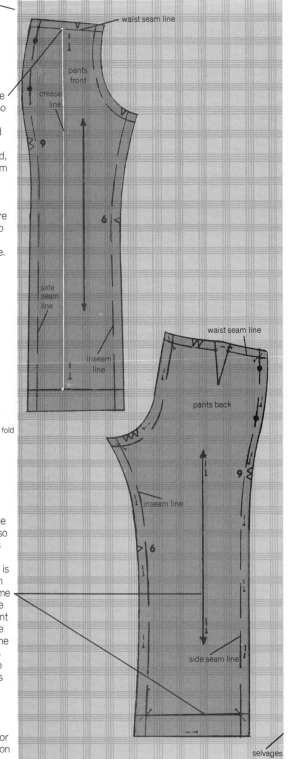

3. Adjust the position of the pants-front pattern piece so that the crease line you drew (page 37) is centered on a dominant vertical stripe. If the fabric is a plaid, also position the waist seam line so that it is centered between two dominant horizontal stripes. If the seam line is curved, be sure no portion of it extends into the dominant horizontal stripes. Pin to hold in place.

4. Adjust the position of the pants-back pattern piece so that the grain-line arrow is centered on a dominant vertical stripe. If the fabric is a plaid, also place the hem edge so that it is in the same position on the plaid as the hem edge of the pants-front piece. Then check to make sure that the notches on the inner and outer leg seams (here No. 6 and No. 9) also are in the same position as their numbered counterparts on the pants front. Pin to hold in place.

5. Follow the instructions for laying out a pants pattern on solid fabric (page 38, Steps 5-7).

A LAYING OUT THE PATTERN

1. Fold the fabric, following the instructions for folding plaid or striped fabric (*page 35*).

2. Follow the instructions for laying out a jacket pattern on solid-colored fabric (*page 39, Steps 2-6*), using the illustration shown here as a guide rather than the cutting guide supplied with the pattern. Make sure to place the pattern pieces for the jacket front and the front facing near the selvages.

3. If you are working with a striped fabric, adjust the front, back, upper-sleeve, undersleeve and any side pattern pieces so that the grain-line arrows are parallel to the stripes. On the front piece, also position the straight middle part of the front seam line so that it is centered between two dominant stripes. On the back piece, position the top of the center-back seam line and the bottom of the vent fold line so that they are centered between two dominant stripes. Pin to hold in place. Then skip to Step 10.

4. On a plaid fabric, select the point where you want the hemline of the jacket to be. If the plaid is large or bold, it should be centered between two dominant horizontal stripes to avoid overemphasizing the hem edge. If the plaid is small or subtle, it may be centered on any horizontal stripe.

5. Adjust the jacket-front pattern so that the hemline is in the position you decided on in Step 4. Then, place the straight middle part of the front seam line in the same location on the vertical stripes as the hemline is on the horizontal stripes. Pin to hold.

6. Adjust the jacket-back pattern so that the hemline is in the same position as the hemline of the jacket-front piece. Then center the top of the center-back seam line and the bottom of the vent fold line on the same vertical stripe as the front edge of the jacket-front piece. Pin to hold.

7. If you have a separate side piece, as shown here, adjust the piece so that the hemline is in the same position as the hemline of the front piece. Then check that the notch on the side-front seam (*here No. 2*) is in the same position as its numbered counterpart on the jacket front. The notch on the side-back seam (*here No. 5*) must also be in the same position as its counterpart on the jacket back. Pin to hold.

8. Adjust the upper-sleeve pattern so that the grain-line arrow is parallel to the vertical stripes. Place the notch on the sleeve cap (*here No. 3*) in the same position on a horizontal stripe as its numbered counterpart on the jacket front. Pin to hold.

9. Adjust the undersleeve piece so that the grain-line arrow is parallel to the vertical stripes. Place the notch on the outer arm seam (*here No. 8*) in the same position on a horizontal stripe as its counterpart on the upper-sleeve piece. Pin to hold.

10. Adjust the upper collar piece so that the line marked "center fold" or "place on fold" is on the fold of the fabric. If the outer seam line is straight (*page 37*) on a plaid fabric, also place it in the same position as the hemline of the front piece. Pin to hold.

11. If you are making a woman's jacket, adjust the pattern piece for the back neck facing so that the line marked "place on fold" is on the fold of the fabric. Adjust the undercollar pattern piece so that the grain-line arrow is parallel to the selvages. Pin to hold.

12. If the jacket will have patch pockets, adjust the pattern piece so that the seam lines are in the same position on the vertical stripes—and on the horizontal stripes on a plaid fabric—as the pocket placement lines on the jacket-front pattern piece. Pin to hold.

13. Adjust the front-facing pattern piece so that the upper and front seam lines are in the same position on the stripe or plaid as the front pattern piece. Also, check to be sure that the notch on the front edge (*here No. 1*) is in the same position as its numbered counterpart on the jacket-front piece. Pin to hold.

14. Pin all pattern pieces diagonally at the corners; then pin them just inside—and parallel to—the cutting lines.

15. If you are making a man's jacket, follow the instructions in Step 9 for laying out a jacket on solid fabric (*page 39*).

16. To provide the extra fabric necessary for shaping the plaid or stripes to the curve of the lapel, cut out the front-facing piece loosely around all edges—except the front edge. Make the cut several inches outside the pattern cutting lines. Do not trim away any fabric extending beyond the front edge of the pattern.

17. To finish all pieces except the front facing, follow the instructions in Steps 10-12 for laying out the jacket on solid-colored fabric (*page 39*).

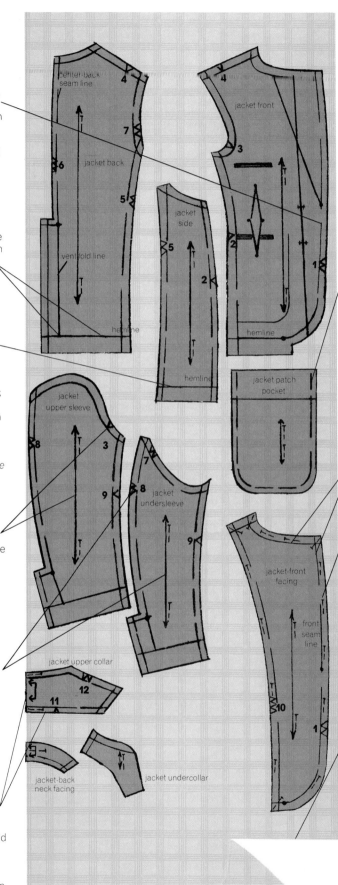

B | SHAPING THE LAPEL CURVE OF THE FRONT FACING

18. Cut along a vertical stripe, trimming off the selvages 1/2 inch beyond the front edge of the pattern piece for the front facing.

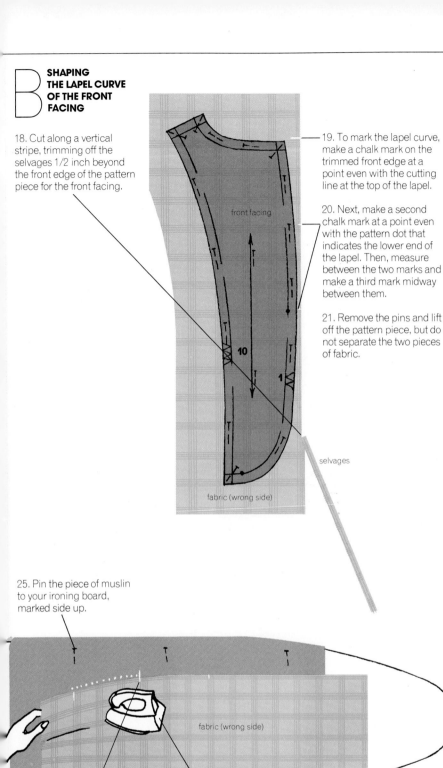

fabric (wrong side)

selvages

19. To mark the lapel curve, make a chalk mark on the trimmed front edge at a point even with the cutting line at the top of the lapel.

20. Next, make a second chalk mark at a point even with the pattern dot that indicates the lower end of the lapel. Then, measure between the two marks and make a third mark midway between them.

21. Remove the pins and lift off the pattern piece, but do not separate the two pieces of fabric.

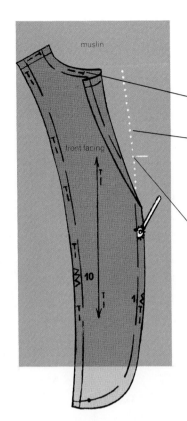

muslin

front facing

22. To prepare a guide for shaping the lapel curve, cut a piece of muslin—or other scrap fabric—slightly larger than the lapel area of the front-facing pattern piece. Pin the pattern piece to the muslin.

23. Then, using a tracing wheel and dressmaker's carbon paper (page 40), mark the front seam line between the top of the lapel and the dot indicating the lower end of the lapel.

24. Remove the pattern and mark the midpoint of the line.

25. Pin the piece of muslin to your ironing board, marked side up.

fabric (wrong side)

26. With the two front-facing fabric pieces still together, place them on the muslin so that the middle mark on the front edge of the fabric lines up with the midpoint mark on the muslin.

27. To shape the straight vertical stripes near the front edge of the fabric to the curved line on the muslin, steam press the lapel area, working on half of the curve at a time. Begin to press along the front edge and work gradually from the midpoint marking toward one end of the curve, pulling the edge of the fabric little by little into the shape of the curve.

28. Then, shrink in the excess fabric that forms on the lapel by gradually steam pressing from the edge inward. To avoid creasing or puckering the fabric, work on a small area at a time.

29. Repeat Steps 27 and 28 to shape the other half of the lapel curve.

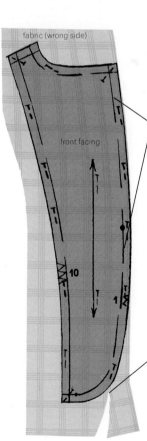

fabric (wrong side)

front facing

30. Repin the pattern piece to the fabric pieces, following the instructions in Steps 13 and 14. This time, make sure that both the curved lapel portion and the straight portion of the front seam line are in the same position on a vertical stripe.

31. Trim the pieces along the cutting lines; transfer pattern markings, using tailor tacks (page 40).

32. To cut out the lining for the jacket, follow the instructions for laying out a jacket pattern on solid-colored fabric (page 39, Steps 13 and 14).

Special tips for interfacings

Tailors make jackets with distinctly shaped interfacings that are quite unlike those that come with most of the standard commercial patterns. Therefore, if the pattern pieces for the interfacings are not identical to the shapes diagramed here, set them aside. Instead use the adaptations shown on the following pages of the actual jacket pattern pieces.

Before cutting, determine how much interfacing fabric you will need. In a man's jacket the two front sections are stiffened with wool interfacing fabric, haircloth and cover cloth. To determine the amount of wool interfacing fabric needed for each front section, measure the jacket-front pattern from shoulder to hemline, and add 8 inches to allow for cutting on the bias. For the haircloth and cover cloth, measure from the shoulder to about an inch below the top of the waistline dart.

A woman's jacket, on the other hand, is supported in front with two layers of wool interfacing fabric —one large and one small—and in back with one layer. For the larger front pieces, measure from the neckline to the hem; then use scraps from this material to cut out the smaller front pieces. The back interfacing extends from the shoulder to a point 3 inches below the armhole. Its width should be equal to twice the distance from the top of the side seam line to the center-back line.

A MARKING THE WOOL INTERFACING PIECES

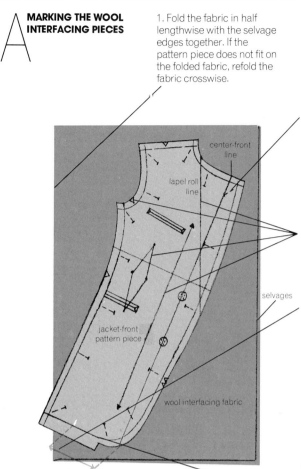

1. Fold the fabric in half lengthwise with the selvage edges together. If the pattern piece does not fit on the folded fabric, refold the fabric crosswise.

2. Place the jacket-front pattern piece on the fabric so that the grain-line arrow on the pattern is at an angle halfway between the straight lengthwise grain and the true bias of the fabric. On most patterns, the lapel roll line will be almost parallel with the selvage edge when correctly positioned. Pin.

3. Using dressmaker's carbon paper (page 40), transfer the markings for the armhole notch, the lapel roll line, the waistline dart and the grain-line arrow. The latter will enable you to use the interfacing as a pattern for the haircloth interfacing in Box C.

4. To mark the bottom cutting line of the interfacing, begin by measuring in 7 inches along the hemline from an imaginary extension of the center-front line (or, if the pattern piece has a square corner at the lower front edge, the actual center-front line). Mark the point on the pattern.

5. Then, using a tracing wheel and dressmaker's carbon paper, mark along the hemline from the mark you made in Step 4 to the front cutting line.

6. To draw the shoulder cutting line for the interfacing, measure up from the shoulder cutting line on the pattern, and mark 1 inch at the armhole edge and 1/2 inch at the neckline edge. Connect the marks, duplicating the shape of the pattern cutting line as much as possible.

7. Following the pattern, draw the armhole cutting line on the fabric. Begin at the new shoulder line and end at the underarm cutting line as shown. If your pattern has an underarm dart instead of a separate side panel, end the armhole cutting line 5/8 inch beyond the first stitching line for the dart.

8. Again following the pattern, draw the front cutting line on the fabric. Start at the new shoulder line, go around the neck and lapel, and then down the front to the hemline. Remove the pattern piece.

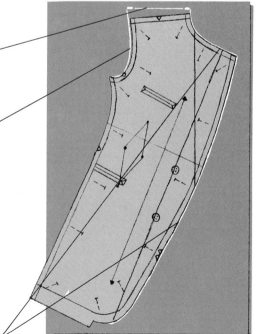

B CUTTING THE WOOL INTERFACING PIECES

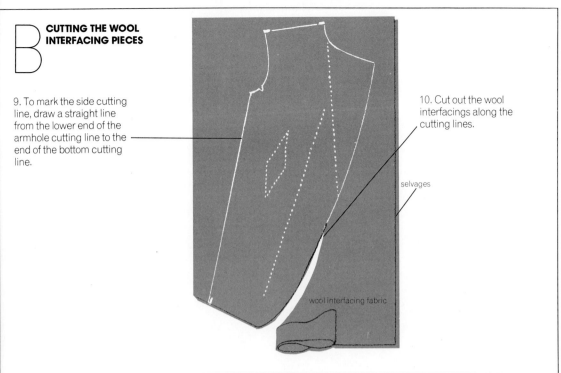

9. To mark the side cutting line, draw a straight line from the lower end of the armhole cutting line to the end of the bottom cutting line.

10. Cut out the wool interfacings along the cutting lines.

selvages

wool interfacing fabric

C MARKING AND CUTTING THE HAIRCLOTH INTERFACING PIECES

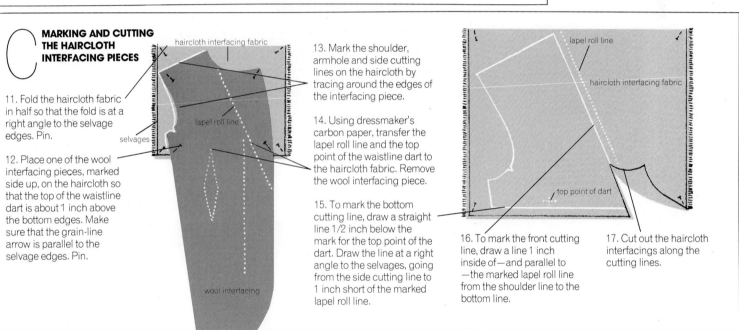

haircloth interfacing fabric

lapel roll line

selvages

wool interfacing

lapel roll line

haircloth interfacing fabric

top point of dart

11. Fold the haircloth fabric in half so that the fold is at a right angle to the selvage edges. Pin.

12. Place one of the wool interfacing pieces, marked side up, on the haircloth so that the top of the waistline dart is about 1 inch above the bottom edges. Make sure that the grain-line arrow is parallel to the selvage edges. Pin.

13. Mark the shoulder, armhole and side cutting lines on the haircloth by tracing around the edges of the interfacing piece.

14. Using dressmaker's carbon paper, transfer the lapel roll line and the top point of the waistline dart to the haircloth fabric. Remove the wool interfacing piece.

15. To mark the bottom cutting line, draw a straight line 1/2 inch below the mark for the top point of the dart. Draw the line at a right angle to the selvages, going from the side cutting line to 1 inch short of the marked lapel roll line.

16. To mark the front cutting line, draw a line 1 inch inside of—and parallel to—the marked lapel roll line from the shoulder line to the bottom line.

17. Cut out the haircloth interfacings along the cutting lines.

D MARKING AND CUTTING THE COVER-CLOTH PIECES

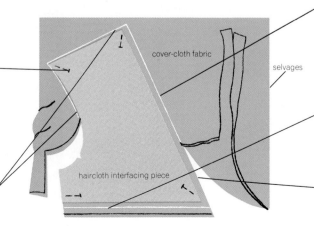

cover-cloth fabric

selvages

haircloth interfacing piece

18. Fold the cover-cloth fabric in half so that the selvage edges are together.

19. Place one of the haircloth interfacing pieces on the fabric so that the bottom edge of the interfacing is at a right angle to the selvages. Pin.

20. Mark the shoulder, armhole and side cutting lines by tracing around the interfacing. Extend the lines slightly beyond the edges at each end.

21. To mark the front cutting line, draw a line 1/2 inch outside of—and parallel to—the front edge of the interfacing, connecting the shoulder line and the bottom line.

22. To mark the bottom cutting line, draw a line 1 inch below—and parallel to—the bottom edge of the interfacing, extending the line slightly beyond the front edge.

23. Cut out the cover-cloth pieces along the cutting lines. Remove the haircloth interfacing piece.

A MARKING THE FRONT-INTERFACING PIECES

1. Fold the wool interfacing fabric in half lengthwise, selvage edges together. If the pattern piece does not fit, refold the fabric crosswise.

2. Place the jacket-front pattern piece on the fabric with the grain-line arrow parallel to the selvage. Pin.

3. Mark the armhole, front-edge and shoulder-neckline cutting lines on the fabric.

4. Mark the side cutting line from the armhole cutting line to a point 2 1/2 inches below it.

5. To determine the width of the bottom cutting line for the interfacing, measure the pattern from the center-front line to the nearest stitching line on the waistline dart at its widest point. Then subtract 1/2 inch.

6. To mark the bottom cutting line, measure in along the hemline the distance determined in Step 5 from an imaginary extension of the center-front line (or from the actual center-front line if the lower front edge is square).

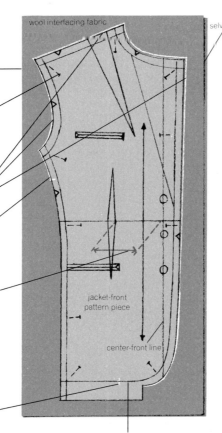

wool interfacing fabric

selvages

jacket-front pattern piece

center-front line

7. Then, using dressmaker's carbon paper, run a tracing wheel (page 40) along the hemline from the mark you made in Step 6 to the front cutting line.

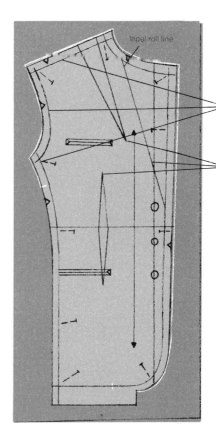

lapel roll line

8. Using a tracing wheel and dressmaker's carbon paper, mark the shoulder and armhole seam lines and the side seam line along the marked part of the side cutting line.

9. Then, mark the lapel roll line, the top point of the waistline dart—and the shoulder-dart stitching lines if there is a shoulder dart.

10. Remove the pattern.

B CUTTING OUT THE FRONT-INTERFACING PIECES

11. To mark the remaining cutting lines, begin by drawing a vertical line —parallel to the selvage edge—from the end of the bottom cutting line to a point even with the marking for the top point of the waistline dart.

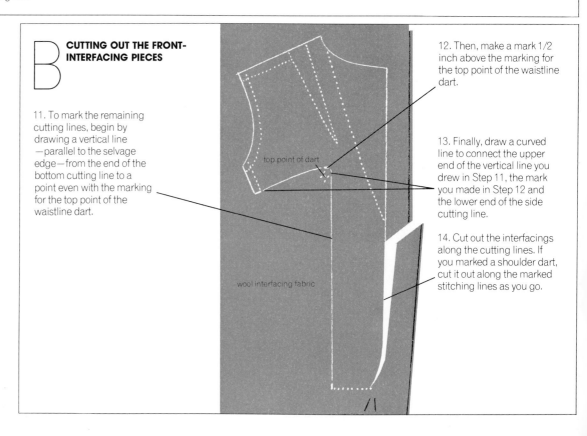

top point of dart

wool interfacing fabric

12. Then, make a mark 1/2 inch above the marking for the top point of the waistline dart.

13. Finally, draw a curved line to connect the upper end of the vertical line you drew in Step 11, the mark you made in Step 12 and the lower end of the side cutting line.

14. Cut out the interfacings along the cutting lines. If you marked a shoulder dart, cut it out along the marked stitching lines as you go.

C ▸ MARKING AND CUTTING THE ARMHOLE REINFORCEMENTS

15. Using a piece of interfacing fabric large enough to cover the armhole area of both interfacings, fold the fabric in half so that the selvage edges are together—or arrange two layers of scrap fabric so that the grains are aligned.

16. Place the armhole section of one of the front interfacings, marked side up, on the fabric and align the grains. Pin.

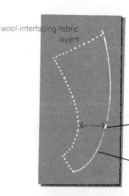

wool-interfacing-fabric layers

front-interfacing piece

17. To mark the shoulder cutting line for the reinforcement, use a tracing wheel and dressmaker's carbon paper to transfer the shoulder seam line of the interfacing between the armhole seam line and a point about 4 inches beyond it, depending on the size of the jacket. If necessary, extend the line across any shoulder-dart opening.

18. To mark the armhole and side cutting lines, transfer the armhole and the side seam lines of the interfacing.

19. Remove the interfacing.

wool-interfacing-fabric layers

20. To mark the front cutting line, begin by finding the point on the armhole cutting line where it starts to curve sharply. This will be approximately two thirds of the way down. Starting at that point, measure in about 3 1/2 inches along the crosswise grain of the fabric and make a mark.

21. Then, draw a gently curved line to connect the end of the shoulder cutting line with the mark you made in Step 20 and the end of the side cutting line.

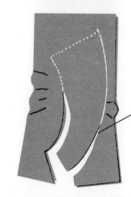

22. Cut out the armhole reinforcements along the cutting lines.

D ▸ MARKING AND CUTTING THE BACK INTERFACING PIECE

23. Fold the fabric in half, lengthwise, so that the selvage edges are together.

24. Place the upper half of the jacket-back pattern piece on the fabric so that the upper part of the center-back seam line is along the fold. Pin.

25. Along the center-back seam line, measure down 5 inches from the neck seam line and make a mark on the folded edge of the fabric as a guide for drawing the bottom cutting line in Steps 33 and 34.

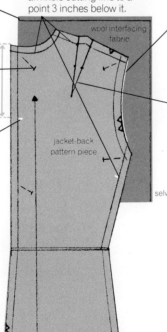

wool interfacing fabric

jacket-back pattern piece

selvages

26. Use dressmaker's carbon paper to transfer the neck and shoulder seam lines on the pattern to the interfacing. Then, transfer the side seam line from the armhole cutting line to a point 3 inches below it.

27. To mark the armhole cutting line, trace the pattern-armhole cutting line.

28. If there are markings for a shoulder dart, use dressmaker's carbon paper to transfer the stitching lines —even though you crossed them out and did not use them on the garment.

29. Remove the pattern. If you marked a shoulder dart, skip to Step 34.

30. To determine the position of the shoulder dart if you did not mark one, measure in along the shoulder cutting line 1 1/2 inches from the neck cutting line and make a mark.

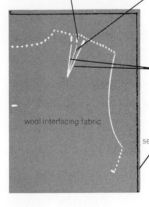

wool interfacing fabric

selvages

31. Starting at the mark, draw a line, 3 inches long, parallel to the upper part of the armhole cutting line. This is the center line of the dart.

32. On each side of the center line—and 1/4 inch away from it—make a mark on the shoulder line. Draw lines to connect the marks with the end of the center line.

33. To mark the bottom cutting line, begin by drawing a straight line—at a right angle to the folded edge—from the mark you made on the folded edge in Step 25 to a point even with the end of the dart.

34. Continue the line by curving it downward so that it is parallel to the lower armhole line. Then, curve it around to the end of the side line. The shape may be approximated because the interfacing will not be visible on the finished jacket.

35. Cut out the interfacing along the lines, cutting out the dart as you go.

48

3

FIRST STEP TO A PERFECT FIT

When Bill Blass, still a couple of decades away from becoming a top couturier, was inducted into the Army during World War II, he was appalled by the Sad Sack fit of his GI uniform. At the first opportunity he took it to Brooks Brothers, New York's ancient bastion of men's wear, and had the pants and jacket altered to give him a trim, flattering silhouette. Today in the Seventh Avenue offices and

THE SECRETS OF A PREMIER DESIGNER

workrooms of his design establishment, Blass still evidences that passion for perfection of fit. And he has achieved it for a generation of customers, who consider him a master fitter in the ready-to-wear industry.

Although fit is perhaps the most important single element in tailoring, it is nonetheless a subjective and personal value, so that even Blass and his fellow craftsmen find it hard to define in precise terms. At the same time, as with sex appeal and the ability to carry a tune, its absence is painfully apparent. "People acquire clothes to give them pleasure," Blass says, "and this means that a garment must both look beautiful and feel comfortable."

But precise fit does not mean a slavish duplication of the body's outline. A suit that fits like a second skin would not let its wearer move freely and comfortably. "Obviously," says Blass, "you can't get pleasure from something you can't sit in, or dance in, or walk in, or drink in."

Nevertheless, if comfort and freedom were achieved simply by making everything a bit too large, the wearer would look lumpy and ludicrous. In fact, according to Blass, an obsession with roominess is the most common fault with the way American men choose their clothes—which he feels tend to be two sizes too big, for comfort's sake. But with proper fit, a man's or a woman's garment can be trimly flattering while feeling perfectly comfortable.

This subtle balance can be achieved by the home seamstress, just as it is by Blass —whose facilities are more substantial than those in most homes but whose methods can be easily duplicated. Starting with a basic pattern for a new creation, Blass fits it to the model who will introduce it. If the model happens to be a woman, the process of adaptation involves more steps than with a man, whose straight-line contours are relatively simple to fit. With a woman, however, the more complex curves of the figure require closer attention—some nipping in here, some easing there. The surest way for the home tailor to bring the pattern into ex-act harmony with these curves is to baste a muslin mockup of the ultimate garment. Then this muslin can be used to make the myriad adjustments needed before taking the irretrievable step of cutting the actual material for the garment.

When Blass sets out to create the ideal fit for one of his originals, he uses a live mannequin known as the "sample model." She is selected not because she is a perfect size 8 or size 10 or size anything, says Blass, but "because she'll be stunning in this particular garment —and because she loves the dress. Fashion is an emotional thing; how a woman feels about a dress has a lot to do with how she'll look in it. A sympathetic attitude is essential for a sample model."

Thus, as his fitter fusses over the garment, Blass observes not so much where the pins or bastings go, but how the girl reacts after each new adjustment snugs the material along her body. And he lets her pretty much command the fitting herself.

However, Blass himself concentrates on two particular areas of the garment. One is the shoulder. "It's the shoulder, and with it the setting of the sleeve into the armhole, that fundamentally makes clothes work," he says. "If a jacket doesn't fit in the shoulders, forget it." For proper shoulder fit, the crucial measurements are the width of the shoulder from neck to tip, and the depth of the armhole. "If a woman has a size 12 shoulder and is size 14 elsewhere," says Blass, "I much prefer that she buy a 12. We can let out the hipline much more easily than we can take in the lines of the shoulder and armhole, the place where the fit must *always* be snug."

Another tricky measurement is the one around the pelvis and seat. When the pants are being fitted, Blass always asks the model to sit down. "How does it feel?" he asks. And when she tells him it feels fine he has her cross her legs.

"I can tell a model how an outfit looks, but she must tell me how it feels," he says. And he adds a clear message for the home seamstress: "The only one who can really fit you is you yourself. But the need for an outside eye poses a problem for a woman tailoring her own garment. She's the one who knows how it feels; she can test the hip fit by sitting down at will. But she also must be eyed objectively when she has made all those adjustments that feel right. She needs an aide whose eye she can trust."

After all hands have agreed that the muslin has reached the perfect fit, the mockup garment must be disassembled and its measurements meticulously transferred to the real fabric. Then the project enters its second phase—cutting and basting the garment fabric. Here, too, there will be some adjustments that demand the combination of instinctive feel and an objective eye to reach the ultimate in perfect fit. "Your eye must tell you that your look is precisely the look you want," says Bill Blass. "If the outfit also makes you feel 10 pounds lighter —that's quality tailoring."

Fitting a muslin mockup of a Bill Blass suit, a tailor adjusts the trouser length so that the cuff just brushes the toe of the shoe. Then *(clockwise from top)* he studies the jacket's shoulders, inspects the set of the all-important armhole, fits the sleeve, adjusts the side seam—and winds up with a superbly fitted garment.

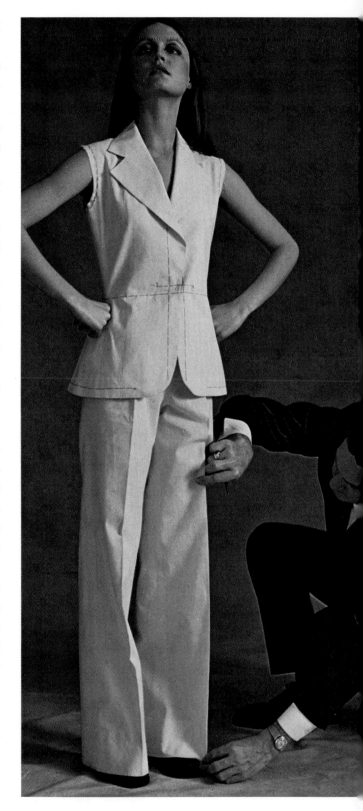

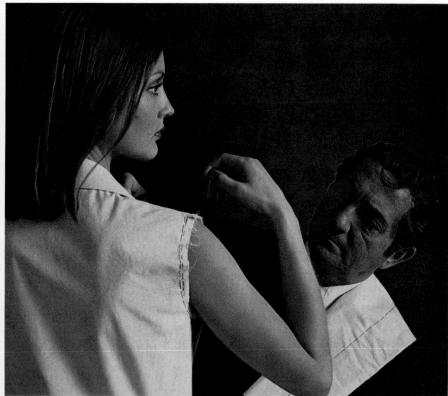

Mapping your figure

To transform an ordinary commercial pattern into a distinctive suit with a custom-tailored fit, you must start as a professional tailor does, by measuring your body precisely.

The red and blue bands on the figures at right show the measurements that you will need for buying the pattern and for altering it to your own specifications. Select the pattern for a man's jacket on the basis of the chest measurement, and the pattern for a woman's jacket according to the bustline. Pattern adjustments for men are then made for length and for the critical area around the shoulders. Other adjustments such as the fit of collar and body are eventually made on the jacket itself. Women need only adjust for length since the other alterations will be made on a muslin prototype *(overleaf)*.

Patterns for trousers are also handled differently according to the sex of the wearer. For men the key measurement is the waistline, and for women it is the hip size. But the crucial adjustment is the same for both —the crotch length, or rise.

A man should be measured in trousers and shirt, a woman in the kind of undergarments she will wear with the suit. While measuring, stand in a normal posture, with your weight evenly on both feet. You can take some measurements—such as waist size—yourself; but you will need help for most of the others.

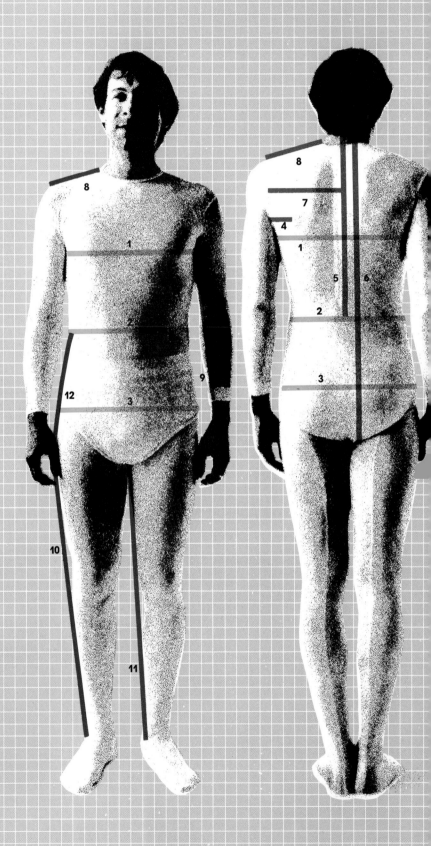

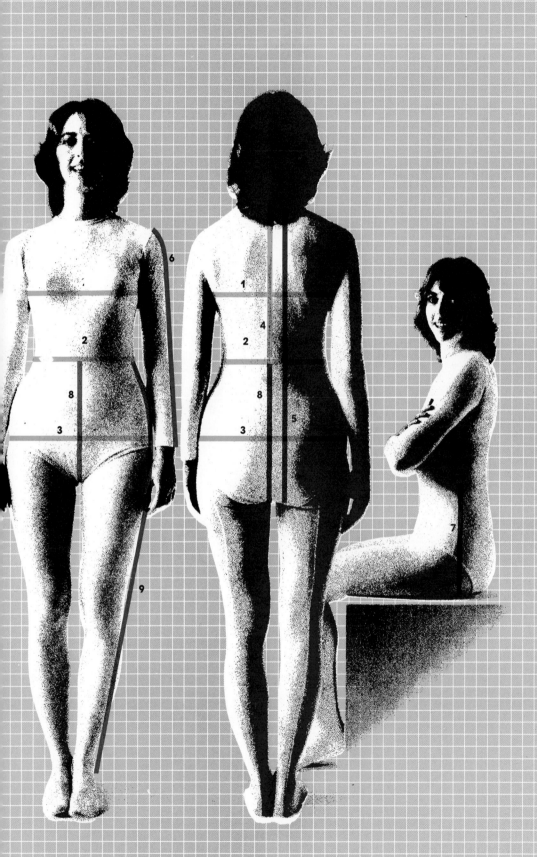

TAKING MEASUREMENTS

The red lines on the figures at left indicate measurements on standard pattern envelopes; the blue lines are additional measurements to be used for further fitting.

WOMEN'S MEASUREMENTS

1. BUST: Measure around the fullest part, with the tape slightly raised in back.

2. WAIST: Tie a cord around the narrowest part and leave it on as a marker. Measure the waist.

3. HIP: Measure around the fullest part, usually 7 to 9 inches down from the waist.

4. BACK-WAIST LENGTH: Measure from the bone at the base of the neck to the waistline cord.

5. FINISHED JACKET LENGTH: Measure from the bone at the base of the neck to the desired length, according to the style of the garment.

6. ARM LENGTH: Keeping the arm slightly bent, measure from the shoulder along the outside of the arm over the elbow to the wristbone.

7. CROTCH LENGTH: Sitting on a hard surface, measure from the waistline cord to the surface.

8. FULL CROTCH LENGTH: Measure from the waistline in back between the legs to the waistline in front—not too tightly.

9. SIDE-SEAM LENGTH: Measure from the waist down the side of the leg to the top of the shoe heel.

MEN'S MEASUREMENTS

1. CHEST CIRCUMFERENCE: With two fingers under the tape to provide optimum slack for comfort, measure under the arms high enough to cross the shoulder blades in back.

2. WAIST CIRCUMFERENCE: With two fingers inside the tape to allow for wearing ease, measure the waist just above the hipbone.

3. SEAT OR HIP: Measure around the hips 6 inches down from the waist, again with two fingers inside the tape.

4. ARMHOLE DEPTH: Position a 12-inch ruler under the armpit, parallel to the floor. Put a pin or a chalk mark at the top of the ruler in back of the armpit. This is the armhole depth, used as a reference point for other measurements.

5. WAIST LENGTH: Measure from the bone at the base of the neck to the hollow of the back.

6. BACK LENGTH OR FINISHED JACKET LENGTH: Measure from the base of the neck to the jacket's desired length—usually just below the buttocks.

7. BACK WIDTH: Make a mark on the center back at the same level as the armhole depth (*above*). Determine the halfway point between this mark and the neckbone. Measure from here to the armhole seam.

8. SHOULDER WIDTH: Wearing a jacket that fits well, measure from the edge of the undercollar to the armhole seam.

9. SLEEVE LENGTH: On the same jacket, measure the inseam from the armhole to the desired length—or to a point even with the wristbone. If you want some shirt cuff to show (half an inch is customary) shorten the jacket sleeve accordingly.

10. OUTSEAM: Wearing trousers that fit well, measure from the waistline to the top of the shoe heel.

11. INSEAM: Measure from the crotch seam of the trousers to the top of the shoe heel.

12. RISE: The distance from waist to crotch. Subtract the length of the inseam on the trousers from the outseam.

A muslin fitting for a woman

Because a woman's body tends to be rounded, several fittings may be required to reconcile her curves to the lines of a tailored garment. In order to spare the garment fabric from repeated bastings and rippings, this fitting process is best done on an inexpensive muslin.

To make a muslin for fitting, first compare your own measurements (page 54) with those on the pattern envelope, and lengthen or shorten the paper piece along the pattern adjustment lines. Then cut out, mark and assemble a jacket muslin as explained at right. For a pants muslin, cut out and machine baste the pieces together according to the pattern instructions, substituting a grosgrain ribbon for the waistband.

Wearing a blouse or sweater under the jacket and appropriate shoes with the pants, try the muslin on for fit. Make the necessary adjustments, following the instructions on these pages. Rebaste and try on the muslin again. Continue revising the fit until it looks right and feels comfortable. Only then should you transfer the adjustments onto the pattern pieces for the jacket, the lining, the facing and the interfacing.

Now the garment can be cut out and sewed. Regardless of how skillful a job you do on the muslin, you may still have to make adjustments on the actual garment because the real fabric drapes differently. Such changes will, however, be minor.

ASSEMBLING THE MUSLIN FOR A WOMAN'S JACKET

1. Following the pattern cutting guide, lay out and pin the modified pattern pieces (pages 36-39) on the muslin fabric. Use only the jacket-front, back, side, undercollar, upper-sleeve and undersleeve pieces.

2. Mark new cutting lines 1 inch outside the side-front, side-back, center-back, shoulder and armhole seam lines of the front, back and side pieces. Repeat along the seam line of the sleeve cap.

3. Cut out the pieces, and transfer all stitching lines, notches and circles to the wrong sides of the pieces, using a tracing wheel and dressmaker's carbon (page 40).

4. Transfer all pocket, buttonhole, waistline and center-front markings to the outside of the muslin pieces. Also, transfer all grain-line arrows and extend them the length of the pieces. At the base of the sleeve cap, mark a horizontal grain line at a right angle to the grain-line arrow.

5. To take up the ease along the shoulder seam lines of the back piece, machine baste—6 stitches to the inch—just outside the seam lines. Then gather the ease by pulling the ends of the bastings. Repeat along the seam lines of the sleeve caps.

6. Close the waistline and shoulder darts by machine basting. Press.

7. To assemble the muslin, machine baste the front, side and back pieces together along the seam lines. Then machine baste the sleeve pieces together. Press open all the seams.

8. Hand baste the sleeves into the armholes, distributing the ease evenly.

9. Machine baste the undercollar pieces together. Then pin the undercollar to the muslin along the neck seam line.

10. Press the muslin.

11. If the jacket you are making has shoulder pads, place them inside the shoulders so that the straight edge of each pad is aligned with the armhole seam and the corner opposite the edge is on the shoulder seam. (Most of the pad will be in back of the seam.) Pin.

12. Turn up and pin the hem of the muslin jacket body and sleeves.

13. Try on the muslin, and pin the fronts together at the buttonhole markings.

14. To evaluate the fit, look in a mirror and check that the vertical grain-line markings are at right angles to the floor and that the horizontal grain-line markings on the sleeve are parallel to the floor. Check the overall fit, and make any alterations needed according to the instructions on the following pages.

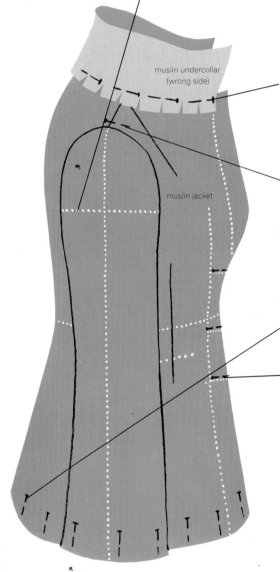

muslin undercollar (wrong side)

muslin jacket

IF THE BACK NECKLINE IS TIGHT

A SYMPTOMS OF A TIGHT NECKLINE

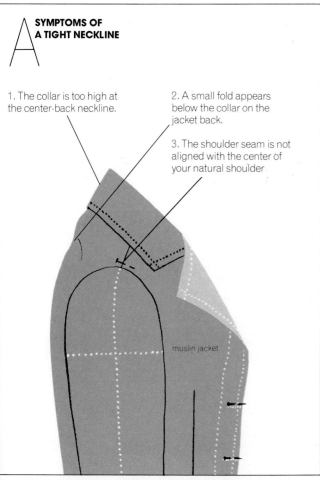

1. The collar is too high at the center-back neckline.

2. A small fold appears below the collar on the jacket back.

3. The shoulder seam is not aligned with the center of your natural shoulder.

muslin jacket

B LETTING OUT THE SHOULDER SEAM AT THE NECKLINE

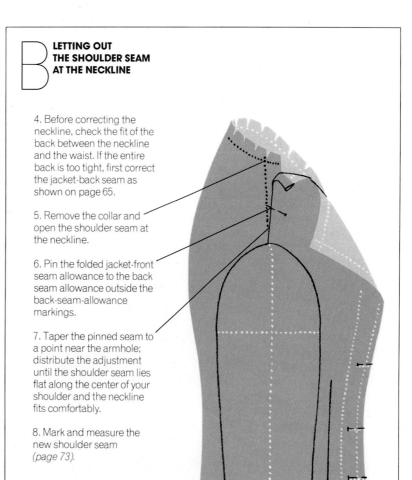

4. Before correcting the neckline, check the fit of the back between the neckline and the waist. If the entire back is too tight, first correct the jacket-back seam as shown on page 65.

5. Remove the collar and open the shoulder seam at the neckline.

6. Pin the folded jacket-front seam allowance to the back seam allowance outside the back-seam-allowance markings.

7. Taper the pinned seam to a point near the armhole; distribute the adjustment until the shoulder seam lies flat along the center of your shoulder and the neckline fits comfortably.

8. Mark and measure the new shoulder seam (page 73).

C ADJUSTING THE PATTERN

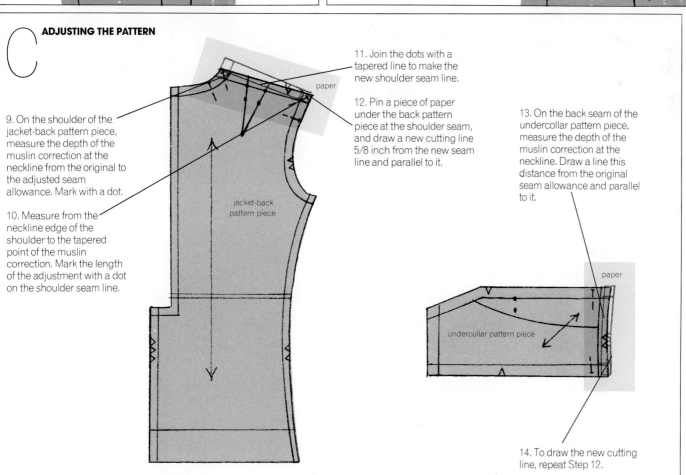

9. On the shoulder of the jacket-back pattern piece, measure the depth of the muslin correction at the neckline from the original to the adjusted seam allowance. Mark with a dot.

10. Measure from the neckline edge of the shoulder to the tapered point of the muslin correction. Mark the length of the adjustment with a dot on the shoulder seam line.

11. Join the dots with a tapered line to make the new shoulder seam line.

12. Pin a piece of paper under the back pattern piece at the shoulder seam, and draw a new cutting line 5/8 inch from the new seam line and parallel to it.

13. On the back seam of the undercollar pattern piece, measure the depth of the muslin correction at the neckline. Draw a line this distance from the original seam allowance and parallel to it.

14. To draw the new cutting line, repeat Step 12.

paper

jacket-back pattern piece

paper

undercollar pattern piece

IF THE BACK NECKLINE IS LOOSE

A SYMPTOMS OF A LOOSE NECKLINE

1. The collar and the neckline seam stand away from the back of the neck.

2. The shoulder seam lies in front of the center of your natural shoulder.

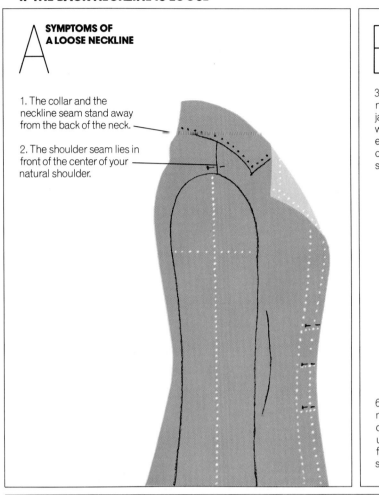

B TAKING IN THE SHOULDER SEAM AT THE NECKLINE

3. Before correcting the neckline, check the fit of the jacket back between the waist and the neckline. If the entire back is too wide, correct the center-back seam as shown on pages 64-65.

4. Remove the collar and open the shoulder seam from the neckline edge.

5. Repin the folded jacket-front seam allowance to the back seam, inside the seam-allowance markings.

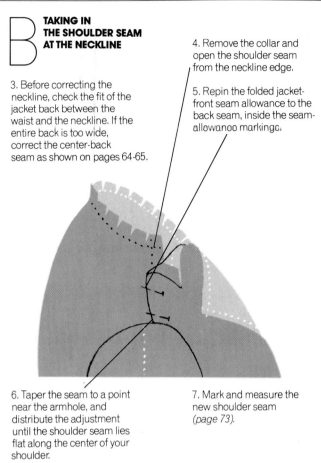

6. Taper the seam to a point near the armhole, and distribute the adjustment until the shoulder seam lies flat along the center of your shoulder.

7. Mark and measure the new shoulder seam (page 73).

C ADJUSTING THE PATTERN

8. On the shoulder of the jacket-back pattern piece, measure the depth of the muslin correction at the neckline from the original to the adjusted seam allowance. Mark with a dot.

9. Measure from the neckline edge of the shoulder seam to the tapered point of the muslin correction. Mark the length of the adjustment with a dot on the shoulder seam line.

10. To make the new shoulder seam line, join the dots with a tapered line.

11. Draw a new cutting line 5/8 inch from the new seam line and parallel to it.

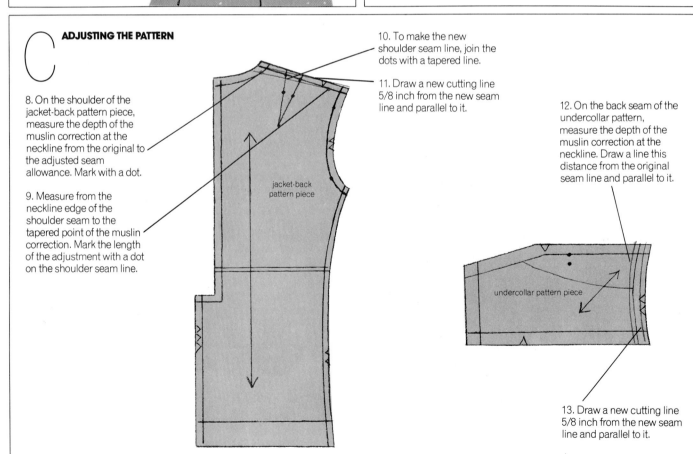

jacket-back pattern piece

undercollar pattern piece

12. On the back seam of the undercollar pattern, measure the depth of the muslin correction at the neckline. Draw a line this distance from the original seam line and parallel to it.

13. Draw a new cutting line 5/8 inch from the new seam line and parallel to it.

IF THE JACKET SHOULDER SEAM IS SQUARE

A SYMPTOMS OF A SQUARE SHOULDER SEAM

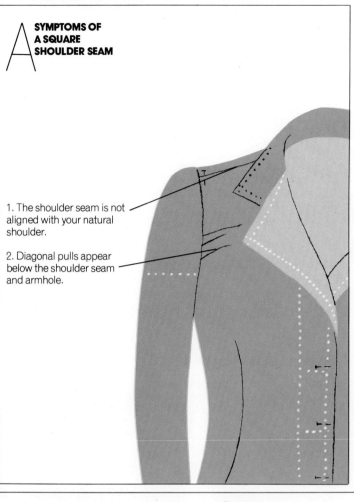

1. The shoulder seam is not aligned with your natural shoulder.

2. Diagonal pulls appear below the shoulder seam and armhole.

B LETTING OUT THE SHOULDER SEAM

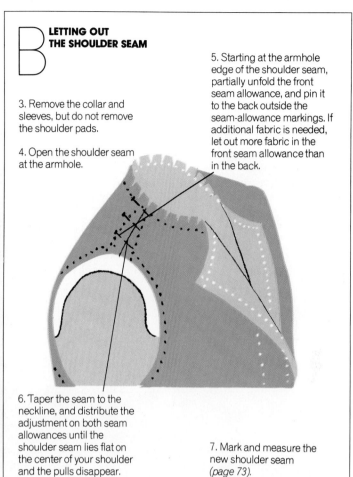

3. Remove the collar and sleeves, but do not remove the shoulder pads.

4. Open the shoulder seam at the armhole.

5. Starting at the armhole edge of the shoulder seam, partially unfold the front seam allowance, and pin it to the back outside the seam-allowance markings. If additional fabric is needed, let out more fabric in the front seam allowance than in the back.

6. Taper the seam to the neckline, and distribute the adjustment on both seam allowances until the shoulder seam lies flat on the center of your shoulder and the pulls disappear.

7. Mark and measure the new shoulder seam (*page 73*).

C ADJUSTING THE PATTERN

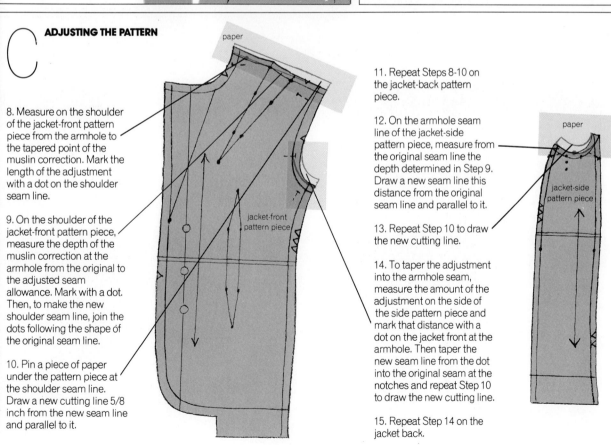

8. Measure on the shoulder of the jacket-front pattern piece from the armhole to the tapered point of the muslin correction. Mark the length of the adjustment with a dot on the shoulder seam line.

9. On the shoulder of the jacket-front pattern piece, measure the depth of the muslin correction at the armhole from the original to the adjusted seam allowance. Mark with a dot. Then, to make the new shoulder seam line, join the dots following the shape of the original seam line.

10. Pin a piece of paper under the pattern piece at the shoulder seam line. Draw a new cutting line 5/8 inch from the new seam line and parallel to it.

11. Repeat Steps 8-10 on the jacket-back pattern piece.

12. On the armhole seam line of the jacket-side pattern piece, measure from the original seam line the depth determined in Step 9. Draw a new seam line this distance from the original seam line and parallel to it.

13. Repeat Step 10 to draw the new cutting line.

14. To taper the adjustment into the armhole seam, measure the amount of the adjustment on the side of the side pattern piece and mark that distance with a dot on the jacket front at the armhole. Then taper the new seam line from the dot into the original seam at the notches and repeat Step 10 to draw the new cutting line.

15. Repeat Step 14 on the jacket back.

IF THE JACKET SHOULDER SEAM SLOPES

A — SYMPTOMS OF A SLOPING SHOULDER SEAM

1. The shoulder seam and sleeve cap stand above the natural shoulder and wrinkles appear below the shoulder.

2. Horizontal folds appear at the underarm.

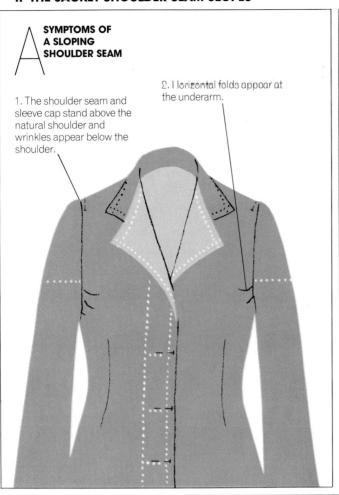

B — TAKING IN THE SHOULDER SEAM

3. Remove the collar and sleeves but do not remove shoulder pads.

4. Open the shoulder seam at the armhole.

5. Repin the folded jacket front seam allowance to the back, inside the original seam allowance on the jacket back.

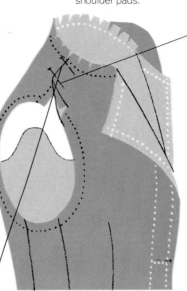

6. Taper the seam to the neckline, and distribute the adjustment until the shoulder seam lies flat along the center of your shoulder and the horizontal folds disappear.

7. Mark and measure the new shoulder seam *(page 73)*.

C — ADJUSTING THE PATTERN

8. Measure from the armhole to the tapered point of the muslin correction. Mark the length of the adjustment with a dot on the shoulder seam line.

9. On the shoulder of the jacket-front pattern piece, measure the depth of the muslin correction at the armhole from the original to the adjusted seam allowance. Mark with a dot, and make the new shoulder seam line by joining the dots following the shape of the original seam line.

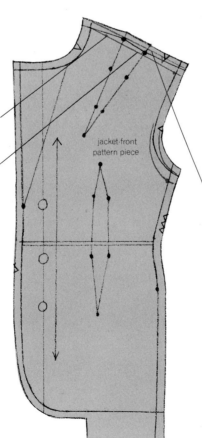

jacket-front pattern piece

10. Draw a new cutting line 5/8 inch from the new seam line and parallel to it.

11. Repeat Steps 8-10 on the jacket-back pattern piece.

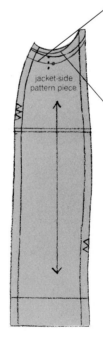

jacket-side pattern piece

12. On the armhole seam line of the jacket-side pattern piece, measure from the armhole seam line the depth determined in Step 9. Draw a new seam line this distance from the original seam line and parallel to it.

13. Repeat Step 10 to draw the new cutting line.

14. To taper the new seam and cutting lines into the original armhole seam, repeat Steps 14 and 15, Box C, for the square shoulder, lowering both lines.

IF THE TOP OF THE SLEEVE IS LOOSE

A. SYMPTOMS OF A LOOSE SLEEVE CAP OR LONG SHOULDER

1. If the shoulder is too long, the shoulder seam droops below the natural shoulder line.

2. If the sleeve cap is loose, it rolls up above the shoulder seam to create a puffed effect.

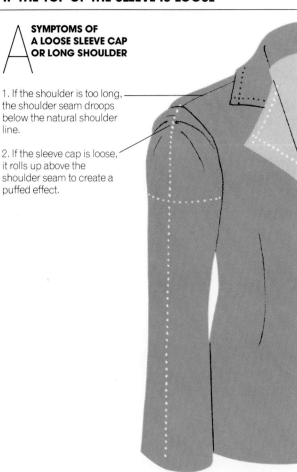

B. TAKING IN THE SLEEVE TOP

3. Open the armhole seam around the top of the sleeve cap, releasing at least 4 inches of the sleeve cap on either side of the shoulder seam.

4. Smooth the sleeve cap up over your upper arm to meet the shoulder seam. Fold under the excess fabric inside the original seam line at the center edge of the sleeve cap, and pin the folded edge to the armhole of the jacket so that it meets the natural shoulder at the armhole seam.

5. Continue to pin the folded edge of the sleeve cap around the armhole seam, tapering it into the original seam line midway down the armhole.

6. Mark and measure the new armhole and shoulder seam (page 73).

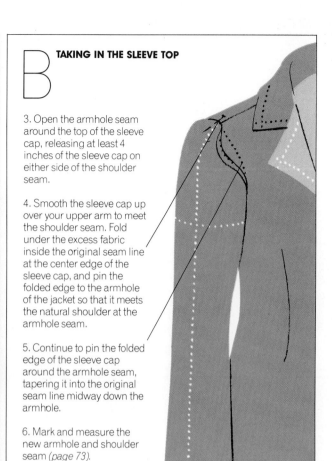

C. ADJUSTING THE PATTERN

7. On the cap of the sleeve pattern piece, measure the depth of the muslin correction from the original to the adjusted seam allowance. Mark with a dot below the original dot indicating the center of the sleeve cap.

8. On each side of the sleeve-cap pattern, measure the distance from the dot made in Step 7 to the end of the adjustment. Mark with a dot on each side.

9. To make the new seam line, join the three dots following the curve of the original seam line.

10. Draw a new cutting line 5/8 inch outside the new seam line and parallel to it.

11. On the armhole seam line of the jacket-front pattern piece, measure from the original shoulder seam line to the tapered point on the corrected muslin. Mark with a dot.

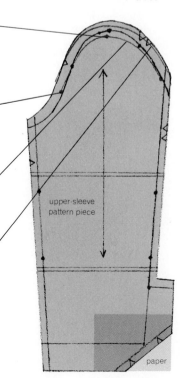

upper-sleeve pattern piece

paper

12. On the shoulder of the jacket-front pattern piece, measure the depth from the original shoulder seam line to the new seam line on the muslin correction. Mark with a dot.

13. To make the new armhole seam line, join the two dots with a line, following the curve of the original seam line.

14. Draw a new cutting line 5/8 inch outside the new seam line and parallel to it.

15. Repeat Steps 11-14 for the jacket-back pattern piece.

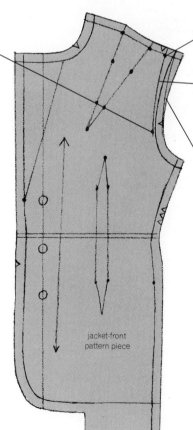

jacket-front pattern piece

IF THE TOP OF THE SLEEVE IS TIGHT

A SYMPTOMS OF A SHORT SLEEVE CAP OR NARROW SHOULDER

1. If the shoulder is too narrow, the sleeve cap pulls up from the natural shoulder line.

2. If the sleeve cap is short, it feels snug around the upper arm. Pulls appear on the sleeve cap.

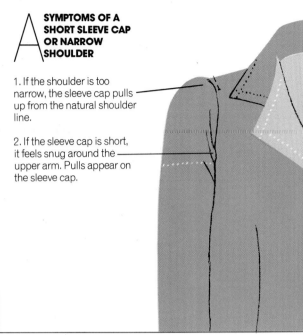

B LETTING OUT THE SLEEVE CAP

3. Open the armhole seam around the top of the sleeve cap, releasing at least 4 inches on either side of the shoulder seam.

4. Smooth the sleeve cap up over the upper arm until the wrinkles disappear. Fold under the seam allowance on the cap. Pin it to the shoulder. You may have to pin it outside the original seam line to align the adjusted sleeve cap with the natural shoulder line.

5. Continue to pin the folded seam allowance of the sleeve cap around the jacket armhole, tapering it into the original seam line midway down the armhole.

6. Mark and measure the new armhole and shoulder seam (page 73).

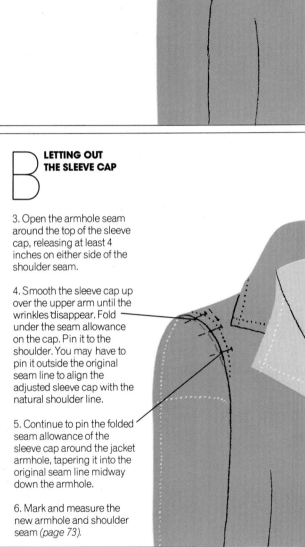

C ADJUSTING THE PATTERN

7. On the cap of the sleeve pattern piece, measure the depth of the muslin correction from the original to the adjusted seam allowance. Mark with a dot above the original dot indicating the center of the sleeve cap.

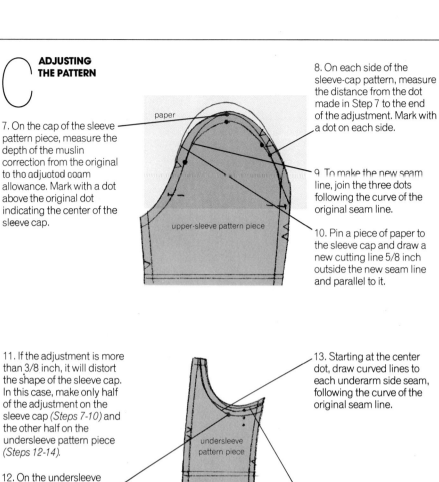

8. On each side of the sleeve-cap pattern, measure the distance from the dot made in Step 7 to the end of the adjustment. Mark with a dot on each side.

9. To make the new seam line, join the three dots following the curve of the original seam line.

10. Pin a piece of paper to the sleeve cap and draw a new cutting line 5/8 inch outside the new seam line and parallel to it.

11. If the adjustment is more than 3/8 inch, it will distort the shape of the sleeve cap. In this case, make only half of the adjustment on the sleeve cap (Steps 7-10) and the other half on the undersleeve pattern piece (Steps 12-14).

12. On the undersleeve pattern piece, measure 1/2 of the muslin correction found in Step 7 between the original and the adjusted seam allowance. Mark with a dot in the center of the underarm below the seam line.

13. Starting at the center dot, draw curved lines to each underarm side seam, following the curve of the original seam line.

14. Draw a new cutting line 5/8 inch outside the new underarm seam line and parallel to it.

15. On the armhole seam line of the jacket-front pattern piece, measure the distance down from the original shoulder seam line to the tapered point on the corrected muslin. Mark with a dot on the armhole seam line.

16. On the shoulder of the jacket-front pattern piece, measure the depth from the original shoulder seam line to the new seam line on the muslin correction. Mark with a dot on the shoulder seam line.

17. To make the new armhole seam line, join the two dots with a line, following the curve of the original seam.

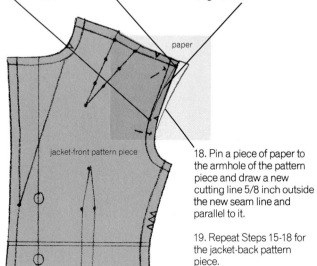

18. Pin a piece of paper to the armhole of the pattern piece and draw a new cutting line 5/8 inch outside the new seam line and parallel to it.

19. Repeat Steps 15-18 for the jacket-back pattern piece.

IF THE UPPER BACK IS LONG

A — SYMPTOM OF A LONG UPPER BACK

1. Horizontal wrinkles form on the jacket back between the shoulders.

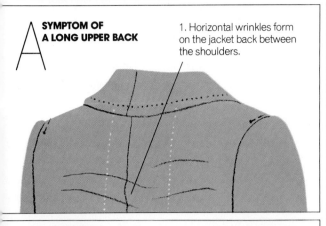

B — TAKING IN THE UPPER BACK

2. Starting in the center back of the jacket at the loose area, pin the excess fabric into a horizontal tuck.

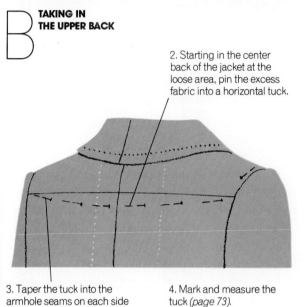

3. Taper the tuck into the armhole seams on each side and insert pins as you go.

4. Mark and measure the tuck (*page 73*).

C — ADJUSTING THE PATTERN

5. On the jacket-back pattern piece, measure from the neckline to the top of the tuck, and mark this distance with a dot on the center-back seam line. Then draw a straight line from the dot to the armhole seam.

6. Measure from the dot the depth of the tucked muslin correction, down the center-back seam line. Mark with a dot. Then draw a line from the second dot to the point where the line made in Step 5 intersects the armhole seam.

7. Fold the pattern along the line made in Step 6, turning the folded edge up so that it meets the line made in Step 5. Taper the tuck to a point at the armhole seam line; pin it flat.

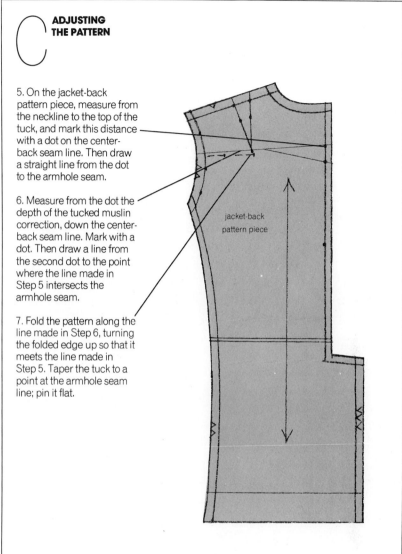

jacket-back pattern piece

IF THE UPPER BACK IS SHORT

A — SYMPTOMS OF A SHORT UPPER BACK

1. The jacket feels snug and rides up over the shoulders.

2. Wrinkles radiate from the center of the upper back toward the armhole.

3. The hem of the jacket hikes up in the back.

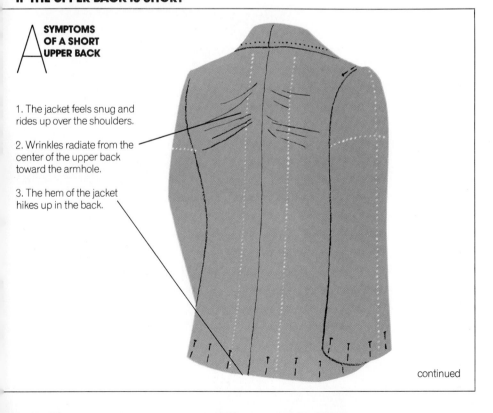

continued

B SLASHING THE UPPER BACK

4. Cut across the upper back in a horizontal line, from one armhole seam to the other, in the area that is snug.

5. Insert a piece of muslin under the slash. Spread the slashed edges of the jacket back apart until the jacket feels comfortable and the wrinkles disappear.

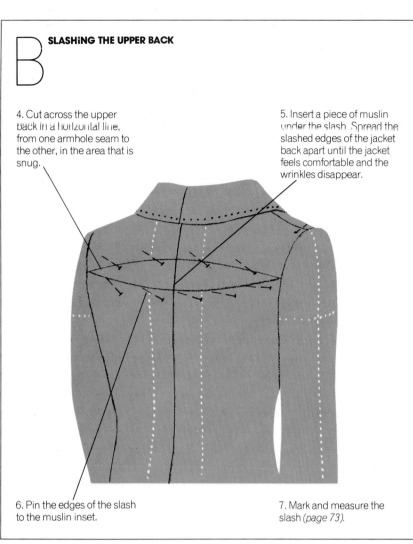

6. Pin the edges of the slash to the muslin inset.

7. Mark and measure the slash (page 73).

C ADJUSTING THE PATTERN

8. On the jacket-back pattern piece, measure from the neckline seam to the top of the slashed muslin correction. Mark with a dot on the center-back seam line. Then draw a line from the dot straight across to the armhole seam.

9. Cut along the line drawn in Step 8, up to but not through the edge of the pattern piece.

10. Place a piece of paper under the slash. Spread the cut edges apart until the distance between the edges of the slash at the center-back seam line is equal to the depth of the slashed muslin correction. Pin the insert in place.

11. Draw a seam line at the center back to connect the original seam lines on the pattern.

12. Draw a new cutting line 5/8 inch outside the new seam line and parallel to it.

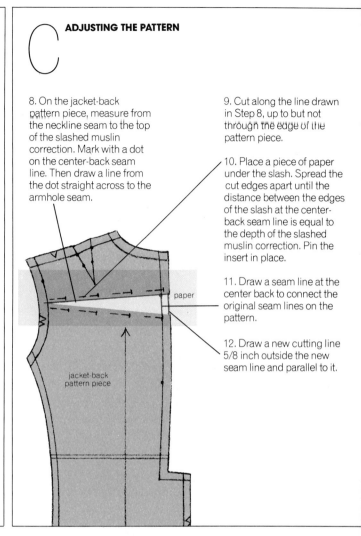

paper

jacket-back pattern piece

IF THE BACK OR SIDE IS LOOSE

A SYMPTOMS OF A LOOSE CENTER-BACK OR SIDE SEAM

1. If the back is too loose, lengthwise wrinkles form between the neckline and the waist.

2. If the side seam is too loose, the jacket falls away from the body at the bust, waist or hips.

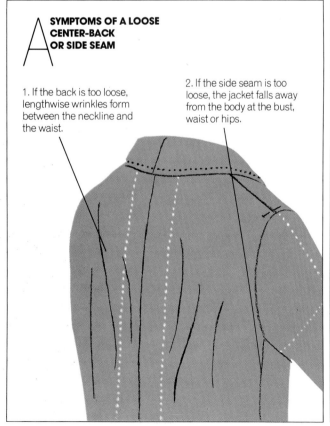

B TUCKING THE CENTER-BACK OR SIDE SEAM

3. Remove the collar. Starting at the back neckline on the center seam, pinch the excess fabric into a vertical tuck, and pin.

4. Extend the tuck on the center-back seam. Taper it to a point at the waistline, and insert pins as you go.

5. Mark and measure the tucked seam (page 73).

6. Tuck the excess fabric on the side seam in the area that is too loose, and taper the tuck into the original side seam, inserting pins as you go.

7. Mark and measure the tucked seam (page 73).

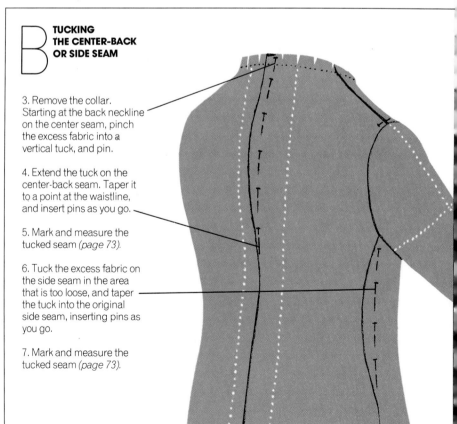

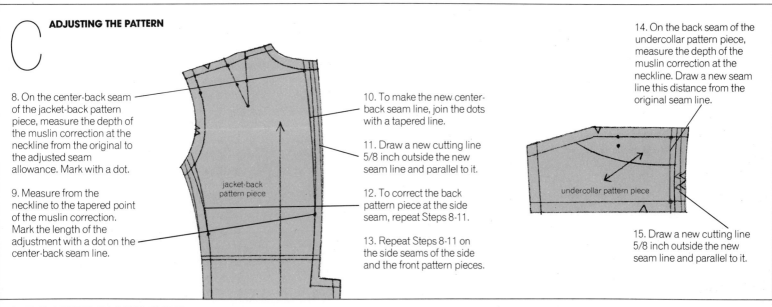

C ADJUSTING THE PATTERN

8. On the center-back seam of the jacket-back pattern piece, measure the depth of the muslin correction at the neckline from the original to the adjusted seam allowance. Mark with a dot.

9. Measure from the neckline to the tapered point of the muslin correction. Mark the length of the adjustment with a dot on the center-back seam line.

jacket-back pattern piece

10. To make the new center-back seam line, join the dots with a tapered line.

11. Draw a new cutting line 5/8 inch outside the new seam line and parallel to it.

12. To correct the back pattern piece at the side seam, repeat Steps 8-11.

13. Repeat Steps 8-11 on the side seams of the side and the front pattern pieces.

14. On the back seam of the undercollar pattern piece, measure the depth of the muslin correction at the neckline. Draw a new seam line this distance from the original seam line.

undercollar pattern piece

15. Draw a new cutting line 5/8 inch outside the new seam line and parallel to it.

IF THE CENTER BACK IS TIGHT

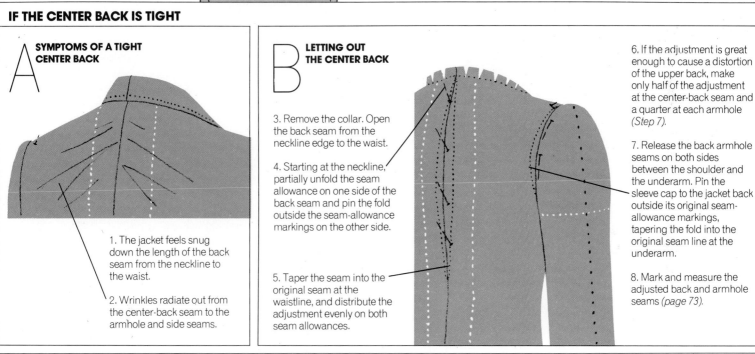

A SYMPTOMS OF A TIGHT CENTER BACK

1. The jacket feels snug down the length of the back seam from the neckline to the waist.

2. Wrinkles radiate out from the center-back seam to the armhole and side seams.

B LETTING OUT THE CENTER BACK

3. Remove the collar. Open the back seam from the neckline edge to the waist.

4. Starting at the neckline, partially unfold the seam allowance on one side of the back seam and pin the fold outside the seam-allowance markings on the other side.

5. Taper the seam into the original seam at the waistline, and distribute the adjustment evenly on both seam allowances.

6. If the adjustment is great enough to cause a distortion of the upper back, make only half of the adjustment at the center-back seam and a quarter at each armhole *(Step 7)*.

7. Release the back armhole seams on both sides between the shoulder and the underarm. Pin the sleeve cap to the jacket back outside its original seam-allowance markings, tapering the fold into the original seam line at the underarm.

8. Mark and measure the adjusted back and armhole seams *(page 73)*.

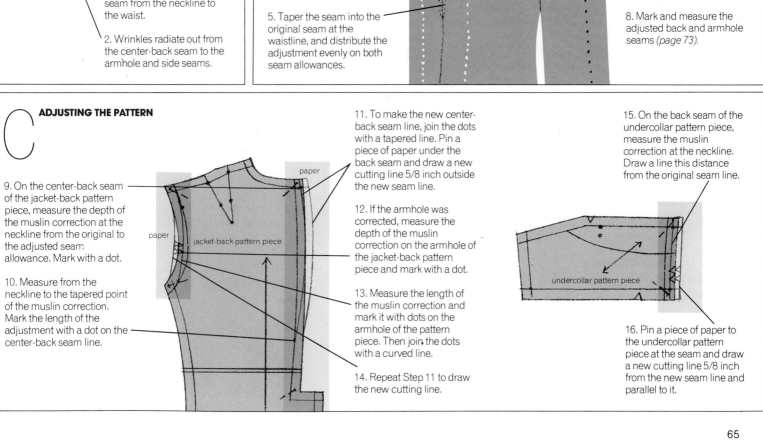

C ADJUSTING THE PATTERN

9. On the center-back seam of the jacket-back pattern piece, measure the depth of the muslin correction at the neckline from the original to the adjusted seam allowance. Mark with a dot.

10. Measure from the neckline to the tapered point of the muslin correction. Mark the length of the adjustment with a dot on the center-back seam line.

paper

jacket-back pattern piece

paper

11. To make the new center-back seam line, join the dots with a tapered line. Pin a piece of paper under the back seam and draw a new cutting line 5/8 inch outside the new seam line.

12. If the armhole was corrected, measure the depth of the muslin correction on the armhole of the jacket-back pattern piece and mark with a dot.

13. Measure the length of the muslin correction and mark it with dots on the armhole of the pattern piece. Then join the dots with a curved line.

14. Repeat Step 11 to draw the new cutting line.

15. On the back seam of the undercollar pattern piece, measure the muslin correction at the neckline. Draw a line this distance from the original seam line.

undercollar pattern piece

16. Pin a piece of paper to the undercollar pattern piece at the seam and draw a new cutting line 5/8 inch from the new seam line and parallel to it.

IF THE PANTS ARE LOOSE AT THE SIDE SEAM

A. SYMPTOMS OF A LOOSE WAIST, HIP OR LEG

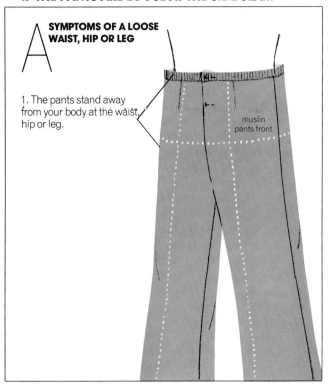

1. The pants stand away from your body at the waist, hip or leg.

B. TUCKING THE SIDE SEAM

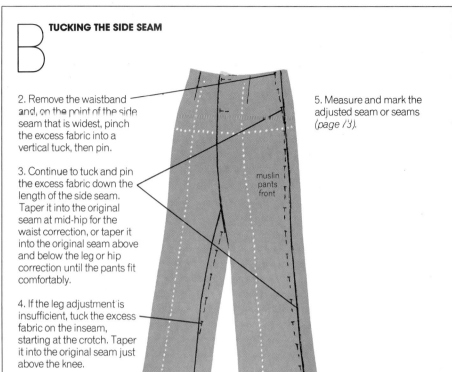

2. Remove the waistband and, on the point of the side seam that is widest, pinch the excess fabric into a vertical tuck, then pin.

3. Continue to tuck and pin the excess fabric down the length of the side seam. Taper it into the original seam at mid-hip for the waist correction, or taper it into the original seam above and below the leg or hip correction until the pants fit comfortably.

4. If the leg adjustment is insufficient, tuck the excess fabric on the inseam, starting at the crotch. Taper it into the original seam just above the knee.

5. Measure and mark the adjusted seam or seams *(page 73)*.

C. ADJUSTING THE PATTERN

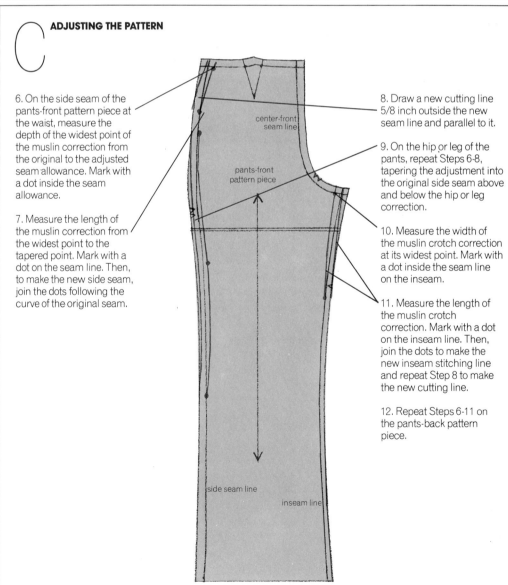

6. On the side seam of the pants-front pattern piece at the waist, measure the depth of the widest point of the muslin correction from the original to the adjusted seam allowance. Mark with a dot inside the seam allowance.

7. Measure the length of the muslin correction from the widest point to the tapered point. Mark with a dot on the seam line. Then, to make the new side seam, join the dots following the curve of the original seam.

8. Draw a new cutting line 5/8 inch outside the new seam line and parallel to it.

9. On the hip or leg of the pants, repeat Steps 6-8, tapering the adjustment into the original side seam above and below the hip or leg correction.

10. Measure the width of the muslin crotch correction at its widest point. Mark with a dot inside the seam line on the inseam.

11. Measure the length of the muslin crotch correction. Mark with a dot on the inseam line. Then, join the dots to make the new inseam stitching line and repeat Step 8 to make the new cutting line.

12. Repeat Steps 6-11 on the pants-back pattern piece.

IF THE PANTS ARE TIGHT AT THE SIDE SEAM

A SYMPTOMS OF A TIGHT WAIST, HIP OR LEG

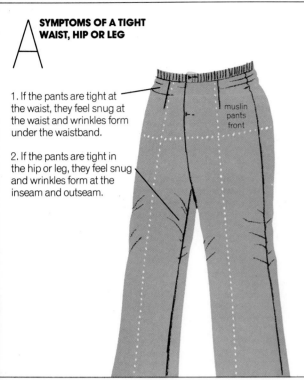

1. If the pants are tight at the waist, they feel snug at the waist and wrinkles form under the waistband.

2. If the pants are tight in the hip or leg, they feel snug and wrinkles form at the inseam and outseam.

muslin pants front

B LETTING OUT THE SIDE SEAM

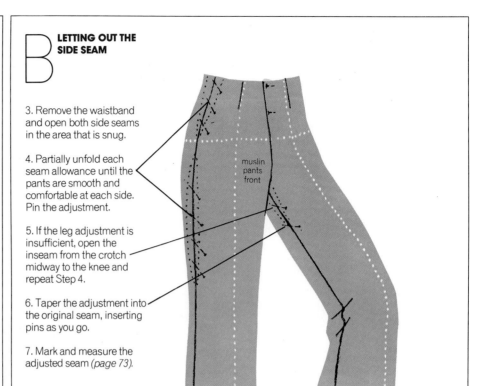

3. Remove the waistband and open both side seams in the area that is snug.

4. Partially unfold each seam allowance until the pants are smooth and comfortable at each side. Pin the adjustment.

5. If the leg adjustment is insufficient, open the inseam from the crotch midway to the knee and repeat Step 4.

6. Taper the adjustment into the original seam, inserting pins as you go.

7. Mark and measure the adjusted seam (page 73).

muslin pants front

C ADJUSTING THE PATTERN

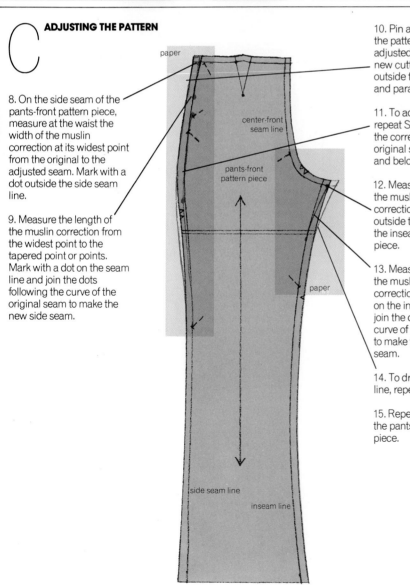

8. On the side seam of the pants-front pattern piece, measure at the waist the width of the muslin correction at its widest point from the original to the adjusted seam. Mark with a dot outside the side seam line.

9. Measure the length of the muslin correction from the widest point to the tapered point or points. Mark with a dot on the seam line and join the dots following the curve of the original seam to make the new side seam.

10. Pin a piece of paper to the pattern piece in the adjusted area and draw a new cutting line 5/8 inch outside the new seam line and parallel to it.

11. To adjust the hip or leg, repeat Steps 8-10, tapering the correction into the original side seam above and below the correction.

12. Measure the width of the muslin crotch correction. Mark with a dot outside the seam line on the inseam of the pattern piece.

13. Measure the length of the muslin crotch correction. Mark with a dot on the inseam line. Then join the dots, following the curve of the original seam to make the new crotch seam.

14. To draw a new cutting line, repeat Step 10.

15. Repeat Steps 8-14 on the pants-back pattern piece.

paper

center-front seam line

pants-front pattern piece

paper

side seam line

inseam line

IF THE PANTS ARE TIGHT AT THE HIPBONE

A SYMPTOMS OF TIGHT UPPER HIP

1. The pants feel snug across the hipbone and wrinkles radiate out from the side seams.

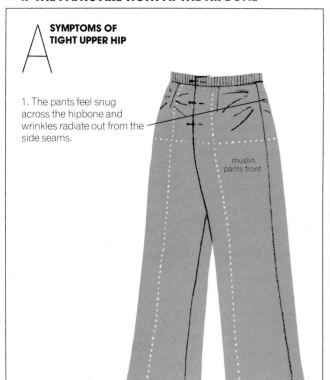

muslin pants front

B LETTING OUT THE HIPLINE

2. Open both side seams from the waist to the hip.

3. Starting at the waist, smooth the pants front and back together until they meet comfortably at each side.

4. Unfold enough of the pants-front seam allowance to overlap the back seam allowance. Pin the fold outside the original seam-allowance markings. Let out more fabric in the front than in the back seam allowance if necessary.

5. Taper the adjusted seam into the original seam, inserting pins as you go.

6. Open the front darts, and repin to fit the contours of the body.

7. Mark and measure the adjusted side seam and the dart (page 73).

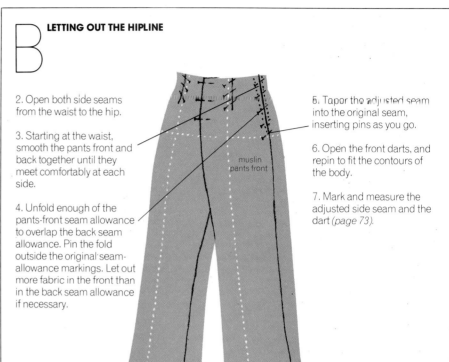

muslin pants front

C ADJUSTING THE PATTERN

8. On the waistline of the pants-front pattern piece, measure the width of the muslin correction from the original to the adjusted seam. Mark with a dot at the side seam.

9. Measure on the side seam the length from the waistline to the tapered point of the muslin correction. Mark the length of the adjustment with a dot on the seam line. Then join the dots with a line following the curve of the original seam to make the new side seam.

10. Pin a piece of paper on the side seam, and draw a new cutting line 5/8 inch outside the new seam line and parallel to it.

11. Repeat Steps 8-10 on the pants-back pattern piece.

12. Distribute the amount of the dart adjustment from the muslin correction on both sides of the original dart markings. Mark with a dot on the outside of the original dart markings at the waistline.

13. Taper a line from each dot to a point below the original point of the dart.

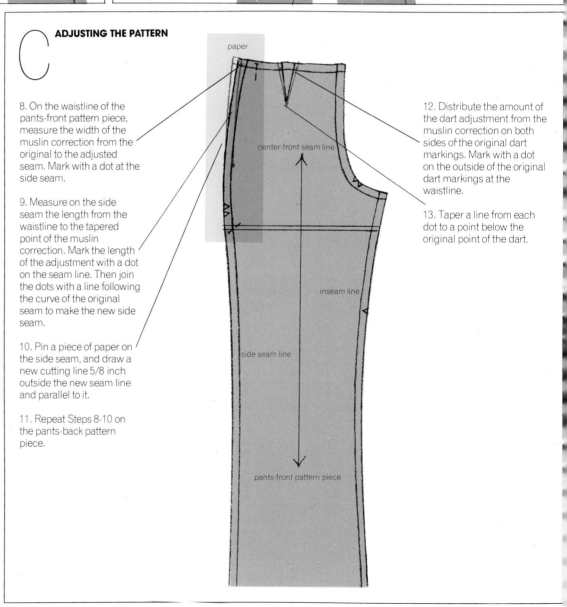

paper

center-front seam line

inseam line

side seam line

pants-front pattern piece

IF THE PANTS-BACK WAIST IS HIGH

A SYMPTOMS OF A HIGH WAIST

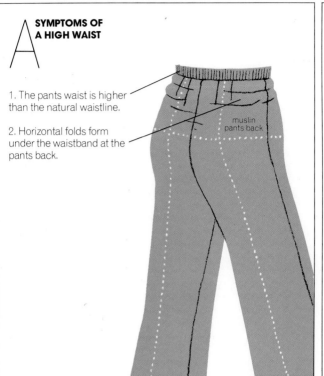

1. The pants waist is higher than the natural waistline.

2. Horizontal folds form under the waistband at the pants back.

muslin pants back

B TUCKING THE BACK

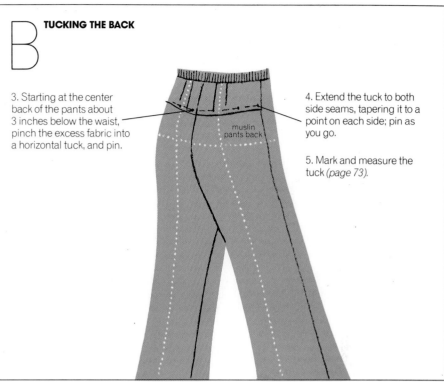

3. Starting at the center back of the pants about 3 inches below the waist, pinch the excess fabric into a horizontal tuck, and pin.

4. Extend the tuck to both side seams, tapering it to a point on each side; pin as you go.

5. Mark and measure the tuck (page 73).

muslin pants back

C ADJUSTING THE PATTERN

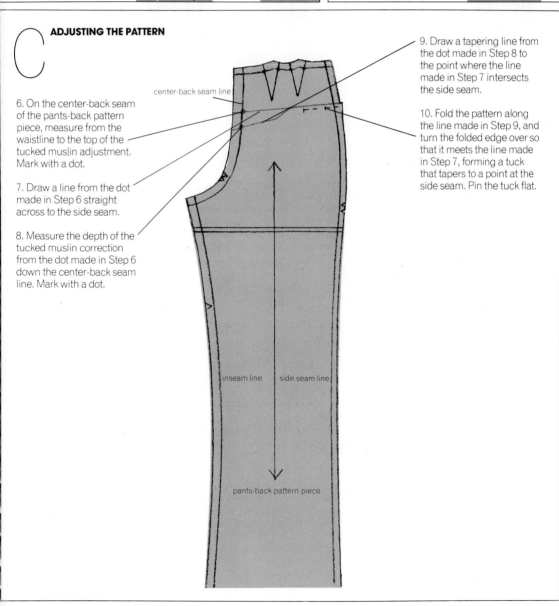

6. On the center-back seam of the pants-back pattern piece, measure from the waistline to the top of the tucked muslin adjustment. Mark with a dot.

7. Draw a line from the dot made in Step 6 straight across to the side seam.

8. Measure the depth of the tucked muslin correction from the dot made in Step 6 down the center-back seam line. Mark with a dot.

9. Draw a tapering line from the dot made in Step 8 to the point where the line made in Step 7 intersects the side seam.

10. Fold the pattern along the line made in Step 9, and turn the folded edge over so that it meets the line made in Step 7, forming a tuck that tapers to a point at the side seam. Pin the tuck flat.

center-back seam line

inseam line   side seam line

pants-back pattern piece

IF THE CROTCH OR ABDOMEN IS TIGHT

A. SYMPTOMS OF A TIGHT CROTCH OR ABDOMEN

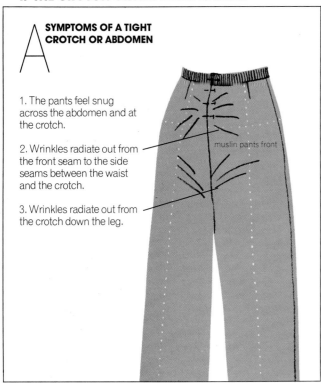

1. The pants feel snug across the abdomen and at the crotch.

2. Wrinkles radiate out from the front seam to the side seams between the waist and the crotch.

3. Wrinkles radiate out from the crotch down the leg.

muslin pants front

B. SLASHING THE ABDOMEN AND CROTCH

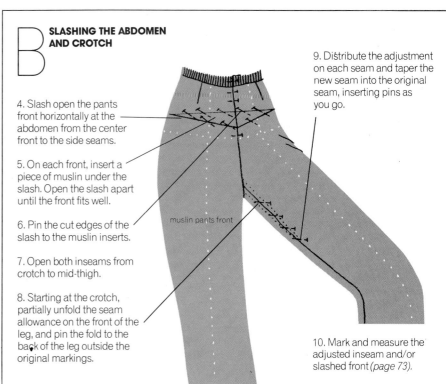

4. Slash open the pants front horizontally at the abdomen from the center front to the side seams.

5. On each front, insert a piece of muslin under the slash. Open the slash apart until the front fits well.

6. Pin the cut edges of the slash to the muslin inserts.

7. Open both inseams from crotch to mid-thigh.

8. Starting at the crotch, partially unfold the seam allowance on the front of the leg, and pin the fold to the back of the leg outside the original markings.

9. Distribute the adjustment on each seam and taper the new seam into the original seam, inserting pins as you go.

muslin pants front

10. Mark and measure the adjusted inseam and/or slashed front (page 73).

C. ADJUSTING THE PATTERN

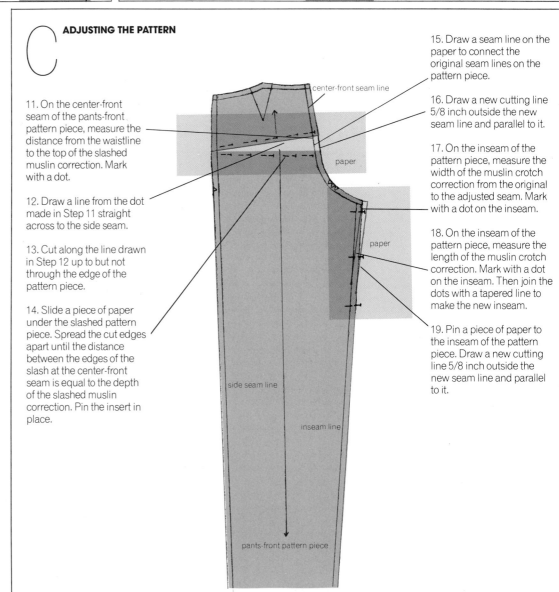

11. On the center-front seam of the pants-front pattern piece, measure the distance from the waistline to the top of the slashed muslin correction. Mark with a dot.

12. Draw a line from the dot made in Step 11 straight across to the side seam.

13. Cut along the line drawn in Step 12 up to but not through the edge of the pattern piece.

14. Slide a piece of paper under the slashed pattern piece. Spread the cut edges apart until the distance between the edges of the slash at the center-front seam is equal to the depth of the slashed muslin correction. Pin the insert in place.

15. Draw a seam line on the paper to connect the original seam lines on the pattern piece.

16. Draw a new cutting line 5/8 inch outside the new seam line and parallel to it.

17. On the inseam of the pattern piece, measure the width of the muslin crotch correction from the original to the adjusted seam. Mark with a dot on the inseam.

18. On the inseam of the pattern piece, measure the length of the muslin crotch correction. Mark with a dot on the inseam. Then join the dots with a tapered line to make the new inseam.

19. Pin a piece of paper to the inseam of the pattern piece. Draw a new cutting line 5/8 inch outside the new seam line and parallel to it.

center-front seam line

paper

paper

side seam line

inseam line

pants-front pattern piece

IF THE PANTS ARE LOOSE AT THE SEAT

A SYMPTOMS OF A LOOSE SEAT

1. The seat of the pants droops, and folds appear at the seat back and the back of the pants legs.

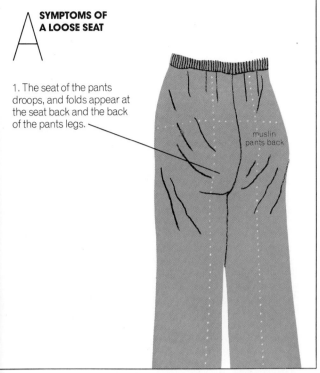

muslin pants back

B TUCKING THE PANTS BACK

2. Starting at the center-back seam about 4 inches below the waist, pinch the excess fabric into a horizontal tuck, and pin.

3. Extend the tuck to both side seams; taper it to a point on each side, and insert pins as you go.

4. If the seat is still too loose, start at the crotch and pinch the excess fabric into a vertical tuck down the inseam. Pin the tuck.

5. Extend the tuck down the inseam; taper it to a point midway down the thigh, inserting pins as you go.

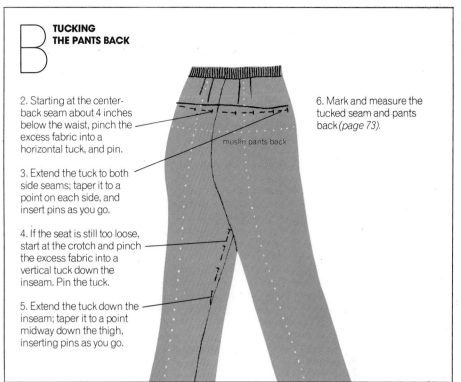

muslin pants back

6. Mark and measure the tucked seam and pants back (*page 73*).

C ADJUSTING THE PATTERN

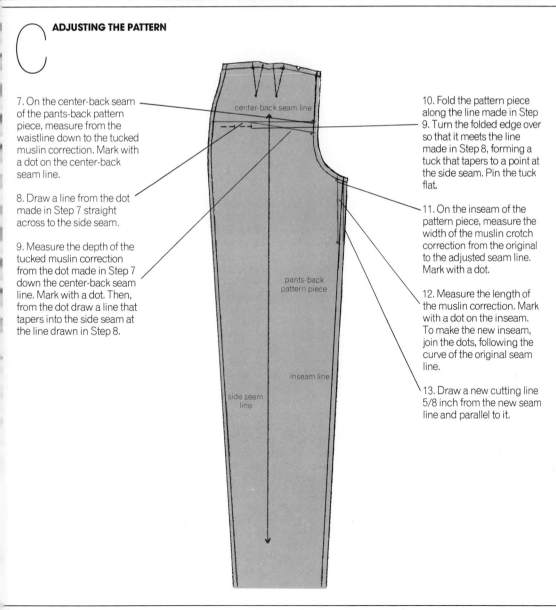

center-back seam line

pants-back pattern piece

inseam line

side seam line

7. On the center-back seam of the pants-back pattern piece, measure from the waistline down to the tucked muslin correction. Mark with a dot on the center-back seam line.

8. Draw a line from the dot made in Step 7 straight across to the side seam.

9. Measure the depth of the tucked muslin correction from the dot made in Step 7 down the center-back seam line. Mark with a dot. Then, from the dot draw a line that tapers into the side seam at the line drawn in Step 8.

10. Fold the pattern piece along the line made in Step 9. Turn the folded edge over so that it meets the line made in Step 8, forming a tuck that tapers to a point at the side seam. Pin the tuck flat.

11. On the inseam of the pattern piece, measure the width of the muslin crotch correction from the original to the adjusted seam line. Mark with a dot.

12. Measure the length of the muslin correction. Mark with a dot on the inseam. To make the new inseam, join the dots, following the curve of the original seam line.

13. Draw a new cutting line 5/8 inch from the new seam line and parallel to it.

IF THE PANTS ARE TIGHT AT THE SEAT

A SYMPTOMS OF A TIGHT SEAT

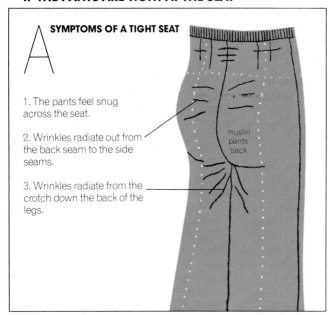

1. The pants feel snug across the seat.

2. Wrinkles radiate out from the back seam to the side seams.

3. Wrinkles radiate from the crotch down the back of the legs.

B SLASHING THE PANTS BACK

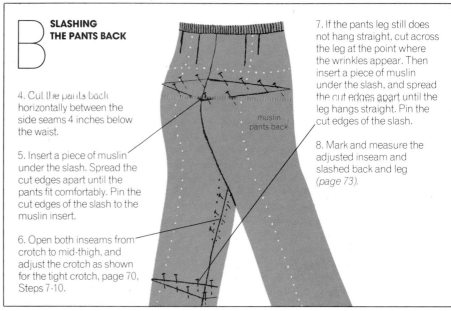

4. Cut the pants back horizontally between the side seams 4 inches below the waist.

5. Insert a piece of muslin under the slash. Spread the cut edges apart until the pants fit comfortably. Pin the cut edges of the slash to the muslin insert.

6. Open both inseams from crotch to mid-thigh, and adjust the crotch as shown for the tight crotch, page 70, Steps 7-10.

7. If the pants leg still does not hang straight, cut across the leg at the point where the wrinkles appear. Then insert a piece of muslin under the slash, and spread the cut edges apart until the leg hangs straight. Pin the cut edges of the slash.

8. Mark and measure the adjusted inseam and slashed back and leg (page 73).

C ADJUSTING THE PATTERN

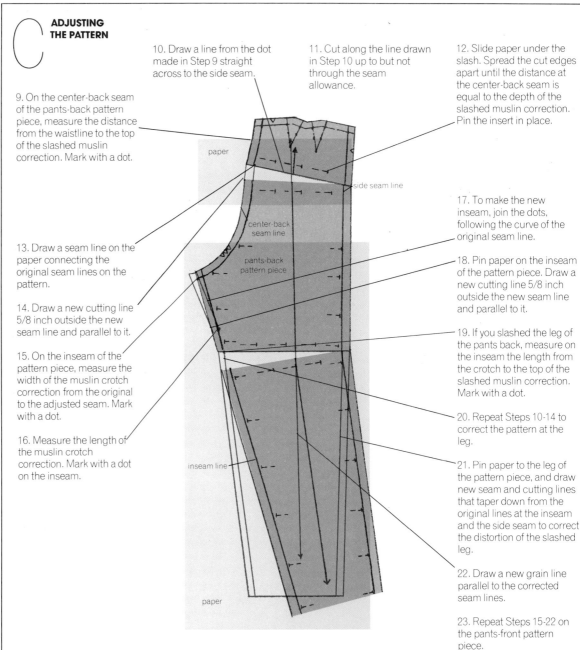

9. On the center-back seam of the pants-back pattern piece, measure the distance from the waistline to the top of the slashed muslin correction. Mark with a dot.

10. Draw a line from the dot made in Step 9 straight across to the side seam.

11. Cut along the line drawn in Step 10 up to but not through the seam allowance.

12. Slide paper under the slash. Spread the cut edges apart until the distance at the center-back seam is equal to the depth of the slashed muslin correction. Pin the insert in place.

13. Draw a seam line on the paper connecting the original seam lines on the pattern.

14. Draw a new cutting line 5/8 inch outside the new seam line and parallel to it.

15. On the inseam of the pattern piece, measure the width of the muslin crotch correction from the original to the adjusted seam. Mark with a dot.

16. Measure the length of the muslin crotch correction. Mark with a dot on the inseam.

17. To make the new inseam, join the dots, following the curve of the original seam line.

18. Pin paper on the inseam of the pattern piece. Draw a new cutting line 5/8 inch outside the new seam line and parallel to it.

19. If you slashed the leg of the pants back, measure on the inseam the length from the crotch to the top of the slashed muslin correction. Mark with a dot.

20. Repeat Steps 10-14 to correct the pattern at the leg.

21. Pin paper to the leg of the pattern piece, and draw new seam and cutting lines that taper down from the original lines at the inseam and the side seam to correct the distortion of the slashed leg.

22. Draw a new grain line parallel to the corrected seam lines.

23. Repeat Steps 15-22 on the pants-front pattern piece.

MARKING AND MEASURING MUSLIN ADJUSTMENTS

IF THE MUSLIN WAS TUCKED...

1. Baste the tuck along its base and remove the pins. Then baste the tuck flat.

2. Measure the depth of the tuck at its widest point.

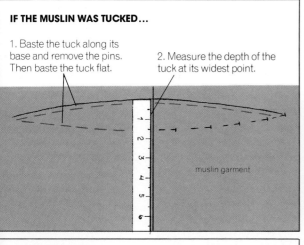

IF THE MUSLIN WAS SLASHED...

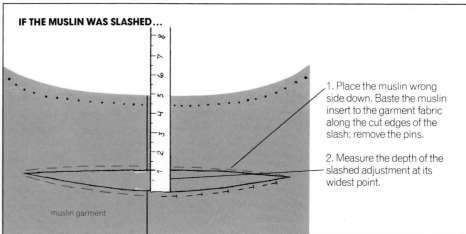

1. Place the muslin wrong side down. Baste the muslin insert to the garment fabric along the cut edges of the slash; remove the pins.

2. Measure the depth of the slashed adjustment at its widest point.

IF THE MUSLIN WAS TUCKED AT A SEAM...

1. Turn the muslin wrong side out and fold the garment along the tucked seam.

2. With your fingers, locate the pins along the folded line of the muslin. Mark this position with chalk.

3. Mark the beginning and end of the tuck with chalk lines at right angles to the seam line.

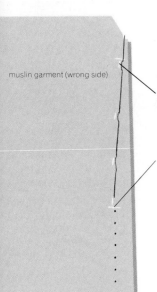

4. Unpin the tuck to make the new seam line; connect the chalk marks made in Step 2.

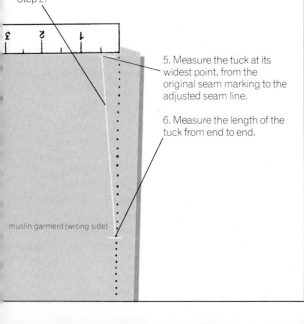

5. Measure the tuck at its widest point, from the original seam marking to the adjusted seam line.

6. Measure the length of the tuck from end to end.

IF THE MUSLIN SEAM WAS LET OUT...

1. Mark both edges of the pinned seam along the fold with chalk lines at 2-inch intervals.

2. Mark the ends of the adjusted seam with chalk lines at right angles to the seam line.

3. Unpin the seam and open the seam 1 inch below the end of the correction. Connect the chalk marks with a smooth line, tapering the line into the original seam line.

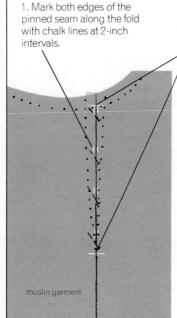

4. Measure the width of the adjustment at its widest point, from the original to the adjusted seam line.

5. Measure the length of the adjustment from end to end.

IF THE MUSLIN SEAM WAS TAKEN IN...

1. Mark both edges of the pinned seam with chalk lines at 1-inch intervals.

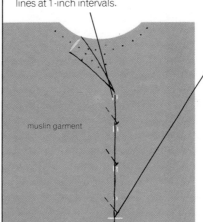

2. Mark the ends of the adjusted seam with chalk lines at right angles to the seam line.

3. To complete marking and measuring the adjustment, repeat Steps 3-5 for letting out the seam. Mark inside the original seam allowance.

A direct fitting for a man

Men's jackets and trousers are likely to require less drastic fitting adjustments than women's, since a man's figure conforms more closely than does a woman's to the straight-lined ideals of tailoring. And those adjustments that are necessary can be made directly on the garment fabric.

Before cutting the fabric for a jacket or trousers, however, compare the proper body measurements *(page 54)* with those listed on the pattern envelope, and wherever needed, lengthen or shorten the pattern pieces along the adjustment lines. Before measuring for the pants-leg length, make sure to turn up the cuff on the fold line of the pattern.

The actual fitting will be done in two phases. For the first, baste together the jacket's basic elements —the front, the back, the undercollar and the interfacing *(pages 108-111).* Try on that baste-up and mark any adjustments as shown on the pages that follow. For the second and final jacket fitting, baste the basic elements together again after the jacket front is assembled—this time adding the sleeves *(page 127).*

Trousers need fitting only once during construction: after the pockets, the zipper and the waistband have been attached, and before the crotch seam is stitched *(page 197).*

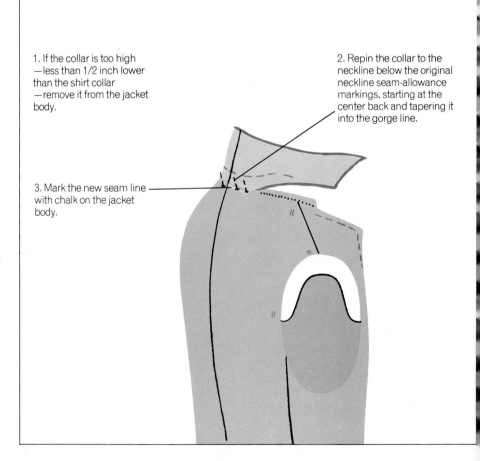

ADJUSTING A LOOSE NECKLINE

1. If the collar and neckline are loose, raise the collar above the jacket back to reveal the center-back seam.

2. Starting at the neckline, pinch the excess fabric into a vertical tuck at the center-back seam, and pin.

3. Pin the tuck evenly up the collar to its top edge, and then taper and pin the tuck down the center-back seam.

4. To mark the new center-back seam, draw chalk lines on both sides of the adjustment tuck.

undercollar

shoulder pad

center-back seam

jacket

ADJUSTING A HIGH COLLAR

1. If the collar is too high —less than 1/2 inch lower than the shirt collar —remove it from the jacket body.

2. Repin the collar to the neckline below the original neckline seam-allowance markings, starting at the center back and tapering it into the gorge line.

3. Mark the new seam line with chalk on the jacket body.

ADJUSTING
A LOW COLLAR

1. If the collar is too low —more than 1/2 inch below the shirt collar—remove it from the jacket body.

2. Repin the collar to the neckline above the original neckline seam-allowance markings, starting at the center back and tapering it into the gorge line.

3. Mark the new seam line with chalk on the jacket body.

ADJUSTING
A SLOPING SHOULDER

1. Check the fit at both shoulder seams. Often only one shoulder slopes.

2. Raise the collar above the jacket and open the shoulder seam at the armhole.

3. Pin the folded jacket-back shoulder seam allowance inside the jacket-front seam allowance, taking in more fabric in the back seam allowance than on the front, and taper the adjustment into the original seam at the neckline, inserting pins as you go.

4. Distribute the adjustment along the shoulder seam until it lies flat along the center of your natural shoulder.

5. Mark the new seam lines on the jacket back and front with chalk.

6. Repin the collar.

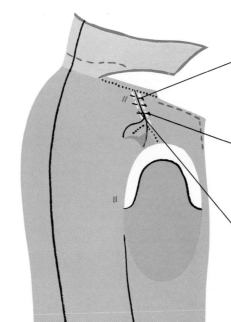

ADJUSTING
A SQUARE SHOULDER

1. If the shoulder is square, remove the collar and open the shoulder seam at the armhole.

2. Partially unfold the jacket-back shoulder seam allowance and pin it to the jacket-front seam allowance, letting out more fabric from the back seam than the front and tapering the adjustment into the original seam at the neckline. Insert pins as you go.

3. Distribute the adjustment along the shoulder seam until it lies flat along the center of the natural shoulder.

4. Mark the new seam lines on the back and front with chalk.

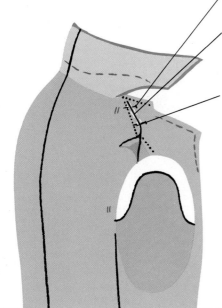

ADJUSTING A LOOSE BACK

1. If the jacket back is too loose across the shoulders, raise the collar above the jacket. Starting on the center seam, pinch the excess fabric into a vertical tuck, and pin.

2. Extend the tuck on the center-back seam. Taper it into the original seam to a point at the waistline, and insert pins as you go.

3. Mark the adjusted seam line with chalk down the length of both sides of the tuck.

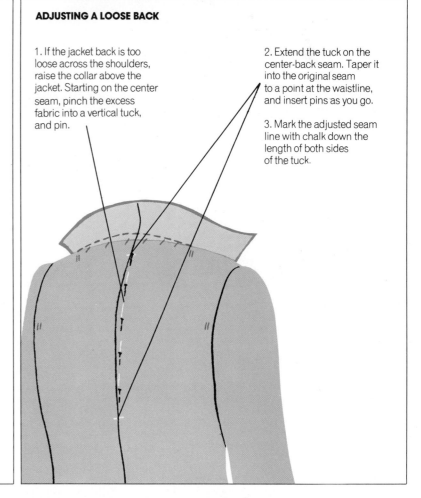

ADJUSTING A NARROW BACK

1. If the jacket back is too narrow across the shoulders, raise the collar above the jacket. Open the center-back seam in the shoulder area, from about 3 inches below the neckline to the underarm.

2. Partially unfold the seam allowance on one side of the back opening. Pin the folded edge to the other side, up to 3/8 inch outside the original seam-allowance markings. Distribute the adjustment evenly on both sides.

3. Taper the adjusted seam into the original seam, inserting pins as you go.

4. Mark the adjusted seam lines on both sides of the adjustment with chalk.

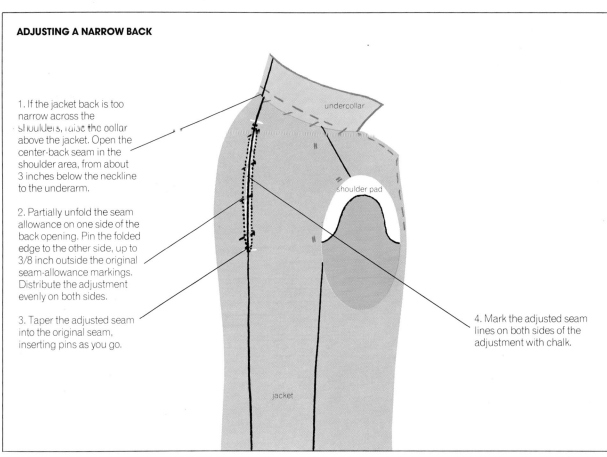

ADJUSTING A LONG BACK

1. If the jacket back is too long, remove the collar, and open the shoulder seam from the neckline to the armhole.

2. Starting at the neckline, fold under the excess fabric in the jacket-back shoulder seam allowance. Pin the folded edge to the jacket front along the original shoulder seam markings.

3. Repin the collar to the jacket below the original neckline seam markings. Start at the center back and taper it into the gorge line.

4. Draw a new collar seam line on the jacket back with chalk.

5. Mark the new shoulder seam on both sides of the folded edge with chalk.

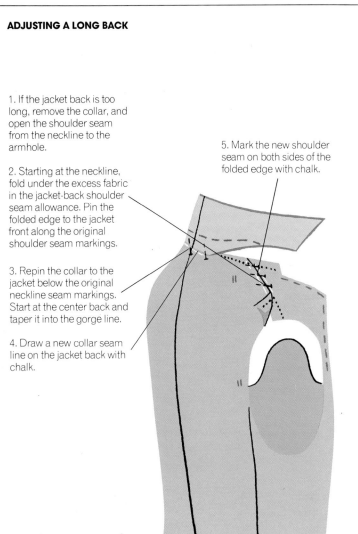

ADJUSTING A SHORT BACK

1. If the jacket back is too short, remove the collar. Open the shoulder seam from the neckline to the armhole.

2. Starting at the neckline, partially unfold the jacket-back seam allowance at the shoulder. Pin the folded edge to the jacket front along the original seam-allowance markings.

3. Repin the collar to the jacket above the original neckline seam-allowance markings, starting at the center back and tapering into the gorge line.

4. Draw a new collar seam on the jacket back with chalk.

5. Mark the adjusted shoulder seam on both sides of the folded edge with chalk.

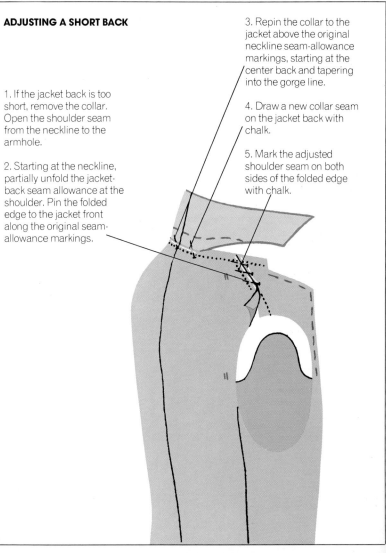

ADJUSTING A LOOSE JACKET BODY

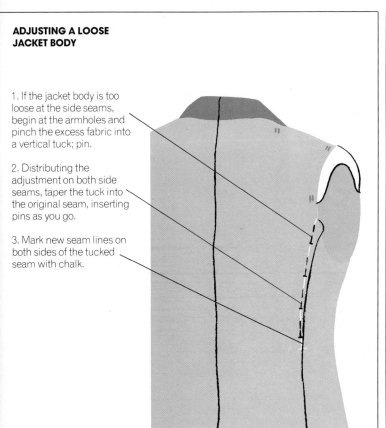

1. If the jacket body is too loose at the side seams, begin at the armholes and pinch the excess fabric into a vertical tuck; pin.

2. Distributing the adjustment on both side seams, taper the tuck into the original seam, inserting pins as you go.

3. Mark new seam lines on both sides of the tucked seam with chalk.

ADJUSTING A NARROW JACKET BODY

1. If the jacket body is too tight at the side seams, open the side seams from the armhole to the waist.

2. Starting at the armhole, unfold the jacket-back side seam allowance. Pin the folded edge to the jacket front outside the original seam-allowance markings.

3. Taper the adjusted seam into the original seam at the waist, inserting pins as you go.

4. Mark the new seam lines on both sides of the adjustment with chalk.

THE SECOND JACKET FITTING

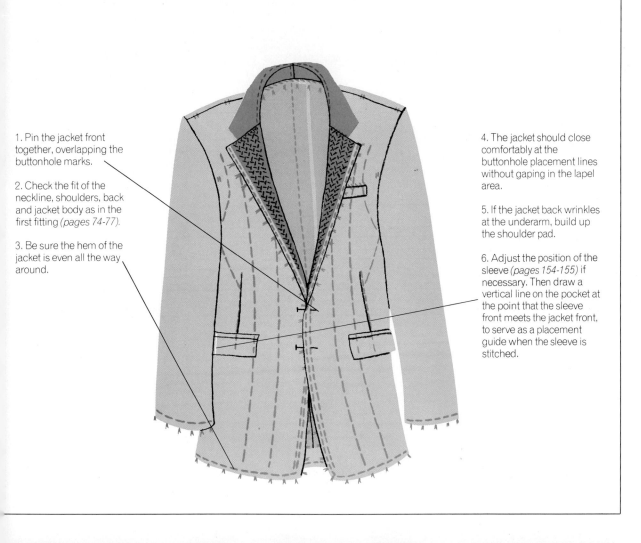

1. Pin the jacket front together, overlapping the buttonhole marks.

2. Check the fit of the neckline, shoulders, back and jacket body as in the first fitting (pages 74-77).

3. Be sure the hem of the jacket is even all the way around.

4. The jacket should close comfortably at the buttonhole placement lines without gaping in the lapel area.

5. If the jacket back wrinkles at the underarm, build up the shoulder pad.

6. Adjust the position of the sleeve (pages 154-155) if necessary. Then draw a vertical line on the pocket at the point that the sleeve front meets the jacket front, to serve as a placement guide when the sleeve is stitched.

ADJUSTING A LOOSE WAIST

A SYMPTOM OF A LOOSE WAIST

1. If the waist is loose, the pants stand away from your natural waist at the back.

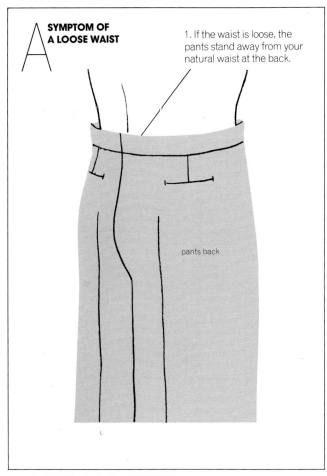

pants back

B REFITTING THE CENTER-BACK SEAM

2. Starting at the center-back seam at the top edge of the waist, pinch the excess fabric into a vertical tuck, and pin.

3. Continue to tuck and pin the excess fabric down the length of the back seam, tapering into the original seam at the seat of the pants.

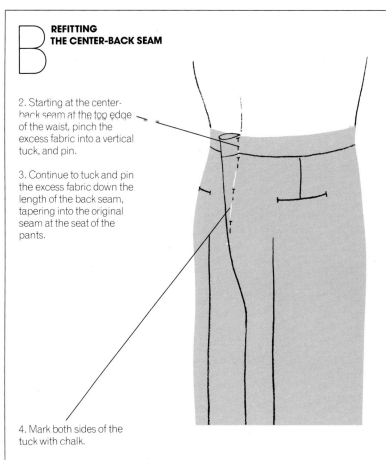

4. Mark both sides of the tuck with chalk.

ADJUSTING A TIGHT WAIST

A SYMPTOM OF A TIGHT WAIST

1. If the pants are snug in the waist, wrinkles form around the waistband.

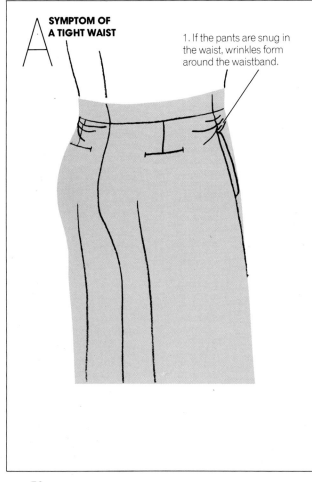

B REFITTING THE CENTER-BACK SEAM

2. Open the back seam from the waist to the seat of the pants—about 6 inches.

3. Starting at the waistband on the center-back seam, partially unfold the seam allowance on one side and pin the fold outside the seam-allowance markings on the other side, until the seam is aligned at the center back and the waist is comfortable.

4. Taper the adjustment into the original seam, inserting pins as you go.

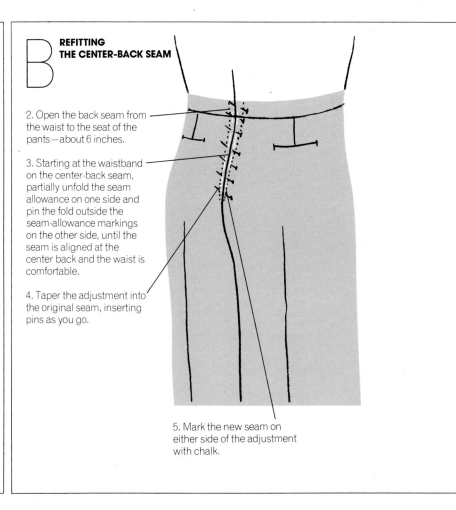

5. Mark the new seam on either side of the adjustment with chalk.

ADJUSTING A LOOSE SEAT

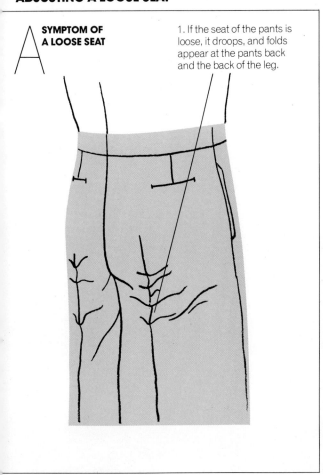

A | **SYMPTOM OF A LOOSE SEAT**

1. If the seat of the pants is loose, it droops, and folds appear at the pants back and the back of the leg.

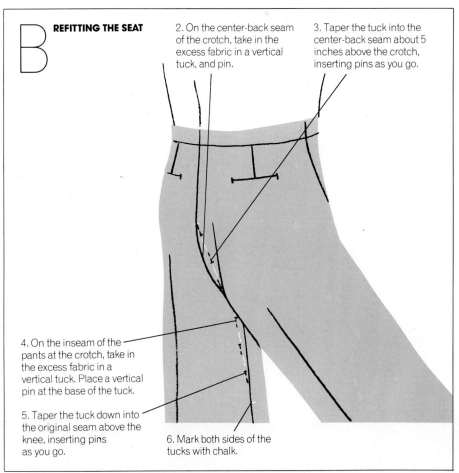

B | **REFITTING THE SEAT**

2. On the center-back seam of the crotch, take in the excess fabric in a vertical tuck, and pin.

3. Taper the tuck into the center-back seam about 5 inches above the crotch, inserting pins as you go.

4. On the inseam of the pants at the crotch, take in the excess fabric in a vertical tuck. Place a vertical pin at the base of the tuck.

5. Taper the tuck down into the original seam above the knee, inserting pins as you go.

6. Mark both sides of the tucks with chalk.

ADJUSTING A TIGHT SEAT

A | **SYMPTOM OF A TIGHT SEAT**

1. If the pants are snug across the seat, wrinkles radiate from the back seam and from the crotch down the back of the legs.

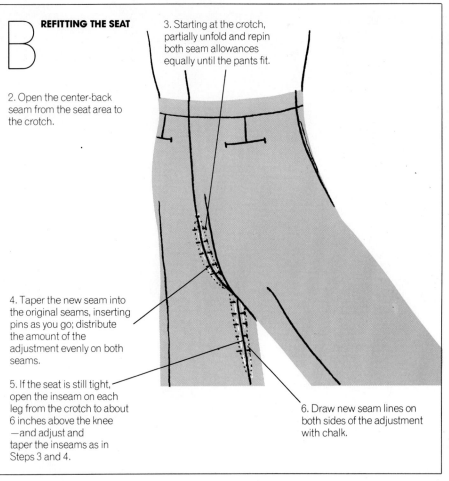

B | **REFITTING THE SEAT**

2. Open the center-back seam from the seat area to the crotch.

3. Starting at the crotch, partially unfold and repin both seam allowances equally until the pants fit.

4. Taper the new seam into the original seams, inserting pins as you go; distribute the amount of the adjustment evenly on both seams.

5. If the seat is still tight, open the inseam on each leg from the crotch to about 6 inches above the knee —and adjust and taper the inseams as in Steps 3 and 4.

6. Draw new seam lines on both sides of the adjustment with chalk.

4
MASTERWORKS OF TAILORING

A craftsman at Huntsman's, one of
London's oldest custom tailors, adjusts the
shoulder of a scarlet hunting coat, whose
wearer bestrides a saddle kept on the
premises to help in fitting riding clothes.

Back when His Royal Highness the Duke of Edinburgh was still a gad-about bachelor, he needed a new suit. But how to go about finding one? Though a great grandson of Queen Victoria and a grandson of Greece's King George I, Prince Philip (then a lieutenant in the Navy) hesitated to stride without introduction into one of London's venerable custom tailoring establishments. So he appealed to his uncle Lord Louis Mountbatten,

THE CUSTOM CLOTHIERS' ELEGANT WORLD

who armed him with a letter to the firm of Hawes & Curtis Ltd., which was pleased to outfit him then and has done so ever since.

Like Prince Philip, most men approach the great-name tailors with diffidence and even awe. One executive from a Madison Avenue advertising company—where top management is not noted for its bashfulness—walked firmly to the threshold of a London tailor's shop and then turned on his heels and bolted. "I thought maybe you had to be invited," he explained later.

Small wonder. In London, the walls of the best tailoring establishments display as many as 26 royal "By Appointment" warrents, and the back rooms stay busy filling orders from emperors, kings, shahs and oil-rich sheiks. It is the same with other top-drawer tailors the world over. In New York, Dunhill Tailors' clients include Rockefellers, Whitneys, board chairmen and star quarterbacks. In Rome, Angelo Litrico used to outfit his good friend Nikita Khrushchev, whom he often visited on the Premier's home grounds. So privileged was Litrico that Khrushchev gave him a camera and unprecedented liberty to photograph anyplace in the Soviet Union.

Such privilege emanates not only from the unquestionably artistic service that a master tailor renders, but from the mystique that envelops the upper stratum of custom tailoring. (Even the proper British designation of the profession—it is called "bespoke" rather than "custom" tailoring—has a majestic ring.) And the bespoke tailor does indeed work a kind of magic, making his client appear stronger and slimmer and younger and often richer than the truth warrants. To attain those ends, the tailor must be an anatomist, a psychologist and an artist—as well as a master craftsman.

Nowhere is the aura of mystique thicker than in London's Savile Row, the world capital of custom tailoring. Savile Row, a term that embraces the Row itself and some of its side streets, originated as an elegant residential development promoted in 1735 by the Earl of Burlington and named for the Earl's wife, Lady Dorothy Savile. For nearly a century London's best doctors practiced there, to be close to their gouty patients. They left in disdain when Henry Poole, a tailor whose father had grown rich supplying uniforms to the warriors of Waterloo, set up shop there in 1846, and was followed by similar establishments.

Poole acquired the patronage of King Edward VII when that monarch was still Prince of Wales. The Prince had gone to the theater, where a French actor was playing an adventurous rogue. The actor's costume was a ragged, much patched affair. But the Prince, deeply interested in fashion, noted a touch of genius in the costume's cut.

Who had made the thing? the Prince asked the actor. Poole, was the answer. And Poole's, thereafter enjoying the Prince's patronage, became a rendezvous for the day's dandies. "It was more like a club than a shop," one memoirist recalled, "whither from 3:30 p.m. to 5 p.m. flocked many of the Lords Dundreary and Tomnoddy from Rotten Row, to sip Pooley's monstrous fine Claret and hock and to pull Pooley's cigars."

When Henry Poole died in 1876, he had attained such fame that a New York newspaper published as his epitaph:

Yes, Poole's my tailor. Poole! You know!
Who makes the Prince of Wales's things.
He's tailor (as his billheads show) to half
    the Emperors and Kings.
An introduction is required
At Poole's before they take your trade.
No common people are desired
However promptly bills are paid.

Poole's is still in business and employs a

staff of 80—but for a time it was a close thing. The firm verged on bankruptcy when Edward VII died, not because of his lost patronage but because he owed the shop so much money. Nevertheless, prompt payment is considered a dubious virtue in a Savile Row customer, even today. Although a few tailors now ask for payment within 30 days, most view such unseemly haste as a sign that the customer is dissatisfied and will place future business elsewhere.

Savile Row tailors still adhere to the 19th Century injunction to "be urbane and deferential without being familiar, ingratiating without being obsequious . . . till the customer is smiled out of the door."

Despite the traditional manners, Savile Row's tailors have taken on a modern —though still highly dignified—outlook. They no longer turn out, except on emphatic demand, suits to be worn with gaiters and button shoes. Trousers are made for belts rather than suspenders, unless the customer protrudes hopelessly in front and back and could not keep his pants up without braces. Vests, once obligatory, may now be dispensed with. Lightweight materials, long scorned by Savile Row tailors on the ground that they would not keep their shape, have become acceptable. "No one survives these days unless he keeps up with the times," says Colin Hammick, a director of H. Huntsman & Sons, Ltd., the biggest and most expensive—at $625 a suit—of Savile Row firms. "Young men used to be influenced by what their fathers wore. Today the fathers are influenced by their sons."

Hammick himself exemplifies the trend to modernity. Though Huntsman's dates back to a gaiter and breeches maker who was doing business in 1809, Hammick has been named both Designer of the Year and the Best-Dressed Man in an England recently beset by the mod revolution. Although changing fashion thus gets an acknowledging nod, fads are still overshadowed in the making of a properly tailored suit by the individual line that best befits the customer.

The modernity of Huntsman's outlook is scarcely apparent to a patron who enters the shop for the first time. In the reception area, stags' heads flank a big mirror, and the main window displays seven royal crests, including those of Edward VII, George V and Prince Bernhard of The Netherlands.

In a wood-paneled, Old Worldish fitting room, a riding saddle bestrides a stand (pages 80-81). It is there for customers ordering hunting pinks, the de rigueur garb for riding to hounds in pursuit of the fox. (Pinks, though usually an off-shade of red, are named for a long-departed tailor, a Mr. Pink, and may be of any color to which the maker will consent.) Gaslights were removed from Huntsman's back rooms only in 1973. They had survived because a few older tailors, who still sit on tables and stitch cloth on their laps, preferred the soft glow of gas to the glare of electricity.

In ordering a suit, the customer initiates a process that will require three months. It begins with a conference between the client and Hammick or one of his lieutenant generals on the suit's purpose—business wear? travel? sports?—and the selection of an appropriate material from among the bolts of cloth arrayed with seeming casualness on tables in the reception area. Next the client is measured for dozens of dimensions, all carefully noted. (They will be stored indefinitely in dusty archives with measurements of five generations of clients.) Then the tailor retires to create a suit.

Backstage, Huntsman craftsmen, each of them a specialist, start to work. Here the sense of tradition is strongest of all, because the techniques—and even the tools *(pages 90-95)*—of fine tailoring have scarcely changed since the early days of the Savile Row shops. First, a cutter transforms the measurements into a brown paper pattern. Guided by the pattern, a subordinate cutter called a striker cuts the cloth by hand, using a pair of extra-heavy tailor's shears. As the project gets fully underway, one artisan works only on the wool or hair interfacing for the body of the jacket—cutting it, shrinking it, and then shaping it both with darts and by pressing. Another will work only on lapel interfacing; he eases the canvas, which is slightly larger than the cloth it reinforces, into the jacket's front with row upon row of tiny hand stitches. This meticulous exercise endows that part of the suit with a permanent spring so that after years of wear it will retain its original shape.

In some Savile Row shops a single master craftsman works on a suit from start to finish. But whatever the methods, a Savile Row suit is distinguished by impeccable

The great tailoring houses of London's Savile Row presented an awesomely dignified face to the public in 1901, when this photograph was taken. The plaque on the second door from the left marks the oldest shop,

Henry Poole's, described by a contemporary as "one of the buttresses of the British Constitution—eternal, immoveable, immutable." But in 1961, Poole's moved to Cork Street and a garage was put up in its place.

workmanship, most of it in concealed hand stitches. When the suit is finished, after a number of fittings and subsequent alterations in which it may be completely dismantled and sewn together anew, it will be ready for 20 years of wear. During this time its unmistakably individualistic line will prevent it from ever going out of style. The suit can prevent its wearer from seeming unstylish, too. "Almost everyone needs to be improved," says Colin Hammick, and in making these improvements the master tailor finds ultimate expression for his talent.

One globe-trotting journalist, exulting in his first Savile Row suit, asked his tailor if he had met any special problems. Hesitantly, the tailor conceded: "Well, sir, you have a rather long body, and that's the thing we had to try to minimize. We had to lengthen your legs, so to speak, and to shorten your body. Nothing serious, really." Aware suddenly of "this particular defect in my structure," the writer studied himself in a mirror. "It was impossible to tell now where my short legs ended and my long body began."

But how is a man who does not have Lord Louis Mountbatten for an uncle to obtain the services of a Savile Row paragon? It is no longer so difficult as it once seemed. An American going to London may write beforehand and introduce himself: an appointment will be arranged. He does not, in fact, even have to go to London. Savile Row firms dispatch ambassadors to the former colonies each year, and a letter of inquiry will bring a reply announcing the ambassador's arrival. "But we notice," one master tailor remarks, "that our customers feel more comfortable if they come with introductions."

A windowful of seals indicating royal patronage marks the entrance *(above)* to Huntsman's, one of Savile Row's most distinguished tailors. At right, co-director Colin Hammick *(in cream suit)* and a clerk confer with clients.

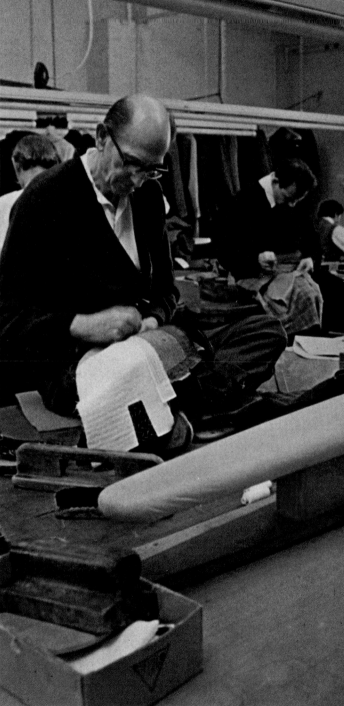

A cutter at Huntsman's checks the outlines he will follow in scissoring fabric for a client's new suit. The outlines have been painstakingly chalked on a bolt of Scots tweed from a paper pattern made to the client's measure.

In a workroom devoted to coats and jackets, a tailor stitches fabric reinforcement to a jacket. By sitting cross-legged atop his table—as tailors have for centuries—he brings the work into his lap, making it easier to sew.

After a preliminary fitting on the client, a foreman uses a dummy to adjust the construction and fit of a jacket. Here he marks the excess fabric to be trimmed from the shoulders and armholes before the sleeves are set in.

The basic tools of tailoring

The craft of tailoring requires an assortment of simple tools that have remained basically unchanged for more than a century. Many of the implements, like the open-tipped thimble shown here, are variations on standard sewing devices. Others are straight duplicates, but with odd names: Sharps and Betweens for types of needles, gimp for the cord used to reinforce buttonholes.

Each has a precise function. For example, small scissors are used for most detail work, and heavy shears for cutting fabric. In choosing your instruments, select only the best.

HOW TO USE THE BASIC TOOLS

TAILOR'S THIMBLE: A special thimble that, together with the distinctive sewing technique used with it, allows the needlecrafter to push through heavy fabrics and interfacings. The thimble, made from sturdy metal and open at the top for comfort, should be worn on the middle finger of the hand that holds the needle. Choose a thimble in a size that covers your finger down to the first joint, but leaves the fingertip exposed. When sewing, use only the fingernail side of the thimble, and push the needle through all layers of fabric in a long, smooth motion, using the whole arm.

BENT-HANDLED TAILOR'S SHEARS: Used for nearly all cutting operations. Tailoring shears have long, heavy blades and a handle that bends upward so that the bottom blade can rest firmly on the cutting table. (A 10- or 12-inch pair is handiest.) Cut with a long, steady closure, using the entire blade. If the shears become stiff, put a drop of sewing-machine oil on the bolt. Do not use the sheers to cut paper; to do so will dull the blades.

SCISSORS: Use a 3-inch pair for cutting in small areas, and for trimming in hard-to-reach areas.

TAILOR'S CHALK: Flat squares made of wax, stone or clay, used to transfer pattern markings or adjustments onto fabric. For marking wool or other natural fibers, use wax chalk in a contrasting color; the wax can be easily removed by pressing lightly with a steam iron. For pattern pieces and interfacings, black wax shows up best. On synthetic fabrics or blends, use stone or clay chalk; when the marks are no longer needed, simply brush them off.

TAPE MEASURE: For taking body measurements and aligning pattern pieces on the fabric. Select a tape measure made of oilcloth, fiber glass or plastic (cloth shrinks), with metal tips at each end.

YARDSTICK AND RULER: The yardstick is for checking fabric grain lines, and measuring fabric yardage. The shorter ruler is for measuring buttonholes, and assuring accuracy when placing pattern pieces on the fabric. Select a yardstick of hardwood, and a 6- or 12-inch wooden ruler with a metal strip at one edge.

NEEDLES: Needles come in a wide range of sizes, designated by numbers: low-numbered needles are longer and thicker; high-numbered ones are shorter and thinner. You will need an assortment of long to medium-length round-eyed needles called Sharps, and some short, stubby needles called Betweens. Sharps are used for most hand-sewing tasks: Size 3 for sewing through many thicknesses; Size 3 or 4 for marking stitches such as tailor tacks; Size 5 or 6 for basting, padding stitches on interfacing and on medium-weight lapels; Sizes 5-8 for sewing garment fabric or linings; Size 8 or 9 for fine details such as hemming and padding stitches on lightweight lapels. Betweens, being stronger, are for sewing extra-thick fabrics: Size 4 for basting; Sizes 5 and 6 for sewing on buttons; Sizes 6 and 7 for hand working buttonholes; and Sizes 6-9 for fine hand sewing, such as padding stitches.

THREAD: For most sewing tasks, use pure silk or mercerized cotton thread in No. 0 to 00; for basting, white glazed cotton thread, No. 40 or 50; for making tailor tacks and marking special areas such as the lapel roll line, cotton marking-stitch thread or lightweight cotton crochet thread; and linen or strong cotton button thread for sewing on buttons. Work the buttonholes with silk buttonhole twist, separating the twisted strands as needed. On men's suits, use Nos. 8-10 silk tailor's twist, if available; if not, substitute No. D silk buttonhole twist—which is also the standard twist for women's clothes. In all tailoring operations, choose a matching or slightly darker color for permanent or visible stitches; white or a contrasting color for basting or mark stitching. To give extra strength to permanent hand stitching, coat the thread with beeswax.

NOTIONS: Any items such as buttons, hooks and zippers, needed to finish the garment. Buttons are measured in units called lines; 40 lines equal 1 inch. Use 24-line buttons on sleeves, vest and the back trouser pocket; 30-line buttons on single-breasted jackets; 34-line buttons on double-breasted ones; 27-line suspender buttons and small fly buttons. For the trouser waistband, select a strong hook and eye and use a sturdy fly zipper with metal teeth. Use a nylon zipper only with synthetics, or for lightweight women's pants.

GIMP: Heavy cord made of silk, cotton or wool strands threaded with metal wire, used to reinforce hand-worked buttonholes. Use buttonhole twist if gimp is not available—or for a softer buttonhole.

TAILOR'S BODKIN: A slender, 4-inch-long pointed ivory stick, used to pull basting threads, and to round out the eyelets of hand-worked buttonholes.

Tailor's implements include, from left: yardstick and ruler; Betweens in various sizes; an ivory bodkin for removing bastings; scissors and shears; buttons and fasteners and an open-ended tailor's thimble; gimp tied in a bow; silk, cotton and linen threads; a zipper; 60-inch measuring tape.

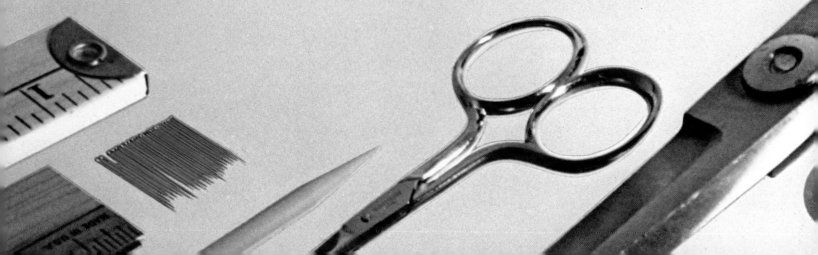

Essentials for shaping and fit

Master tailors, like good professional housebuilders, put their finest efforts into laying foundations. Beneath the surface of every tailored suit is a multilayered arrangement of reinforcing and structuring materials, like the ones at left, that help determine the garment's ultimate shape. These underpinnings, called "findings" in the trade, include the fabric interfacings that sculpt a jacket's front, the shoulder padding and the curved linen band that gives a collar its graceful roll. Like the tailor's tools, these foundation materials should be of top quality.

HOW TO SELECT THE FINDINGS

WOOL INTERFACING: A strong, highly resilient fabric made of a mixture of cotton, wool and/or goat hair. Also called hair or foundation canvas. The interfacing is used on a jacket to help shape and support the fabric, and to keep the jacket from stretching, wrinkling or sagging. Use mediumweight interfacing with most suit fabrics, and lightweight for summer tropicals. Select the best quality interfacing available, made of natural fibers only. Test the quality by crushing the fabric in your hand; when released, it will spring back to shape and not show any wrinkles. Avoid burlap interfacing, which is scratchy and stiff.

HAIRCLOTH INTERFACING: A wiry, extra-resilient interfacing fabric that is a mixture of strong cotton fibers and tough horsehair, used over the wool interfacing to reinforce the chest and shoulder areas of a jacket. Select haircloth made of natural fibers only, if available.

COVER CLOTH: A loosely woven material, preferably cotton flannel, with a slightly fuzzy, or napped, surface; sewed over haircloth to prevent the sharp ends of the horsehair from protruding. The fabric adds extra padding that helps round out the shape of the jacket. If flannel is not available, substitute soft, lightweight felt.

COLLAR INTERFACING: Stiff, firmly woven linen interfacing material sewed between the collar surface and the undercollar. It helps give the collar shape and firmness, allowing it to turn over smoothly at the roll line, and permitting it to set neatly and accurately at the neck. If linen canvas is not available, use wool interfacing. In fact, some tailors prefer wool, to achieve a softer effect. Avoid cotton canvas treated with a chemical finish called sizing; it will not stand up to dry cleaning.

UNDERCOLLAR FABRIC: Sewed to the collar interfacing to form the underside of the collar. For most women's jackets the garment fabric itself is used. For men's jackets, which are usually of heavier material, a strong, durable wool fabric called melton cloth is preferable. Melton cloth gives the collar extra reinforcement and longer wear. And because it is less bulky than most heavy garment fabric, melton allows the collar to be shaped and to roll more easily. It is also used with loose weaves to provide sharp collar edges. Melton cloth comes in a variety of colors to match, contrast or harmonize with the suit fabric color.

WIGAN: A loosely woven, durable interfacing fabric used around the bottom of sleeves to reinforce the hem. (It is named after the town of Wigan, England, where it was first produced.) Select pure cotton wigan, if available. If not, substitute a polyester and cotton blend, jacket pocketing, or a lightweight, nonwoven interfacing fabric.

POCKETING FABRIC: Tightly woven twilled cotton fabric, treated with a satiny finish to make the material soft. Pocketing fabric is available in different weights and is used to form not only pockets on jackets and pants, but also to reinforce the crotch, and to make the fly and waistband facing. It may also be substituted for wigan to reinforce sleeve hemlines. The softest and most durable pocketing material is a pure cotton twill called silesia. If silesia is not available, substitute a polished cotton or a blend of cotton and polyester. Avoid stiff cotton pocketing treated with sizing.

TWILL TAPE: A thin, extra-strong strip of twilled linen or cotton fabric, also called stay tape; sewed along the lapel roll line of the jacket to prevent stretching, and to keep the jacket front from buckling away from the chest. The tape is also used to reinforce the edges of the lapels, and to ensure flat, sharp edges that do not pucker or stretch. The narrowest width of tape available —preferably 3/8 inch wide—will produce the neatest lapel roll and edges. Before using, preshrink the tape by dipping it in water. Avoid nontwilled seam binding and tape treated with sizing.

WAISTBAND INTERFACING, FACING AND TROUSER CURTAIN: Waistband interfacing is a strip of strong, canvas-like fabric sewed to the waistband to reinforce it and to help hold its shape. The waistband facing is another strip of softer fabric that covers the interfacing and forms the waistband's lining. The trouser curtain is an extra piece of fabric that extends below the waistband to keep the waist area from stretching, to cover the waistband seam and to hold trouser pleats in place. Ready-made waistband parts, sold by the yard, are available, some already joined. If you make your own, select firm but pliable linen canvas for the interfacing. (Avoid harsh nylon and sized, or chemically treated, cotton stiffening.) For the facing and the trouser curtain, select soft, durable cotton such as pocketing fabric or a cotton and polyester blend.

SHOULDER PADS AND SLEEVE HEADS: Shoulder pads are usually made of triangular pieces of muslin or cotton wadding, which is a kind of nonwoven cotton fabric. The triangles form the outer layers of a cloth sandwich, which is filled with lamb's-wool fleece or raw cotton batting. The pads are used to shape and build up the shoulders of a jacket, and must be carefully fitted before they are inserted. Sleeve heads are 2-inch-wide strips of cotton wadding or lamb's-wool fleece placed around the top of the sleeve to create a smooth line and to support the roll at the sleeve cap. They will also improve and help maintain the hang of the sleeve. Ready-made shoulder pads and sleeve heads are available. If you make your own, shape the pads carefully and join the layers, using hand padding stitches or machine zigzag stitches.

The tailor's findings, which provide the hidden strengths of a jacket, are, from top to bottom: ready-made shoulder pads resting on horsehair cloth, strips of cotton and linen interfacings, a commercial sleeve head, pocketing fabric, twill tape, collar pieces and, finally, wool interfacing.

Special pressing equipment

A skilled tailor puts as much artistry into wielding a hot iron as he gives to plying a needle. As soon as he finishes a seam he presses it flat, and at virtually every stage of a jacket's assembly he molds the fabric and interfacing with his iron.

The most essential pressing tools, of course, are a first-rate steam iron and an adjustable ironing board with a scorch-resistant cover. In addition, the specialized pressing boards and forms shown here allow the needle-crafter to do the extra-fine shaping and molding that help give a tailored garment its distinctive look.

THE PRESSING EQUIPMENT AND HOW TO USE IT

SLEEVE BOARD: A miniature ironing board for pressing small areas—such as sleeve and neck seams—that will not fit over the end of a regular ironing board. The sleeve board may also be used when pressing straight darts and when shrinking out puckers along the armhole seams. The best sleeve boards for tailoring rest on a sturdy wooden platform. They should be well padded and covered with a firmly woven twilled cotton fabric called cotton drill cloth. Wash the drill-cloth cover before using it to remove all sizing or starch—which would otherwise cause the iron to stick and would also adhere to the garment fabric.

PRESSING CLOTH: A piece of fabric, preferably cotton drill cloth, that is placed between the iron and the garment when pressing. For all pressing operations while the garment is being made, use a dry cloth; enough steam from your iron will pass through the cloth to shape the fabric. For final pressing, use a damp cloth to remove any gloss or shine the fabric has picked up during construction. Wash all new pressing cloths before using to remove the sizing. If cotton drill cloth is not available, substitute white paper towels.

TAILOR'S HAM: An oval, ham-shaped cushion with built-in curves that conform to the general contours of the body. Use the ham when pressing areas that require shaping, such as the curved darts on the jacket front, and seams at the bust, chest, shoulder and hip. The ham is also a convenient aid for pressing collars into shape, for sculpting the roll line of lapels, for pressing open the armhole seam and for shrinking out fullness at the armhole. Select a ham that is firmly stuffed, smoothly rounded and with a surface free of lumps. One half should be covered with cotton drill cloth, to be used when pressing most fabrics. The other half should be covered with soft, lightweight wool—which must always be used when pressing woolen fabric to prevent shine.

PRESS MITT: A soft, padded thumbless mitten that fits over the entire hand. It is used to give a light pressing to small, curved areas—such as sleeve caps—that do not fit over the tailor's ham or the regular ironing board. It may also be slipped over the narrow end of the sleeve board to provide extra padding. As in the tailor's ham, one side of the mitt should be covered with cotton drill cloth and the other side with soft, lightweight wool.

POINT PRESSER: A narrow, hardwood board mounted on its side and shaped into a fine point at one end. Also called a seam or tailor's board. Used for pressing open small seams in narrow or hard-to-reach places such as collars, lapel peaks or points, and waistbands. Since the point presser is bare wood, not covered by padding or drill cloth, it also provides a firm, hard surface for pressing open regular seams on worsteds or other hard fabrics that do not flatten easily. Before using, make sure that the hardwood surface and edges of the presser are completely smooth, with no nicks or splinters that could cause damage to the fabric. Point pressers and clappers (below) are frequently combined into a single piece of equipment.

TAILOR'S SLEEVE CUSHION: A long, flat pad with a sleevelike silhouette; sometimes inserted into a completed sleeve to prevent wrinkling the underside or forming undesired creases when pressing. Since sleeve cushions are not generally available outside tailor's specialty shops, you may have to make do with an ordinary ironing board. Simply lay the sleeve on the ironing board and press it down the center, being careful not to crease the edges. Then roll the sleeve slightly and again run the iron down the center. Continue in this manner until the entire sleeve is pressed.

SPONGE: For dampening a pressing cloth—or the fabric itself if you need extra moisture to flatten a stubborn seam. The sponge is also handy to wipe up water spillage from an overfull steam iron. Keep the sponge clean, and let it dry out frequently to avoid mildewing; never store it near metal tools, to avoid rusting them.

TAILOR'S CLAPPER: An oblong or rectangular piece of hardwood; also called a beater, striker or pounding block. As these names imply, the clapper is wielded like a paddle to slap parts of the garment in order to shape them. Typically, it is used to flatten the edges of collars, hems and lapels, to form trouser creases and pleats—or any other areas where a crisp, sharp edge is desired. When working with very heavy fabrics, use the clapper to smooth and reduce the bulk of seams. Before using the clapper, cover the fabric to be shaped with a press cloth and apply steam from the iron until the fabric is thoroughly moistened. Remove the cloth, and pound the area until the fabric is dry and the desired edge has become distinct. Because the clapper, like the point presser (above), has no cloth covering, make sure that its surface and the edges are smooth and splinter free, to avoid damaging the fabric.

This assortment of oddly shaped but useful pressing aids includes, clockwise from top left: a tailor's ham, covered in wool and cotton drill cloth, used for shaping; a combination hardwood point presser and clapper to flatten seams; a sponge; a press cloth; a sleeve cushion; and a sleeve board.

Stitching by hand for precision

To accomplish the precision and fine detail essential to tailoring, you must master a small repertory of unique and precise hand stitches—in addition to the basic dressmaking stitches shown in the Appendix.

Among these tailoring stitches are two that are temporary: a two-handed basting technique and a marking stitch called a tailor tack. The two-handed basting technique facilitates stitching in straight, even lines and is less tiring than the standard one-handed style. This is particularly important in tailoring since tailors frequently baste without pinning, relying on the adhering qualities of most tailoring fabrics. The other temporary stitch, the so-called tailor tack, is used to transfer pattern markings to both sides of one or more layers of fabrics; tailor tacks enable you to mark quickly and precisely and will not remain on the fabric permanently, as chalk might.

Among the tailor's repertoire of permanent hand stitches is the padding stitch, which is concealed within the layers of collars and lapels and helps give them body and shape, and the chain stitch, often used to reinforce the underarm. Finally, another group of stitches known as tacks—the arrowhead tack, bar tack and French tack—finishes the ends of pockets, pleats and buttonholes securely and decoratively.

TWO-HANDED BASTING: For temporarily joining fabrics, underlining and interfacing

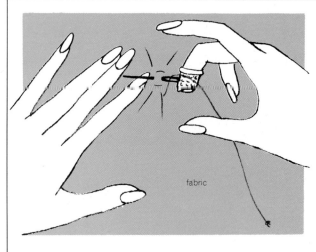

1. With your left hand, hold in place the fabric pieces to be joined 1/4 to 1/2 inch to the left of where your first stitch will enter. Using knotted white basting thread, take a stitch down and up through all fabric thicknesses, bringing the point of the needle out just in front of your left index finger. Then push the needle all the way through the fabric with the front side of your thimble, and pull the thread through.

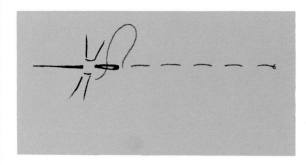

2. Continue the process, taking stitches at least 1 inch long and 1/2 inch apart. Pull the thread through firmly but loosely enough not to pucker the fabric.

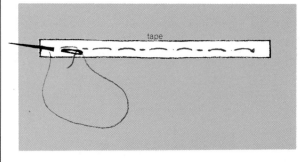

3. When basting tape on fabric, or basting two fabrics that may shift, interrupt the basting stitches at several intervals with short fastening stitches (*Appendix*). End the row with another fastening stitch through all the fabric layers.

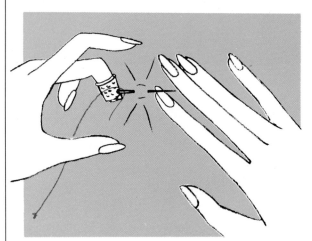

IF YOU ARE LEFT-HANDED...
Following the directions in Steps 1-3, proceed from left to right as shown.

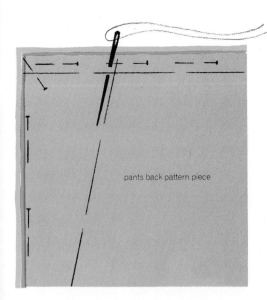

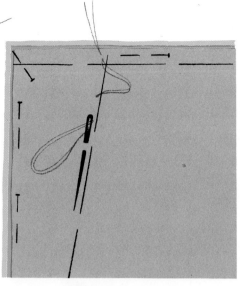

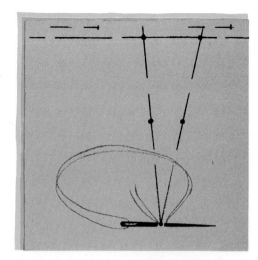

1. Using a double strand of unknotted mark-stitching thread, take a 1/2-inch-long stitch from right to left just outside and at the far right edge of the line to be marked. Adjust the threads so that they are even, then stitch through the paper pattern and both fabric layers.

2. Pull the threads through, leaving a 2-inch loose end. Then take a 1-inch-long stitch at least 1/2 inch to the left of the previous stitch. Push the needle all the way through the fabric with the front part of the thimble as shown for two-handed basting, Step 1. Pull the thread through gently, leaving a 2-inch loop on top of the pattern piece. Continue the process, ending the row of tailor tacks with at least 2 inches of loose thread so that the thread does not pull through.

3. If marking only one point, such as the tip of a dart, take a 1/4-inch-long stitch, leaving 2-inch-long loose ends. Then take another stitch through the same point and pull the thread through, leaving a 2-inch loop on top of the pattern piece. End with at least 2 inches of loose thread.

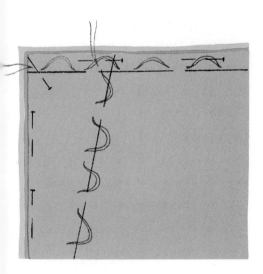

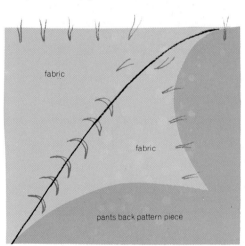

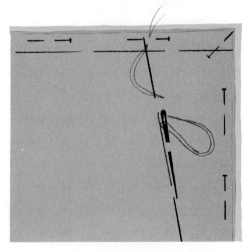

4. Similarly mark all pattern markings. Do not stitch around corners, but after marking one line, begin another at a right angle to the first.

5. Remove all pins and clip through the loops of thread on the top of the pattern. Then separate the pattern piece from the fabric layers. Carefully pull back the top layer of fabric and clip through the exposed threads with the tip of a pair of sharp scissors.

IF YOU ARE LEFT-HANDED...
Follow the directions in Steps 1-5, starting at the left edge of the line to be marked and stitching from left to right as shown.

THE PADDING STITCH: To add body and hold interfacing in place

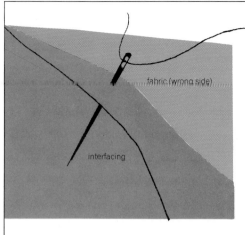

1. Place in your lap the garment section to be padded. Thread the needle with knotted cotton thread; then begin by bringing out the needle between the interfacing and the upper layer of fabric at the top right of the area to be padded. Now pull the needle through.

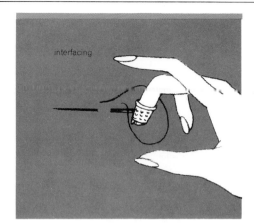

2. Bring the needle down at least 1/4 inch (the distance should be equal to the length desired for the diagonal padding stitch). Keeping the thread to the right of the needle, take a horizontal stitch from right to left so that the needle emerges directly below the point where the thread first emerged. The stitch should be equal to half the length of the diagonal stitch.

3. Push the needle through with the front of the thimble.

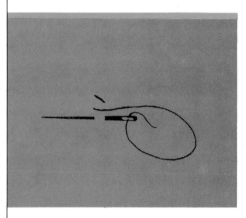

4. Bring the needle down the same distance as in Step 2 and, still keeping the thread to the right of the needle, take another horizontal stitch from right to left directly under the previous stitch.

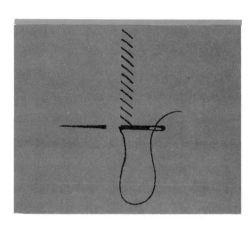

5. After taking the last stitch at the end of the row, insert the needle back where it last emerged. To begin the next parallel row—which will be to the left of the original row—take another stitch from right to left. You will now be ready to work from bottom to top.

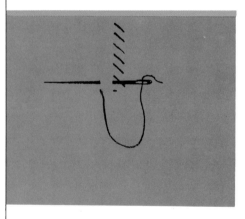

6. Bring the needle up so that it is just short of the top of the corresponding diagonal stitch on the previous row, and take a stitch from right to left directly above the previous stitch. Continue the process.

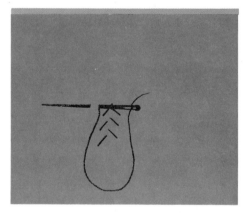

7. At the top of the row, repeat Step 5. This will start the next row. Then bring the needle down and take a horizontal stitch from right to left, directly below the previous stitch as in Step 2. Secure the end of the thread with a fastening stitch (*Appendix*). Start again with a new thread length by embedding its knot between the layers as in Step 1.

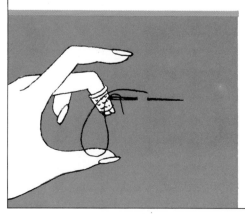

IF YOU ARE LEFT-HANDED...
Follow the directions in Steps 1-7, taking horizontal stitches from left to right, as shown.

CHAIN STITCH: To reinforce an area of stress

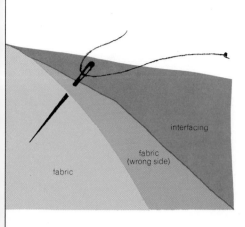

1. Using knotted, coarse-weight thread or buttonhole twist, bring the needle out from underneath the top layer of fabric. This will embed the knot between the fabric layers. Pull the thread through.

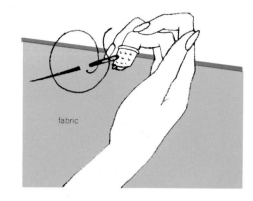

2. Insert the needle 1/8 inch above the point where the thread emerged. Holding the long strand of thread to the left and above the stitch with your thumb, bring the needle out 1/4 inch to the left of the first stitch. Push the needle through the fabric with the front of the thimble.

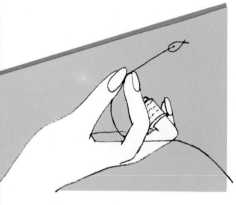

3. To complete the first chain, pull the thread through the loop that formed in the previous step.

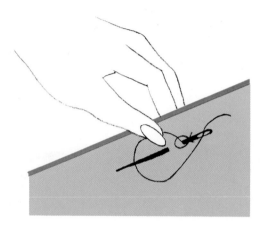

4. Again, holding the thread above and to the left of your stitches with your thumb, insert the needle inside the previous chain, and bring it out 1/4 inch to the left. Pull it through as in Step 3 to complete the second chain.

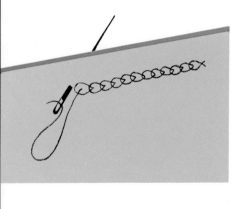

5. Continue the process across the row, ending by inserting the needle down outside the last loop so it emerges on the wrong side of the fabric.

6. Secure the stitches with a small fastening stitch (Appendix) on the wrong side.

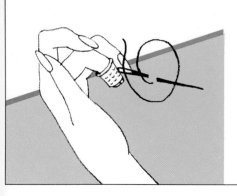

IF YOU ARE LEFT-HANDED...
Follow the directions in Steps 1-6, holding the thread to the right of the stitch and bringing the needle out to the right as shown. Continue the chain from left to right.

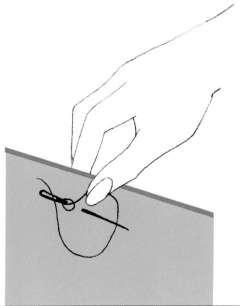

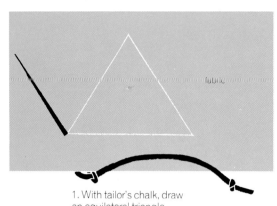

1. With tailor's chalk, draw an equilateral triangle, placing the base at the edge to be tacked. Using knotted buttonhole twist, bring the needle up from the wrong side of the fabric at the lower left-hand corner of the triangle.

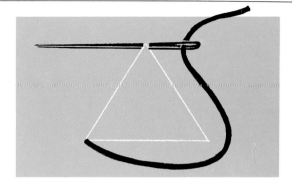

2. Insert the needle at the top of the triangle, and take a small stitch from right to left.

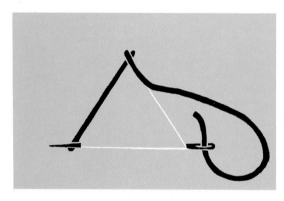

3. Insert the needle into the lower right-hand corner of the triangle and bring it out across the base to the left, just inside the lower left-hand corner.

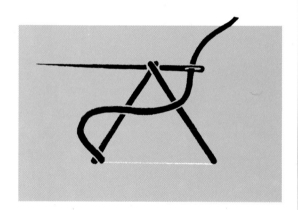

4. Repeat Step 2, taking a small stitch from right to left at the top of the triangle just below and outside the stitch made in Step 2.

5. Repeat Step 3, taking parallel stitches just inside the previous ones. Continue to fill in the triangle by repeating Steps 2 and 3. Secure the thread of the finished arrowhead tack with a fastening stitch (Appendix) on the wrong side of the fabric.

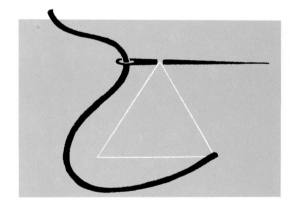

IF YOU ARE LEFT-HANDED...
Follow the directions in Steps 1-5, beginning at the far right corner and stitching from left to right as shown.

THE BAR TACK: To reinforce the ends of pockets or buttonholes

1. To make the thread bar part of the bar tack, use a double thread, or one strand of buttonhole twist, knotted at the end, and bring the needle out from the wrong side of the fabric.

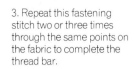

2. Insert it back 1 inch—or however long you want the bar tack to be. Bring out the needle where the thread first emerged.

3. Repeat this fastening stitch two or three times through the same points on the fabric to complete the thread bar.

fabric

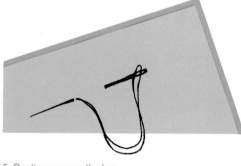

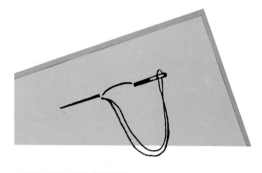

4. Insert the needle under the thread bar at its left edge, and pull it through, tightening the stitch as close to the edge as possible.

5. Continue across the bar, tightening the thread as close to the previous stitch as possible. At the end of the row, insert the needle down to the wrong side of the fabric and secure with a fastening stitch *(Appendix)*.

IF YOU ARE LEFT-HANDED...
Follow the directions in Steps 1-5, working from right to left as shown.

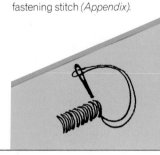

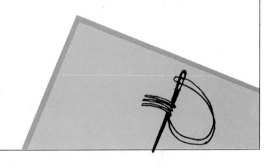

THE FRENCH TACK: To connect a hemmed lining to a garment

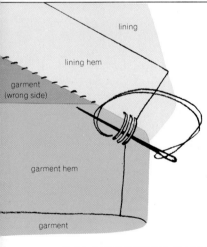

lining

lining hem

garment (wrong side)

garment hem

garment

1. At each vertical seam, make a thread bar (see bar tack, Steps 1 and 2) between the lining and the garment hem. Begin by taking a stitch in the middle of the lining hem, then pick up a few threads of the under layer of the garment hem. Repeat this two or three times in the same place, and end with a fastening stitch *(Appendix)* on the hem of the garment.

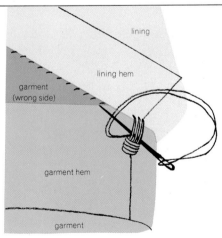

lining

lining hem

garment (wrong side)

garment hem

garment

2. Make the chain part of the French tack by inserting the needle through the loops of thread as in the buttonhole stitch *(Appendix).*

Timelessness of a tailored jacket

Padded and lined, shaped and fitted, the tailored jacket is always in fashion. The cut of its lapels may alter subtly from decade to decade. The shoulders may require slightly more or less padding as times change, but no matter. The basic look survives. And almost every jacket in a man's wardrobe—or a woman's—remains a variation on a tailoring theme that has been essentially constant for a century or more.

When the modern hip-length jacket first appeared in 1859 it was dubbed a sack coat and sold to men only. Before then, most men had worn sweeping frock coats, with fitted bodies and separately cut, flaring skirts that sometimes reached the knees. Or they wore tail coats, with skirts around the back. By contrast, the new style looked loose and chopped off—sacklike. Its body and skirt, cut as one piece, hung straight down from the shoulders to the hem with no waistline seam. Its lapels were tiny and its shoulder padding lavish.

Nevertheless the sack coat—as professional tailors still term it—was easy to wear and caught on immediately. Shortly it proliferated into dozens of variations that today are the predominant sellers in everyday wear. Made from serge or flannel, the sack, in either its single- or double-breasted version, serves as a businessman's suit jacket. In tweed or plaid, it is a sports jacket; in linen or seersucker, a tropical or summer jacket.

Cut from solid-colored or striped fabric, adorned with metal buttons and perhaps a braid edging, the sack coat becomes a blazer. Add box pleats front and back, put a belt around the waist and it's a Norfolk jacket; lengthen the skirt and flare out the bottom from a fitted waist, and the sack coat is a hacking or riding jacket. Fashioned from black or white mohair or worsted, with matching satin or grosgrain lapels, the sack becomes a dinner jacket—or a tuxedo, as it came to be called after it first appeared as a less formal replacement for white tie and tails at a fancy ball in Tuxedo Park, New York, in 1886.

In all its utilitarian versions the modern sack coat, long since adopted by women, displays not only the basic lines of its common parent but also some distinctive vestiges of more remote ancestors. The traditional V-shaped neckline with its notched lapels, as one example, was inspired originally by the high-collared military tunic. When a soldier flopped the top of his tunic open at the neck, the edges of the flaps extended out beyond the base of the collar, and the break between the flaps and the ends of the collar formed a notch at either side. Notched lapels retain this effect, and in most jackets also preserve the top buttonhole that used to be visible when the neck of the tunic was opened.

Equally nonfunctional, although subtly decorative, are the buttons at the wrists of a tailored jacket—relics of a time when men opened their sleeves and turned them back to display lace-trimmed shirt cuffs. Today the only possible significance of sleeve buttons is as a rough gauge of the formality of a jacket. Custom tailors often suggest using three or possibly four buttons at each wrist for city suits, two for country suits and one for sports jackets.

The center vent in the back skirt of a tailored jacket once enabled a horseback rider to spread his coattails comfortably at either side of his saddle. Now the vent is simply a fashion convention—though it also has the happy attribute of making rear trouser pockets more accessible. And although most of the pockets on the original sack coat have survived as practical receptacles for wallets, keys and such, the snappy little change pocket that was once routinely set above the right-hand side pocket has been streamlined away on most contemporary jackets.

To create any variation on the sack coat, the home tailor should anticipate setting aside several weeks for a challenging and satisfying experience. And though a well-made sack represents perhaps the epitome in tailoring, the basic art of jacket-making is as straightforward as any other aspect of custom sewing. The methods—as described in complete detail on the following pages—are well within the capability of any accomplished needlecrafter.

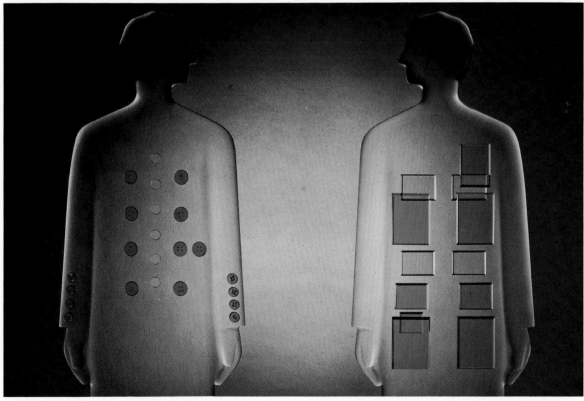

The dots and squares on these two plastic models represent the buttons and pockets on a double-breasted jacket *(green)* and vest *(yellow)*. Of the 23 buttons, only eight are used—the top five on the vest; and on the jacket, the bottom pair on the wearer's left side and an inner button on his right. While all the pockets can be used, some are outmoded, e.g., the pair on the vest that were originally meant for a pocket watch and chain.

Constructing the foundation

The first step in tailoring a jacket is to construct the contoured foundation of stiffening material—shown in the open jacket at left—that will give shape to its body. In a man's jacket this foundation is made of wool interfacing, horsehair and cover cloth. In a woman's jacket, with its softer contours, wool alone is sufficient. When these structuring materials have been stitched together, the jacket body is assembled temporarily for its initial fitting *(page 108)*.

PREPARING THE INTERFACING FOR THE MAN'S JACKET

A CUTTING THE INSERT AND DARTS IN THE WOOL INTERFACING

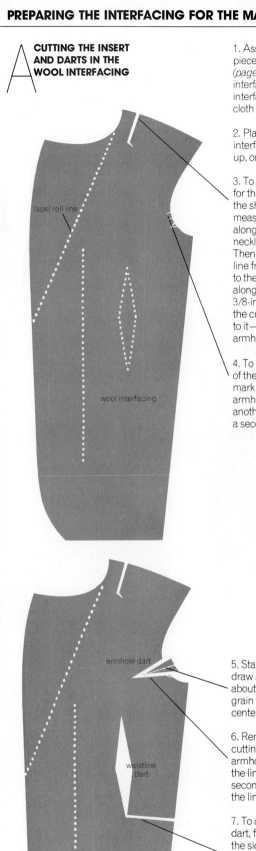

lapel roll line

wool interfacing

armhole dart

waistline dart

1. Assemble the interfacing pieces you cut out earlier (*pages 44-45*): two wool interfacings, two haircloth interfacings and two cover cloth pieces.

2. Place one of the wool interfacings, marked side up, on a flat surface.

3. To determine the position for the cut you will make for the shoulder inset, first measure in 1 1/2 inches along the shoulder from the neckline edge and mark. Then draw a 3-inch-long line from the mark parallel to the lapel roll line. Cut along the line. Then make a 3/8-inch clip at the end of the cut—and at a 45° angle to it—going toward the armhole edge.

4. To determine the position of the armhole dart, make a mark 1/2 inch above the armhole notch. Measure up another 1/2 inch and make a second mark.

5. Starting at the first mark, draw a 3-inch-long line at about a 45° angle to the grain line. This line is the center line of the dart.

6. Remove the dart fabric by cutting first from the armhole notch to the end of the line and then from the second mark to the end of the line.

7. To cut out the waistline dart, first make a cut from the side edge to the bottom point of the dart, cutting at a right angle to the edge. Then cut out the dart along the marked seam lines.

8. Using the wool interfacing as a guide, make the same cuts at the armhole and the shoulder on one of the haircloth interfacings.

B CLOSING THE ARMHOLE AND WAISTLINE DARTS

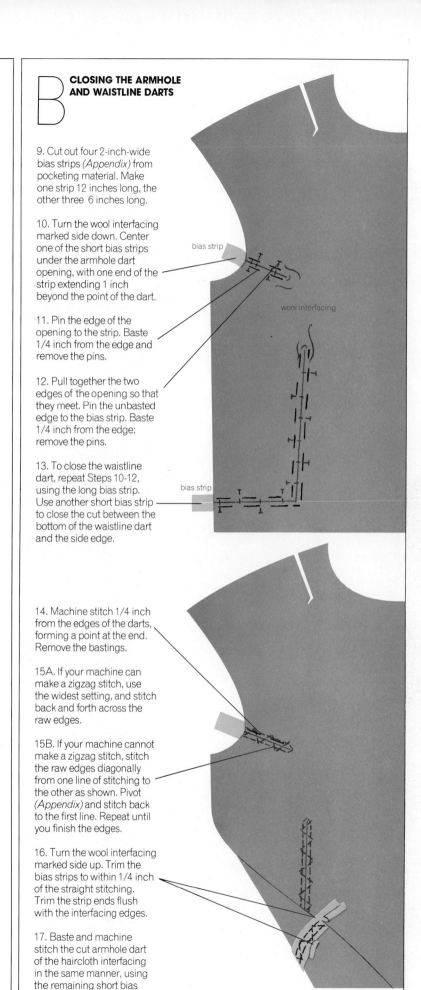

bias strip

wool interfacing

bias strip

9. Cut out four 2-inch-wide bias strips (*Appendix*) from pocketing material. Make one strip 12 inches long, the other three 6 inches long.

10. Turn the wool interfacing marked side down. Center one of the short bias strips under the armhole dart opening, with one end of the strip extending 1 inch beyond the point of the dart.

11. Pin the edge of the opening to the strip. Baste 1/4 inch from the edge and remove the pins.

12. Pull together the two edges of the opening so that they meet. Pin the unbasted edge to the bias strip. Baste 1/4 inch from the edge; remove the pins.

13. To close the waistline dart, repeat Steps 10-12, using the long bias strip. Use another short bias strip to close the cut between the bottom of the waistline dart and the side edge.

14. Machine stitch 1/4 inch from the edges of the darts, forming a point at the end. Remove the bastings.

15A. If your machine can make a zigzag stitch, use the widest setting, and stitch back and forth across the raw edges.

15B. If your machine cannot make a zigzag stitch, stitch the raw edges diagonally from one line of stitching to the other as shown. Pivot (*Appendix*) and stitch back to the first line. Repeat until you finish the edges.

16. Turn the wool interfacing marked side up. Trim the bias strips to within 1/4 inch of the straight stitching. Trim the strip ends flush with the interfacing edges.

17. Baste and machine stitch the cut armhole dart of the haircloth interfacing in the same manner, using the remaining short bias strip you cut in Step 9.

continued

C | ATTACHING THE SHOULDER INSET

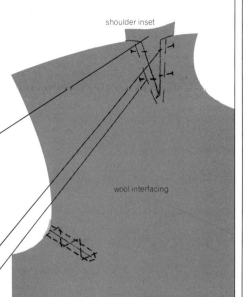

shoulder inset

wool interfacing

18. For the shoulder inset, cut a bias piece 3 inches wide and 5 inches long from wool interfacing material.

19. Turn the wool interfacing marked side down. Place the inset under the cut in the shoulder so that one edge of the cut overlaps one side of the inset by 1/2 inch. The inset should extend 1 inch beyond the bottom of the opening.

20. Pin the edge of the cut nearest the neckline to the inset. Baste 1/4 inch from the edge and remove the pins.

21. Spread the cut open so that the edges are 1 inch apart at the top. Pin the other edge of the cut to the inset. Baste 1/4 inch from the edge; remove the pins.

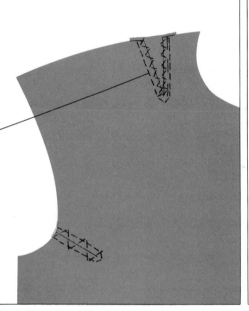

22. Machine stitch 1/4 inch from the edges of the opening, forming a point at the end. Remove the basting. Then finish the raw edges as you did in Step 15 and trim the inset, following the instructions in Step 16.

23. Using haircloth, cut out a second shoulder inset and attach it to the haircloth interfacing in the same manner.

D | ATTACHING THE HAIRCLOTH INTERFACING TO THE WOOL INTERFACING

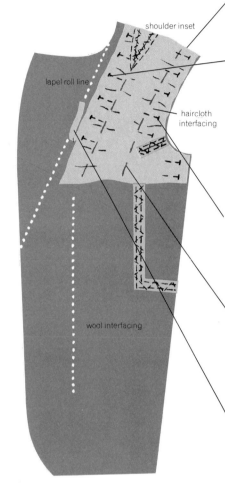

shoulder inset

lapel roll line

haircloth interfacing

wool interfacing

24. With the wool interfacing marked side up, place the haircloth interfacing over it. Align the shoulder, armhole and side edges, and pin.

25. To provide extra fullness for shaping in the chest and shoulders, first ease in the haircloth 1/8 inch from the lapel roll line so that the haircloth buckles slightly. Pin at 1-inch intervals. Then run a line of basting stitches parallel to the lapel roll line, from the shoulder inset to the bottom edge of the haircloth interfacing. Remove the pins.

26. Remove the pins along the armhole edge. Ease in the haircloth interfacing 1/4 inch toward the line of basting, then repin at 1-inch intervals.

27. Run a second line of basting 3 inches inside —and parallel to—the first line of basting. Start at the shoulder edge and baste to the bottom edge of the haircloth interfacing. Remove the pins.

28. Trim the haircloth interfacing if it is closer than 1 inch to the lapel roll line.

E | ATTACHING THE COVER CLOTH

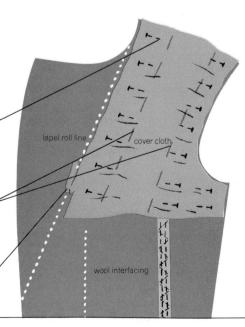

lapel roll line

cover cloth

wool interfacing

29. With the partially assembled front interfacing positioned haircloth side up, place one of the cover cloths on it. Align the shoulder, armhole and side edges of the cover cloth with those of the wool interfacing. Pin.

30. To ease and baste the cover cloth into position, repeat Steps 25-27.

31. Trim the cover cloth if it is closer than 1/2 inch to the lapel roll line.

32. To mark the shoulder-pad area, first measure 4 1/2 inches from the intersections of the armhole and shoulder edges, and mark each edge. Then draw a curved line to connect the marks.

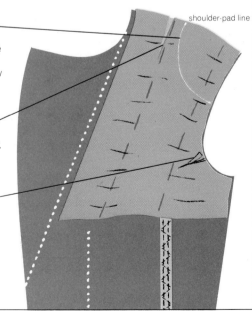

shoulder-pad line

33. Make a 3-inch-long cut in the cover cloth over the center of the shoulder inset.

34. Make another cut in the cover cloth, this time 2 inches long and centered over the underarm dart. Trim away any overlap.

35. Place the assembled interfacing cover-cloth side up. Hand stitch a row of 1/2-inch-long padding stitches *(page 98)* just inside the bottom of the cover cloth. Start at the edge nearest the lapel roll line and end at the side edge. Make sure to sew through all three layers of fabric.

36. Continue making rows of padding stitches over the entire cover cloth, except for the marked shoulder-pad area. As you sew, the padding stitches will take up the ease in the layers of fabric. Remove the bastings.

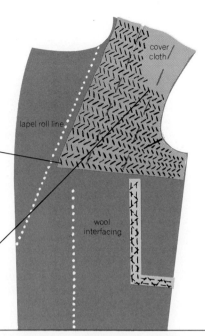

37. Place the interfacing, cover-cloth side up, on your ironing board. To press in the contour of the chest area, first hold up one long edge of the interfacing so that it is gently curved. Then steam press the padding-stitched area, taking the time to steam the ease into the required shape. Repeat on the other half of the padded area.

38. Continue the shaping by turning the assembled interfacing cover-cloth side down, with half of the padded area hanging over the edge of the ironing board. Steam press, then turn the interfacing around and steam press the other half in the same manner.

39. Repeat Steps 2-38 to assemble the other half of the interfacing.

PREPARING THE INTERFACING FOR A WOMAN'S JACKET

A **ASSEMBLING
THE FRONT INTERFACING**

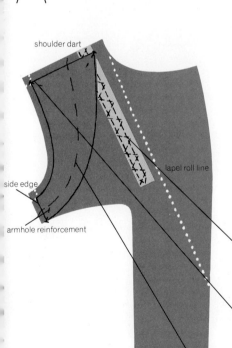

1. Assemble the interfacing pieces you cut out earlier *(pages 46-47)*: two front interfacings, two front armhole reinforcements and one back interfacing.

2. If your jacket front does not have a shoulder dart, skip to Step 4. If there is a shoulder dart, cut out two bias strips *(Appendix)* from pocketing fabric. Make each strip 2 inches wide and 2 inches longer than the shoulder dart.

3. Place one of the interfacings marked side down. Close the dart opening, following the instructions for closing the armhole dart in a man's jacket interfacing on page 105, Steps 10-16, omitting Step 13.

4. Turn the interfacing marked side up. Place one of the armhole reinforcements on it. Then align the shoulder, armhole and side edges of the reinforcement with the corresponding seam lines of the interfacing. Pin.

5. Starting at the shoulder edge, run a curved line of basting through the center of the reinforcement to the side edge. Remove the pins.

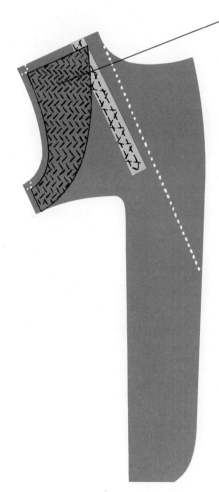

6. Again starting at the shoulder edge, cover the reinforcement with 1/2-inch-long padding stitches *(page 98)*, sewing along the crosswise grain of the fabric. Make sure to sew through both layers of fabric. Remove the basting.

7. Steam press the padding-stitched area.

8. Turn the assembled interfacing over, reinforcement side down, and press the other side of the padding-stitched area.

9. Repeat Steps 3-8 to assemble the other interfacing.

continued

B FINISHING THE BACK INTERFACING

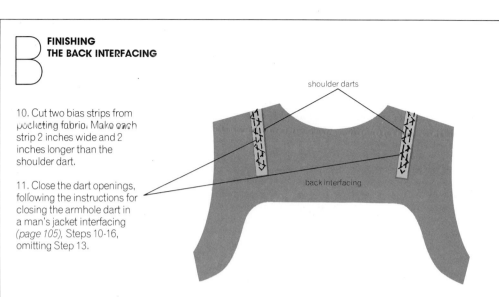

shoulder darts

back interfacing

10. Cut two bias strips from pocketing fabric. Make each strip 2 inches wide and 2 inches longer than the shoulder dart.

11. Close the dart openings, following the instructions for closing the armhole dart in a man's jacket interfacing *(page 105),* Steps 10-16, omitting Step 13.

ASSEMBLING THE JACKET FOR THE FIRST FITTING

A PREPARING THE JACKET FRONT

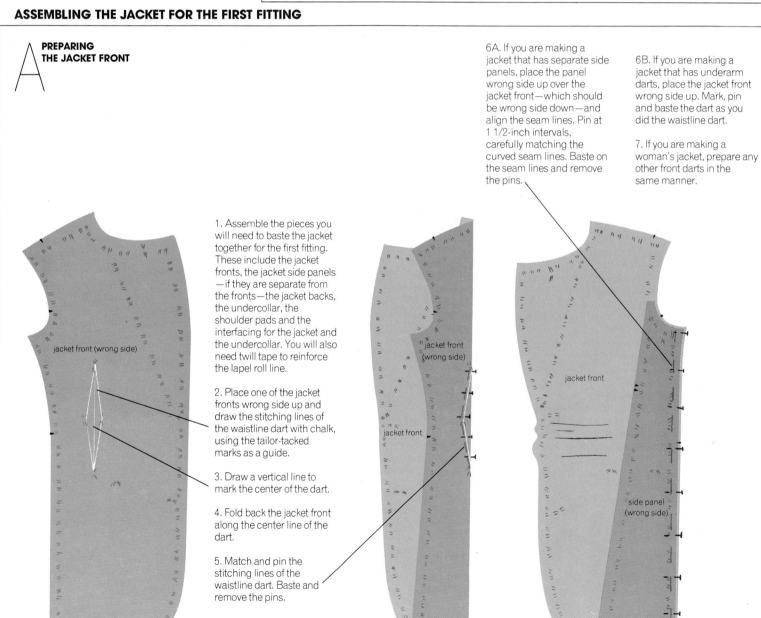

jacket front (wrong side)

jacket front (wrong side)

jacket front

jacket front

side panel (wrong side)

1. Assemble the pieces you will need to baste the jacket together for the first fitting. These include the jacket fronts, the jacket side panels —if they are separate from the fronts—the jacket backs, the undercollar, the shoulder pads and the interfacing for the jacket and the undercollar. You will also need twill tape to reinforce the lapel roll line.

2. Place one of the jacket fronts wrong side up and draw the stitching lines of the waistline dart with chalk, using the tailor-tacked marks as a guide.

3. Draw a vertical line to mark the center of the dart.

4. Fold back the jacket front along the center line of the dart.

5. Match and pin the stitching lines of the waistline dart. Baste and remove the pins.

6A. If you are making a jacket that has separate side panels, place the panel wrong side up over the jacket front—which should be wrong side down—and align the seam lines. Pin at 1 1/2-inch intervals, carefully matching the curved seam lines. Baste on the seam lines and remove the pins.

6B. If you are making a jacket that has underarm darts, place the jacket front wrong side up. Mark, pin and baste the dart as you did the waistline dart.

7. If you are making a woman's jacket, prepare any other front darts in the same manner.

B | BASTING THE INTERFACING TO THE JACKET FRONT

8. Lay the assembled front interfacing marked side down; place the prepared jacket front, wrong side down, over it. Align the lapel roll lines, the front edges and—if you are making a man's jacket—the waistline darts. Smooth out the front portions of the pieces, letting the fabric bunch up along the side edge.

9. Starting 3 inches below the shoulder edge, run a line of 1-inch basting stitches to within 3 inches of the hemline. The stitches should be 4 inches in from, and parallel to, the lapel roll line at the top and a similar distance from the lower front edge at the bottom.

10. Run another line of 1-inch-long basting stitches, first along the lapel roll line and then 1 inch inside the lower front edge to the hemline. Smooth the fabric away from the first line of basting toward the front edge as you stitch.

11. Run a third line of 1-inch-long basting stitches around the armhole 1 inch from the seam line, starting 3 inches below the shoulder edge and going to the underarm seam or dart. This time smooth the fabric away from the first line of basting toward the back edge as you stitch.

12. If you are making a man's jacket, turn and continue the line of basting diagonally to within 1 inch of the bottom tip of the waistline dart.

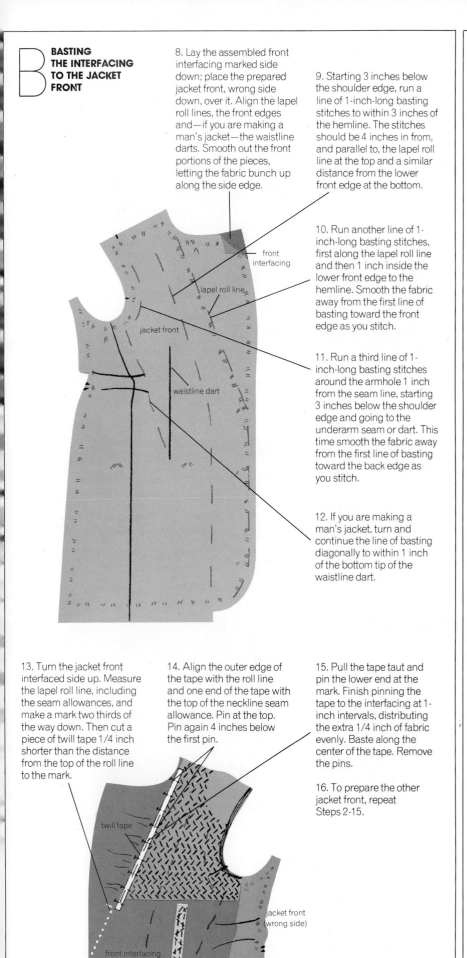

front interfacing

lapel roll line

jacket front

waistline dart

13. Turn the jacket front interfaced side up. Measure the lapel roll line, including the seam allowances, and make a mark two thirds of the way down. Then cut a piece of twill tape 1/4 inch shorter than the distance from the top of the roll line to the mark.

14. Align the outer edge of the tape with the roll line and one end of the tape with the top of the neckline seam allowance. Pin at the top. Pin again 4 inches below the first pin.

15. Pull the tape taut and pin the lower end at the mark. Finish pinning the tape to the interfacing at 1-inch intervals, distributing the extra 1/4 inch of fabric evenly. Baste along the center of the tape. Remove the pins.

16. To prepare the other jacket front, repeat Steps 2-15.

twill tape

front interfacing

jacket front (wrong side)

C | PREPARING THE JACKET BACK

17. Align the center-back seam lines and pin the jacket backs together, wrong sides out. Baste from the neck edge to the hemline and remove the pins.

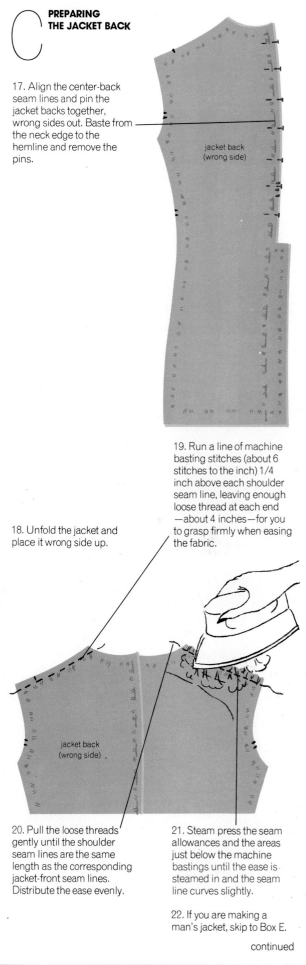

jacket back (wrong side)

18. Unfold the jacket and place it wrong side up.

19. Run a line of machine basting stitches (about 6 stitches to the inch) 1/4 inch above each shoulder seam line, leaving enough loose thread at each end —about 4 inches—for you to grasp firmly when easing the fabric.

jacket back (wrong side)

20. Pull the loose threads gently until the shoulder seam lines are the same length as the corresponding jacket-front seam lines. Distribute the ease evenly.

21. Steam press the seam allowances and the areas just below the machine bastings until the ease is steamed in and the seam line curves slightly.

22. If you are making a man's jacket, skip to Box E.

continued

D ATTACHING THE BACK INTERFACING FOR A WOMAN'S JACKET

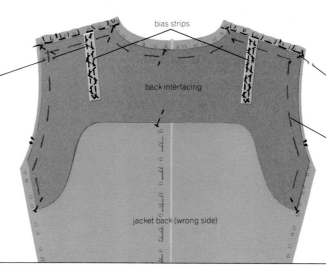

bias strips

back interfacing

jacket back (wrong side)

23. Place the jacket back wrong side up and lay the back interfacing over it, making sure that the side with the bias strips on the darts faces up. Align the edges of the interfacing with the shoulder seam lines on the jacket back, and pin.

24. To create the same fullness in the interfacing as you have in the jacket at the shoulders, ease the interfacing slightly in from each armhole. Pin.

25. Baste 1 inch inside the edges of the interfacing, except the lower edge. Remove the pins.

E ASSEMBLING THE BODY OF THE JACKET

26. Place one jacket front wrong side down and lay the jacket back, wrong side up, over it. Align the side seam lines and pin. Baste and remove the pins. Attach the other jacket front in the same manner.

27. Unfold the jacket front so that it is wrong side up.

31. Refold the jacket fronts under the jacket back. Align the shoulder seam lines. Pin and baste, being careful not to catch the front interfacing. Remove the pins.

jacket front

jacket back (wrong side)

front interfacing

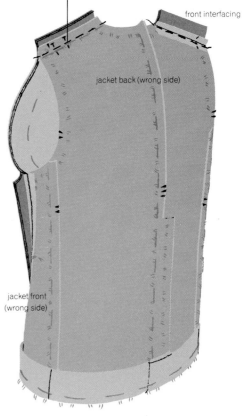

front interfacing

jacket back (wrong side)

jacket front (wrong side)

28. Fold along the hemline, turning the side seam allowances toward the back, and the center-back seam allowance to one side. Pin.

29. Baste 1/2 inch from the folded edge of the hemline. Remove the pins.

30. Turn up the seam allowances along the front edges from the hemline to the top of the lapel. Baste flat.

PREPARING
THE UNDERCOLLAR

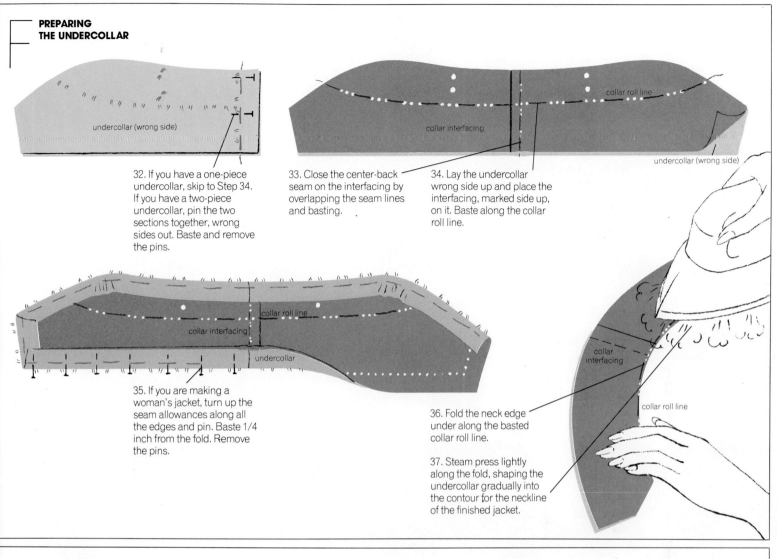

undercollar (wrong side)

collar interfacing

collar roll line

undercollar (wrong side)

collar interfacing

collar roll line

collar interfacing

undercollar

collar interfacing

collar roll line

32. If you have a one-piece undercollar, skip to Step 34. If you have a two-piece undercollar, pin the two sections together, wrong sides out. Baste and remove the pins.

33. Close the center-back seam on the interfacing by overlapping the seam lines and basting.

34. Lay the undercollar wrong side up and place the interfacing, marked side up, on it. Baste along the collar roll line.

35. If you are making a woman's jacket, turn up the seam allowances along all the edges and pin. Baste 1/4 inch from the fold. Remove the pins.

36. Fold the neck edge under along the basted collar roll line.

37. Steam press lightly along the fold, shaping the undercollar gradually into the contour for the neckline of the finished jacket.

FINISHING
THE PREPARATORY
ASSEMBLY

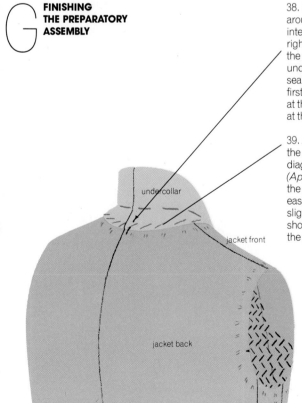

undercollar

jacket front

jacket back

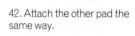

shoulder pad

38. Place the undercollar around the neck so that the interfacing is against the right side of the jacket. Align the neck edge of the undercollar with the neck seam line. Match and pin first at the center back, next at the front edges and then at the shoulder seams.

39. Attach the undercollar to the jacket with small diagonal basting stitches (*Appendix*) 1/4 inch above the edge. As you baste, ease the undercollar fabric slightly on both sides of the shoulder seams. Remove the pins.

40. Insert a shoulder pad in the armhole so that its outer edge aligns with the edge of the armhole and two thirds of the pad is behind the shoulder seam. For a man's jacket, insert the pad between the cover cloth and the haircloth interfacing; for a woman's jacket, insert it on the interfacing, not between the interfacing and the jacket.

41. Use a fastening stitch (*Appendix*) to attach the shoulder pad to the jacket at all three corners of the pad and at the edge of the shoulder seam. As you stitch, catch only the top layer of the shoulder pad.

42. Attach the other pad the same way.

43. Try on the jacket and adjust for fit (*pages 74-77*).

44. When the jacket fits properly, take it apart by removing all the bastings except those for the center back seam, the collar roll line and, in a woman's jacket, the back interfacing. Then construct the jacket front (*page 113*).

Starting the jacket front

When the first fitting is completed and the jacket has been taken apart work begins on the front of the jacket, shown here completed. The tasks include putting in waistline darts stitching the underarm seam and assembling the pockets.

Of all work on the jacket front, putting in pockets is the most demanding. The classic welt pocket, shown here on the jacket's left breast, is named for the wide welt, or doubled-over strip of fabric, that edges the opening. The two flap pockets on the sides have edgings of narrow welts, which tailors call piping—one below at the lip of the pocket opening, and another one above where the flap is attached to the jacket.

After the pockets are on, the interfacing is permanently attached to the front. Then the jacket body is reassembled—again temporarily—for the jacket's final fitting. This time the sleeves are included.

Veteran tailors never use pins basting the pieces directly together as they work. Beginners, however, may have more success if they pin first, as indicated in the directions that follow.

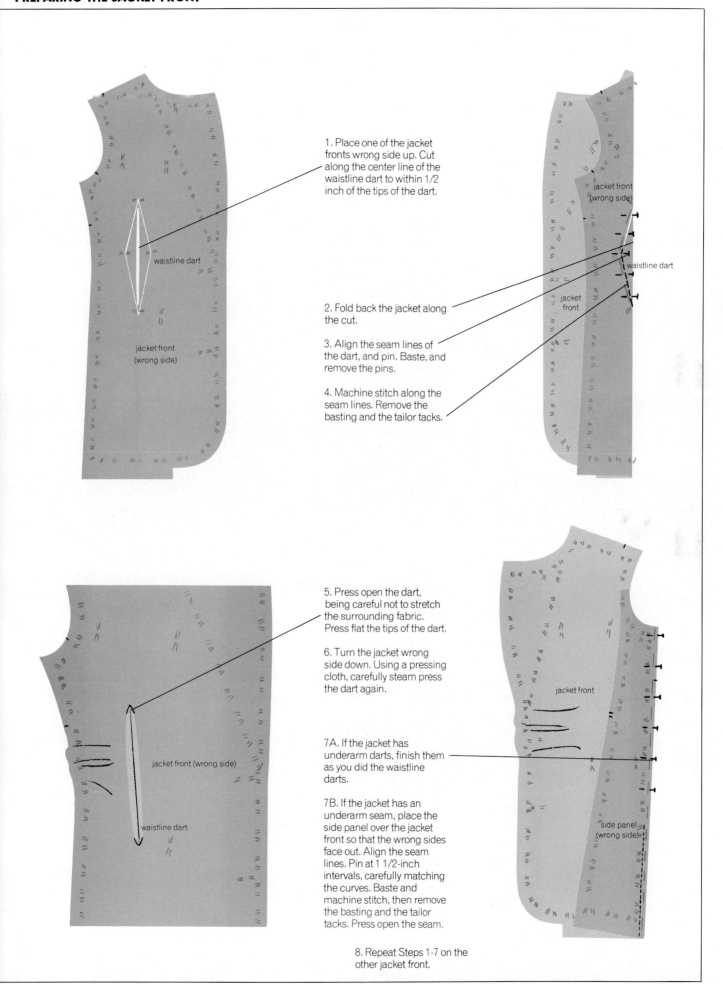

1. Place one of the jacket fronts wrong side up. Cut along the center line of the waistline dart to within 1/2 inch of the tips of the dart.

2. Fold back the jacket along the cut.

3. Align the seam lines of the dart, and pin. Baste, and remove the pins.

4. Machine stitch along the seam lines. Remove the basting and the tailor tacks.

5. Press open the dart, being careful not to stretch the surrounding fabric. Press flat the tips of the dart.

6. Turn the jacket wrong side down. Using a pressing cloth, carefully steam press the dart again.

7A. If the jacket has underarm darts, finish them as you did the waistline darts.

7B. If the jacket has an underarm seam, place the side panel over the jacket front so that the wrong sides face out. Align the seam lines. Pin at 1 1/2-inch intervals, carefully matching the curves. Baste and machine stitch, then remove the basting and the tailor tacks. Press open the seam.

8. Repeat Steps 1-7 on the other jacket front.

waistline dart

jacket front (wrong side)

jacket front (wrong side)

waistline dart

jacket front (wrong side)

waistline dart

jacket front

jacket front

side panel (wrong side)

THE WELT POCKET

A CUTTING AND MARKING THE WELT AND FACING

1. If your pattern indicates making both sides of the welt from the garment fabric, you will need to revise the welt pattern piece before proceeding. To do so, draw a 1-inch seam allowance below the fold line, and 1/4-inch allowances along each of the sides.

2. Cut along the new seam allowances and discard the bottom part of the pattern piece.

welt pattern piece

fold line

3. Place the left jacket front wrong side down and draw a chalk mark to connect the tailor tacks that indicate the position of the pocket.

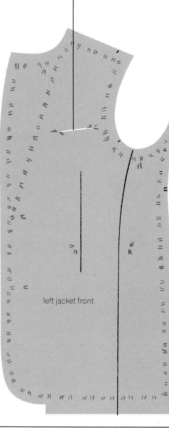

left jacket front

4. If you are working with a striped or plaid fabric, position the welt pattern on the jacket front, so that the lower seam line is directly over the chalk line. With a pencil, indicate the position of the stripes or plaids.

5. Place two pieces of garment fabric, wrong side out, on a flat surface. Pin the revised welt pattern to both layers of fabric, matching the direction of the nap—if any. On striped or plaid fabric, place the pattern marked side down and match the design. Then cut out the pieces.

6. Turn back the pattern. Mark the top piece with an "X"; this piece will be the welt. The lower piece will be used for the facing.

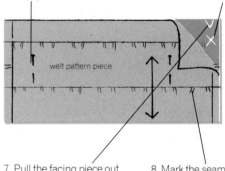

welt pattern piece

7. Pull the facing piece out from below the welt piece and turn it wrong side up. With chalk, mark each piece with a "V" on the top edge.

8. Mark the seam lines on the welt piece with tailor tacks (page 97). Remove the pattern.

B CUTTING OUT AND MARKING THE POCKET PIECES

9. Cut out two squares from pocketing fabric: the length of each side should be equal to the length of the finished welt, plus 2 inches. Be sure to follow the grain of the fabric. These squares will become the pocket itself.

10. Mark a 1/4-inch seam allowance along one side of each square.

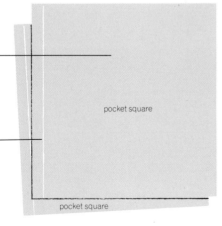

pocket square

pocket square

11. To make a reinforcement patch for the pocket, cut out another piece of pocketing fabric the same width as the squares cut out in Step 9, but only 2 1/2 inches deep.

12. Using the reinforcement patch as a pattern, cut out the pocket lining from a piece of the same lining used for the jacket.

13. Turn up the wrong side of the pocket lining, and draw a 1/4-inch seam allowance along one of its long edges.

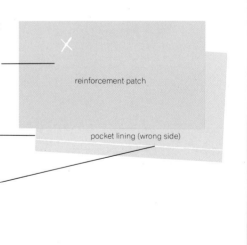

reinforcement patch

pocket lining (wrong side)

C ASSEMBLING THE WELT AND FACING SECTIONS

14. Place the welt wrong side down, with the chalk-marked "V" at the top. Position one pocket square over it so that the seam allowance on the pocket piece is at the top. Then align the top edges.

15. Baste along the seam line, then machine stitch on the seam line. Remove the basting.

16. Steam press the seam allowances toward the pocket square.

17. Repeat Steps 14-16 with the other pocket square and the facing piece.

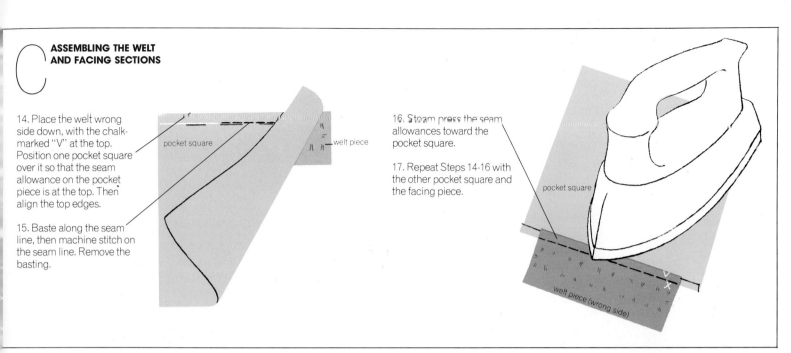

D LINING THE WELT SECTION

18. Turn the welt section wrong side down. Place the lining, wrong side up, over the welt itself. Then align the marked edge of the lining with the seam on the welt section.

19. Pin the pieces together; baste along the chalked seam line, and remove the pins.

20. Machine stitch on the seam line and remove the basting.

21. Fold back the lining, and press the seam flat.

22. Fold under the unattached edge of the lining 3/8 inch, and pin.

23. Next baste the folded edge of the lining to the pocket square. Remove the pins.

24. Machine stitch as close to the folded edge as possible. Remove the bastings.

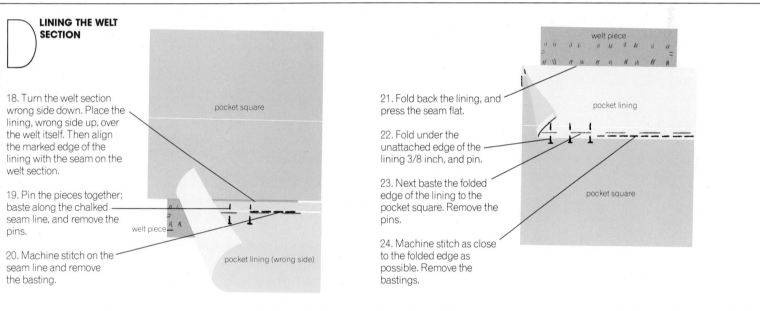

E FINISHING THE WELT SECTION

25. Fold the welt over the lining along the tailor-tacked line nearest the lining. Pin.

26. Ease in the sides of the welt slightly so that the finished welt will be somewhat curved. Then pin along the sides.

27. Baste and remove the pins.

28. Machine stitch on the side seam lines. Remove the bastings and also the tailor tacks on the top fold and side seams.

29. Trim the side seam allowances to 1/8 inch; then cut diagonally to the bottom corners of the lining.

30. Turn the welt right side out.

31. Using unknotted thread, insert a needle into the stitching at one corner. Pull the needle through. Then gently tug on the doubled thread to pull out the corners. Repeat until the corner is square.

32. Square the other corner in the same manner.

33. To keep the sides straight, baste through all layers 1/8 inch from the three finished welt edges.

34. Check the size of the welt against the pattern. Then steam press lightly on both sides using a pressing cloth. Remove the basting.

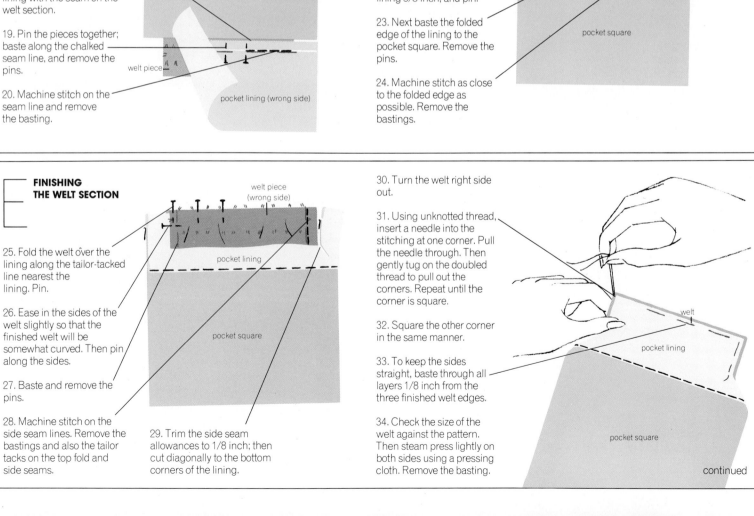

continued

F ATTACHING THE REINFORCEMENT PATCH TO THE JACKET

35. With the left jacket front wrong side up, center the reinforcement patch over the two tailor tacks that indicate the position of the pocket.

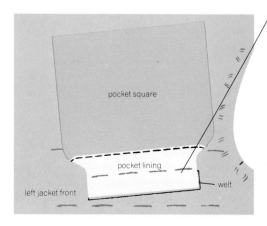

left jacket front (wrong side)

36. Baste along the top and bottom edges of the reinforcement patch.

G ATTACHING THE WELT TO THE JACKET

37. Starting at the lower edge of the welt side seam, use a seam ripper to remove the stitches made in Step 28. Stop just past the tailor-tacked seam line on the welt. Repeat on the other side seam.

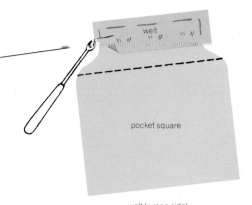

welt

pocket square

38. Turn the jacket wrong side down. With the pocket square turned away from the welt, position the welt on the jacket so that the seam line is aligned with the chalk line indicating the pocket position on the jacket. Pin, then baste along the seam line and remove the pins.

39. To check the position of the basted seam line, fold up the welt and pocket square. Adjust the placement if necessary.

40. Machine stitch on the seam line, backstitching twice at both ends to anchor the welt firmly to the jacket front. Remove the basting.

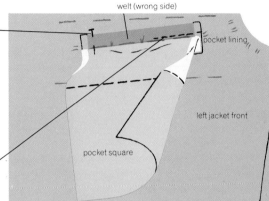

welt (wrong side)

pocket lining

left jacket front

pocket square

41. Trim the welt seam allowance to 3/8 inch, then trim the corners diagonally.

42. Fold the seam allowance over the seam, sandwiching it between the pocket square and the welt. Baste the seam allowance flat against the welt, taking care not to catch the pocket square as you sew.

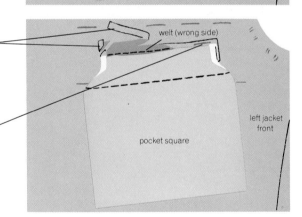

welt (wrong side)

left jacket front

pocket square

H SECURING THE LINING TO THE JACKET

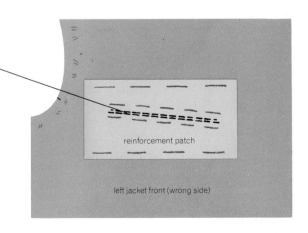

pocket square

pocket lining

left jacket front

welt

43. Turn the pocket square toward the top of the jacket and baste it to the jacket, just above the welt layers.

44. Turn the jacket wrong side up. Run a line of machine stitching on the reinforcement patch directly above—but slightly shorter than—the stitching made in Step 40.

45. Steam press, and remove all remaining basting except the lines at the top and bottom of the reinforcement patch.

reinforcement patch

left jacket front (wrong side)

ATTACHING THE FACING TO THE JACKET

46. Turn the jacket front wrong side down, and fold the pocket square down over the welt.

47. With the facing section wrong side up, align its raw edge with the fold along the seam of the welt.

48. Baste the facing to the jacket 3/8 inch from the raw edge.

49. Indicate on the facing the sides of the welt by drawing 1/4-inch vertical chalk lines at both sides. To mark a seam line, connect the ends of the lines.

50. Machine stitch on the chalked seam line, starting and ending 1/4 inch from the vertical lines drawn in Step 49. Remove the basting.

51. Fold the seam allowance toward the facing. Press.

52. Turn the jacket front wrong side up. Make a slash halfway between the two widely spaced lines of stitching on the reinforcement patch, cutting through all layers of fabric. The slash should be the same length as the top line of stitching.

53. At the ends of the slash, clip straight up to—but not through—the ends of the top seam.

54. Clip the ends of the slash again, this time cutting diagonally down to—but again not through—the ends of the bottom line of stitching.

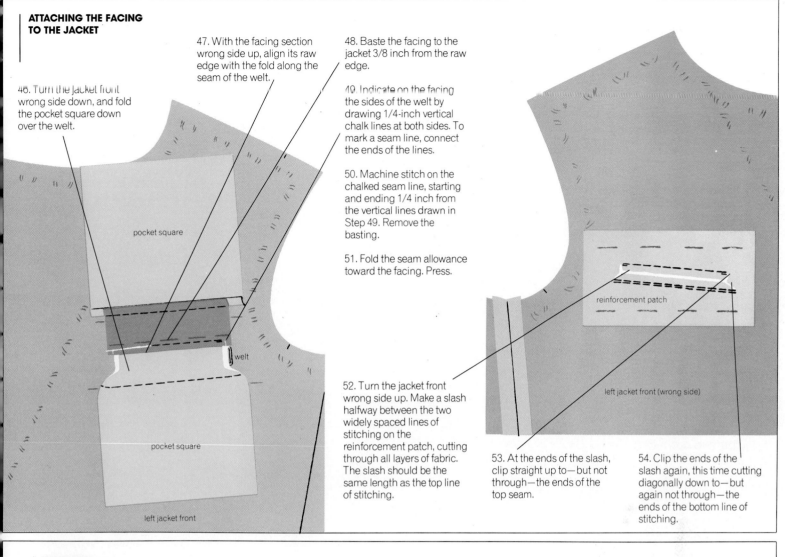

FINISHING THE POCKET SQUARES

55. Turn the jacket front wrong side down. Tuck first the facing section and then the welt section through the slash to the wrong side of the jacket front.

56. Turn up the welt so that the lining side is down; baste it to the jacket front along the top and the two sides, concealing the slash. Make sure to match any plaids or stripes.

57. Turn the jacket wrong side up. Fold under the top of the jacket along the welt seam.

58. Turn the pocket squares away from the jacket and smooth them flat. The top square will be shorter than the other; baste the two squares together at the edge of the shorter one.

59. Beginning at one end of the welt seam, machine stitch for 3/8 inch as close as possible to the seam. Pivot (Appendix), then stitch diagonally until you are 3/8 inch from the edge of the pocket. Pivot again and continue stitching around the pocket, maintaining a 3/8-inch seam allowance and stitching around the corners in a curve. Finish the other side as you began the first. Remove all bastings.

60. Trim the seam allowances of the longer pocket square to within 1/4 inch of the seams.

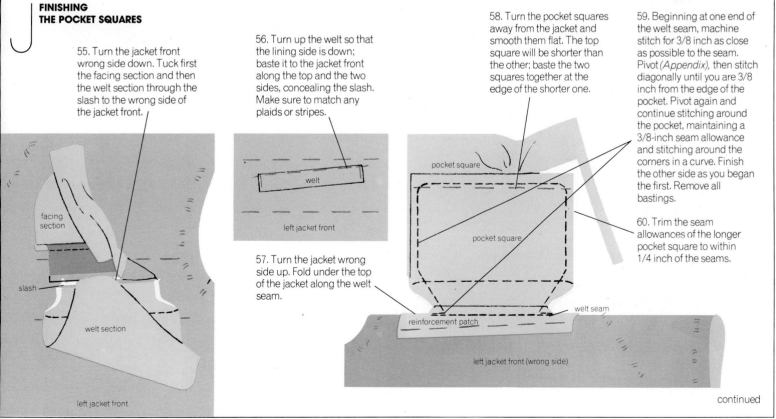

continued

FINISHING THE WELT

61. Unfold the jacket and turn the pocket toward the bottom of the jacket. Clip at each end of the outer seam allowance of the facing, so that both facing seam allowances are the same length. Then steam press the seam allowances open.

62. Turn the jacket wrong side down. Sew the sides of the welt to the jacket with tiny blind hemming stitches (Appendix), concealing the lining as you sew.

63. Remove all the bastings. Then steam press the welt using a pressing cloth.

64. To keep the welt in place, sew it to the jacket front with diagonal basting stitches (Appendix); do not remove these stitches until you have completed the jacket.

65. Turn the jacket wrong side up. Reinforce the sides of the welt with a row of 1/8-inch fastening stitches (Appendix), making sure to sew through as many layers as possible without catching the outside layer. Sew a second row of stitches directly over the first row.

66. If you are making a woman's jacket with front shoulder darts or bust darts, finish them as you did the waistline dart in preparing the jacket front (page 113).

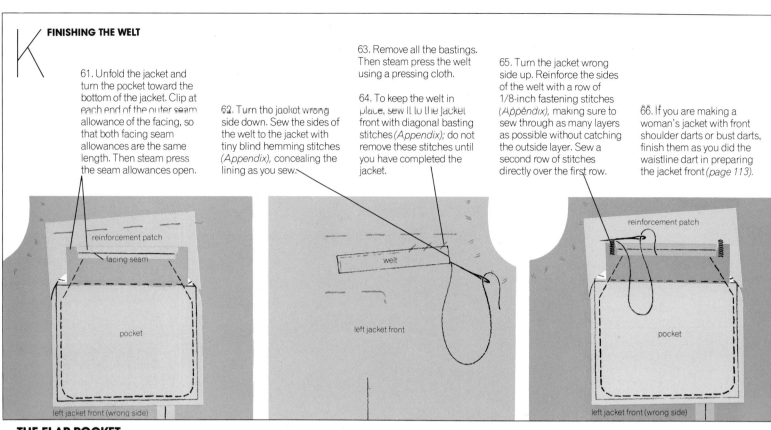

THE FLAP POCKET

CUTTING OUT THE POCKET PIECES

1. Place the jacket fronts wrong sides down on a flat surface. Draw chalk marks to connect the tailor tacks that indicate the position of the pockets. Then baste along the chalk lines.

2. On one of the jacket fronts, measure the distance of the chalk line between the tailor tacks.

3. Measure the distance between the tailor tack marking the front edge of the pocket and the hemline.

4. Cut out two rectangles from pocketing fabric. The length should be equal to twice the vertical measure determined in Step 3 less 2 inches. The width should be equal to the distance measured in Step 2 plus 2 inches. These pieces will become the pocket bodies.

5. To make the reinforcement patches for the pockets, cut out two more rectangles from pocketing fabric, each patch the same width as the rectangles cut out in Step 4 —but only 3 inches deep.

6. Using one reinforcement patch as a pattern, cut out four strips on the straight grain of the garment fabric. These will be the piping above and below the pocket openings. If your fabric is a plaid or a stripe, match the fabric strips to the pattern on the garment at the pocket line.

7. With chalk, indicate with an "X" the wrong side of each strip, and make an arrow showing the direction of the nap, if any.

8. From the jacket lining material, cut out two strips for pocket lining, each strip the same width as the reinforcement patch but 1 inch deeper. Mark the wrong sides with an "X."

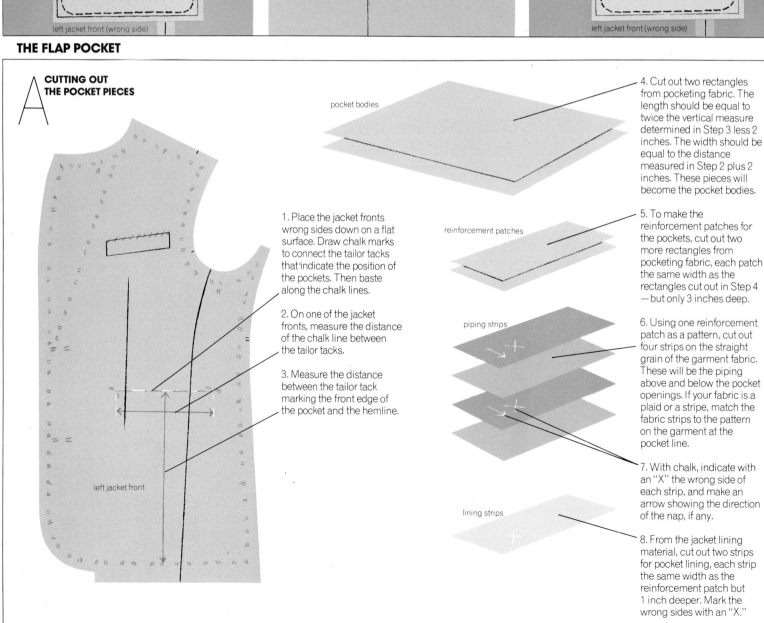

B CUTTING THE FLAP PIECES

9. If your pattern calls for making both sides of the flap from the garment fabric you will need to revise the pattern before proceeding. To do so, draw 1/4-inch seam allowances below the fold line and along each of the sides.

10. Cut along the new seam allowances and discard the bottom part of the pattern piece.

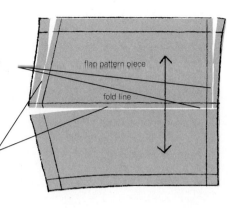

11A. If you are working with a solid-colored fabric, place two pieces of garment fabric together, wrong sides out, on a flat surface.

12A. Pin the revised pattern to both layers of fabric and cut out the flap pieces.

13A. Mark with tailor tacks (page 97) the seam lines of both flap pieces. Remove the pattern.

14A. With chalk, mark an "X" on the wrong sides of the pieces.

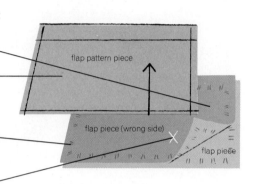

11B. If you are working with a striped or plaid fabric, position the flap pattern on one of the jacket fronts so that the upper seam line on the flap is directly over the chalk line on the jacket. With a pencil, indicate the position of the stripes or plaids.

12B. Place a piece of the garment fabric, wrong side down, on a flat surface. Pin the revised flap pattern to the fabric, matching any stripes or plaid and the direction of the nap—if any. Then cut out the flap piece. Mark the seam lines with tailor tacks (page 97). Remove the pattern.

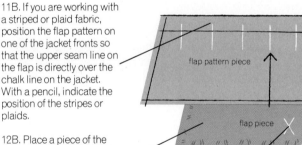

13B. With chalk, mark an "X" on the wrong side of the piece.

14B. Repeat Steps 11B-13B to cut out and mark the second flap piece.

15. Place the two pieces of jacket lining fabric, wrong sides out, on a flat surface. Using the revised flap pattern as a guide, cut out the lining pieces for the flaps. Then mark the wrong sides with an "X."

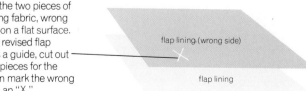

C ASSEMBLING THE FLAP

16. Working on one pocket at a time, place the flap lining wrong side down and cover it with the flap piece, wrong side up. Pin the two together.

17. Baste the lining to the flap about 3/8 inch in from the edges. Ease the flap piece in slightly from the edges as you proceed.

18. Machine stitch around the seam lines of the sides and bottom of the flap. At the front corner, curve the line of stitching to produce a slightly rounded corner. Remove the basting and the tailor tacks.

19. Trim the corners close to the machine stitching.

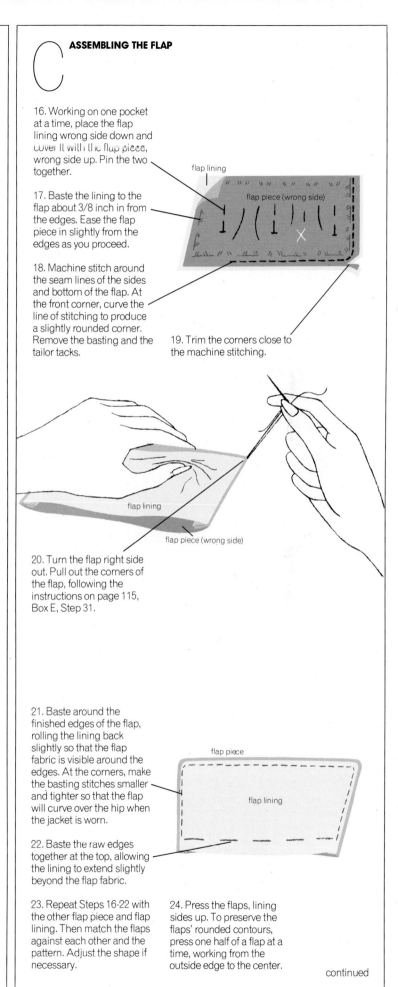

20. Turn the flap right side out. Pull out the corners of the flap, following the instructions on page 115, Box E, Step 31.

21. Baste around the finished edges of the flap, rolling the lining back slightly so that the flap fabric is visible around the edges. At the corners, make the basting stitches smaller and tighter so that the flap will curve over the hip when the jacket is worn.

22. Baste the raw edges together at the top, allowing the lining to extend slightly beyond the flap fabric.

23. Repeat Steps 16-22 with the other flap piece and flap lining. Then match the flaps against each other and the pattern. Adjust the shape if necessary.

24. Press the flaps, lining sides up. To preserve the flaps' rounded contours, press one half of a flap at a time, working from the outside edge to the center.

continued

D LINING THE POCKET

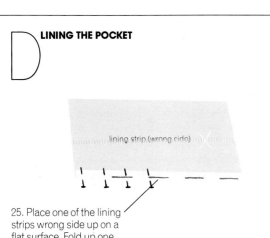

lining strip (wrong side)

25. Place one of the lining strips wrong side up on a flat surface. Fold up one long side to make a 3/8-inch hem. Then pin, baste, remove the pins and press the hem.

pocket body

lining strip

26. Place the lining strip wrong side down over one of the pocket bodies, aligning the unbasted edge of the lining with the pocket edge. Pin. Baste 1/2 inch from the edge.

27. Baste the folded edge of the lining to the pocket, then machine stitch along the fold. Remove the bastings.

E ATTACHING THE PIPING STRIPS

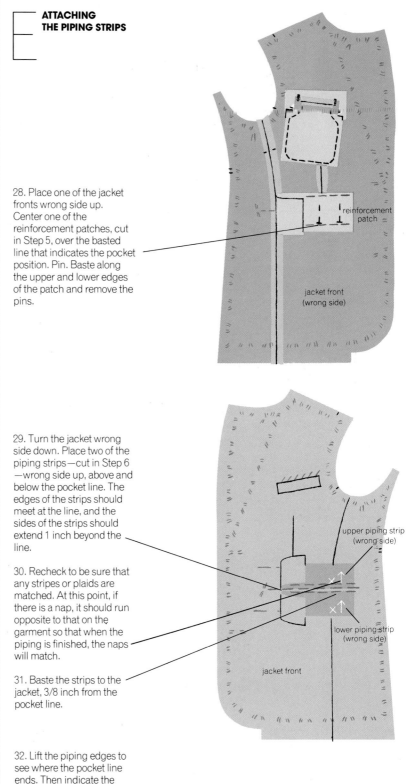

reinforcement patch

jacket front (wrong side)

28. Place one of the jacket fronts wrong side up. Center one of the reinforcement patches, cut in Step 5, over the basted line that indicates the pocket position. Pin. Baste along the upper and lower edges of the patch and remove the pins.

upper piping strip (wrong side)

lower piping strip (wrong side)

jacket front

29. Turn the jacket wrong side down. Place two of the piping strips—cut in Step 6 —wrong side up, above and below the pocket line. The edges of the strips should meet at the line, and the sides of the strips should extend 1 inch beyond the line.

30. Recheck to be sure that any stripes or plaids are matched. At this point, if there is a nap, it should run opposite to that on the garment so that when the piping is finished, the naps will match.

31. Baste the strips to the jacket, 3/8 inch from the pocket line.

32. Lift the piping edges to see where the pocket line ends. Then indicate the ends of the pocket line with 1/4-inch chalk lines on both strips.

33. To create seam lines, connect the ends of the lines on both strips.

34. Machine stitch on the two seam lines made in Step 33. Make the lower line of stitches 1/16 inch shorter at each end than the upper line. If you are using a stretchy fabric such as camel's hair or some tweeds, which will spread when pressed, stitch just inside the seam lines. Remove the bastings and the tailor tacks.

upper piping strip (wrong side)

lower piping strip (wrong side)

35. Turn the jacket wrong side up. Slash along the pocket line to within 3/8 inch of the ends of the lines of stitching. Cut only the jacket fabric and the reinforcement patch, not the seam allowances of the piping strips on the other side of the jacket. Then cut diagonally up to, but not into, the ends of both lines of stitching.

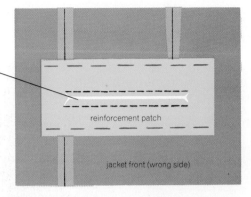

39. Turn the jacket front wrong side down. Push one of the piping strips through the slash again, folding the strip over the top seam allowance. This fold will become the piping on the pocket. If the ends of the piping bulge, recheck the diagonal cuts you made in Step 35 to be sure you have cut all the way to the piping stitching lines.

40. Baste through both layers of the piping strip between the fold and the seam, taking care that the piping itself is an even 1/4 inch all the way across. (If the fabric is stretchy, make the piping slightly narrower.)

41. Repeat Steps 39 and 40 on the other piping strip.

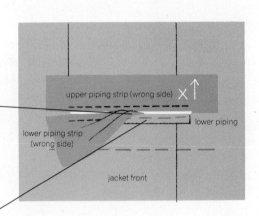

36. Reach into the slash and pull the lower piping strip through the slash. Then smooth the strip and steam press open the seam allowances.

37. Push the lower piping strip back through the slash.

38. Repeat Steps 36 and 37 to press open the seam allowances of the upper piping strip.

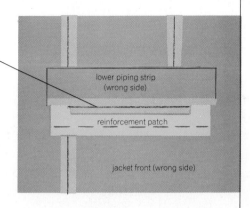

42. Fold up the jacket along the lower piping seam. Turn the lower piping strip away from the jacket, so that the line of stitching on the reinforcement patch is visible.

43. Secure the lower piping strip to the seam allowances with a line of machine stitches, stitching as close as possible to the seam.

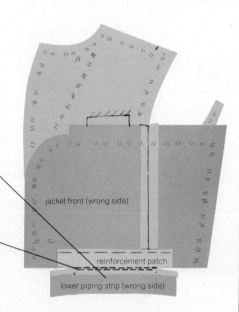

44. Unfold the jacket so that it is wrong side down. Push through the pocket opening the small fabric triangles that were created at each end when you cut the slash.

45. Insert the raw edges of the flap assembly into the pocket opening, so that the top seam line on the flap aligns with the bottom of the upper piping.

46. Pin the flap to the jacket front, checking to see that the flap is straight. The flap should be slightly longer than the pocket opening.

47. Baste along the piping through all the fabric layers, easing the excess flap fabric as you sew so that the flap will curve to the body contour when the jacket is worn. Remove the pins.

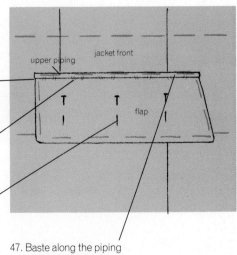

48. Fold the jacket front in half, wrong sides out, along the seam of the upper piping. Turn the upper piping strip away from the jacket so that the line of stitching on the reinforcement patch is visible.

49. Secure the upper piping strip and the flap to the seam allowances with a line of machine stitching, sewing as close to the seam as possible. Remove the basting.

50. Turn the jacket wrong side down and steam press the flap and piping with a pressing cloth, making sure that all the layers underneath are flat.

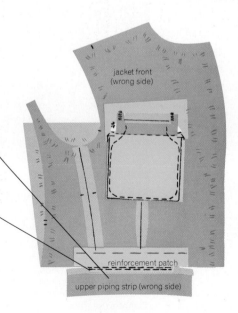

continued

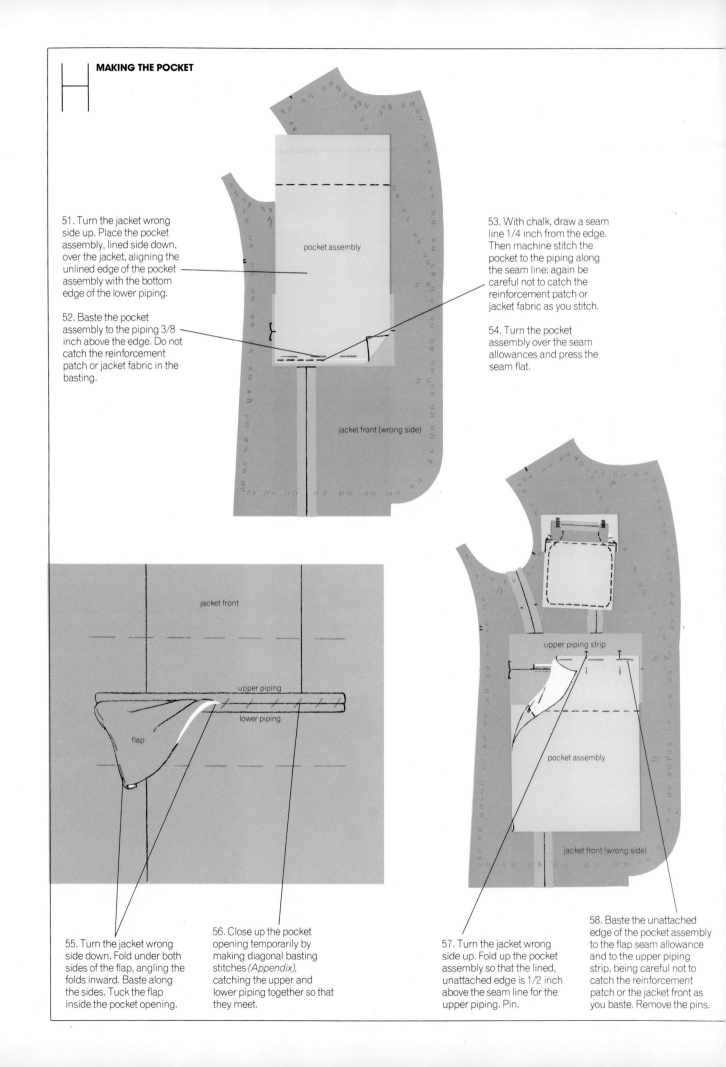

51. Turn the jacket wrong side up. Place the pocket assembly, lined side down, over the jacket, aligning the unlined edge of the pocket assembly with the bottom edge of the lower piping.

52. Baste the pocket assembly to the piping 3/8 inch above the edge. Do not catch the reinforcement patch or jacket fabric in the basting.

53. With chalk, draw a seam line 1/4 inch from the edge. Then machine stitch the pocket to the piping along the seam line; again be careful not to catch the reinforcement patch or jacket fabric as you stitch.

54. Turn the pocket assembly over the seam allowances and press the seam flat.

pocket assembly

jacket front (wrong side)

jacket front

upper piping
lower piping

flap

upper piping strip

pocket assembly

jacket front (wrong side)

55. Turn the jacket wrong side down. Fold under both sides of the flap, angling the folds inward. Baste along the sides. Tuck the flap inside the pocket opening.

56. Close up the pocket opening temporarily by making diagonal basting stitches (Appendix), catching the upper and lower piping together so that they meet.

57. Turn the jacket wrong side up. Fold up the pocket assembly so that the lined, unattached edge is 1/2 inch above the seam line for the upper piping. Pin.

58. Baste the unattached edge of the pocket assembly to the flap seam allowance and to the upper piping strip, being careful not to catch the reinforcement patch or the jacket front as you baste. Remove the pins.

59. Fold the jacket front in half, wrong sides out, along the seam for the upper piping. Turn the upper piping strip away from the jacket so that the lines of stitching on the reinforcement patch are visible.

60. Run a line of machine stitching the length of the seam directly over the line of stitching made in Step 49.

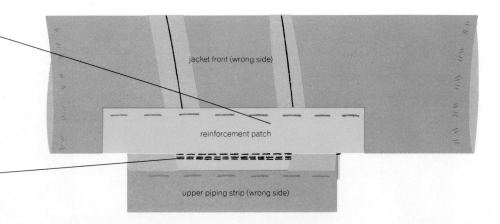

jacket front (wrong side)

reinforcement patch

upper piping strip (wrong side)

61. Turn the jacket wrong side down. Fold back the edge of the pocket opening on one side of the jacket. Smooth flat the pocket and piping.

62. Pull the small, two-layered fabric triangle away from the opening. Then, using the zipper foot (Appendix) on your machine, stitch two or three times across the triangle, reversing the stitching at each end and catching all layers. Stitch parallel with the side seam line, and as close to the pocket as possible.

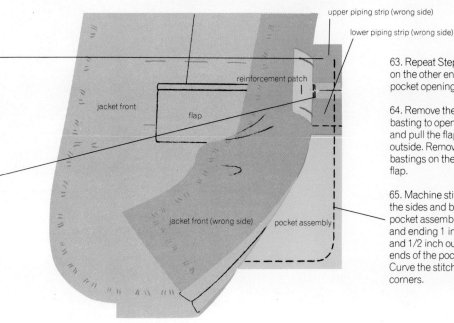

upper piping strip (wrong side)

lower piping strip (wrong side)

reinforcement patch

jacket front

flap

jacket front (wrong side)

pocket assembly

63. Repeat Steps 61 and 62 on the other end of the pocket opening.

64. Remove the diagonal basting to open the pocket and pull the flap to the outside. Remove the bastings on the sides of the flap.

65. Machine stitch around the sides and bottom of the pocket assembly, starting and ending 1 inch above and 1/2 inch outside the ends of the pocket opening. Curve the stitches at the corners.

67. Turn down the flap. Using a pressing cloth, press the flap.

68. Finish each end of the pocket opening by making two vertical stitches with buttonhole twist. Make each stitch from the top corner of the upper piping to the bottom corner of the lower piping. End with a fastening stitch on the wrong side of the jacket.

69. Repeat Steps 25-68 to construct the other pocket.

66. With the jacket wrong side down, lift up the flap and sew the lower piping to the flap lining with diagonal basting stitches (Appendix).

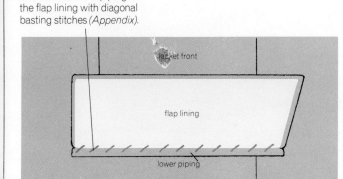

jacket front

flap lining

lower piping

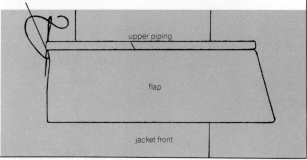

upper piping

flap

jacket front

INTERFACING THE JACKET FRONT

A BASTING THE INTERFACING TO THE JACKET FRONT

1. Place both of the jacket-front interfacing assemblies, cover-cloth sides down, on a flat surface.

2. Position the left jacket front, wrong side down, over one of the interfacings so that the front edges and the lapel roll lines are aligned.

3. To baste the jacket front to the interfacing assembly you will be making several lines of 1-inch-long basting stitches—here and in Box C—that should not be removed until the jacket is finished. Begin the first line of basting about 4 inches below the shoulder edge midway between the lapel roll line and the armhole, and end about 4 inches above the hem. The basting line will pass close to the center of the welt pocket, and will run about 1 inch in front of the waistline dart and directly over the front of the flap pocket.

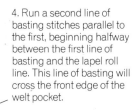

welt pocket
lapel roll line
waistline dart
flap pocket
left jacket front

4. Run a second line of basting stitches parallel to the first, beginning halfway between the first line of basting and the lapel roll line. This line of basting will cross the front edge of the welt pocket.

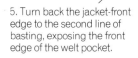

5. Turn back the jacket-front edge to the second line of basting, exposing the front edge of the welt pocket.

6. Fold back the reinforcement patch on the welt pocket to expose the seam allowances of the pocket assembly.

7. Fasten the welt-pocket seam allowances to the interfacing with hemming stitches (Appendix). Turn the edge of the jacket front down again, over the interfacing.

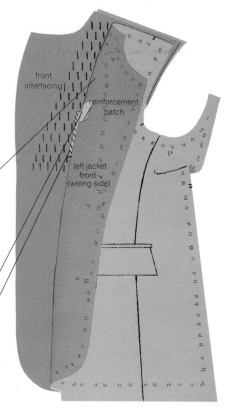

front interfacing
reinforcement patch
left jacket front (wrong side)

8. Run a third line of basting stitches along the length of the lapel roll line, smoothing the garment fabric toward the front edge of the jacket as you proceed.

9. At the lower edge of the lapel roll line continue the basting about 1 1/2 inches from the front edge until you reach the hemline. So that the front of the finished garment will curve to the contours of the body, be sure to ease the garment fabric back from the interfacing edge as you baste. Ease the fabric 1/8 inch for firm fabrics or 1/4 inch for soft fabrics.

10. If you are making a woman's jacket, skip to Box C.

11. If you are making a man's jacket, run a line of basting stitches the length of the waistline dart, smoothing the fabric toward the side seam as you go.

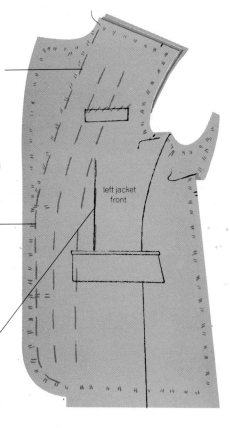

left jacket front

B FASTENING THE WAISTLINE DART TO THE INTERFACING ON A MAN'S JACKET

12. Turn back the jacket fabric from the side to expose the seam allowance of the waistline dart.

13. Fasten the dart seam allowance to the interfacing with hemming stitches. Turn the jacket fabric back down over the interfacing.

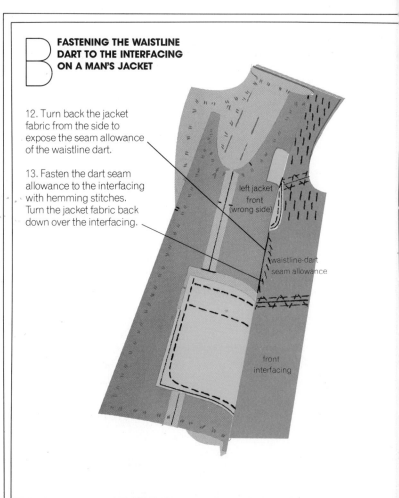

left jacket front (wrong side)
waistline-dart seam allowance
front interfacing

BASTING THE ARMHOLE TO THE INTERFACING

14. Run a line of basting stitches about 2 inches from the armhole edge, starting 4 inches below the shoulder seam and ending at the underarm dart or seam. Smooth the fabric layers toward the armhole as you proceed.

15. If you are making a man's jacket, run a line of basting stitches from the underarm dart or seam to the middle of the waistline dart, curving the line of stitches slightly. Again smooth the fabric layers toward the side seam as you proceed.

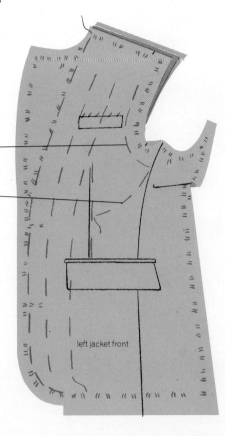

left jacket front

16. Turn back the jacket front at the armhole edge and pull back the reinforcement patch of the welt pocket. Attach the seam allowances of the pocket assembly to the interfacing with hemming stitches.

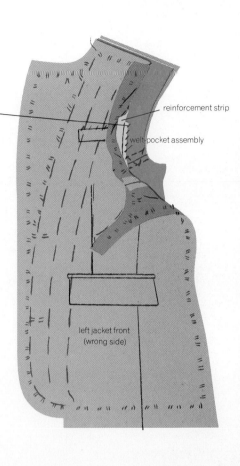

reinforcement strip

welt-pocket assembly

left jacket front (wrong side)

D **TAPING THE LAPEL ROLL LINE**

17. Turn the jacket-front assembly wrong side up. To repin and baste the twill tape to the lapel roll line, follow the instructions on page 109, Box B, Steps 14 and 15.

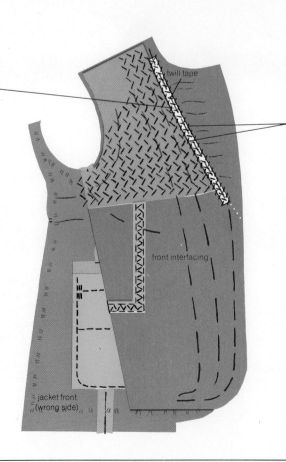

twill tape

front interfacing

jacket front (wrong side)

18. Fasten the edges of the twill tape to the interfacing with 1/4-inch-long padding stitches *(page 98)*. Remove the basting done in Step 17, then make another row of padding stitches down the middle of the tape.

continued

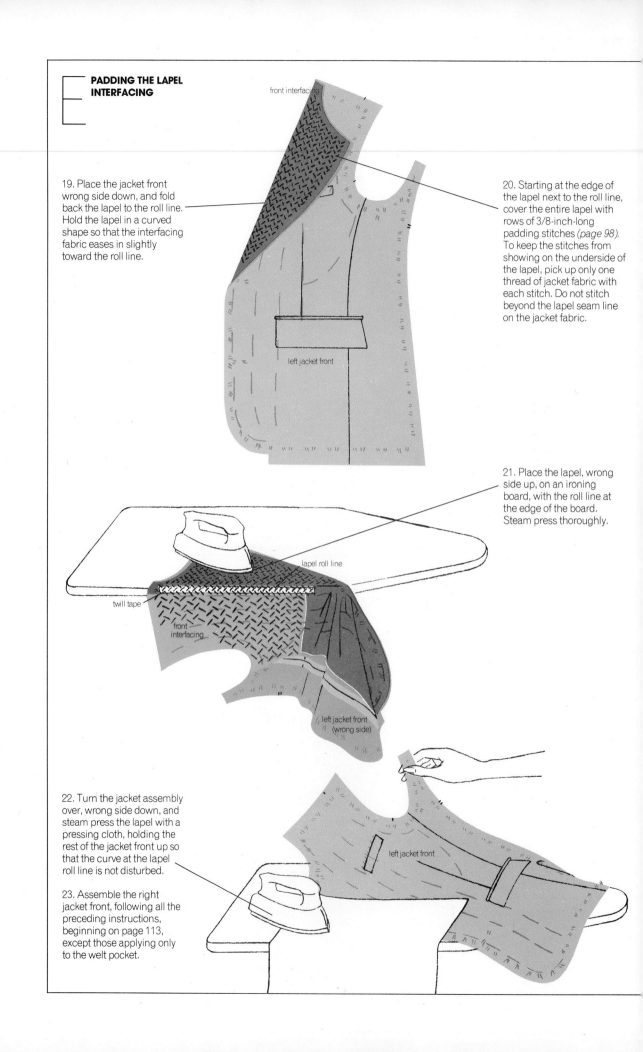

19. Place the jacket front wrong side down, and fold back the lapel to the roll line. Hold the lapel in a curved shape so that the interfacing fabric eases in slightly toward the roll line.

20. Starting at the edge of the lapel next to the roll line, cover the entire lapel with rows of 3/8-inch-long padding stitches *(page 98)*. To keep the stitches from showing on the underside of the lapel, pick up only one thread of jacket fabric with each stitch. Do not stitch beyond the lapel seam line on the jacket fabric.

21. Place the lapel, wrong side up, on an ironing board, with the roll line at the edge of the board. Steam press thoroughly.

22. Turn the jacket assembly over, wrong side down, and steam press the lapel with a pressing cloth, holding the rest of the jacket front up so that the curve at the lapel roll line is not disturbed.

23. Assemble the right jacket front, following all the preceding instructions, beginning on page 113, except those applying only to the welt pocket.

front interfacing

left jacket front

lapel roll line

twill tape

front interfacing

left jacket front (wrong side)

left jacket front

THE SECOND FITTING

A | ASSEMBLING THE SLEEVES

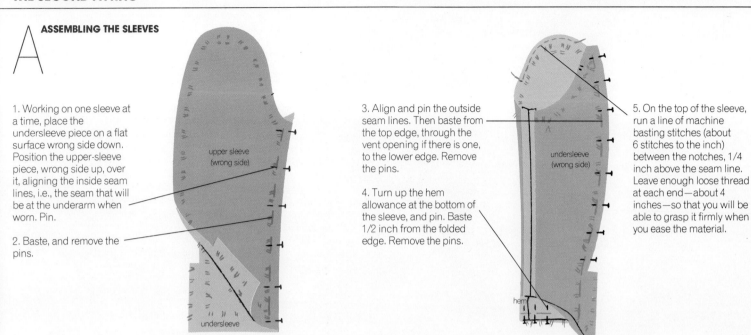

1. Working on one sleeve at a time, place the undersleeve piece on a flat surface wrong side down. Position the upper-sleeve piece, wrong side up, over it, aligning the inside seam lines, i.e., the seam that will be at the underarm when worn. Pin.

2. Baste, and remove the pins.

3. Align and pin the outside seam lines. Then baste from the top edge, through the vent opening if there is one, to the lower edge. Remove the pins.

4. Turn up the hem allowance at the bottom of the sleeve, and pin. Baste 1/2 inch from the folded edge. Remove the pins.

5. On the top of the sleeve, run a line of machine basting stitches (about 6 stitches to the inch) between the notches, 1/4 inch above the seam line. Leave enough loose thread at each end—about 4 inches—so that you will be able to grasp it firmly when you ease the material.

B | FINISHING THE PREPARATORY ASSEMBLY

6. Finish the jacket assembly as you did for the first fitting (pages 109-111, Boxes C-G, Steps 17-39). Then turn the jacket wrong side out.

7. Turn one of the sleeves right side out. Insert the sleeve into its corresponding armhole. Then align the seam lines, matching and pinning at the pattern markings.

8. Pull the loose threads gently to ease in the fullness on the top of the sleeve. Pin. Baste, and remove the pins.

9. Repeat Steps 7 and 8 on the other sleeve.

10. Turn the jacket right side out. Attach the shoulder pads as you did for the first fitting (page 111, Box G, Steps 40-42).

11. Try on the jacket, and following the instructions on page 77, check the fit and make appropriate adjustments.

12. When the jacket fits properly, take it apart by removing the bastings made in Steps 2-10. Then proceed with the construction of the lapel.

Facings that form the lapels

After the jacket's second fitting adjustments have been made and it is again disassembled, the remaining work on the front should be completed. This means adding the facings —lengths of garment fabric that run down the inside of each front section and, when turned outward, form the surface of the lapels.

Attached correctly, the facings help the jacket front keep its shape. Their stability comes from twill-tape reinforcing and from the painstaking basting and structuring procedures described on the following pages. The seam along the front edge between the facing and the jacket front must be rolled slightly so that the stitching will not show. Along the lapel, the seam must be turned under the facing so that it will be hidden by the lapel. Below the lapel it must be turned to the facing side so that it will be inside the jacket.

If the garment is a man's jacket, which is lined piecemeal as each section is finished to ensure that the lining fits precisely and remains wrinkle free, the front linings are sewed in when the facings are being attached. A woman's jacket —which uses lighter weight, more delicate lining fabrics—is lined only after it has been fully constructed.

THE JACKET-FRONT FACING

A | PREPARING THE JACKET FRONT

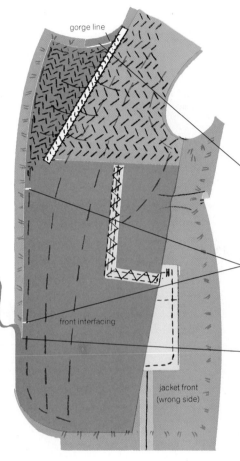

gorge line

front interfacing

jacket front
(wrong side)

1. Bring together one of the interfaced jacket fronts, the corresponding front facing, twill tape and, if you are making a man's jacket, a front lining.

2. Press the lapel area of the jacket front, following the instructions on page 126, Box E, Steps 21 and 22.

3. With the jacket front wrong side up, lift the top edge of the interfacing and locate the tailor tacks marking the gorge line—i.e., the seam line on the top of the lapel to which the collar will be joined. With chalk, transfer the gorge-line marking to the interfacing.

4. Lift up the front edge of the interfacing and transfer the top and bottom button placement marks.

5. Trim the lapel and front edges of the interfacing from the hemline to the front end of the gorge line so that the interfacing is flush with the seam lines on the jacket front. If you are making a man's jacket, skip to Box B.

6. If you are making a woman's jacket—the collar of which will be attached to the neck edge in a different manner from the collar on a man's jacket—continue to trim the interfacing just inside the seam lines along the gorge line and around the neck edge. Be careful not to trim off the twill tape on the lapel roll line.

7. Hand sew along the trimmed gorge line and neck edge with a catch stitch (Appendix). Pick up only one or two threads of the jacket fabric with each stitch.

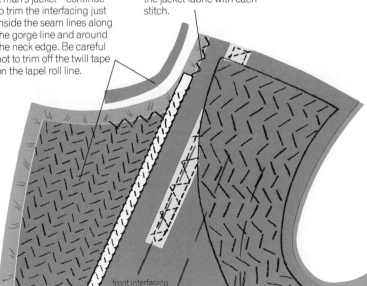

front interfacing

B | PINNING THE REINFORCEMENT TAPE

8. Place twill tape so that its outer edge is aligned with the gorge line, and its end overlaps the tape already on the lapel roll line. Pin at the roll line. Pull the tape taut. Pin along the gorge line.

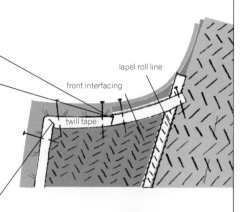

lapel roll line

front interfacing

twill tape

9. At the end of the gorge line, clip the tape from its outer edge up to—but not through—the inner edge. Then align the outer edge of the tape with the trimmed edge of the interfacing along the lapel top. Pin.

10. At the upper corner of the lapel, clip the tape again, this time from the inner edge up to—but not through—the outer edge. Then turn the tape so that the outer edge is aligned with the front edge of the interfacing. Trim the tape at the clip so that the edges just overlap.

11. Keeping the outer edge of the tape aligned with the front edge of the interfacing, pin the tape flat to the interfacing at 4-inch intervals until you reach the top button mark.

12. Pull the tape taut, pin at the lower button mark, then pin between the marks.

13. Continue pinning the tape flat until you are 1 inch above the curved edge at the bottom of the jacket or, if the bottom of the jacket is square, 2 inches above the corner.

14A. If the jacket bottom is curved, pull the tape taut and pin at 1/2-inch intervals around the curve.

14B. If the bottom is square, pull the tape taut and pin at the corner. Turn the corner as you did in Step 10. Pull the tape taut, and pin 2 inches from the corner.

15. Pin the tape flat along the hemline, to 2 inches beyond the end of the interfacing. If you are working with loosely woven material to make a man's jacket, continue pinning the tape as far as the side seam line to reinforce the entire front hemline.

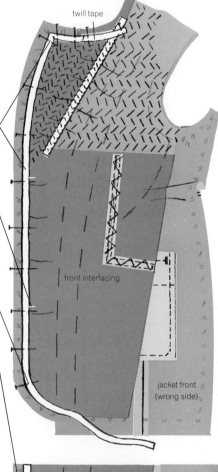

twill tape

front interfacing

jacket front
(wrong side)

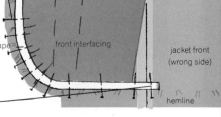

twill tape

front interfacing

jacket front
(wrong side)

hemline

continued

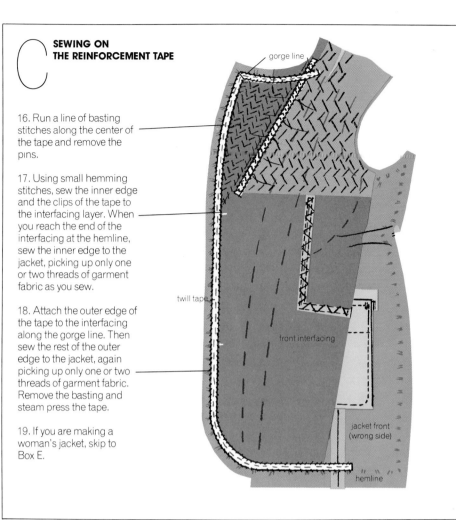

C SEWING ON THE REINFORCEMENT TAPE

16. Run a line of basting stitches along the center of the tape and remove the pins.

17. Using small hemming stitches, sew the inner edge and the clips of the tape to the interfacing layer. When you reach the end of the interfacing at the hemline, sew the inner edge to the jacket, picking up only one or two threads of garment fabric as you sew.

18. Attach the outer edge of the tape to the interfacing along the gorge line. Then sew the rest of the outer edge to the jacket, again picking up only one or two threads of garment fabric. Remove the basting and steam press the tape.

19. If you are making a woman's jacket, skip to Box E.

D ATTACHING THE FRONT LINING TO THE FACING OF THE MAN'S JACKET

20. With the front lining wrong side up, fold the shoulder pleat along the designated line. (On some patterns the pleat is at the armhole edge.) Align the fold with the pleat placement line and pin. Baste 1/4 inch from the fold and remove the pins.

21. Sew any darts in the lining just as you did for the jacket front *(page 113)*. Then press the darts flat toward the side seams.

22. Lay the front facing wrong side down. Place the front lining over it, wrong side up, matching the front seam line of the lining with the inside seam line of the facing. To provide for extra fullness in the chest area, ease the lining down slightly from the shoulder edge, distributing the ease evenly. Pin at 2-inch intervals.

23. Baste along the seam line and remove the pins. Then machine stitch on the seam line from the shoulder edge to 1/8 inch above the lower seam line of the facing. Remove the basting.

24. Press the seam allowances toward the lining.

25. Make the inside pocket with piping edges, following the instructions for making the flap pocket *(pages 118-123)* but omitting the steps for making and inserting the flap.

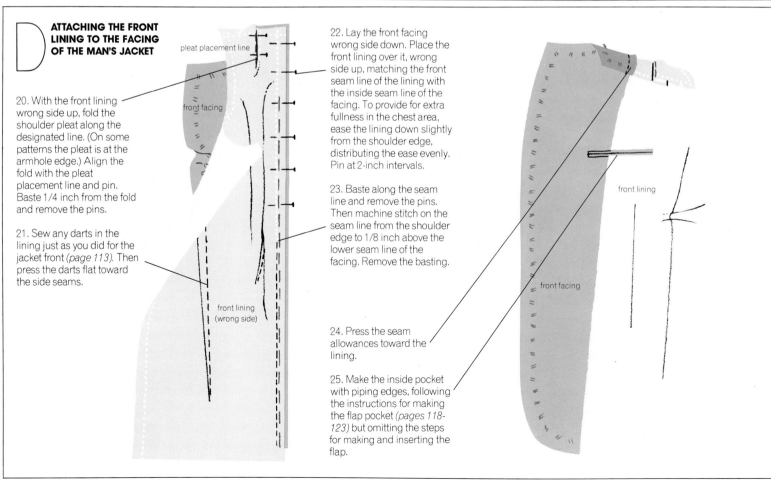

ATTACHING THE FACING TO THE JACKET FRONT

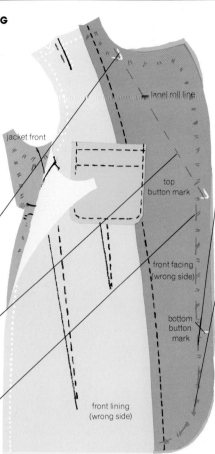

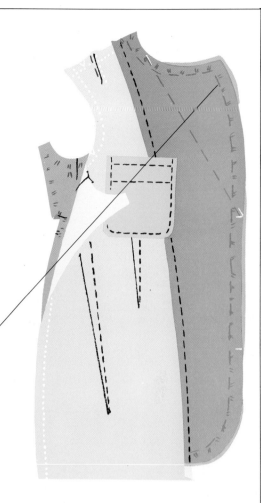

26. With the jacket front lying interfaced side down, place the front facing over it, wrong side up, and align the front seam lines. If you are making a man's jacket, as shown, the front lining is attached to the facing.

27. Lift the edges of the facing; locate the ends of the lapel roll line as well as the top and bottom button marks on the jacket front. With chalk, transfer the marks to the facing.

28. To provide extra fullness in the chest area, ease the facing fabric 1/4 inch down from the upper lapel edge and run a line of 1-inch basting stitches along the lapel roll line. Take up the eased fabric in the first 6 inches.

29. Run a second line of basting 1/2 inch inside the front seam line. Begin at the top button mark; as you baste, ease the facing fabric 1/8 inch in from the front edge between the top and bottom button marks. This easing will provide for extra fabric that will be needed when you make the buttonholes and attach the buttons.

30. Continue the basting below the bottom button mark, this time keeping the edges of the facing and jacket front aligned.

31. As you baste around the edge, pull taut the facing fabric so that the edge will curve slightly toward the body when the jacket is worn. If the front edge of your jacket is square, begin to pull the facing taut about 1 inch above the corner. End the basting at the inner seam—or edge—on the facing.

32. Now make a third line of basting, this time starting at the top button mark and sewing 1 inch inside the lapel edge up to the shoulder edge. For the first 2 inches, ease in the facing fabric 1/8 inch from the front edge. Then align the front edges, and continue basting until you are about 3 inches from the top of the lapel. Next, ease in the facing fabric again 1/8 inch from the edges, and baste around the corner for about 3 inches. Align the edges again, and continue the basting up to the shoulder edge.

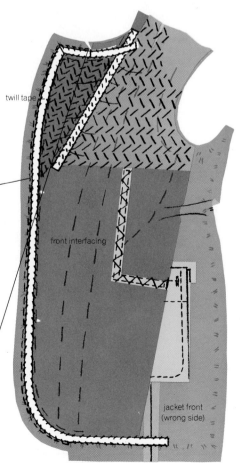

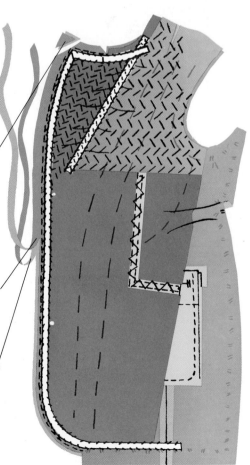

33. Turn over the assembled jacket front so that the interfaced side is up. Machine stitch on the front seam line just outside the twill tape. Stitch between the front end of the gorge line and the inner edge of the bottom of the facing —which is indicated by the end of the basting made in Step 31.

34. At the point where the stitching meets the gorge line, make a diagonal clip in the seam allowances, angling the clip toward the armhole. Clip up to—but not into—the stitching.

35. Remove the tailor tacks and the bastings.

36. Press open the front seam, using a sleeve board or point presser (*pages 94-95*) or a rolled towel.

37. Trim both of the seam allowances diagonally at the lapel corner; and, if you are making a jacket with a square lower corner, trim the lower corner as well.

38. Trim the jacket-front seam allowance to a width of 1/8 inch between the clip made in Step 34 and the front edge of the hem allowance.

39. Trim the seam allowance of the facing between the same points to a width of 1/4 inch.

continued

FINISHING THE FRONT EDGE

40. Turn the assembled jacket front right side out so that the interfacing lies between the facing and the jacket front, with the facing on top.

41. Pull out the lapel corner —and the lower corner, if your jacket has a square corner—following the instructions on page 115, Box E, Step 31.

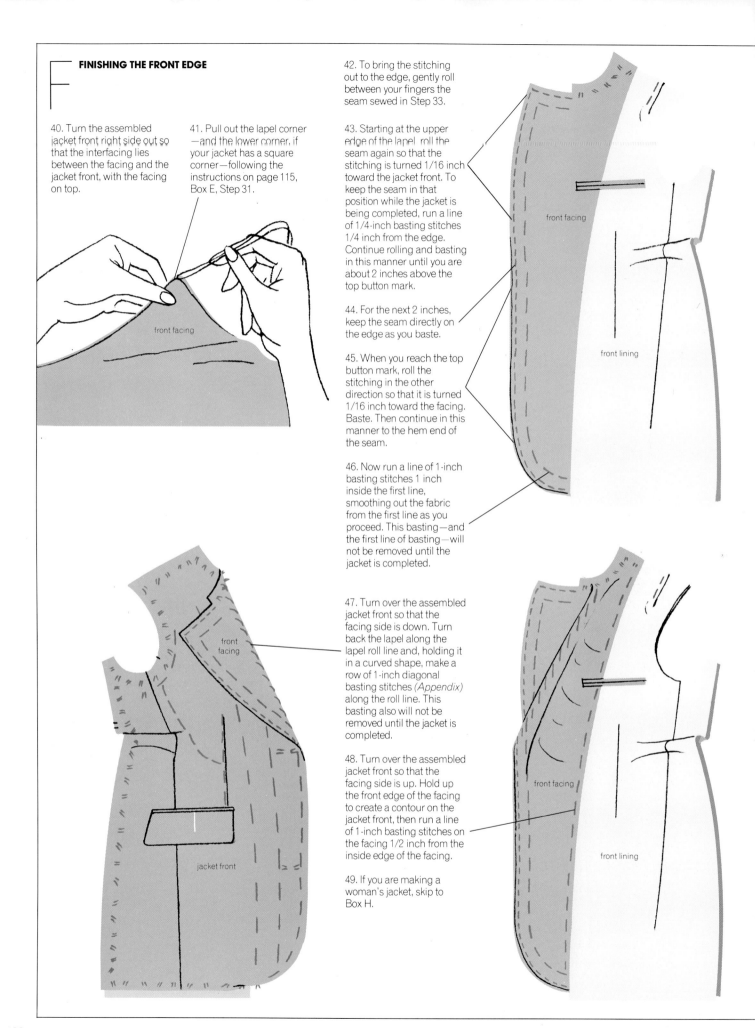

front facing

42. To bring the stitching out to the edge, gently roll between your fingers the seam sewed in Step 33.

43. Starting at the upper edge of the lapel, roll the seam again so that the stitching is turned 1/16 inch toward the jacket front. To keep the seam in that position while the jacket is being completed, run a line of 1/4-inch basting stitches 1/4 inch from the edge. Continue rolling and basting in this manner until you are about 2 inches above the top button mark.

44. For the next 2 inches, keep the seam directly on the edge as you baste.

45. When you reach the top button mark, roll the stitching in the other direction so that it is turned 1/16 inch toward the facing. Baste. Then continue in this manner to the hem end of the seam.

46. Now run a line of 1-inch basting stitches 1 inch inside the first line, smoothing out the fabric from the first line as you proceed. This basting—and the first line of basting—will not be removed until the jacket is completed.

47. Turn over the assembled jacket front so that the facing side is down. Turn back the lapel along the lapel roll line and, holding it in a curved shape, make a row of 1-inch diagonal basting stitches (Appendix) along the roll line. This basting also will not be removed until the jacket is completed.

48. Turn over the assembled jacket front so that the facing side is up. Hold up the front edge of the facing to create a contour on the jacket front, then run a line of 1-inch basting stitches on the facing 1/2 inch from the inside edge of the facing.

49. If you are making a woman's jacket, skip to Box H.

front facing

front lining

front facing

front facing

front lining

jacket front

G FINISHING THE FACING AND FRONT LINING ON A MAN'S JACKET

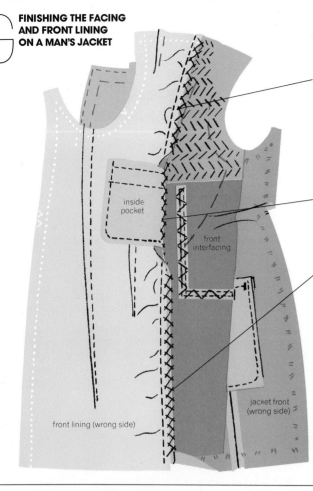

front lining (wrong side)

inside pocket

front interfacing

jacket front (wrong side)

50. If you are making a man's jacket, turn back the lining and hand stitch the seam allowances of the lining and the facing to the interfacing with a catch stitch (Appendix). Sew from the shoulder edge to 1 inch above the inside pocket, being careful not to pick up the jacket-front fabric in your stitches.

51. Catch stitch the pocket to the interfacing, being careful to pick up only the inside layer of the pocket fabric as you stitch.

52. Finish catch stitching the seam allowances to the interfacing from 1 inch below the pocket to 3 inches above the hemline.

53. Turn the lining back over the jacket. To allow for later shrinkage, ease in the lining fabric 1/4 inch from the edges at the armhole, side and hem. Pin.

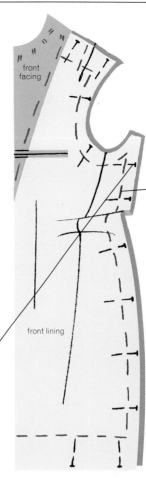

front facing

front lining

54. To hold the lining in position as you continue the jacket construction, run a line of 1-inch-long basting stitches around the lining. Starting and ending at the seam between the lining and the facing, baste 2 inches from the armhole and side edges and 4 inches from the hemline. Remove the pins.

55. Attach the facing for the other jacket front in the same manner.

H FINISHING THE FACING ON A WOMAN'S JACKET

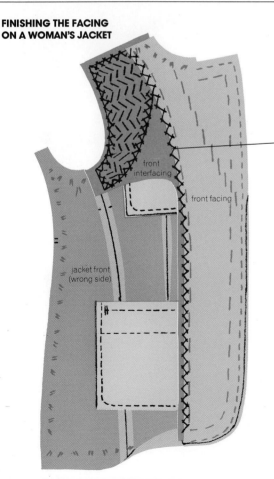

front interfacing

front facing

jacket front (wrong side)

56. If you are making a woman's jacket, use a catch stitch (Appendix) to attach the inner edge of the facing to the interfacing, ending 3 inches above the hem edge. Be careful not to catch the jacket-front fabric in your stitches.

57. Attach the facing for the other jacket front in the same manner.

Joining
back to front

Styling details of the back, which differ in men's and women's jackets, dictate slightly different assembly procedures. A man's jacket, for example, is almost always vented—its back skirt split, as shown here—to provide easy access to the pants pockets. The slit must be reinforced with twill tape before the vent and center seam can be stitched.

This done, the jacket back is sewed to the fronts along the side seams. (Since the finishing of the hem will be easier if the jacket sections can be spread out flat, the shoulder seams are not sewed until later.) If the fabric is a soft one, such as camel's hair or one of the novelty tweeds, the hem must also be reinforced with twill tape to keep it from stretching. Then, after a man's jacket is hemmed, the lining is put in.

A woman's jacket may or may not have vents and is not lined until it has been fully constructed. But the back does require interfacing around the shoulders. And if its fabric is soft, the hem, too, must be reinforced with interfacing cut on the bias.

MAN'S JACKET BACK

A | JOINING THE JACKET BACKS

1. To join and line the back of the man's jacket, first assemble the pieces: the jacket backs, the back linings, the lined and faced jacket fronts, together with twill tape and a scrap of pocketing material to reinforce the vent.

2A. If your jacket backs are still basted together from the last fitting, remove the basting from the hemline to the top of the vent.

2B. If your jacket backs are not basted together, place the two backs together, wrong sides out, and pin along the center-back and vent-top seam lines. Then baste along all these seam lines and remove the pins.

3. Make a reinforcement patch for the top of the vent by cutting—on the straight of the grain—a rectangle 2 inches long and 1 inch wide from pocketing material.

4. With the jacket backs together, wrong sides out, and with the left-back facing up, center the patch over the end of the center-back seam line. Pin at the corners.

5. Baste 1/4 inch inside the long edges and remove the pins.

6. Machine stitch along the center-back seam line, starting at the neck edge. When you reach the vent, pivot (Appendix) and stitch along the vent-top seam line, stopping just inside the seam allowance. Remove the bastings and the tailor tacks.

7. To reinforce the vent edge on the left back, first measure the vent fold line from the vent-top seam to the hemline and cut a piece of twill tape to fit.

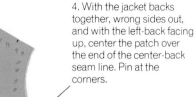

left jacket back (wrong side)

reinforcement patch

8. Align the inner edge of the tape with the fold line and pin it to the left back at 2-inch intervals. Baste along the center of the tape and remove the pins.

9. Hand sew around all edges of the tape with a small hemming stitch (Appendix). So that the stitching will not be visible on the finished jacket, catch only one or two threads on the top layer of jacket fabric with each stitch. Remove the basting.

B | FINISHING THE VENT REINFORCEMENT

10. Open the assembled jacket back so that the wrong side is up, and steam press the center-back seam open. When you reach the vent, turn out of the way the vent edge on the right jacket back and fold the left jacket vent along the fold line. Baste 1/4 inch from the fold. Then steam press the fold, using a pressing cloth.

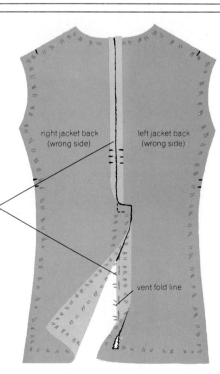

right jacket back (wrong side)

left jacket back (wrong side)

vent fold line

11. Place the right jacket-vent edge over the left jacket vent; steam press the seam allowances flat where they curve toward the left jacket back at the top of the vent.

12. To reinforce the vent seam line on the right jacket back, first measure the seam line from the top edge of the vent to the hemline, and cut a piece of twill tape to fit. Then repeat Steps 8 and 9 along the seam line rather than the fold line.

13. Fold the seam allowance over the tape. Pin. Baste 1/4 inch from the folded edge and remove the pins.

14. Using a pressing cloth, steam press along the folded edge.

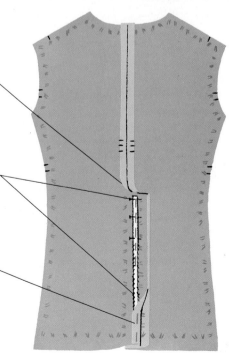

continued

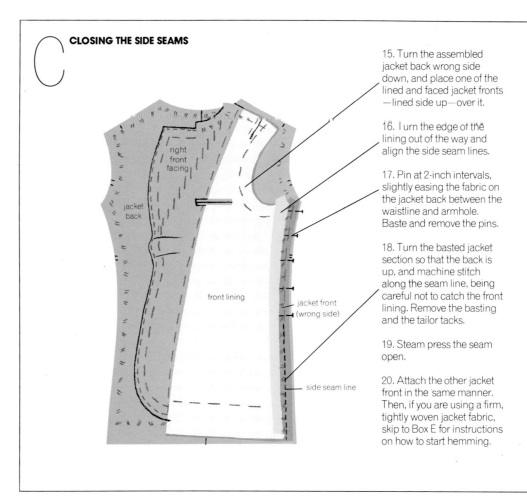

C CLOSING THE SIDE SEAMS

15. Turn the assembled jacket back wrong side down, and place one of the lined and faced jacket fronts —lined side up—over it.

16. Turn the edge of the lining out of the way and align the side seam lines.

17. Pin at 2-inch intervals, slightly easing the fabric on the jacket back between the waistline and armhole. Baste and remove the pins.

18. Turn the basted jacket section so that the back is up, and machine stitch along the seam line, being careful not to catch the front lining. Remove the basting and the tailor tacks.

19. Steam press the seam open.

20. Attach the other jacket front in the same manner. Then, if you are using a firm, tightly woven jacket fabric, skip to Box E for instructions on how to start hemming.

right front facing

jacket back

front lining

jacket front (wrong side)

side seam line

D REINFORCING THE HEM ON A JACKET MADE WITH SOFT FABRIC

21. If you are using a soft jacket fabric such as camel's hair or some tweeds, place the assembled jacket wrong side up and measure along the hemline on the right jacket back, from the side seam to the edge of the tape at the vent. Cut a piece of twill tape to that measurement.

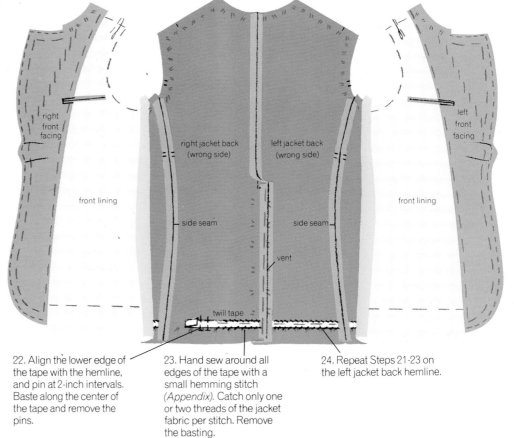

right front facing

front lining

right jacket back (wrong side)

left jacket back (wrong side)

left front facing

front lining

side seam

side seam

vent

twill tape

22. Align the lower edge of the tape with the hemline, and pin at 2-inch intervals. Baste along the center of the tape and remove the pins.

23. Hand sew around all edges of the tape with a small hemming stitch (Appendix). Catch only one or two threads of the jacket fabric per stitch. Remove the basting.

24. Repeat Steps 21-23 on the left jacket back hemline.

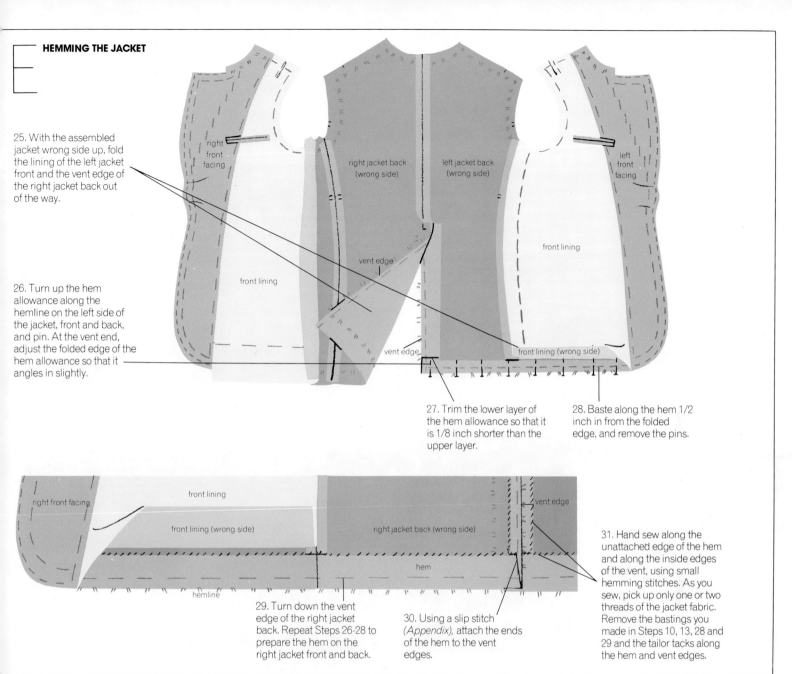

HEMMING THE JACKET

25. With the assembled jacket wrong side up, fold the lining of the left jacket front and the vent edge of the right jacket back out of the way.

26. Turn up the hem allowance along the hemline on the left side of the jacket, front and back, and pin. At the vent end, adjust the folded edge of the hem allowance so that it angles in slightly.

27. Trim the lower layer of the hem allowance so that it is 1/8 inch shorter than the upper layer.

28. Baste along the hem 1/2 inch in from the folded edge, and remove the pins.

29. Turn down the vent edge of the right jacket back. Repeat Steps 26-28 to prepare the hem on the right jacket front and back.

30. Using a slip stitch (*Appendix*), attach the ends of the hem to the vent edges.

31. Hand sew along the unattached edge of the hem and along the inside edges of the vent, using small hemming stitches. As you sew, pick up only one or two threads of the jacket fabric. Remove the bastings you made in Steps 10, 13, 28 and 29 and the tailor tacks along the hem and vent edges.

PREPARING THE BACK LINING

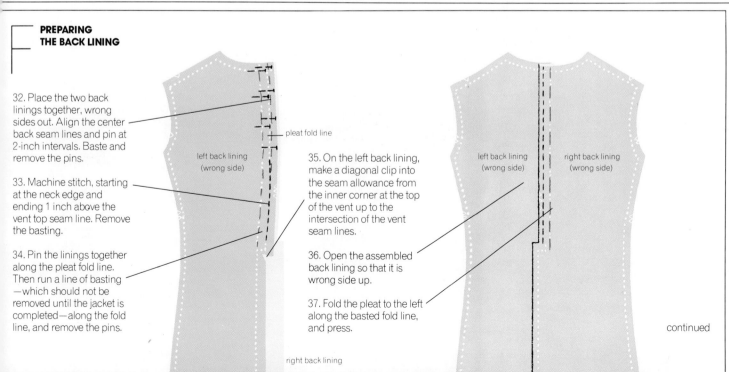

32. Place the two back linings together, wrong sides out. Align the center back seam lines and pin at 2-inch intervals. Baste and remove the pins.

33. Machine stitch, starting at the neck edge and ending 1 inch above the vent top seam line. Remove the basting.

34. Pin the linings together along the pleat fold line. Then run a line of basting —which should not be removed until the jacket is completed—along the fold line, and remove the pins.

35. On the left back lining, make a diagonal clip into the seam allowance from the inner corner at the top of the vent up to the intersection of the vent seam lines.

36. Open the assembled back lining so that it is wrong side up.

37. Fold the pleat to the left along the basted fold line, and press.

continued

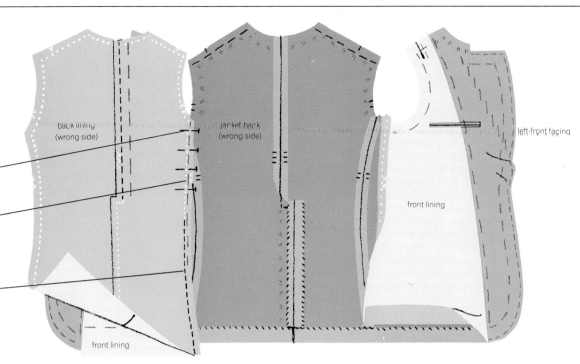

38. Lay out the assembled jacket body wrong side up; place the assembled back lining, wrong side up, over the right-front jacket lining. Align the side seam lines of the linings and pin, being careful not to catch other layers of fabric.

39. Baste along the seam line, and remove the pins.

40. To allow for ease in the lining, machine stitch 1/4 inch outside the seam line, holding the outer layers of fabric out of the way as you stitch. Remove the basting.

41. Press the seam open.

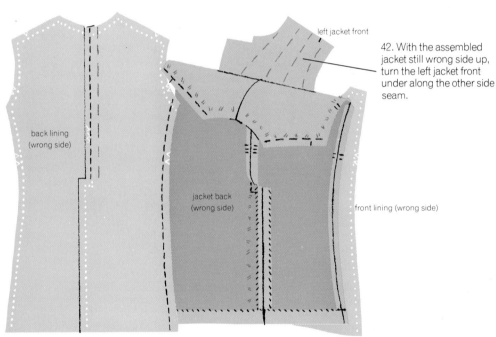

42. With the assembled jacket still wrong side up, turn the left jacket front under along the other side seam.

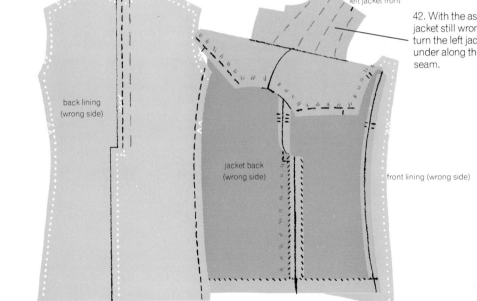

43. Then turn the back and the left jacket front under along the right side seam. The unattached edge of the left front lining should now be under the unattached edge of the back lining.

44. Align the side seam lines of the left-front lining and the back lining, and pin.

45. Baste along the seam line, being careful not to catch the other layers of fabric. Remove the pins.

46. Again allowing for ease in the lining, machine stitch 1/4 inch outside the seam line. Remove the basting.

47. With a sleeve board or a rolled towel placed under the lining, press the seam open.

48. To turn the jacket right side out, insert your arm under the back lining from the hem edge and grab the tops of the other layers of fabric. Pull them down and out.

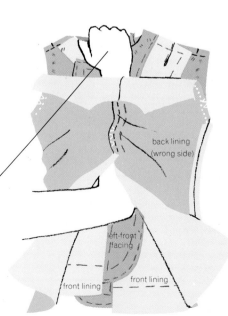

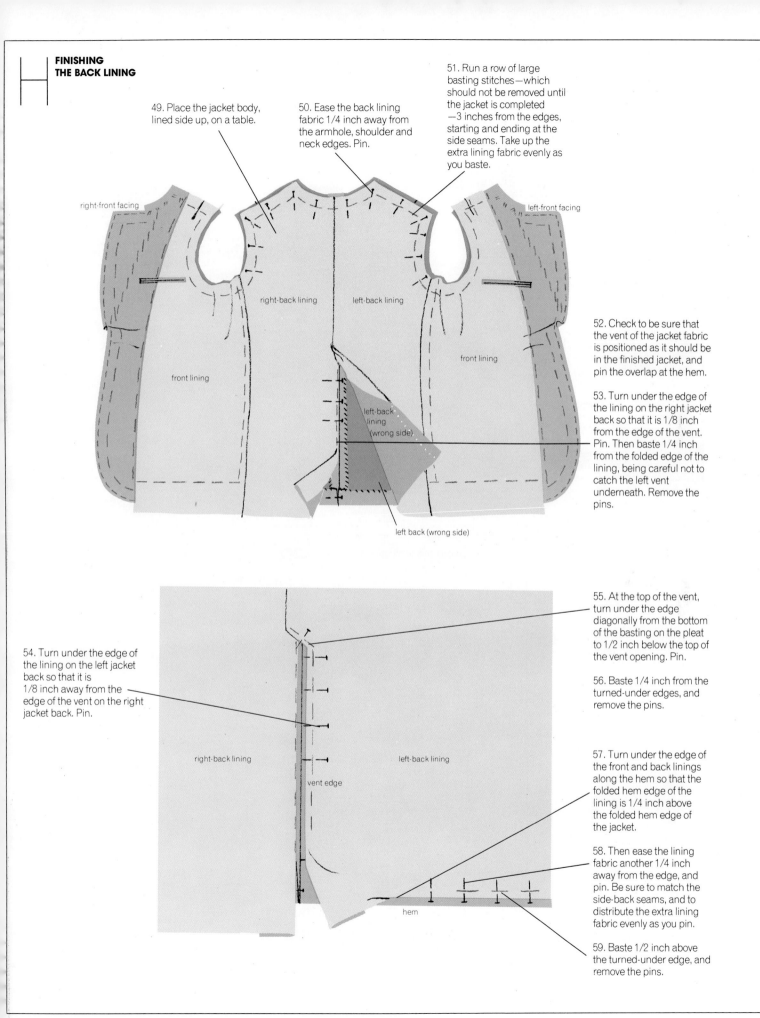

49. Place the jacket body, lined side up, on a table.

50. Ease the back lining fabric 1/4 inch away from the armhole, shoulder and neck edges. Pin.

51. Run a row of large basting stitches—which should not be removed until the jacket is completed—3 inches from the edges, starting and ending at the side seams. Take up the extra lining fabric evenly as you baste.

right-front facing

left-front facing

right-back lining

left-back lining

front lining

front lining

front lining

left-back lining (wrong side)

left back (wrong side)

52. Check to be sure that the vent of the jacket fabric is positioned as it should be in the finished jacket, and pin the overlap at the hem.

53. Turn under the edge of the lining on the right jacket back so that it is 1/8 inch from the edge of the vent. Pin. Then baste 1/4 inch from the folded edge of the lining, being careful not to catch the left vent underneath. Remove the pins.

54. Turn under the edge of the lining on the left jacket back so that it is 1/8 inch away from the edge of the vent on the right jacket back. Pin.

right-back lining

left-back lining

vent edge

hem

55. At the top of the vent, turn under the edge diagonally from the bottom of the basting on the pleat to 1/2 inch below the top of the vent opening. Pin.

56. Baste 1/4 inch from the turned-under edges, and remove the pins.

57. Turn under the edge of the front and back linings along the hem so that the folded hem edge of the lining is 1/4 inch above the folded hem edge of the jacket.

58. Then ease the lining fabric another 1/4 inch away from the edge, and pin. Be sure to match the side-back seams, and to distribute the extra lining fabric evenly as you pin.

59. Baste 1/2 inch above the turned-under edge, and remove the pins.

THE WOMAN'S JACKET BACK

A ASSEMBLING THE JACKET BACK

1, Assemble the pieces needed for joining and interfacing the back of the jacket: the jacket backs, the back interfacing and the faced jacket fronts. If your jacket has a vent, you will also need twill tape and a scrap of pocketing fabric to reinforce the vent. If you are using a soft fabric, you will need a piece of wool interfacing to reinforce the hem.

2A. To join the jacket backs and reinforce the vent, if there is one, follow the instructions for the man's jacket back (page 135, Steps 2-14).

2B. To join the jacket backs if there is no vent, place the two backs together, wrong sides out. Pin and baste along the center-back seam line. Remove the pins. Then machine stitch and remove the basting. Steam press the seam open.

left jacket back (wrong side)

3. Place the jacket back wrong side up and lay the back interfacing over it, making sure that the side with the bias strips on the darts faces up. Align the edges of the interfacing with the shoulder seam lines on the jacket back, and pin.

4. To create the same fullness in the interfacing as you have in the jacket at the shoulders, ease in the interfacing slightly away from each armhole edge. Pin.

5. Baste 1 inch inside all the edges of the interfacing, except the lower edge. Remove the pins.

6. Hand sew along the shoulder, neck and side edges with a catch stitch (Appendix). Pick up only one or two threads of the jacket fabric with each stitch.

7. Remove the bastings except for those along the armholes.

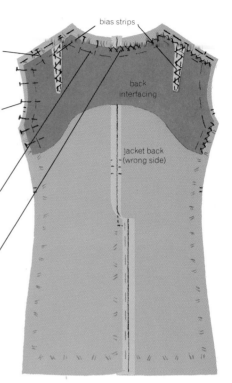

bias strips

back interfacing

jacket back (wrong side)

B CLOSING THE SIDE SEAMS

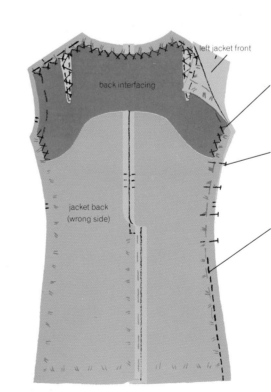

left jacket front

back interfacing

jacket back (wrong side)

8. Place one of the jacket fronts facing side down, and place the assembled jacket back, interfacing side up, over it. Align the side seam lines.

9. Pin at 2-inch intervals, slightly easing the fabric of the jacket back between the waistline and the armhole. Baste and remove the pins.

10. Machine stitch, being careful not to catch the edge of the back interfacing. Remove the basting.

11. Steam press the seam open.

12. To attach the other jacket front, repeat the above process. If you are using a firm, tightly woven jacket fabric, skip to Box D for instructions on how to start hemming.

C REINFORCING THE HEM ON A JACKET MADE WITH SOFT FABRIC

13. If you are using a soft jacket fabric such as camel's hair or some tweeds, you will need to reinforce the hem. To do so, begin by placing the jacket assembly wrong side up and measuring along the hemline. If your jacket does not have a vent, measure the distance along the hemline between the front facings. If your jacket has a vent, measure each half of the hemline from the front facing to the tape on the vent edge.

14. Cut from wool interfacing material a bias strip—or strips, if you have a vent—the length determined in Step 13 and 1 inch wider than your hem allowance.

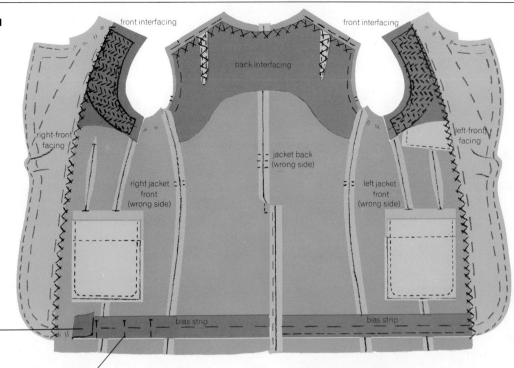

15. Place the strip along the hem, so that the lower edge of the strip extends 1/2 inch below the hemline. Pin.

16. Baste along the center of the strip, and remove the pins.

17. Hand sew along the hemline with running stitches (Appendix). With each stitch, pick up only one or two threads of the jacket fabric. Remove the basting.

D HEMMING THE JACKET

18. Place the assembled jacket wrong side up.

19A. If your jacket has a vent, fold the vent edge of the right jacket back out of the way. Then prepare the hem of the jacket, following the instructions for the man's jacket back (page 137, Steps 26-30). Next, hand sew with a hemming stitch (Appendix) along the inner sides of the vent. As you sew, pick up only one or two threads of the jacket fabric.

19B. If your jacket does not have a vent, turn up the hem allowance along the hemline and pin. Baste 1/4 inch from the folded edge, and remove the pins.

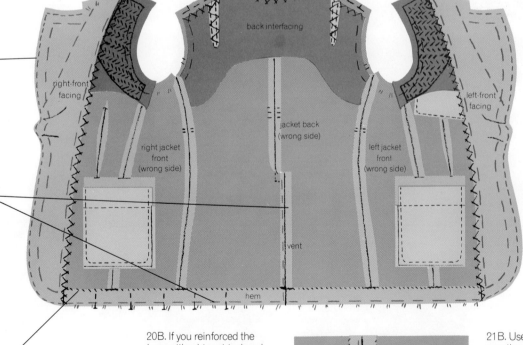

20A. If you did not reinforce the hem, hand sew along the unattached edge of the hem with small hemming stitches. With each stitch, catch only one or two threads of the jacket fabric. Remove the basting and the tailor tacks.

21A. Steam press the hem edge with a pressing cloth.

20B. If you reinforced the hem with a bias strip, hand sew the unattached edge of the hem to the bias strip with small hemming stitches (Appendix), being careful not to catch the jacket fabric. Remove the basting and the tailor tacks. Then steam press the hem edge with a pressing cloth.

21B. Use a catch stitch to sew the edge of the bias strip to the jacket fabric. With each stitch, catch only one or two threads of the jacket fabric.

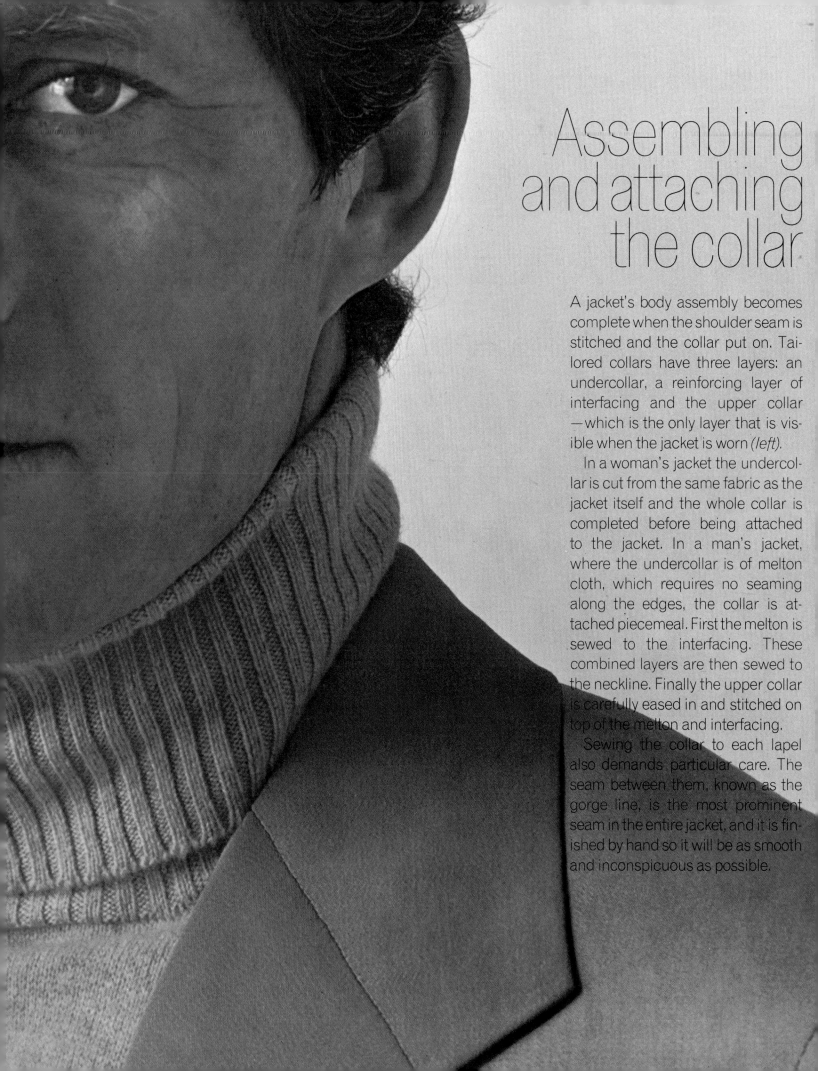

Assembling and attaching the collar

A jacket's body assembly becomes complete when the shoulder seam is stitched and the collar put on. Tailored collars have three layers: an undercollar, a reinforcing layer of interfacing and the upper collar —which is the only layer that is visible when the jacket is worn (left).

In a woman's jacket the undercollar is cut from the same fabric as the jacket itself and the whole collar is completed before being attached to the jacket. In a man's jacket, where the undercollar is of melton cloth, which requires no seaming along the edges, the collar is attached piecemeal. First the melton is sewed to the interfacing. These combined layers are then sewed to the neckline. Finally the upper collar is carefully eased in and stitched on top of the melton and interfacing.

Sewing the collar to each lapel also demands particular care. The seam between them, known as the gorge line, is the most prominent seam in the entire jacket, and it is finished by hand so it will be as smooth and inconspicuous as possible.

THE JACKET SHOULDER

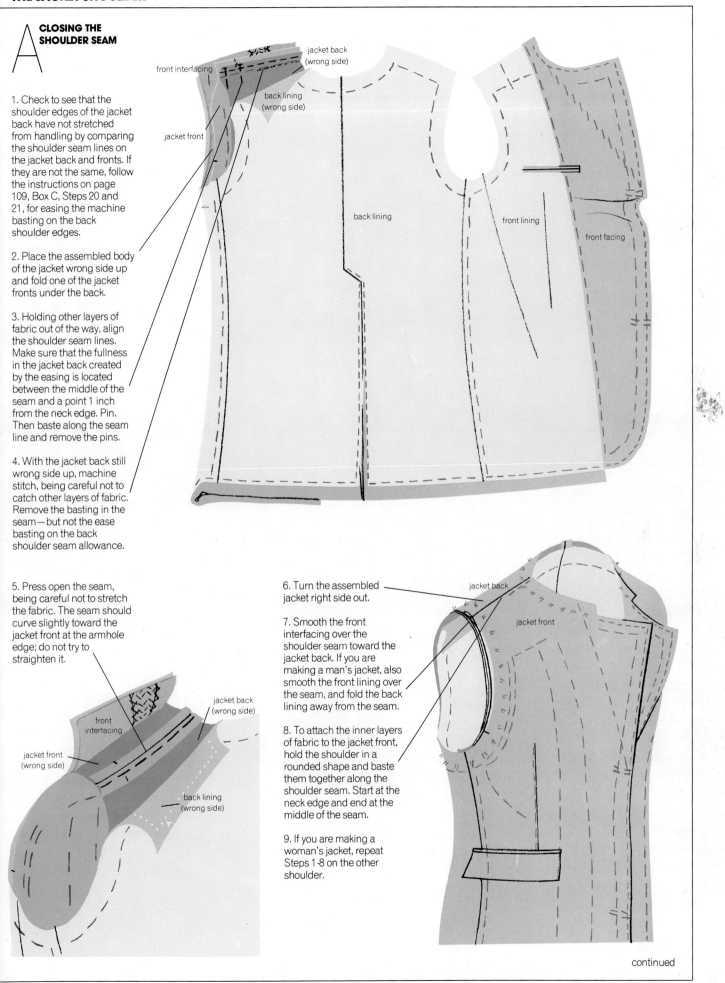

A CLOSING THE SHOULDER SEAM

1. Check to see that the shoulder edges of the jacket back have not stretched from handling by comparing the shoulder seam lines on the jacket back and fronts. If they are not the same, follow the instructions on page 109, Box C, Steps 20 and 21, for easing the machine basting on the back shoulder edges.

2. Place the assembled body of the jacket wrong side up and fold one of the jacket fronts under the back.

3. Holding other layers of fabric out of the way, align the shoulder seam lines. Make sure that the fullness in the jacket back created by the easing is located between the middle of the seam and a point 1 inch from the neck edge. Pin. Then baste along the seam line and remove the pins.

4. With the jacket back still wrong side up, machine stitch, being careful not to catch other layers of fabric. Remove the basting in the seam—but not the ease basting on the back shoulder seam allowance.

5. Press open the seam, being careful not to stretch the fabric. The seam should curve slightly toward the jacket front at the armhole edge; do not try to straighten it.

6. Turn the assembled jacket right side out.

7. Smooth the front interfacing over the shoulder seam toward the jacket back. If you are making a man's jacket, also smooth the front lining over the seam, and fold the back lining away from the seam.

8. To attach the inner layers of fabric to the jacket front, hold the shoulder in a rounded shape and baste them together along the shoulder seam. Start at the neck edge and end at the middle of the seam.

9. If you are making a woman's jacket, repeat Steps 1-8 on the other shoulder.

continued

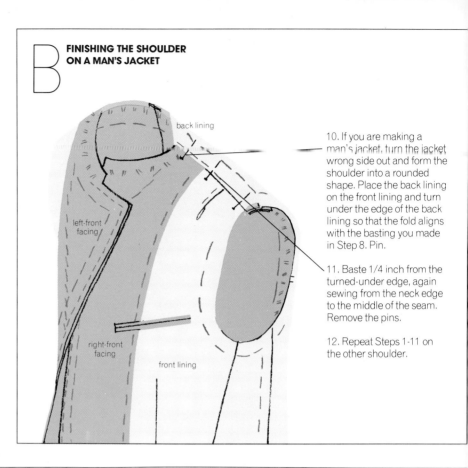

FINISHING THE SHOULDER ON A MAN'S JACKET

10. If you are making a man's jacket, turn the jacket wrong side out and form the shoulder into a rounded shape. Place the back lining on the front lining and turn under the edge of the back lining so that the fold aligns with the basting you made in Step 8. Pin.

11. Baste 1/4 inch from the turned-under edge, again sewing from the neck edge to the middle of the seam. Remove the pins.

12. Repeat Steps 1-11 on the other shoulder.

THE MAN'S JACKET COLLAR

A PREPARING THE UNDERCOLLAR

1. Assemble the pieces for making and attaching the collar: the body of the jacket, undercollar, collar interfacing and upper collar.

2. If the undercollar and interfacing have center-back seams, baste the seams, following the instructions on page 111, Box F, Steps 32 and 33. Machine stitch. Remove the bastings.

3. Press open the seam allowances on the undercollar only. Trim the seam allowance of the interfacing to 1/4 inch.

4. Baste the interfacing to the undercollar, and steam press into a horseshoe shape, following the instructions on page 111, Box F, Steps 34, 36 and 37.

7. Finish attaching the interfacing to the undercollar below the roll line, using rows of padding stitches parallel to the roll line. In doing so, begin and end the rows 1/8 inch from the gorge-line edges (the line along which the collar will be attached to the front facing).

8. When you reach the notch area, begin and end the stitches 1/2 inch from the notch edges. Do not make padding stitches closer than 1/2 inch from the outer edge.

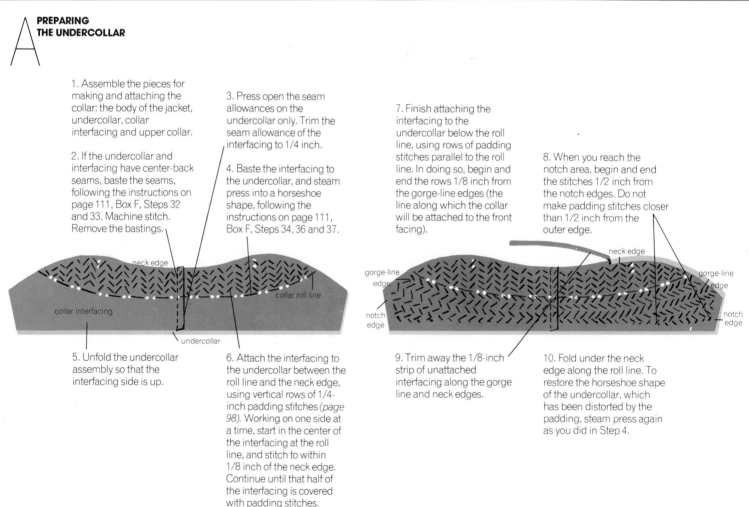

5. Unfold the undercollar assembly so that the interfacing side is up.

6. Attach the interfacing to the undercollar between the roll line and the neck edge, using vertical rows of 1/4-inch padding stitches (page 98). Working on one side at a time, start in the center of the interfacing at the roll line, and stitch to within 1/8 inch of the neck edge. Continue until that half of the interfacing is covered with padding stitches. Repeat on the other side.

9. Trim away the 1/8-inch strip of unattached interfacing along the gorge line and neck edges.

10. Fold under the neck edge along the roll line. To restore the horseshoe shape of the undercollar, which has been distorted by the padding, steam press again as you did in Step 4.

**ATTACHING
THE UNDERCOLLAR**

11. Turn the jacket right side out and fold it along the upper back.

12. Place the undercollar assembly, interfacing side down, around the neckline and align the neck edge of the undercollar with the corresponding seam line on the jacket.

13. Match and pin, beginning at the center back and being careful not to catch the back lining.

14. Working on one side, pull taut the edge of the undercollar and pin from the center until you are 1 inch from the shoulder seam.

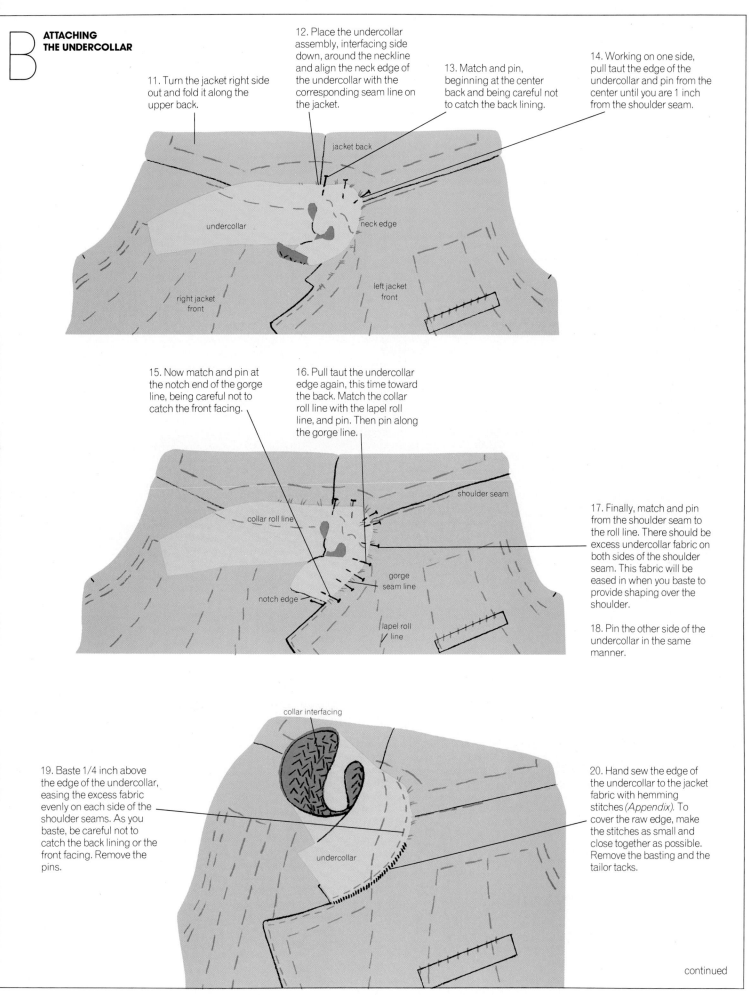

jacket back

undercollar

neck edge

right jacket front

left jacket front

15. Now match and pin at the notch end of the gorge line, being careful not to catch the front facing.

16. Pull taut the undercollar edge again, this time toward the back. Match the collar roll line with the lapel roll line, and pin. Then pin along the gorge line.

17. Finally, match and pin from the shoulder seam to the roll line. There should be excess undercollar fabric on both sides of the shoulder seam. This fabric will be eased in when you baste to provide shaping over the shoulder.

18. Pin the other side of the undercollar in the same manner.

shoulder seam

collar roll line

gorge seam line

notch edge

lapel roll line

collar interfacing

19. Baste 1/4 inch above the edge of the undercollar, easing the excess fabric evenly on each side of the shoulder seams. As you baste, be careful not to catch the back lining or the front facing. Remove the pins.

undercollar

20. Hand sew the edge of the undercollar to the jacket fabric with hemming stitches (Appendix). To cover the raw edge, make the stitches as small and close together as possible. Remove the basting and the tailor tacks.

continued

C FINISHING THE UNDERCOLLAR

21. Spread out the jacket wrong side up, with the undercollar extended away from the jacket.

22. With the edges of the back lining and the front facing turned out of the way, catch stitch (Appendix) the neckline edges of the jacket to the undercollar. During this process, sew through the front interfacing and garment fabric on the jacket, but only through the interfacing layer on the undercollar.

23. Fold the undercollar over the jacket along the roll line. Using a pressing cloth to protect the jacket fabric, steam press the undercollar into a horseshoe shape as you did in Step 4.

24. Now turn up the undercollar and fold it in half along the center back, matching the front edges. If the edges do not align, trim to make them identical.

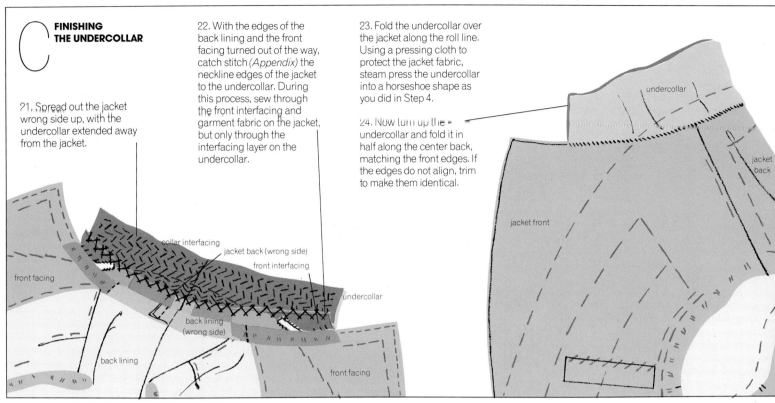

front facing

collar interfacing

jacket back (wrong side)

front interfacing

undercollar

back lining (wrong side)

back lining

front facing

undercollar

jacket back

jacket front

D PINNING THE UPPER COLLAR TO THE UNDERCOLLAR

25. Trim the seam allowances on the notch and outer edges of the upper collar to 3/8 inch, rounding the corners slightly.

26. With the jacket turned right side out, fold it along the upper back so that the undercollar is flat, and the interfacing side is up. Place the upper collar, wrong side down, over the undercollar; align the notch and outer seam lines of the upper collar with the corresponding edges of the undercollar.

27. Match and pin first at the center back.

28. Next, working on one side, pull taut the edge of the upper collar, and pin from the center until you are 1 inch from a point even with the shoulder marking.

29. Now match and pin along the notch seam line, being careful not to catch the seam allowance of the front facing.

30. Finally, pin along the rest of the outer seam line, distributing the excess collar fabric evenly.

31. Pin the other side of the upper collar in the same manner.

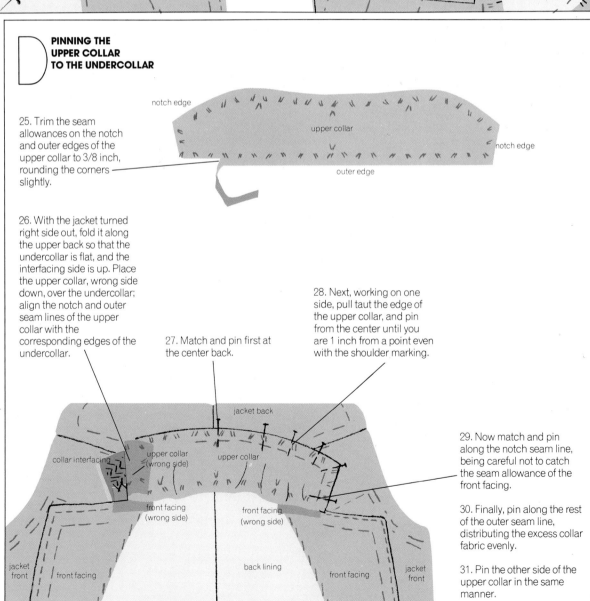

notch edge

upper collar

notch edge

outer edge

collar interfacing

upper collar (wrong side)

jacket back

upper collar

front facing (wrong side)

front facing (wrong side)

jacket front

front facing

back lining

front facing

jacket front

32. Run a line of basting —which should not be removed until the jacket is completed—1 inch inside the pinned edges of the upper collar. Be careful not to catch the front facing at each end. Distribute the ease evenly; remove the pins.

33. Run another line of basting—which also will not be removed until the jacket is completed—1/2 inch inside the first line of basting, being careful to keep the grain of the fabric straight. Again, distribute the ease evenly.

36. Turn under the trimmed gorge-line seam allowance on one facing so that the fold aligns with the upper edge of the twill tape on the top of the lapel interfacing. Pin. Continue folding under and pinning the facing on the seam line between the roll line and the shoulder seam.

37. Now turn under the trimmed gorge-line seam allowance on the upper collar so that it meets the folded edge of the facing. Pin.

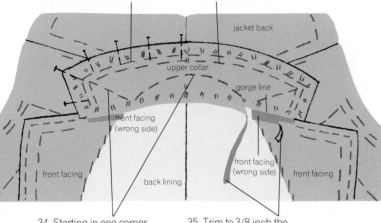

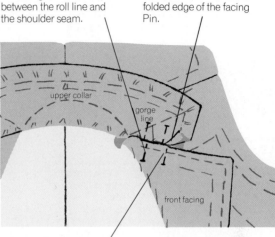

34. Starting in one corner of the collar, baste diagonally to the end of the roll line, which can be felt beneath the upper collar. Next, baste along the roll line and then diagonally to the other corner of the collar. These bastings should not be removed until the jacket is completed.

35. Trim to 3/8 inch the gorge-line and neckline seam allowances on the upper collar and on both front facings.

38. Baste 1/4 inch from both folded edges and remove the pins.

39. Repeat Steps 36-38 along the gorge line on the other side of the collar.

41. Fold under the back neck edge of the upper collar. Align the fold with the bottom edge of the undercollar, which can be felt beneath the jacket neckline. The fold may be below the tailor-tacked seam line; some of the seam allowance may have been used to form the roll of the collar.

44. Turn the collar assembly so that the undercollar faces up. Then fold under the notch edges and outer edges of the upper collar along the seam lines, and insert the edges between the undercollar and the interfacing. Pin.

45. Baste 1/4 inch from the edges of the undercollar and remove the pins.

40. Fold the collar assembly along the roll line. Insert the neck edge of the back lining under the edges of the upper-collar assembly.

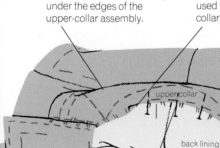

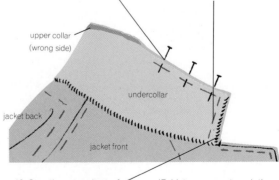

42. Match and pin the folded edge of the upper collar, pulling the fabric taut across the center back and easing in the resulting excess fabric at the shoulders. Baste 1/4 inch from the folded edge and remove the pins.

43. Use tiny blind hemming stitches *(Appendix)* to sew together the folded edges of the upper collar and the facings. Use slip stitches *(Appendix)* to sew the folded edges of the upper collar to the lining and jacket along the neckline. Remove the bastings.

46. Sew the raw edges of the undercollar to the turned-under part of the collar piece with hemming stitches *(Appendix)*. Make the stitches as small and close together as possible to cover the raw edges. Remove the basting and the tailor tacks.

47. Using a pressing cloth, steam press the collar as you did in Step 4.

THE WOMAN'S JACKET COLLAR

A PREPARING THE UNDERCOLLAR

1. Assemble the pieces for making and attaching the collar: the body of the jacket, the undercollar, the collar interfacing, the back-neck facing and the upper collar.

2. Join and press the undercollar and interfacing, following the instructions for the man's jacket collar on page 144, Box A, Steps 2-5.

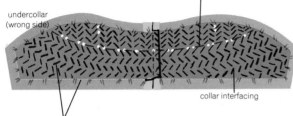

undercollar (wrong side)

collar interfacing

3. Attach the interfacing to the undercollar with padding stitches, following the instructions for the man's jacket collar on page 144, Box A, Steps 6 and 7 —but beginning and ending all the rows of padding stitches 5/8 inch from the edges of the undercollar fabric. Then trim all the interfacing edges even with the seam lines of the undercollar.

4. Remove the basting on the roll line; then fold under the neck edge along the roll line. To restore the horseshoe shape of the undercollar, which has been distorted by the padding stitches, steam press again as you did in Step 2.

B ASSEMBLING THE COLLAR

5. Place the upper collar wrong side down, and position the undercollar assembly, interfacing side up, directly over the upper collar. Align the outer seam lines.

6. Pin the undercollar to the upper collar, following the instructions for the man's jacket collar on page 146, Box D, Steps 26-31, but along the notch and outer edges, align the seam lines on the two pieces instead of the edge and seam line.

7. Baste just inside the seam lines on the outer edges, and remove the pins.

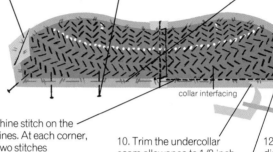

undercollar (wrong side)

collar interfacing

8. Machine stitch on the seam lines. At each corner, make two stitches diagonally across the corner so that the corner will not be bulky when turned. Be careful not to catch the edges of the interfacing as you sew.

9. Steam press the seam open as far as possible, using a point presser or sleeve board (page 95) or a rolled towel.

10. Trim the undercollar seam allowance to 1/8 inch.

11. Trim the upper-collar seam allowance to 1/4 inch.

12. Trim the corners diagonally.

C FINISHING THE OUTER SEAMED EDGE

13. Turn the assembled collar right side out and pull out the corners, following the instructions on page 115, Box E, Step 31.

14. Roll the seamed edges to bring the stitching out to the edge.

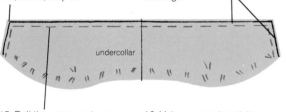

undercollar

15. Roll the seam again so that the stitching is turned 1/16 inch toward the undercollar. To keep the seam rolled under, run a line of 1/4-inch basting stitches—which should not be removed until the jacket is completed—1/4 inch from the edge.

16. Using a pressing cloth, steam press along the seamed edge.

17. Turn the collar assembly so that the undercollar is down. Fold under the neck edge along the roll line. Using a pressing cloth, steam press the assembled collar into a horseshoe shape, as you did for the undercollar in Step 2.

D ATTACHING THE COLLAR

18. Spread out the jacket wrong side down with the neck edge flat. Spread open the collar assembly. Place the undercollar, interfacing side up, on the jacket neck edge, aligning the seam lines.

19. Pin the undercollar to the jacket, following the instructions for the man's jacket collar on page 145, Box B, Steps 13-18, but align the seam lines on the two pieces instead of the undercollar edge and the neck seam line.

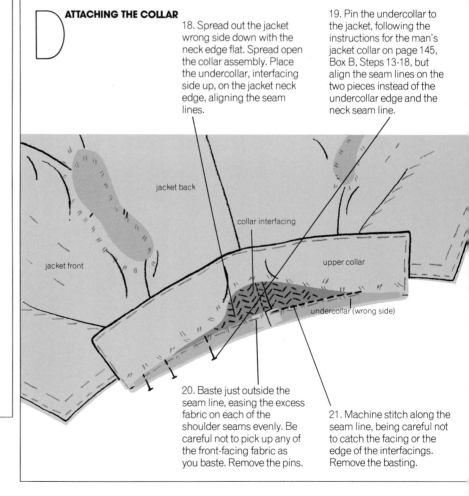

jacket back

collar interfacing

jacket front

upper collar

undercollar (wrong side)

20. Baste just outside the seam line, easing the excess fabric on each of the shoulder seams evenly. Be careful not to pick up any of the front-facing fabric as you baste. Remove the pins.

21. Machine stitch along the seam line, being careful not to catch the facing or the edge of the interfacings. Remove the basting.

E ⎿ FINISHING THE NECKLINE SEAM

22. Turn the jacket wrong side up and spread it out flat. Clip the curved portions of the neckline seam allowance on the jacket.

23. Spread open the attached collar, and steam press the neckline seam open.

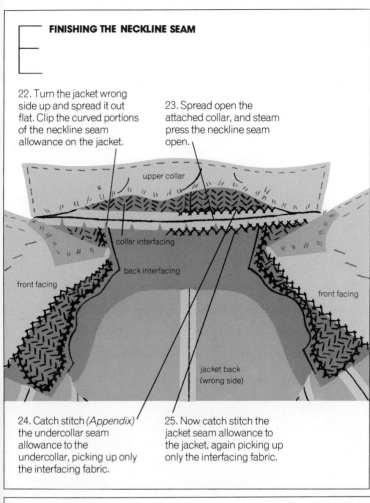

24. Catch stitch (Appendix) the undercollar seam allowance to the undercollar, picking up only the interfacing fabric.

25. Now catch stitch the jacket seam allowance to the jacket, again picking up only the interfacing fabric.

F ⎿ ATTACHING THE BACK NECK FACING

26. Align one of the shoulder seam lines on the back neck facing with the shoulder seam line on one of the front facings; baste them together, wrong sides out.

27. Machine stitch along the seam line, holding other layers of fabric out of the way. Remove the basting and the tailor tacks.

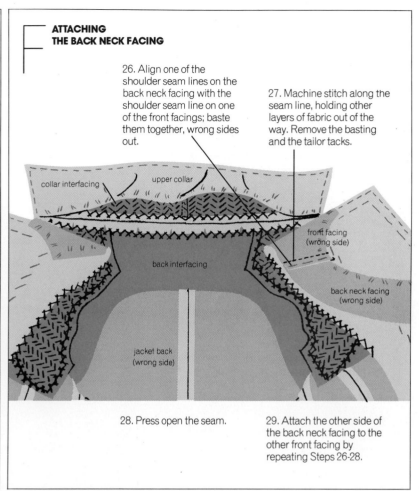

28. Press open the seam.

29. Attach the other side of the back neck facing to the other front facing by repeating Steps 26-28.

G ⎿ FINISHING THE NECK EDGE

30. Turn the back neck facing down, so that its wrong side is on the back interfacing.

31. Clip the curved portions of the neckline seam allowances on the front and back facings.

32. Fold the collar and lapels along the roll lines. Holding the collar in a rounded shape, run a line of diagonal basting stitches (Appendix) along the collar roll line, keeping the grain of the fabric straight. Do not remove this basting until the jacket is completed.

36. Turn under the edge of the front and back facings so that the fold is aligned with the bottom edge of the collar. Pin. Baste 1/4 inch from the folded edge and remove the pins.

37. Using tiny blind hemming stitches (Appendix), hand sew the folded edge of the facings to the folded edge of the upper collar. Remove the bastings and the tailor tacks.

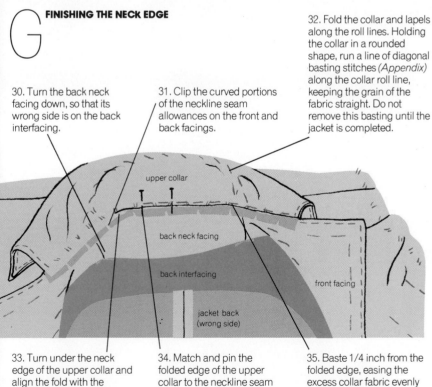

33. Turn under the neck edge of the upper collar and align the fold with the neckline seam on the jacket. Do not worry if the fold is below the tailor-tacked seam line on the upper collar; some of the seam allowance may have been used to form the collar roll.

34. Match and pin the folded edge of the upper collar to the neckline seam as you did when attaching the undercollar (Step 19).

35. Baste 1/4 inch from the folded edge, easing the excess collar fabric evenly on both sides of the shoulder seam markings. Remove the pins.

38. Catch stitch the lower edge of the back neck facing to the jacket back, picking up only the interfacing layer.

Setting in the sleeves

One hallmark of fine tailoring is the perfectly mounted sleeve. First, of course, the sleeves themselves must be constructed. Among other things this entails reinforcing the hems, making the wrist vents and—with a man's jacket—sewing in the lining. (Women's sleeves are lined after the jacket is constructed.)

Attaching the sleeve is a key operation demanding extra pains. The circumference of the sleeve cap is larger than that of the armhole to allow ample fabric for the curve at the top of the sleeve. Careful easing, basting and checking will create a smooth curve and also ensure that the sleeve hangs in perfect balance.

Shoulder pads (optional in a woman's jacket) are inserted to define the shoulder outline characteristic of the tailored look—however slight the squaring desired. Then a strip of supporting fabric called a sleeve head is placed under the cap to preserve its rounded shape.

CONSTRUCTING THE SLEEVE

A PREPARING THE HEM OF THE SLEEVE

1. Baste the inner seam of the sleeve, following the instructions on page 127, Box A, Steps 1 and 2. Then machine stitch and remove the basting and the tailor tacks. Steam press the seam open.

2. With the partially assembled sleeve wrong side up, measure along the hemline. From wigan (page 93), cut a bias strip equal in length to the hemline measurement and 1 inch wider than the hem allowance.

3. Place the bias strip over the sleeve so that the lower edge of the strip extends 1/2 inch below the tailor-tacked hemline. Then align one end of the strip with the vent fold line on the upper sleeve. Pin.

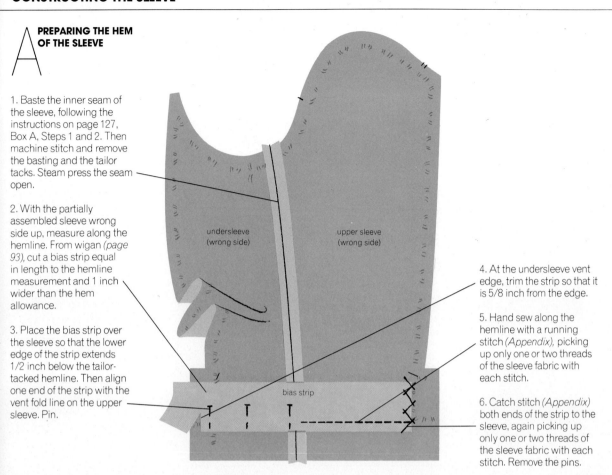

underdsleeve (wrong side)

upper sleeve (wrong side)

bias strip

4. At the undersleeve vent edge, trim the strip so that it is 5/8 inch from the edge.

5. Hand sew along the hemline with a running stitch (Appendix), picking up only one or two threads of the sleeve fabric with each stitch.

6. Catch stitch (Appendix) both ends of the strip to the sleeve, again picking up only one or two threads of the sleeve fabric with each stitch. Remove the pins.

B HEMMING THE SLEEVE

7. Turn up the vent edge of the undersleeve, making the fold along the end of the bias strip. Pin.

8. Baste 1/4 inch from the folded edge between the top edge of the vent and the hemline. Remove the pins.

11. When you reach the vent edges, fold the ends of the hem allowance so that they taper in slightly.

12. Baste along the hem 1/4 inch from the folded edge. Remove the pins.

14. Continue to use small hemming stitches to attach the raw vent edge of the undersleeve to the bias strip and the sleeve fabric.

15. Now sew the raw edge of the vent on the upper sleeve to the bias strip. Do not sew above the top of the strip.

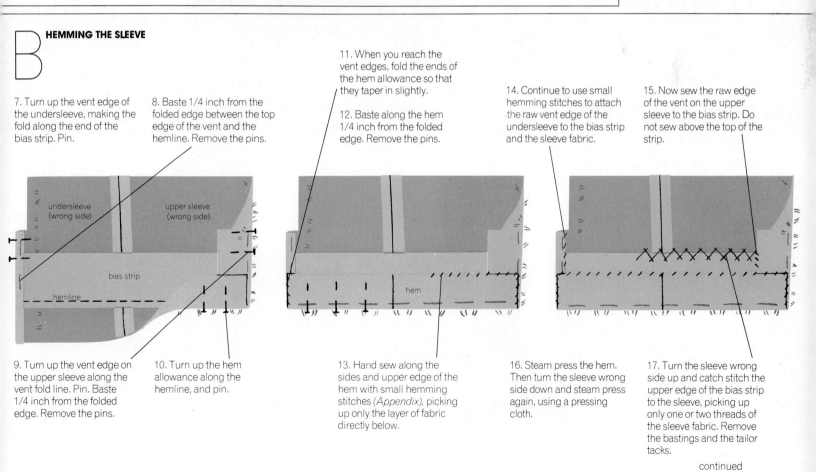

undersleeve (wrong side)

upper sleeve (wrong side)

bias strip

hemline

hem

9. Turn up the vent edge on the upper sleeve along the vent fold line. Pin. Baste 1/4 inch from the folded edge. Remove the pins.

10. Turn up the hem allowance along the hemline, and pin.

13. Hand sew along the sides and upper edge of the hem with small hemming stitches (Appendix), picking up only the layer of fabric directly below.

16. Steam press the hem. Then turn the sleeve wrong side down and steam press again, using a pressing cloth.

17. Turn the sleeve wrong side up and catch stitch the upper edge of the bias strip to the sleeve, picking up only one or two threads of the sleeve fabric. Remove the bastings and the tailor tacks.

continued

C CLOSING THE OUTER SEAM

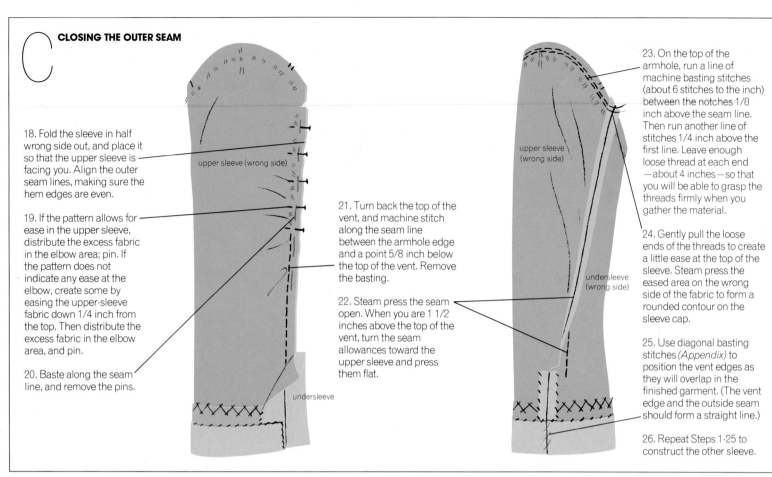

upper sleeve (wrong side)

upper sleeve (wrong side)

undersleeve (wrong side)

undersleeve

18. Fold the sleeve in half wrong side out, and place it so that the upper sleeve is facing you. Align the outer seam lines, making sure the hem edges are even.

19. If the pattern allows for ease in the upper sleeve, distribute the excess fabric in the elbow area; pin. If the pattern does not indicate any ease at the elbow, create some by easing the upper-sleeve fabric down 1/4 inch from the top. Then distribute the excess fabric in the elbow area, and pin.

20. Baste along the seam line, and remove the pins.

21. Turn back the top of the vent, and machine stitch along the seam line between the armhole edge and a point 5/8 inch below the top of the vent. Remove the basting.

22. Steam press the seam open. When you are 1 1/2 inches above the top of the vent, turn the seam allowances toward the upper sleeve and press them flat.

23. On the top of the armhole, run a line of machine basting stitches (about 6 stitches to the inch) between the notches 1/8 inch above the seam line. Then run another line of stitches 1/4 inch above the first line. Leave enough loose thread at each end —about 4 inches—so that you will be able to grasp the threads firmly when you gather the material.

24. Gently pull the loose ends of the threads to create a little ease at the top of the sleeve. Steam press the eased area on the wrong side of the fabric to form a rounded contour on the sleeve cap.

25. Use diagonal basting stitches (*Appendix*) to position the vent edges as they will overlap in the finished garment. (The vent edge and the outside seam should form a straight line.)

26. Repeat Steps 1-25 to construct the other sleeve.

PREPARING THE SLEEVE LINING

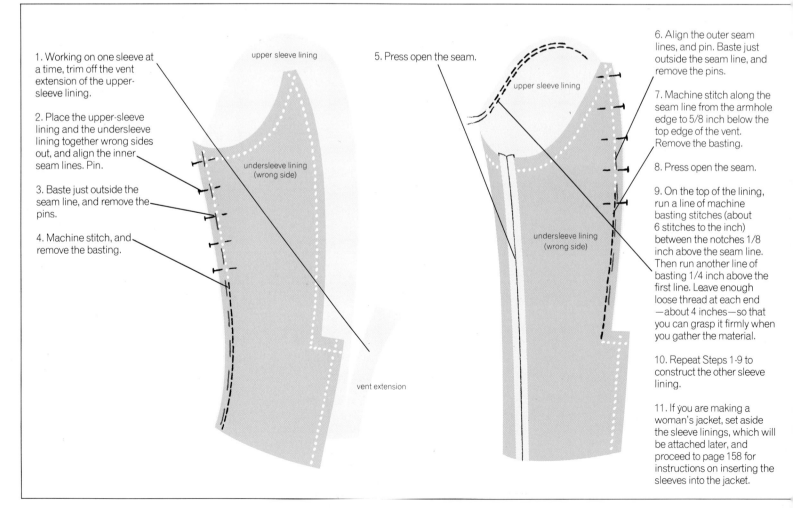

upper sleeve lining

undersleeve lining (wrong side)

vent extension

upper sleeve lining

undersleeve lining (wrong side)

1. Working on one sleeve at a time, trim off the vent extension of the upper-sleeve lining.

2. Place the upper-sleeve lining and the undersleeve lining together wrong sides out, and align the inner seam lines. Pin.

3. Baste just outside the seam line, and remove the pins.

4. Machine stitch, and remove the basting.

5. Press open the seam.

6. Align the outer seam lines, and pin. Baste just outside the seam line, and remove the pins.

7. Machine stitch along the seam line from the armhole edge to 5/8 inch below the top edge of the vent. Remove the basting.

8. Press open the seam.

9. On the top of the lining, run a line of machine basting stitches (about 6 stitches to the inch) between the notches 1/8 inch above the seam line. Then run another line of basting 1/4 inch above the first line. Leave enough loose thread at each end —about 4 inches—so that you can grasp it firmly when you gather the material.

10. Repeat Steps 1-9 to construct the other sleeve lining.

11. If you are making a woman's jacket, set aside the sleeve linings, which will be attached later, and proceed to page 158 for instructions on inserting the sleeves into the jacket.

ATTACHING THE LINING TO A MAN'S JACKET SLEEVE

A JOINING THE SIDE SEAMS

1. With the assembled sleeve wrong side out, fold it along the inner seam, extending the upper-sleeve seam allowance away from the sleeve. Place the assembly so that the undersleeve is facing up.

2. Fold the assembled sleeve lining in the same manner. Then position the lining undersleeve down, so that the inner seams are aligned. Pin together the extended seam allowances of the upper sleeve and its lining.

3. Use running stitches to sew together the upper-sleeve seam allowances from the armhole edge to the upper edge of the bias strip. Remove the pins.

4. Move the sleeve assembly slightly so that the upper sleeve and lining seam allowances are extended on the outer seam. Attach these sleeve and lining seam allowances as you did the inner seam.

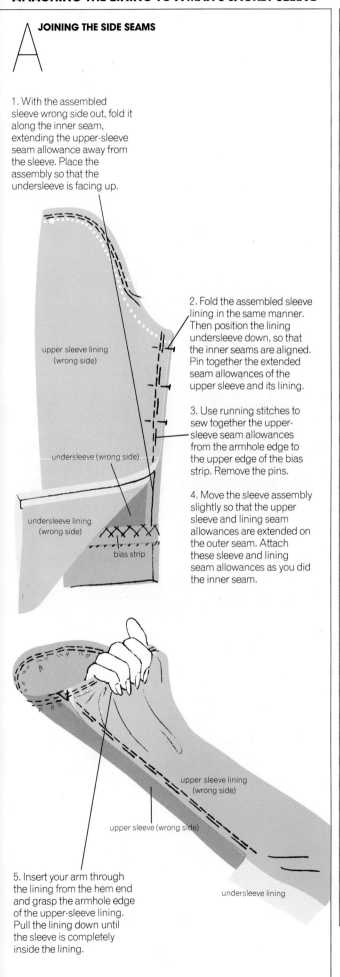

5. Insert your arm through the lining from the hem end and grasp the armhole edge of the upper-sleeve lining. Pull the lining down until the sleeve is completely inside the lining.

B FINISHING THE LINING HEM

6. Turn under the undersleeve lining so that it is 1/8 inch from the edge of the vent. Pin.

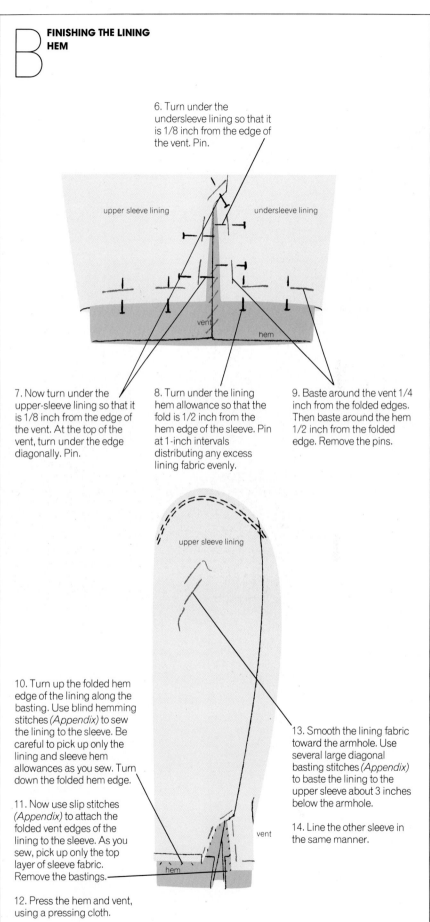

7. Now turn under the upper-sleeve lining so that it is 1/8 inch from the edge of the vent. At the top of the vent, turn under the edge diagonally. Pin.

8. Turn under the lining hem allowance so that the fold is 1/2 inch from the hem edge of the sleeve. Pin at 1-inch intervals distributing any excess lining fabric evenly.

9. Baste around the vent 1/4 inch from the folded edges. Then baste around the hem 1/2 inch from the folded edge. Remove the pins.

10. Turn up the folded hem edge of the lining along the basting. Use blind hemming stitches (*Appendix*) to sew the lining to the sleeve. Be careful to pick up only the lining and sleeve hem allowances as you sew. Turn down the folded hem edge.

11. Now use slip stitches (*Appendix*) to attach the folded vent edges of the lining to the sleeve. As you sew, pick up only the top layer of sleeve fabric. Remove the bastings.

12. Press the hem and vent, using a pressing cloth.

13. Smooth the lining fabric toward the armhole. Use several large diagonal basting stitches (*Appendix*) to baste the lining to the upper sleeve about 3 inches below the armhole.

14. Line the other sleeve in the same manner.

INSERTING THE SLEEVE IN A MAN'S JACKET

A PREPARING THE ARMHOLE

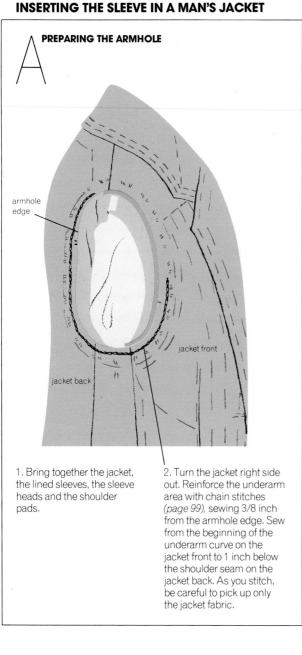

armhole edge

jacket front

jacket back

1. Bring together the jacket, the lined sleeves, the sleeve heads and the shoulder pads.

2. Turn the jacket right side out. Reinforce the underarm area with chain stitches *(page 99),* sewing 3/8 inch from the armhole edge. Sew from the beginning of the underarm curve on the jacket front to 1 inch below the shoulder seam on the jacket back. As you stitch, be careful to pick up only the jacket fabric.

B BASTING ON THE SLEEVE

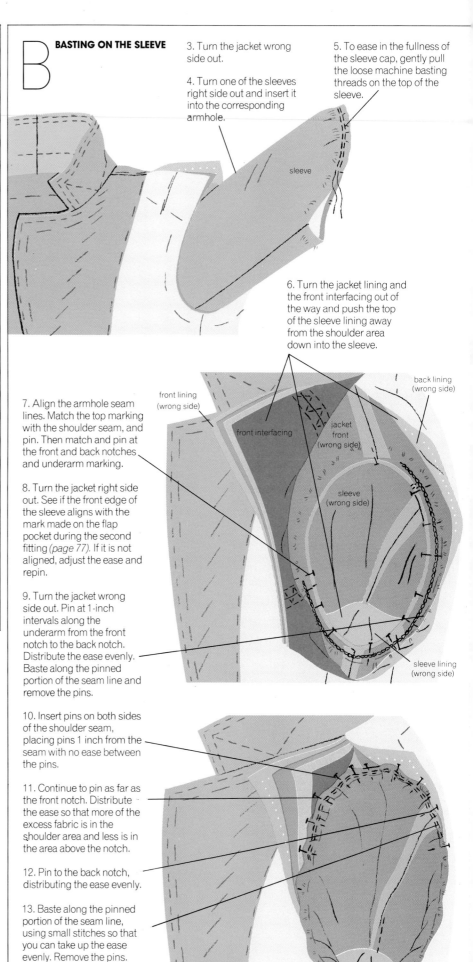

3. Turn the jacket wrong side out.

4. Turn one of the sleeves right side out and insert it into the corresponding armhole.

5. To ease in the fullness of the sleeve cap, gently pull the loose machine basting threads on the top of the sleeve.

sleeve

6. Turn the jacket lining and the front interfacing out of the way and push the top of the sleeve lining away from the shoulder area down into the sleeve.

front lining (wrong side)

front interfacing

back lining (wrong side)

jacket front (wrong side)

sleeve (wrong side)

sleeve lining (wrong side)

7. Align the armhole seam lines. Match the top marking with the shoulder seam, and pin. Then match and pin at the front and back notches and underarm marking.

8. Turn the jacket right side out. See if the front edge of the sleeve aligns with the mark made on the flap pocket during the second fitting *(page 77).* If it is not aligned, adjust the ease and repin.

9. Turn the jacket wrong side out. Pin at 1-inch intervals along the underarm from the front notch to the back notch. Distribute the ease evenly. Baste along the pinned portion of the seam line and remove the pins.

10. Insert pins on both sides of the shoulder seam, placing pins 1 inch from the seam with no ease between the pins.

11. Continue to pin as far as the front notch. Distribute the ease so that more of the excess fabric is in the shoulder area and less is in the area above the notch.

12. Pin to the back notch, distributing the ease evenly.

13. Baste along the pinned portion of the seam line, using small stitches so that you can take up the ease evenly. Remove the pins.

C CHECKING THE SLEEVE

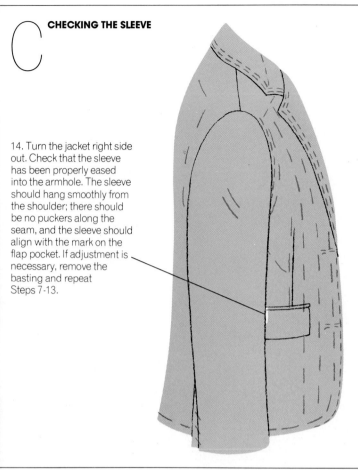

14. Turn the jacket right side out. Check that the sleeve has been properly eased into the armhole. The sleeve should hang smoothly from the shoulder; there should be no puckers along the seam, and the sleeve should align with the mark on the flap pocket. If adjustment is necessary, remove the basting and repeat Steps 7-13.

D SEWING ON THE SLEEVE

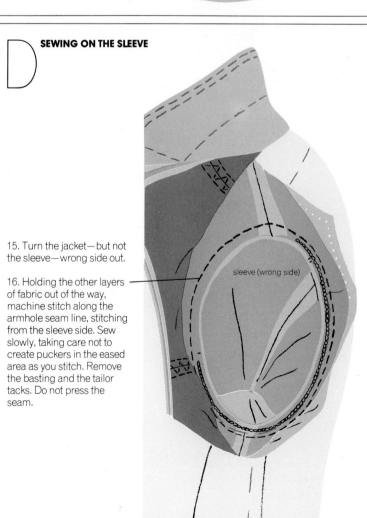

sleeve (wrong side)

15. Turn the jacket—but not the sleeve—wrong side out.

16. Holding the other layers of fabric out of the way, machine stitch along the armhole seam line, stitching from the sleeve side. Sew slowly, taking care not to create puckers in the eased area as you stitch. Remove the basting and the tailor tacks. Do not press the seam.

E ATTACHING THE SHOULDER PAD

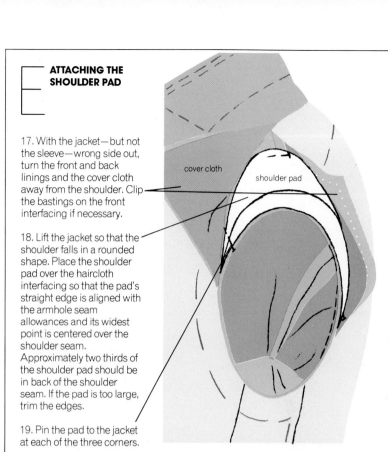

cover cloth

shoulder pad

17. With the jacket—but not the sleeve—wrong side out, turn the front and back linings and the cover cloth away from the shoulder. Clip the bastings on the front interfacing if necessary.

18. Lift the jacket so that the shoulder falls in a rounded shape. Place the shoulder pad over the haircloth interfacing so that the pad's straight edge is aligned with the armhole seam allowances and its widest point is centered over the shoulder seam. Approximately two thirds of the shoulder pad should be in back of the shoulder seam. If the pad is too large, trim the edges.

19. Pin the pad to the jacket at each of the three corners.

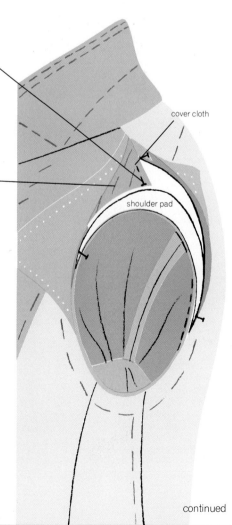

cover cloth

shoulder pad

20. Place the cover cloth over the shoulder pad, and pin.

21. Put your hand between the front interfacing and the jacket fabric and make several 1-inch-long padding stitches (page 98) on the front third of the shoulder-pad area, sewing through the cover cloth, the shoulder pad and the front interfacing. To sew through these thicknesses, insert the needle with a stabbing motion, then pull it through from the other side. If you want to reduce the thickness of the pad, pull the stitches tight.

22. Remove the pins, including those on the pad under the cover cloth.

continued

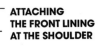

F ATTACHING THE FRONT LINING AT THE SHOULDER

23. Place the front lining over the cover cloth, and pin at the shoulder.

24. Smoothing the lining fabric toward the armhole, run a line of basting around the front of the armhole 1 inch from the edge. Sew from the side seam to the shoulder edge of the front lining. Remove the pins.

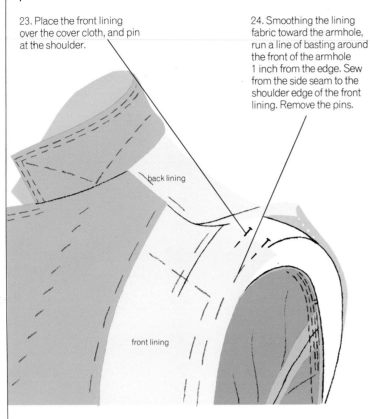

back lining

front lining

25. Turn the jacket right side out. With the back lining turned out of the way, hold the shoulder in a rounded shape again.

26. Smoothing the jacket fabric toward the sleeve, run a line of basting—which should not be removed until the jacket is completed—along the shoulder seam from the collar to the sleeve. Be sure to catch all layers of fabric below. These include the front facing, the front interfacing, the front lining and the shoulder pad. To sew through the pad, insert the needle with a stabbing motion and pull it through from the other side. Do not pull the stitches tight.

27. Again smoothing the jacket fabric toward the sleeve, run a line of basting—which also should not be removed until the jacket is completed—over the shoulder-pad area 1/4 inch inside the armhole seam, attaching the jacket fabric to the interfacing and the top layer of the shoulder pad.

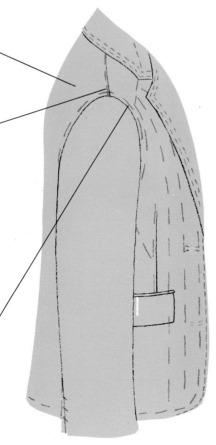

G ATTACHING THE BACK LINING AT THE SHOULDER

28. Turn the jacket—but not the sleeve—wrong side out, and place the back lining over the front lining along the shoulder seam.

29. Smoothing the lining fabric toward the armhole, run a line of basting around the back of the armhole 1 inch from the edge. Sew from the side seam to 1 inch below the shoulder seam.

30. Turn under the shoulder edge of the back lining so that the fold is aligned with the basting you made on the shoulder seam. Pin.

31. Baste 1/4 inch from the folded edge and remove the pins.

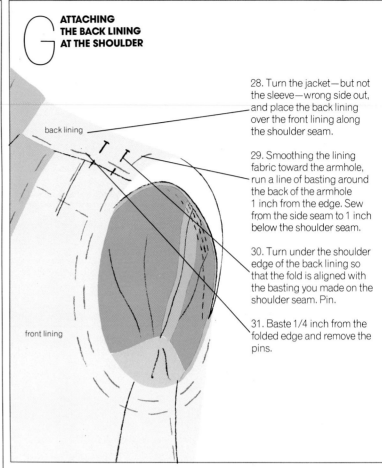

back lining

front lining

H FINISHING THE ARMHOLE SEAM

32. Using 1/2-inch-long running stitches (Appendix), sew around the armhole 1/2 inch from the edges of the seam allowances, stitching through all layers. If you are reducing the thickness of the shoulder pad, pull the stitches tight. Remove the bastings made in Steps 24 and 29.

33. If the front interfacing, the lining or the shoulder pad extends beyond the armhole seam allowance, or has become frayed in handling, trim it flush with the edge of the seam allowance.

34. Spread the armhole seam allowances apart, and trim the haircloth interfacing as close as possible to the running stitches.

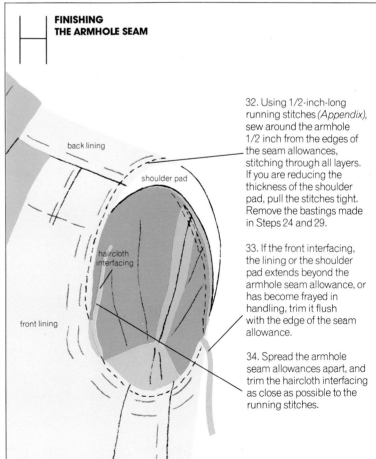

back lining

shoulder pad

haircloth interfacing

front lining

ATTACHING THE SLEEVE HEAD

35. Turn the edges of the sleeve cap and shoulder pad back so that the armhole seam is up around the shoulder area.

36. Place the sleeve head, hemmed side up, around the cap. Align the folded edge of the sleeve head with the armhole seam so that the rest of the sleeve head extends into the sleeve. Pin the sleeve head around the upper third of the armhole.

37. Using a hemming stitch (*Appendix*), hand sew the folded edge of the sleeve head to the sleeve seam allowance, as close to the armhole seam as possible. Remove the pins.

38. To check that the sleeve head fits properly, turn the jacket right side out, making sure that the sleeve head and all the armhole seam allowances are turned into the sleeve. If the sleeve head extends too far into the sleeve or creates too much bulk, trim it along the unattached edge or at the ends.

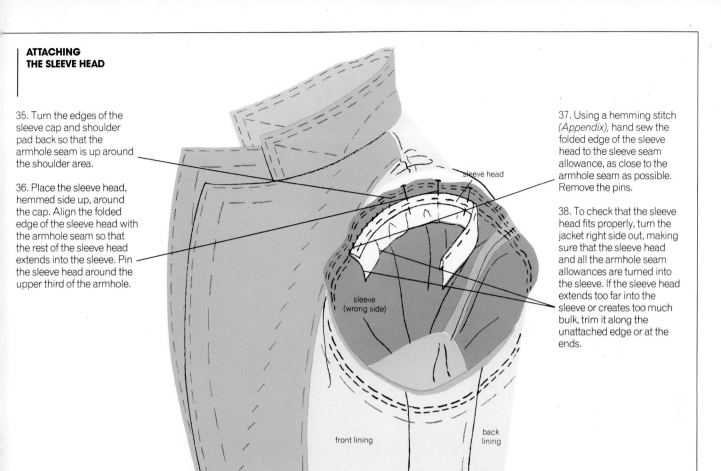

sleeve head

sleeve (wrong side)

front lining

back lining

ATTACHING THE SLEEVE LINING

39. Gently pull the loose machine basting threads on the top of the sleeve lining.

40. Fold under the armhole edge of the sleeve lining so that the machine basting is hidden. Place the sleeve lining on the jacket lining so that the folded edge just covers the running stitches.

41. Pin and distribute the ease as you did when you attached the sleeve (*Steps 7 and 9-12*), basting 1/4 inch from the folded edge. Remove the pins.

42. Repeat Steps 2-41 to attach the other sleeve.

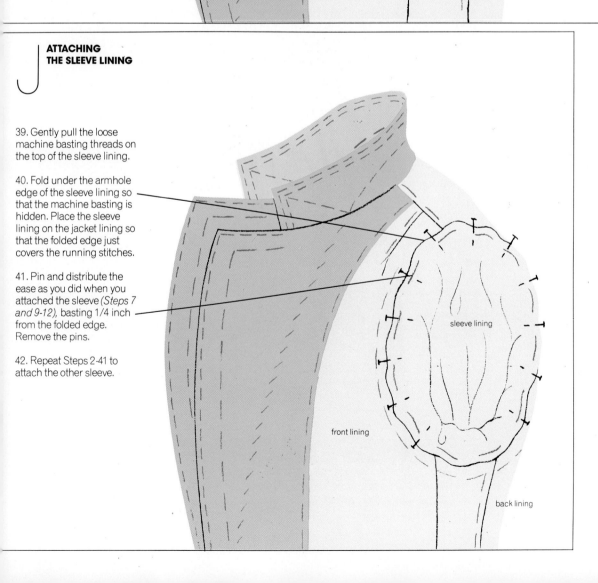

sleeve lining

front lining

back lining

INSERTING THE SLEEVE IN A WOMAN'S JACKET

A — ATTACHING THE SLEEVE

1. Bring together the two sleeves, the jacket, the sleeve heads and, if you are using them, the shoulder pads.

2. Turn the jacket right side out and reinforce the underarm area, following the instructions for a man's sleeve *(page 154, Box A, Step 2).*

3. Turn the jacket wrong side out.

4. Turn one of the sleeves right side out, and insert it into the corresponding armhole.

5. To ease in the fullness, gently pull the loose machine basting threads on the top of the sleeve.

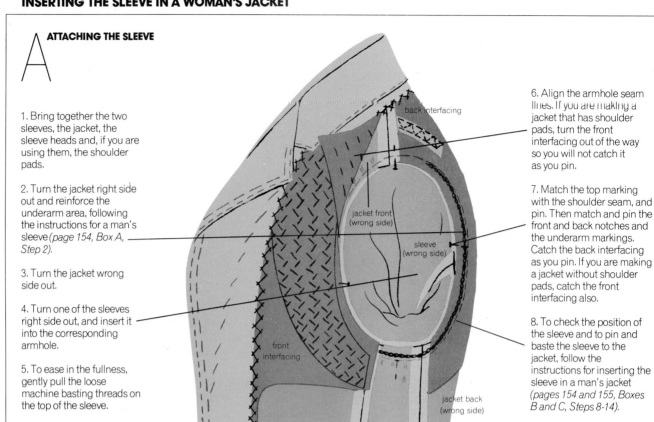

6. Align the armhole seam lines. If you are making a jacket that has shoulder pads, turn the front interfacing out of the way so you will not catch it as you pin.

7. Match the top marking with the shoulder seam, and pin. Then match and pin the front and back notches and the underarm markings. Catch the back interfacing as you pin. If you are making a jacket without shoulder pads, catch the front interfacing also.

8. To check the position of the sleeve and to pin and baste the sleeve to the jacket, follow the instructions for inserting the sleeve in a man's jacket *(pages 154 and 155, Boxes B and C, Steps 8-14).*

B — SEWING ON THE SLEEVE

9. With the jacket—but not the sleeve—wrong side out, machine stitch along the armhole seam line, stitching from the sleeve side. Sew slowly, taking care not to create puckers in the eased area as you stitch. Remove the basting and the tailor tacks.

10. If you are making a jacket that has shoulder pads, skip to Box C.

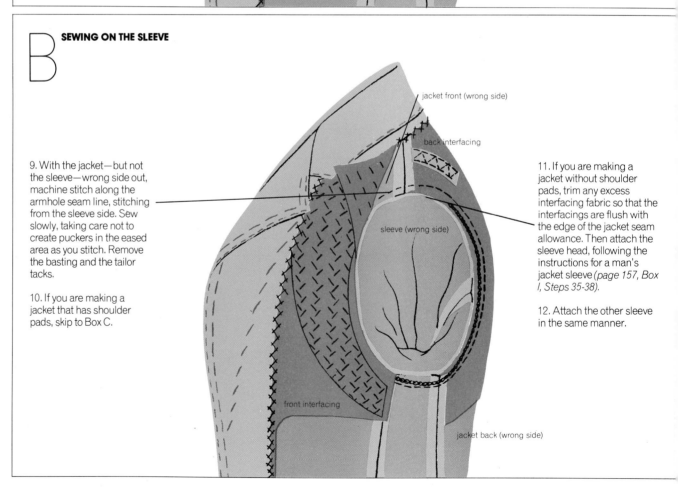

11. If you are making a jacket without shoulder pads, trim any excess interfacing fabric so that the interfacings are flush with the edge of the jacket seam allowance. Then attach the sleeve head, following the instructions for a man's jacket sleeve *(page 157, Box I, Steps 35-38).*

12. Attach the other sleeve in the same manner.

C ATTACHING THE SHOULDER PAD

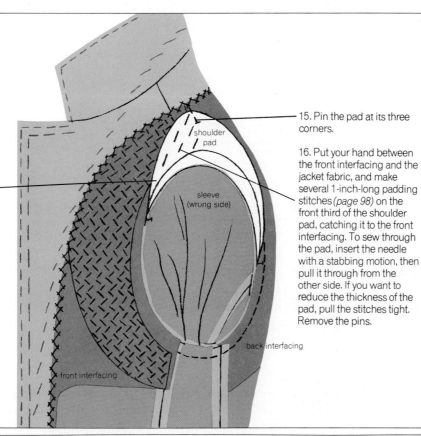

13. With the jacket—but not the sleeve—wrong side out, lift the jacket so that the shoulder falls in a rounded shape.

14. Place the shoulder pad over the interfacings so that the pad's straight edge is aligned with the armhole seam allowances and so that its widest point is centered over the shoulder seam. Approximately two thirds of the shoulder pad should be on the back interfacing. If the pad is too large, trim the edges.

15. Pin the pad at its three corners.

16. Put your hand between the front interfacing and the jacket fabric, and make several 1-inch-long padding stitches *(page 98)* on the front third of the shoulder pad, catching it to the front interfacing. To sew through the pad, insert the needle with a stabbing motion, then pull it through from the other side. If you want to reduce the thickness of the pad, pull the stitches tight. Remove the pins.

D FINISHING THE SHOULDER

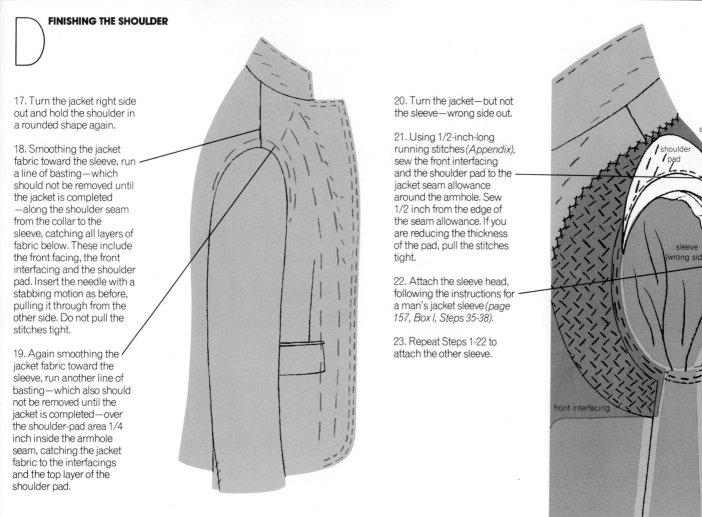

17. Turn the jacket right side out and hold the shoulder in a rounded shape again.

18. Smoothing the jacket fabric toward the sleeve, run a line of basting—which should not be removed until the jacket is completed —along the shoulder seam from the collar to the sleeve, catching all layers of fabric below. These include the front facing, the front interfacing and the shoulder pad. Insert the needle with a stabbing motion as before, pulling it through from the other side. Do not pull the stitches tight.

19. Again smoothing the jacket fabric toward the sleeve, run another line of basting—which also should not be removed until the jacket is completed—over the shoulder-pad area 1/4 inch inside the armhole seam, catching the jacket fabric to the interfacings and the top layer of the shoulder pad.

20. Turn the jacket—but not the sleeve—wrong side out.

21. Using 1/2-inch-long running stitches *(Appendix)*, sew the front interfacing and the shoulder pad to the jacket seam allowance around the armhole. Sew 1/2 inch from the edge of the seam allowance. If you are reducing the thickness of the pad, pull the stitches tight.

22. Attach the sleeve head, following the instructions for a man's jacket sleeve *(page 157, Box I, Steps 35-38)*.

23. Repeat Steps 1-22 to attach the other sleeve.

Final steps for the jacket

The most important last touches on a tailored jacket—and the most visible—are the hand sewing of the buttonholes, and the final pressing. A buttonhole is simply a slit outlined with tiny stitches, but practice is needed to make sure the stitches are identical in size and spacing. Do not start directly on the jacket. Practice on two layers of garment fabric with interfacing between them, to simulate the actual jacket. And remember that men's single-breasted jackets have buttonholes on the left; women's on the right.

After removing the last of the bastings, press the entire jacket to bring out its shape. Tailors may take up to an hour for the task. For a woman's jacket, you now assemble and attach the lining and touch up the pressing. Then sew on the buttons and you have a finished jacket.

FINISHING THE LINING ON A MAN'S JACKET

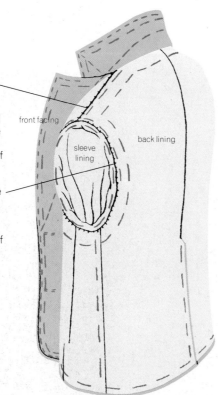

1. Turn the jacket—but not the sleeves—wrong side out.

2. Starting at one armhole edge, use tiny slip stitches (*Appendix*) to sew the folded edge of the back lining to the front lining and to the front facing along the shoulder seam. Be careful not to pick up other layers of fabric in your stitches.

front facing

sleeve lining

back lining

3. Now sew the folded edge of the sleeve lining to the jacket lining around the armhole. Again, be careful not to pick up other layers of fabric.

4. Repeat Steps 2 and 3 on the other shoulder seam and armhole. Remove the bastings.

5. Remove any stitches that attach the top of the hem at the left vent edge. Turn under the raw hem edge 1/8 inch. Pin. Use tiny slip stitches to attach the folded edge to the layer of jacket fabric directly below it. Remove the pins.

6. Attach the folded edges of the lining to the jacket fabric around the vent, again using tiny slip stitches and picking up only the top layer of jacket fabric.

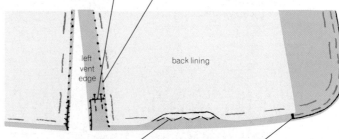

left vent edge

back lining

7. Turn up the folded edge of the lining hem along the basting. Using blind hemming stitches (*Appendix*), attach the turned-up layer of the jacket hem to the turned-under layer of the lining hem. Sew as close to the basting as possible, and be careful not to pick up any other layers of fabric in the stitches. When you are finished, the stitches should be hidden on both sides of the jacket. Remove the basting.

8. Attach the raw edges of the front facings below the lining hem to the top layer of the jacket hem. Use tiny hemming stitches (*Appendix*), and make them as close together as possible, so that the raw edges are completely hidden.

MAKING HAND-WORKED BUTTONHOLES

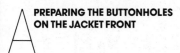

PREPARING THE BUTTONHOLES ON THE JACKET FRONT

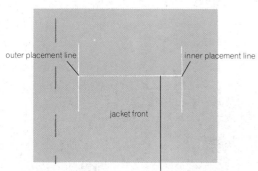

outer placement line

inner placement line

jacket front

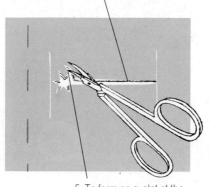

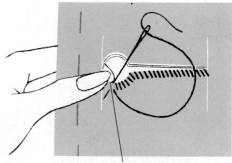

4. Working on one buttonhole at a time, cut with small pointed scissors along the center line. Start in the middle and cut to the inner and outer placement lines.

1. Try on the jacket and check the buttonhole placement (on the left front for a man; on the right for a woman). Adjust if necessary.

2. To determine the length of the buttonhole, measure the diameter of the button you will be using and add 1/8 inch.

3. Using the tailor tacks as a guide, for each buttonhole make center lines (with chalk) equal to the length determined in Step 2. Follow a grain line in the fabric to be sure the center lines are straight. Then draw the inner and outer placement lines and remove the tailor tacks and the bastings in the buttonhole area.

5. To form an eyelet at the outer end of the buttonhole, first make two 1/16-inch diagonal clips on one edge, starting both clips 1/16 inch from the outer placement line. Next make two similar diagonal clips on the other edge. Then trim off the wedges by cutting around the outside of the clips with cuticle scissors.

6. To protect the edges of the buttonhole from fraying, sew around them with 1/16-inch overcast stitches (*Appendix*). As you sew, squeeze the garment and' facing layers of fabric so that the interfacing, which is between the two layers, will not be visible when the buttonhole is finished.

continued

B STITCHING THE BUTTONHOLE

7. Thread your needle with a 30-inch length of knotted buttonhole twist the same color as the garment fabric, and hold the jacket so that the eyelet is away from you. Insert the needle between the interfacing and the facing layers of fabric on the left edge of the buttonhole at the inner placement line. If you are left-handed, insert the needle on the right edge.

8. Bring the needle out 1/8 inch beyond the edge, embedding the knot between the layers of fabric.

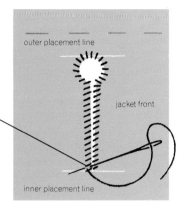

9. Take a 1/8-inch buttonhole stitch (*Appendix*) but do not tighten it.

10. Cut a piece of gimp (*page 90*) or another piece of buttonhole twist that is equal in length to twice the length of the buttonhole plus 2 inches.

11. Lay the gimp or twist along the edge of the buttonhole, and slip 1 inch of it through the untightened buttonhole stitch.

12. To finish the stitch, first pull the thread firmly back toward you. Then pull the thread firmly forward and away from you.

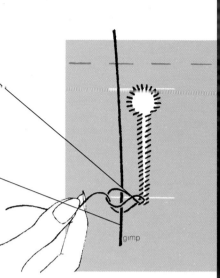

13. Continue making buttonhole stitches along the edge, catching the gimp or twist in the stitches and tightening them as in Step 12.

14. At the outer placement line, make stitches that fan around the eyelet. To tighten each stitch, pull the thread straight up.

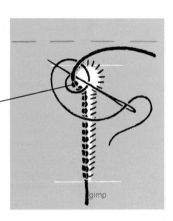

15. Turn the jacket around so that the eyelet is toward you and continue along the other edge, tightening the stitches as you did on the completed edge.

16. At the inner placement line, finish the edge with a bar tack (*page 101*). After you have made the fastening stitches for the bar tack, cut away the loose ends of the gimp. Then finish making the bar tack.

17. Repeat Steps 4-16 to make the remaining buttonholes.

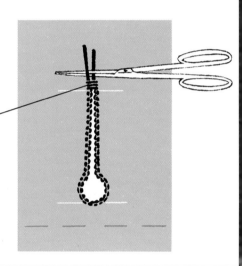

C MAKING THE BUTTONHOLES ON THE SLEEVES

18. To mark the outer placement line for the sleeve-vent buttonholes, draw a chalk line on the upper sleeve 1/2 inch inside the vent edge and parallel to it.

19. For the bottom button, make a mark on the chalk line 1 1/2 to 1 3/4 inches above the hem edge of the sleeve.

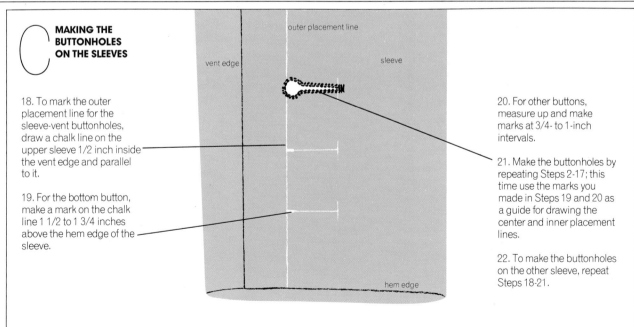

20. For other buttons, measure up and make marks at 3/4- to 1-inch intervals.

21. Make the buttonholes by repeating Steps 2-17; this time use the marks you made in Steps 19 and 20 as a guide for drawing the center and inner placement lines.

22. To make the buttonholes on the other sleeve, repeat Steps 18-21.

THE FINAL PRESS

A PRESSING THE JACKET EDGES

1. Remove all remaining bastings and tailor tacks on the jacket.

2. Use a clothes brush to remove any lint or loose threads on the jacket.

3. Turn the jacket lining side up.

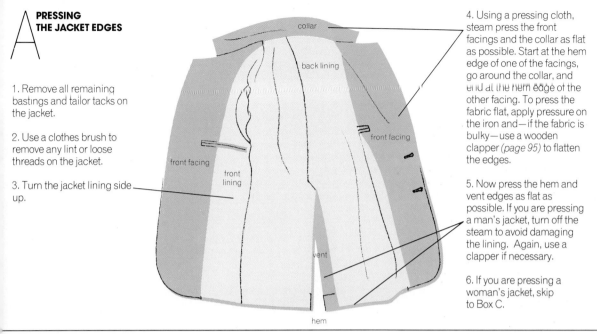

4. Using a pressing cloth, steam press the front facings and the collar as flat as possible. Start at the hem edge of one of the facings, go around the collar, and end at the hem edge of the other facing. To press the fabric flat, apply pressure on the iron and—if the fabric is bulky—use a wooden clapper (page 95) to flatten the edges.

5. Now press the hem and vent edges as flat as possible. If you are pressing a man's jacket, turn off the steam to avoid damaging the lining. Again, use a clapper if necessary.

6. If you are pressing a woman's jacket, skip to Box C.

B PRESSING THE LINING ON A MAN'S JACKET

7. Using a dry iron, press one front lining. Start at the lower edge and press as far as the shoulder area.

8. Press the back lining and the other front lining in the same manner.

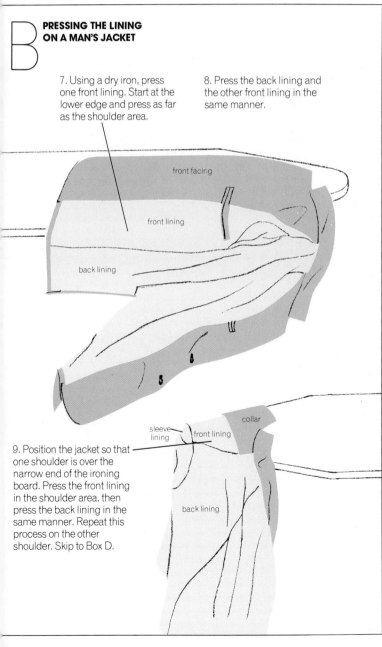

9. Position the jacket so that one shoulder is over the narrow end of the ironing board. Press the front lining in the shoulder area, then press the back lining in the same manner. Repeat this process on the other shoulder. Skip to Box D.

C PRESSING THE INSIDE OF A WOMAN'S JACKET

10. With the jacket wrong side up, steam press one of the jacket fronts as far as the shoulder area.

11. Steam press the back and the other front in the same manner.

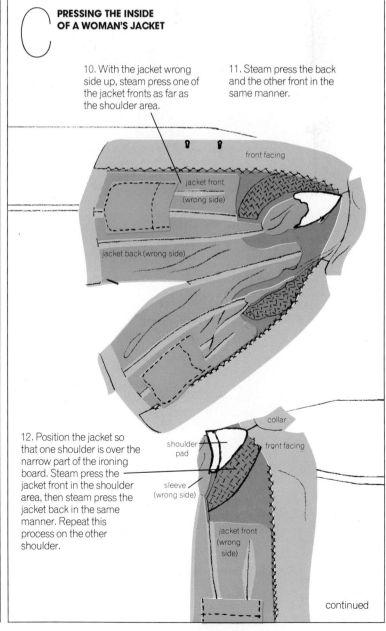

12. Position the jacket so that one shoulder is over the narrow part of the ironing board. Steam press the jacket front in the shoulder area, then steam press the jacket back in the same manner. Repeat this process on the other shoulder.

continued

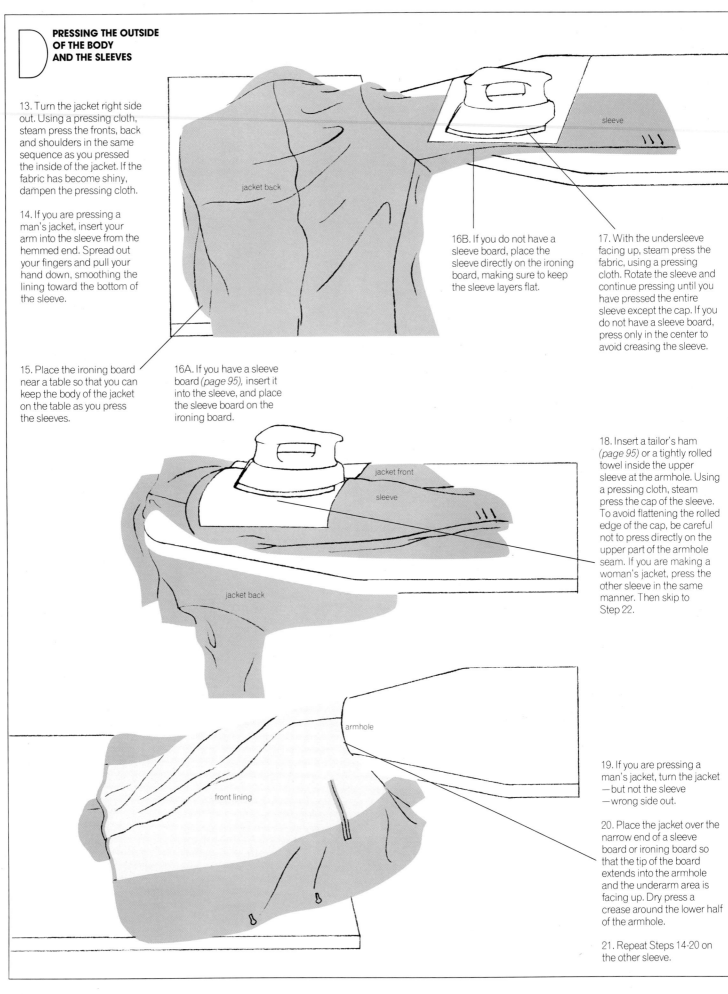

13. Turn the jacket right side out. Using a pressing cloth, steam press the fronts, back and shoulders in the same sequence as you pressed the inside of the jacket. If the fabric has become shiny, dampen the pressing cloth.

14. If you are pressing a man's jacket, insert your arm into the sleeve from the hemmed end. Spread out your fingers and pull your hand down, smoothing the lining toward the bottom of the sleeve.

15. Place the ironing board near a table so that you can keep the body of the jacket on the table as you press the sleeves.

16A. If you have a sleeve board *(page 95),* insert it into the sleeve, and place the sleeve board on the ironing board.

16B. If you do not have a sleeve board, place the sleeve directly on the ironing board, making sure to keep the sleeve layers flat.

17. With the undersleeve facing up, steam press the fabric, using a pressing cloth. Rotate the sleeve and continue pressing until you have pressed the entire sleeve except the cap. If you do not have a sleeve board, press only in the center to avoid creasing the sleeve.

18. Insert a tailor's ham *(page 95)* or a tightly rolled towel inside the upper sleeve at the armhole. Using a pressing cloth, steam press the cap of the sleeve. To avoid flattening the rolled edge of the cap, be careful not to press directly on the upper part of the armhole seam. If you are making a woman's jacket, press the other sleeve in the same manner. Then skip to Step 22.

19. If you are pressing a man's jacket, turn the jacket —but not the sleeve —wrong side out.

20. Place the jacket over the narrow end of a sleeve board or ironing board so that the tip of the board extends into the armhole and the underarm area is facing up. Dry press a crease around the lower half of the armhole.

21. Repeat Steps 14-20 on the other sleeve.

PRESSING THE COLLAR AND THE LAPEL

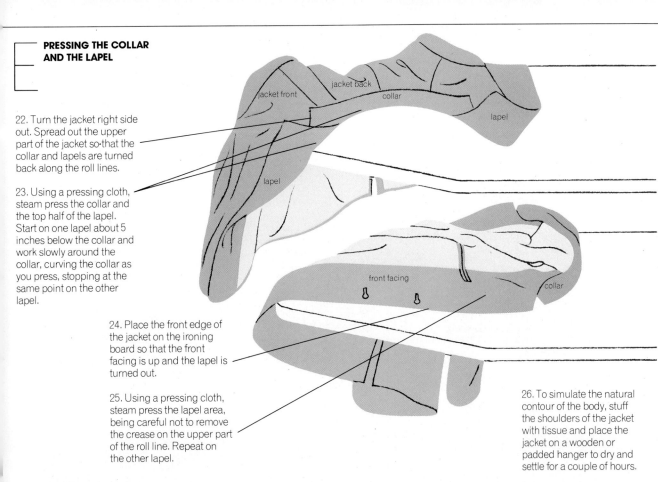

22. Turn the jacket right side out. Spread out the upper part of the jacket so·that the collar and lapels are turned back along the roll lines.

23. Using a pressing cloth, steam press the collar and the top half of the lapel. Start on one lapel about 5 inches below the collar and work slowly around the collar, curving the collar as you press, stopping at the same point on the other lapel.

24. Place the front edge of the jacket on the ironing board so that the front facing is up and the lapel is turned out.

25. Using a pressing cloth, steam press the lapel area, being careful not to remove the crease on the upper part of the roll line. Repeat on the other lapel.

26. To simulate the natural contour of the body, stuff the shoulders of the jacket with tissue and place the jacket on a wooden or padded hanger to dry and settle for a couple of hours.

THE WOMAN'S JACKET LINING

A PREPARING THE LINING

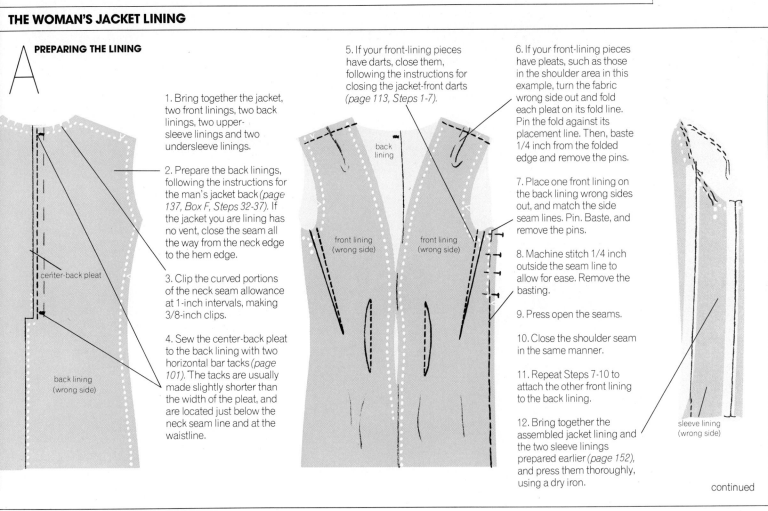

1. Bring together the jacket, two front linings, two back linings, two upper-sleeve linings and two undersleeve linings.

2. Prepare the back linings, following the instructions for the man's jacket back (page 137, Box F, Steps 32-37). If the jacket you are lining has no vent, close the seam all the way from the neck edge to the hem edge.

3. Clip the curved portions of the neck seam allowance at 1-inch intervals, making 3/8-inch clips.

4. Sew the center-back pleat to the back lining with two horizontal bar tacks (page 101). The tacks are usually made slightly shorter than the width of the pleat, and are located just below the neck seam line and at the waistline.

5. If your front-lining pieces have darts, close them, following the instructions for closing the jacket-front darts (page 113, Steps 1-7).

6. If your front-lining pieces have pleats, such as those in the shoulder area in this example, turn the fabric wrong side out and fold each pleat on its fold line. Pin the fold against its placement line. Then, baste 1/4 inch from the folded edge and remove the pins.

7. Place one front lining on the back lining wrong sides out, and match the side seam lines. Pin. Baste, and remove the pins.

8. Machine stitch 1/4 inch outside the seam line to allow for ease. Remove the basting.

9. Press open the seams.

10. Close the shoulder seam in the same manner.

11. Repeat Steps 7-10 to attach the other front lining to the back lining.

12. Bring together the assembled jacket lining and the two sleeve linings prepared earlier (page 152), and press them thoroughly, using a dry iron.

continued

B ATTACHING THE JACKET LINING

13. Turn the jacket—but not the sleeves—wrong side out, and place it on a wooden or padded hanger. Place the lining, turned right side out, over the jacket.

14. On the armhole edges, match the shoulder seams and underarm markings. Pin.

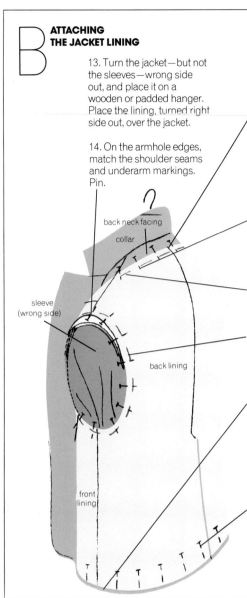

back neck facing

collar

sleeve (wrong side)

back lining

front lining

15. On the neck edge, match the shoulder seams and the center-back markings. If the lining is tight between the pins, release the pin at the armhole and move the lining fabric slightly toward the pin at the neck. Repin. Then pin all around the armholes.

16. Turn under the neck edge of the lining along the seam line, and pin it to the back neck facing at 2-inch intervals.

17. Take the jacket off the hanger. Baste around the neckline 1/4 inch from the folded edge. Remove the pins.

18. Baste around the armholes 1 inch from the edge, catching the lining to the layer of fabric below. Remove the pins.

19. Put the jacket on the hanger again. Turn under the lining so that the fold is 1/4 inch above the folded hem edge of the jacket.

20. Ease in the lining fabric another 1/4 inch and pin, making sure to match the center-back and side seams. If the jacket has a vent, pin the lining around the vent, following the instructions for the man's back lining (page 139, Box H, Steps 52-55).

C FINISHING THE JACKET LINING

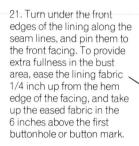

collar

21. Turn under the front edges of the lining along the seam lines, and pin them to the front facing. To provide extra fullness in the bust area, ease the lining fabric 1/4 inch up from the hem edge of the facing, and take up the eased fabric in the 6 inches above the first buttonhole or button mark.

22. If the lining is too tight, release the pins and refold the front edges of the lining, making the fold slightly smaller than before.

23. Remove the jacket from the hanger. Baste along the front edges 1/4 inch from the folded edge.

24. Continue the basting along the hem, sewing 1/2 inch above the folded edge of the lining. If the jacket you are making has a vent, baste around the vent edges 1/4 inch from the folded edges. Remove the pins.

25. Now use slip stitches (Appendix) to sew the folded front and neck edges of the lining to the facings, picking up only the facing layer as you sew.

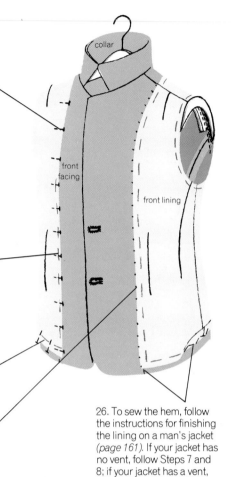

front facing

front lining

26. To sew the hem, follow the instructions for finishing the lining on a man's jacket (page 161). If your jacket has no vent, follow Steps 7 and 8; if your jacket has a vent, follow Steps 5-8.

D ATTACHING THE SLEEVE LINING AT THE ARMHOLE

27. Using running stitches (Appendix), hand sew around each armhole 1/2 inch from the edge of the jacket seam allowance. Attach the lining to the layer of fabric underneath. Remove the basting. If the lining extends beyond the edge of the jacket seam allowance, trim off the excess lining fabric.

28. Place the jacket on a hanger with the jacket—but not the sleeves—wrong side out.

29. Insert the sleeve lining, wrong side out, into the armhole of the jacket.

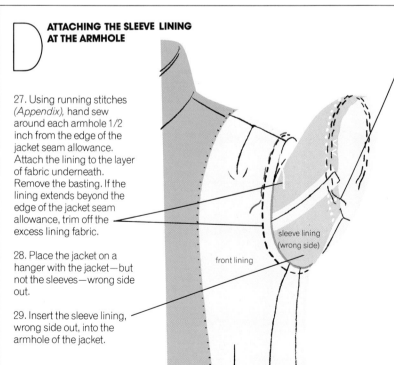

front lining

sleeve lining (wrong side)

30. Gently pull the loose ends of the machine-basting threads at the top of the sleeve lining. Distribute the ease evenly.

31. Turn under the armhole edge of the sleeve lining along the seam line so that the folded edge just covers the running stitches made in Step 27. Match and pin at the pattern markings. Then pin all around, distributing the extra fabric evenly.

32. Remove the jacket from the hanger. Baste 1/4 inch from the folded edge, using small stitches so that you can take up the extra fabric evenly. Remove the pins.

33. Hand sew around the folded edge with a slip stitch (Appendix), catching only the lining layers of fabric. Remove the basting.

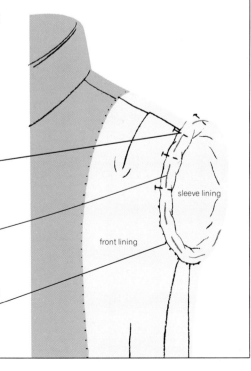

sleeve lining

front lining

HEMMING THE SLEEVE LINING

34. Turn the jacket right side out and place it on the hanger.

35. Pull the sleeve lining out at the bottom of the sleeve and put your arm up the lining. Spread your fingers out and pull your hand down to smooth the lining toward the bottom of the sleeve.

36. Match the seams of the lining and the sleeve. Pin the sleeve to the lining 3 inches above the sleeve edge, distributing the extra lining fabric evenly between the seams. Overlap the vent as it will be when worn, and pin.

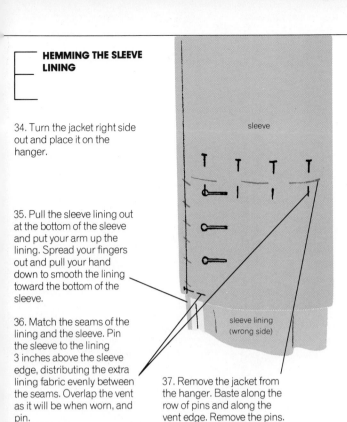

sleeve

sleeve lining (wrong side)

37. Remove the jacket from the hanger. Baste along the row of pins and along the vent edge. Remove the pins.

38. Turn the jacket wrong side out and place it back on the hanger.

39. Turn under the hem allowance of the sleeve lining so that the fold is 1/4 inch above the folded hem edge of the sleeve. Then ease the sleeve lining up another 1/4 inch and pin.

40. Remove the jacket from the hanger and baste 1/2 inch above the folded edge of the lining. Remove the pins.

41. Turn up the folded edge of the lining hem along the basting. Using blind hemming stitches (Appendix), attach the turned-up layer of the sleeve hem to the turned-under layer of the lining hem. Sew as close as possible to the basting. Be careful not to catch other layers of fabric. Remove all the bastings.

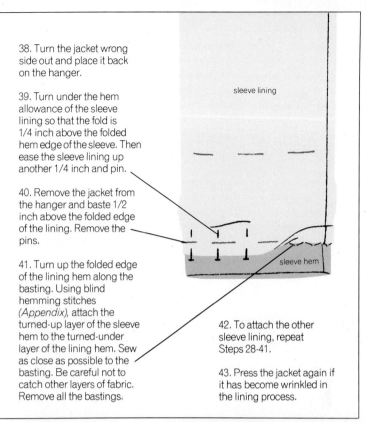

sleeve lining

sleeve hem

42. To attach the other sleeve lining, repeat Steps 28-41.

43. Press the jacket again if it has become wrinkled in the lining process.

SEWING BUTTONS ON A SINGLE-BREASTED JACKET

1. Fold the jacket in half, wrong side out, so that the front edges and the hem edges are aligned.

2. To mark the position for the center of each button, make a chalk mark through the eyelet of the buttonhole.

3. To attach each button, begin by coating a double strand of button thread or buttonhole twist (page 90) with beeswax to prevent knotting.

4. Catching only the outer and interfacing layers of fabric, make a fastening stitch (Appendix) at the chalk mark. Then insert the needle in a hole on the button from the underside and pull it through.

jacket facing

jacket lining

jacket front

5. Place a wooden match on top of the button and sew over it as you make two or three stitches in each hole.

6. To make a shank, remove the match, pull the button up, and tightly wind the thread a few times around the loose threads between the button and fabric.

7. End by making a fastening stitch in the shank.

8. Attach the sleeve buttons by repeating Steps 2-7.

SEWING BUTTONS ON A DOUBLE-BREASTED JACKET

1. Try on the jacket and overlap the fronts so that it fits comfortably, making sure that the hem edges are aligned and the front edge is straight. (On a man's jacket the left front overlaps the right; on a woman's jacket it is the opposite.) Pin the front edge in place.

2. Mark the position of the front edge by making a chalk mark along it. Then, make a horizontal mark next to the front edge and even with each buttonhole.

3. Take off the jacket and, using the chalk marks as a guide, overlap the fronts so that they are in the same position.

4. Follow Steps 2-8 at left to attach all but the top button. Then sew it on, keeping the same spacing, but placing it 1/2 inch closer to the side seam. (This button is decorative; do not use a match to make the shank.)

5. Attach the buttons the same distance from the edge on the other front; do not make shanks. Attach an inside button directly under the middle button; make an extra-long shank.

6. Sew the sleeve buttons, following Steps 2-7 at left.

jacket front

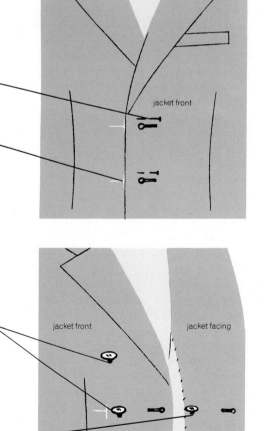

jacket front

jacket facing

5
TAILORED TROUSERS

During the 1940s, that paragon of gentlemen's fashion, the Duke of Windsor, angered British clothiers by traveling to America to buy his trousers. English tailors, said the Duke, refused to give him pants with belt loops. Instead they insisted on producing a high-waisted garment that could be worn only with suspenders—or braces, as they are called in Britain.

In the furor that followed, other turncoats,

BREECHES OF ETIQUETTE: A SOCIAL GAUGE

like couturier Digby Morton, also confessed to taking their trouser trade across the sea. "British trousers look flappy," Morton declared. He then went on to emphasize the role that a well-cut pair of trousers should play in male attire: "Pants are to a man," he said, "what a brassiere is to a woman. They give the figure a line."

Morton's analogy, besides its bizarre anatomical equation, ignored a cardinal rule of traditional trouser etiquette. Heretofore no proper Englishman would have said "pants" when he meant trousers. Upper-crust British folk wisdom had always held that "Girls and Americans wear pants. Gentlemen wear trousers."

Snobbish, perhaps, but snobbery has long been a part of masculine dress. For pants, or trousers, in their various transformations of cut and styling can, indeed, serve as indicators of caste and social outlook—as did their evolutionary ancestors *(pages 172-173)*. Take for example the cuffs. Some time before the turn of the century, England's racing set started turning up their trouser legs while at the track. They did so to keep their bottom hems clear of the mud when visiting the paddock to confer with their jockeys. These gentlemen of Ascot, by virtue of wealth and position, were trend setters. Soon the tailored "turn-up" became a standard in England and, shortly after 1900, the cuff appeared in América.

Creases carry an even more distinguished pedigree. As the story goes, England's King Edward VII once was thrown from his horse into a puddle, whereupon His damp Majesty was hustled off to a nearby cottage to get dry.

The lady of the house tried to steam the water out of his trousers and inadvertently steamed in creases. The King, being a gentleman, wore the transformed trousers, and he found the effect extremely flattering. So did the rest of England's gentry—and not long thereafter, the rest of the world.

Some of the other changes in trouser tailoring, born of pure practicality, were not universally adopted until they received the imprimatur of gentlemanly propriety. A pioneer zipper manufacturer began urging the use of its so-called "C-Curity" fastener for all kinds of garments back in 1905. But not until 1924, when the Duke of Windsor appeared in a pair of zippered trousers, did they became respectable.

While the basic engineering of the modern trouser was thus completed by the mid-'20s, the grament has since undergone many mutations. Among the earliest were Oxford bags. These voluminous trousers, 25 inches wide at the knee, were first worn *over knickers* by defiant British students when the popular plus fours were outlawed by the university. Bags quickly emigrated to America, where they flourished briefly among the Gatsby set.

Enormous trousers then resurfaced in the early days of World War II as the bottom half of the extravagant zoot suit. But the stringent cloth allotments imposed on garment makers during the War erased this wasteful fashion, as it did the cuff and the pleat.

And it also ended forever the upper-class monopoly on determining trouser fashions. The sleek Continental look of the 1950s and 1960s was inaugurated by Italian manufacturers and was aimed at the ordinary man.

The streamlined look is still the most popular one in men's wear—despite the bells and exaggerated flares and other fancies that first caused a rustle during the early '70s. It is the style that is always available from pattern companies, and the one which the home tailor will probably find most manageable as a starter, as the techniques in the following section will show.

Ten centuries of trousers

Men's trousers, throughout most of Western history, have performed double duty: to cover the wearer, while showing off the leg. At the time of the Norman conquest of England in 1066, men wore pajama-like pants held tight with cloth or leather straps.

By 1340, responding to new wealth and leisure, troubadours affected tight, bright hose and a body-hugging tunic. The Elizabethan gentleman of 1560 also wore hose to display his shanks and a bit of thigh; but he shrouded his midriff in trunks stuffed with a material called bombast, creating an effect as pretentious as its name. He was clearly outdone by the English dandy of 1620, whose baggy galligaskins ballooned down to his foppishly gartered calves.

A trim new look had appeared by 1635, which featured the close-fitted knee-length breeches and boots favored by Charles I and his Cavalier followers. Breeches lasted more than a century, and by 1755 they formed the basis of the first three-piece suit —worn with a coat and long waistcoat that would eventually shrink to a vest. During the French Revolution, the breeches extended to the ankles, heralding the modern long trousers. Worn skintight, like those sported by the frock-coated 1805 Londoner, they gave men a last chance to dandify their legs before moving on to loose full-fledged trousers that hid the lines of calf and thigh—as befit the mid-century Victorian mood.

1066 Norman

1340 Gothic

1560 Elizabethan

1755 Georgian

1620 Jacobean

1635 Stuart

1805 Regency

1853 Victorian

Starting off with the pockets

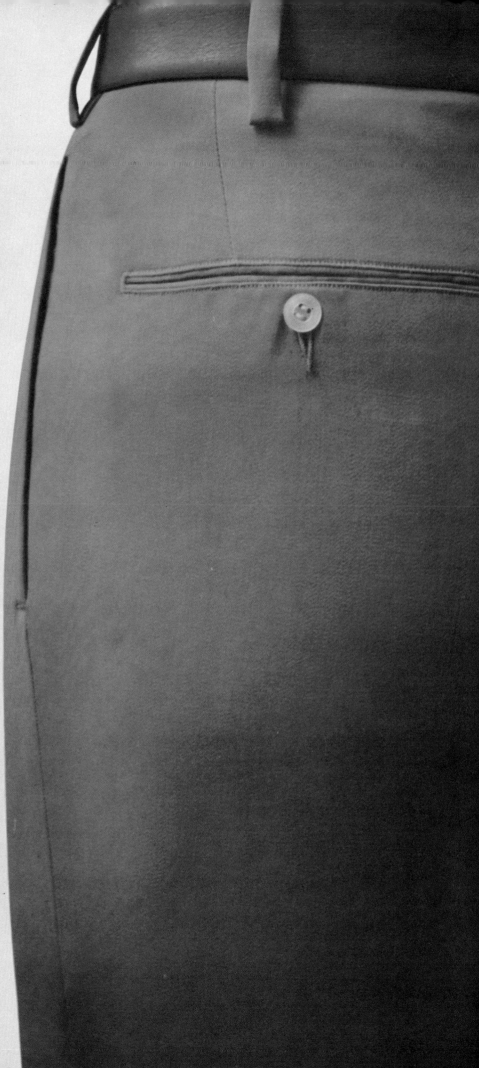

Assembling a pair of trousers begins with putting in their most basic accessory: the pockets. After the four pants sections have been cut out (*page 38*) and before they are sewed together, the back pockets are attached. Their upper and lower pipings should be so narrow that they appear as one, because a well-bred pocket, like a good valet, should be decorously inconspicuous. For easy accessibility the back pocket should be 3 1/2 inches below the waistband. In a man's trousers, the left rear pocket is traditionally used for a wallet; in the final work on the trousers it will acquire a buttonhole.

The side pockets are attached next. They should be roomy and wafer thin, with the back corner slightly curved so that small objects such as coins do not lodge there—and cause the wearer to dig awkwardly when reaching inside.

After the side pockets go in, the trousers' back sections are sewed to the front ones at the outside seam.

PREPARING THE PANTS PIECES

A PREPARING THE PANTS BACK

1. Place one of the pants-back pieces wrong side up on a flat surface.

2. Clip open the waistline dart to within 3/8 inch of its point.

3. Use overcast stitches (*Appendix*) to finish the raw edges of the dart and the other edges of the pants piece—except at the waistline and hem. These edges will be finished when you attach the waistband and make the cuffs.

4. Baste and machine stitch the waistline dart, tying off the threads at the base of the dart; then remove the basting and tailor tacks. Press the dart open and press the point flat.

5. Repeat Steps 1-4 on the other pants-back piece.

B PREPARING THE PANTS FRONT

6. Cut two 6-inch squares of pocketing fabric to be used as crotch stays to reinforce the lower part of the fly. Fold each square on the bias, wrong sides together, to form triangles. Press.

7. Make a pencil mark 3 1/2 inches above the crotch point on the fly edge of the pants-front pattern piece.

8. Make another pencil mark on the inseam edge, 4 inches below the point of the crotch.

9. Place one of the fabric triangles under the crotch point of the pants-front pattern piece. Position the triangle so that the fold is 1 inch inside the edge of the pattern at the top and bottom, and so that the raw edges align with the marks made on the pattern in Steps 7 and 8. Pin the triangle in place.

10. Trace the contour of the pattern onto the fabric, then remove the pins.

11. Trim the triangle along the line made in Step 10.

12. Make a second crotch stay from the other fabric triangle, using the first as a pattern.

13. Pin and baste one of the crotch stays to the wrong side of one of the pants-front pieces at the crotch point. Remove the pins.

14. On women's pants, finish the front waistline darts as you did the back waistline darts (*Steps 2-4*). Then finish the raw edges of the pants-front piece—except at the waistline and hem edges—with an overcast stitch (*Appendix*). Remove the basting from the crotch stay.

15. Repeat Steps 13 and 14 on the other pants-front piece.

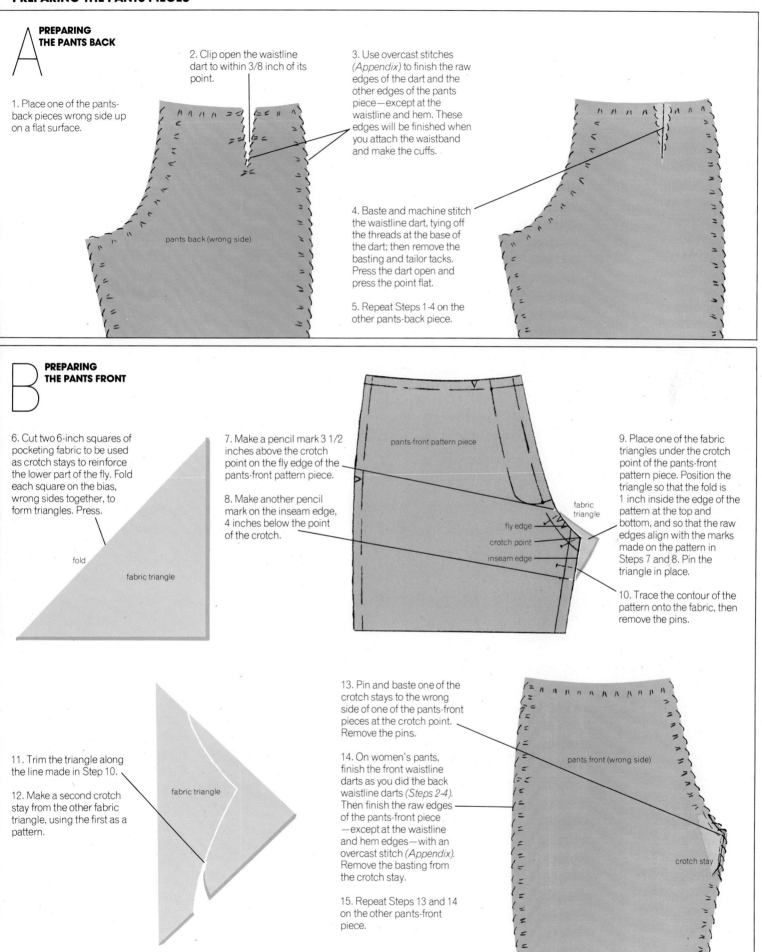

THE BACK POCKET

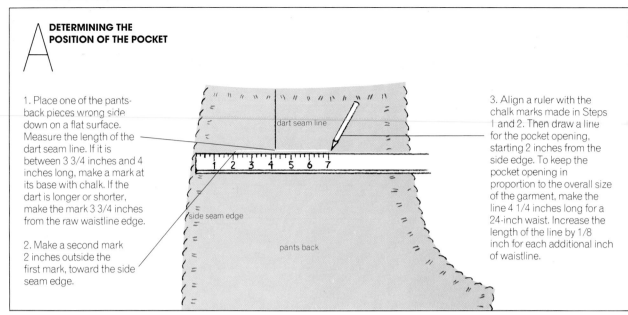

A DETERMINING THE POSITION OF THE POCKET

1. Place one of the pants-back pieces wrong side down on a flat surface. Measure the length of the dart seam line. If it is between 3 3/4 inches and 4 inches long, make a mark at its base with chalk. If the dart is longer or shorter, make the mark 3 3/4 inches from the raw waistline edge.

2. Make a second mark 2 inches outside the first mark, toward the side seam edge.

3. Align a ruler with the chalk marks made in Steps 1 and 2. Then draw a line for the pocket opening, starting 2 inches from the side edge. To keep the pocket opening in proportion to the overall size of the garment, make the line 4 1/4 inches long for a 24-inch waist. Increase the length of the line by 1/8 inch for each additional inch of waistline.

B PREPARING THE POCKET PIECES

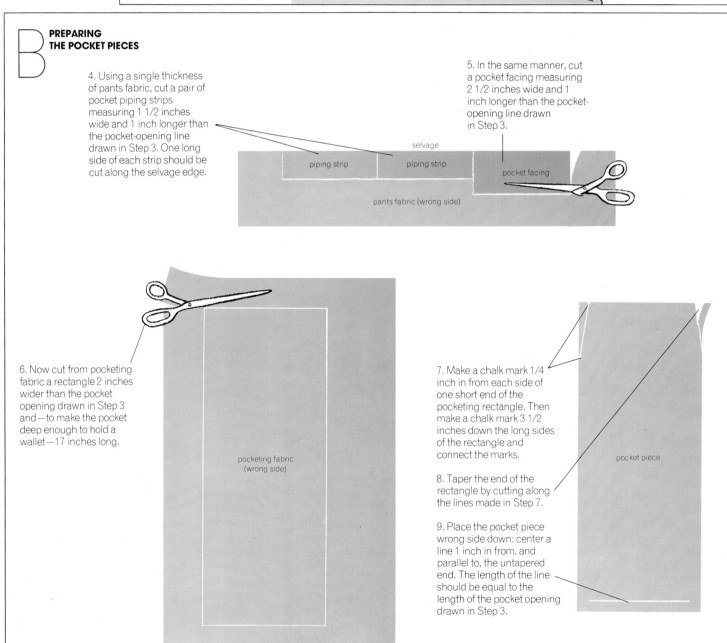

4. Using a single thickness of pants fabric, cut a pair of pocket piping strips measuring 1 1/2 inches wide and 1 inch longer than the pocket-opening line drawn in Step 3. One long side of each strip should be cut along the selvage edge.

5. In the same manner, cut a pocket facing measuring 2 1/2 inches wide and 1 inch longer than the pocket-opening line drawn in Step 3.

6. Now cut from pocketing fabric a rectangle 2 inches wider than the pocket opening drawn in Step 3 and—to make the pocket deep enough to hold a wallet—17 inches long.

7. Make a chalk mark 1/4 inch in from each side of one short end of the pocketing rectangle. Then make a chalk mark 3 1/2 inches down the long sides of the rectangle and connect the marks.

8. Taper the end of the rectangle by cutting along the lines made in Step 7.

9. Place the pocket piece wrong side down; center a line 1 inch in from, and parallel to, the untapered end. The length of the line should be equal to the length of the pocket opening drawn in Step 3.

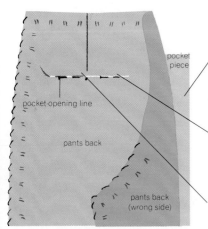

10. Lay the pocket piece, wrong side down, on a flat surface, with the untapered end at the top.

11. Position the pants piece, wrong side down, over the pocket piece, aligning the pocket-opening line on the pants piece with the line drawn on the pocket piece in Step 9. Pin the two pieces of fabric together along the line.

12. Baste and remove the pins.

13. Place a piping strip, wrong side up, just above the basting made in Step 12, with the raw edge of the strip aligned with the stitches. Pin the piping strip in place.

14. On the piping strip, indicate with chalk the ends of the pocket-opening line.

15. Pin the other piping strip, wrong side up, below the row of basting stitches. The raw edges of the two piping strips should meet, concealing the pocket-opening line on the pants back.

16. Baste the piping strips to the pants piece and remove the pins.

17. Beginning and ending at the chalk marks made in Step 14, machine stitch 1/8 inch inside the raw edges of both piping strips, back stitching twice at each end.

18. Remove the basting that marked the pocket-opening line and slash through the pants and pocket pieces along the line. The length of the cut should match the rows of stitching made in Step 17.

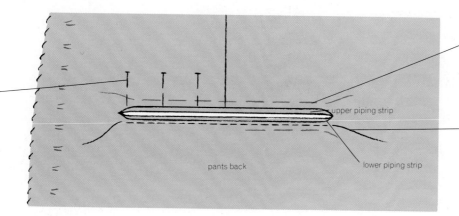

19. Push both piping strips through the slashed opening to the wrong side of the pants piece.

20. Place the pants piece wrong side down. Pinch the top seam of the pocket opening and roll the seam slightly until 1/16 inch of the piping strip shows below the seam. Pin the piping in place.

21. Repeat Step 20 on the bottom piping.

22. Baste both pipings and remove the pins.

23. Run a line of machine stitches 1/16 inch below the seam, along the lower piping. Stitch through the pants piece, the pocket piece and the piping strip. To finish the ends of the row of topstitching, leave about 4 inches of loose thread at each end and tie them off on the wrong side of the fabric. Remove the basting from the lower piping.

24. Turn the pants piece wrong side up. If the pocketing fabric is a different color from the pants fabric, thread the bobbin of your sewing machine with thread that matches the pocketing.

25. Pull the pocket piece away from the pants back and machine stitch the bottom edge of the lower piping strip to the pocket piece.

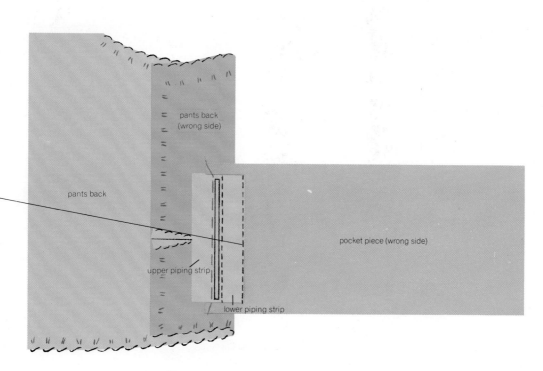

continued

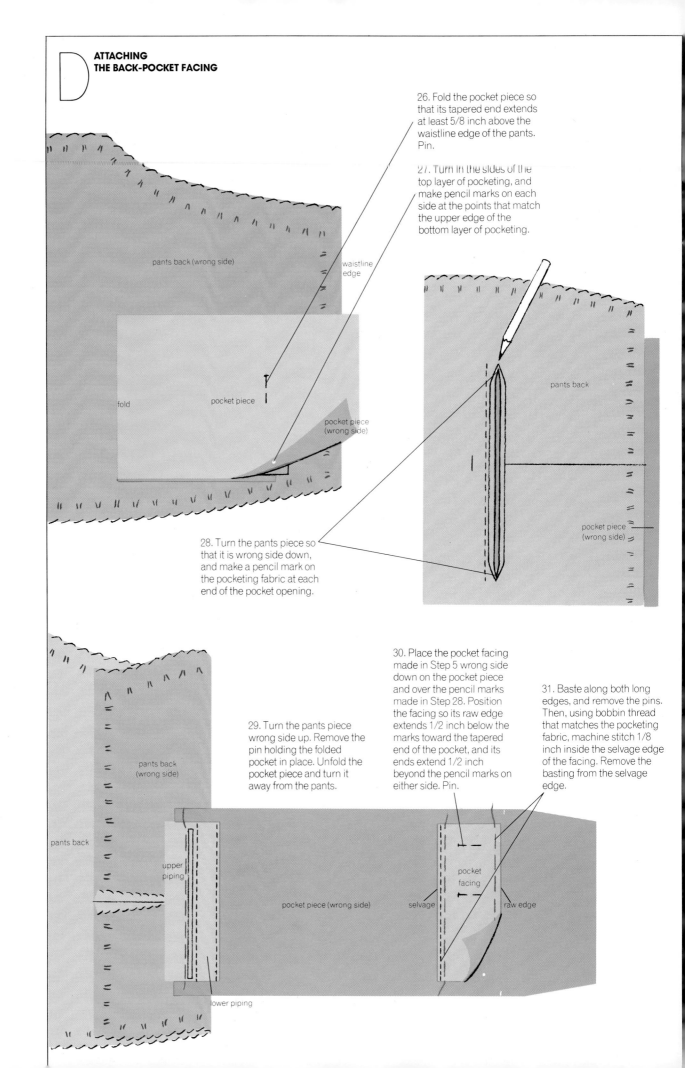

26. Fold the pocket piece so that its tapered end extends at least 5/8 inch above the waistline edge of the pants. Pin.

27. Turn in the sides of the top layer of pocketing, and make pencil marks on each side at the points that match the upper edge of the bottom layer of pocketing.

pants back (wrong side)

waistline edge

fold

pocket piece

pocket piece (wrong side)

pants back

pocket piece (wrong side)

28. Turn the pants piece so that it is wrong side down, and make a pencil mark on the pocketing fabric at each end of the pocket opening.

29. Turn the pants piece wrong side up. Remove the pin holding the folded pocket in place. Unfold the pocket piece and turn it away from the pants.

30. Place the pocket facing made in Step 5 wrong side down on the pocket piece and over the pencil marks made in Step 28. Position the facing so its raw edge extends 1/2 inch below the marks toward the tapered end of the pocket, and its ends extend 1/2 inch beyond the pencil marks on either side. Pin.

31. Baste along both long edges, and remove the pins. Then, using bobbin thread that matches the pocketing fabric, machine stitch 1/8 inch inside the selvage edge of the facing. Remove the basting from the selvage edge.

pants back (wrong side)

pants back

upper piping

pocket piece (wrong side)

pocket facing

selvage

raw edge

lower piping

32. With the pocket still turned away from the pants, turn the pants piece over, wrong side up, and fold the pocket piece so the pocket facing is up.

33. Turning the side of the pants piece out of the way, match the pencil marks on the edges of the top layer of pocketing to the upper edge of the underneath layer.

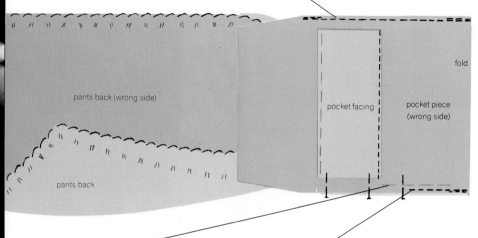

pants back (wrong side)

pants back

fold

pocket facing

pocket piece (wrong side)

37. Turn the pants piece wrong side down, and sew the pipings together with diagonal basting stitches (Appendix).

38. Using bobbin thread that matches the pocketing fabric, topstitch (Appendix) 1/16 inch above the upper piping seam, from one end of the pocket opening to the other. Stitch through the pants piece, the piping strip and both layers of pocketing fabric.

39. Machine stitch between the ends of the top and bottom rows of top stitching. Remove all basting from the pipings and from the facing underneath.

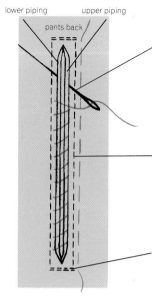

lower piping   upper piping

pants back

34. Pin together the side edges of the pocket piece, then baste and remove the pins.

35. Machine stitch 1/4 inch inside the edge of the fabric, and remove the basting.

36. Turn the pocket piece right side out and toward the bottom edge of the pants piece.

40. Turn back the outside of the pants to expose the pocket edges.

41. At the tapered end of the pocketing, fold in one raw edge of the pocketing 3/8 inch.

42. Baste from the tapered end to the point where the double layer of pocketing begins.

43. Roll the side seam of the pocket between your fingers so that the seam is visible. Continue to baste to the bottom edge of the pocket.

pants back (wrong side)

pocket (wrong side)

pocket (wrong side)

pocket

44. Repeat Steps 41-43 on the opposite side of the pocket.

45. Rethread your sewing machine with thread that matches the pocketing fabric. Topstitch the pocket 1/4 inch inside the fold, starting at one upper edge, continuing across the bottom, and ending at the other upper edge. Remove the basting from the pocket.

46. Turn the pants-back piece wrong side down, and hand stitch bar tacks (page 101) at each end of the topstitching lines.

47. Make a pocket on the other pants-back piece in the same manner.

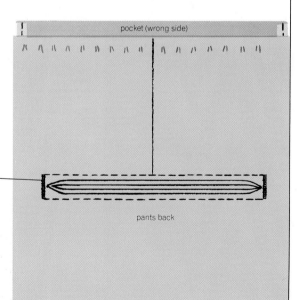

pocket (wrong side)

pants back

THE SIDE POCKET

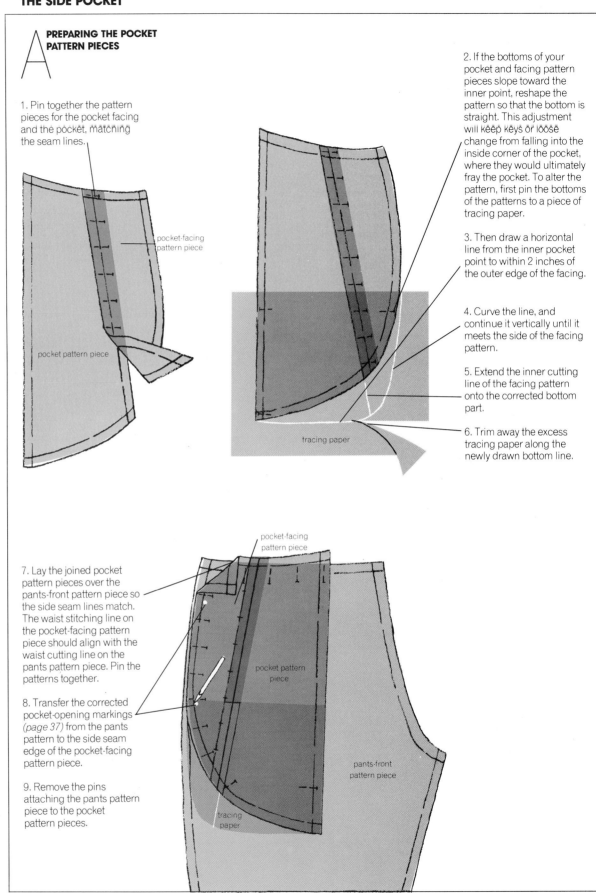

A PREPARING THE POCKET PATTERN PIECES

1. Pin together the pattern pieces for the pocket facing and the pocket, matching the seam lines.

2. If the bottoms of your pocket and facing pattern pieces slope toward the inner point, reshape the pattern so that the bottom is straight. This adjustment will keep keys or loose change from falling into the inside corner of the pocket, where they would ultimately fray the pocket. To alter the pattern, first pin the bottoms of the patterns to a piece of tracing paper.

3. Then draw a horizontal line from the inner pocket point to within 2 inches of the outer edge of the facing.

4. Curve the line, and continue it vertically until it meets the side of the facing pattern.

5. Extend the inner cutting line of the facing pattern onto the corrected bottom part.

6. Trim away the excess tracing paper along the newly drawn bottom line.

pocket-facing pattern piece

pocket pattern piece

tracing paper

7. Lay the joined pocket pattern pieces over the pants-front pattern piece so the side seam lines match. The waist stitching line on the pocket-facing pattern piece should align with the waist cutting line on the pants pattern piece. Pin the patterns together.

8. Transfer the corrected pocket-opening markings (page 37) from the pants pattern to the side seam edge of the pocket-facing pattern piece.

9. Remove the pins attaching the pants pattern piece to the pocket pattern pieces.

pocket-facing pattern piece

pocket pattern piece

pants-front pattern piece

tracing paper

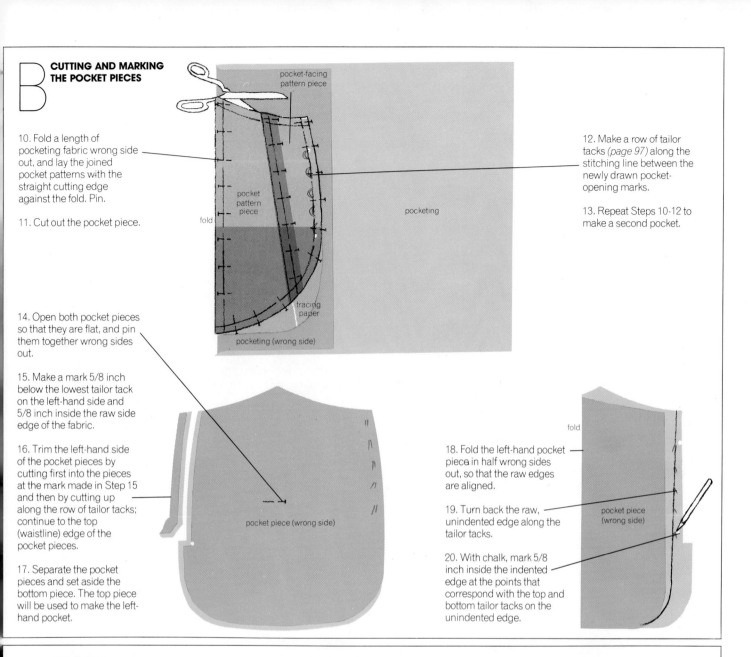

B CUTTING AND MARKING THE POCKET PIECES

10. Fold a length of pocketing fabric wrong side out, and lay the joined pocket patterns with the straight cutting edge against the fold. Pin.

11. Cut out the pocket piece.

14. Open both pocket pieces so that they are flat, and pin them together wrong sides out.

15. Make a mark 5/8 inch below the lowest tailor tack on the left-hand side and 5/8 inch inside the raw side edge of the fabric.

16. Trim the left-hand side of the pocket pieces by cutting first into the pieces at the mark made in Step 15 and then by cutting up along the row of tailor tacks; continue to the top (waistline) edge of the pocket pieces.

17. Separate the pocket pieces and set aside the bottom piece. The top piece will be used to make the left-hand pocket.

12. Make a row of tailor tacks *(page 97)* along the stitching line between the newly drawn pocket-opening marks.

13. Repeat Steps 10-12 to make a second pocket.

18. Fold the left-hand pocket piece in half wrong sides out, so that the raw edges are aligned.

19. Turn back the raw, unindented edge along the tailor tacks.

20. With chalk, mark 5/8 inch inside the indented edge at the points that correspond with the top and bottom tailor tacks on the unindented edge.

C MAKING THE POCKET FACING

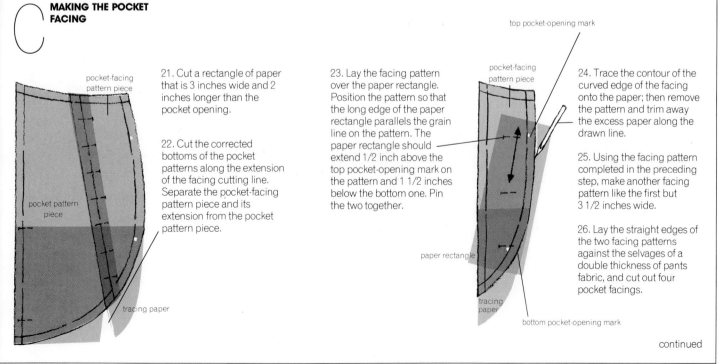

21. Cut a rectangle of paper that is 3 inches wide and 2 inches longer than the pocket opening.

22. Cut the corrected bottoms of the pocket patterns along the extension of the facing cutting line. Separate the pocket-facing pattern piece and its extension from the pocket pattern piece.

23. Lay the facing pattern over the paper rectangle. Position the pattern so that the long edge of the paper rectangle parallels the grain line on the pattern. The paper rectangle should extend 1/2 inch above the top pocket-opening mark on the pattern and 1 1/2 inches below the bottom one. Pin the two together.

24. Trace the contour of the curved edge of the facing onto the paper; then remove the pattern and trim away the excess paper along the drawn line.

25. Using the facing pattern completed in the preceding step, make another facing pattern like the first but 3 1/2 inches wide.

26. Lay the straight edges of the two facing patterns against the selvages of a double thickness of pants fabric, and cut out four pocket facings.

continued

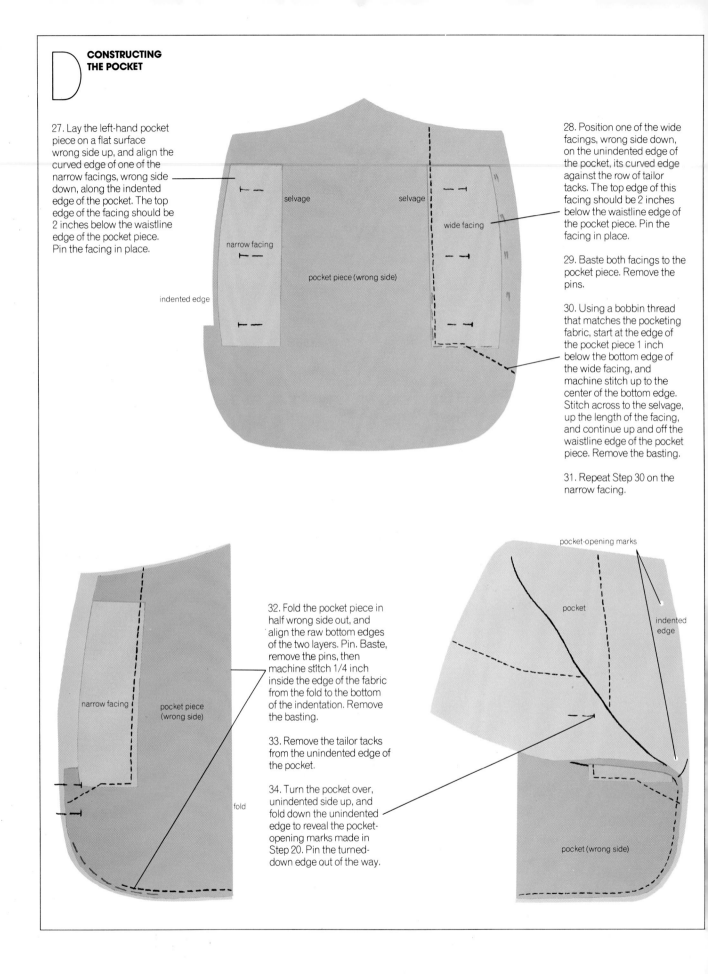

D CONSTRUCTING THE POCKET

27. Lay the left-hand pocket piece on a flat surface wrong side up, and align the curved edge of one of the narrow facings, wrong side down, along the indented edge of the pocket. The top edge of the facing should be 2 inches below the waistline edge of the pocket piece. Pin the facing in place.

28. Position one of the wide facings, wrong side down, on the unindented edge of the pocket, its curved edge against the row of tailor tacks. The top edge of this facing should be 2 inches below the waistline edge of the pocket piece. Pin the facing in place.

29. Baste both facings to the pocket piece. Remove the pins.

30. Using a bobbin thread that matches the pocketing fabric, start at the edge of the pocket piece 1 inch below the bottom edge of the wide facing, and machine stitch up to the center of the bottom edge. Stitch across to the selvage, up the length of the facing, and continue up and off the waistline edge of the pocket piece. Remove the basting.

31. Repeat Step 30 on the narrow facing.

32. Fold the pocket piece in half wrong side out, and align the raw bottom edges of the two layers. Pin. Baste, remove the pins, then machine stitch 1/4 inch inside the edge of the fabric from the fold to the bottom of the indentation. Remove the basting.

33. Remove the tailor tacks from the unindented edge of the pocket.

34. Turn the pocket over, unindented side up, and fold down the unindented edge to reveal the pocket-opening marks made in Step 20. Pin the turned-down edge out of the way.

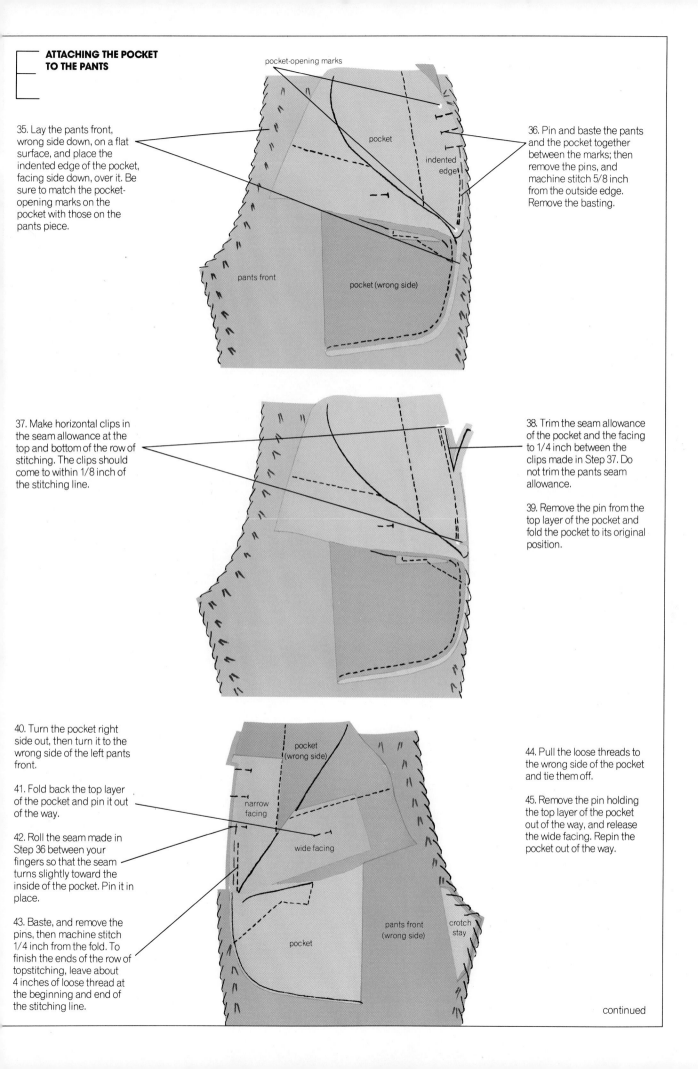

ATTACHING THE POCKET TO THE PANTS

pocket-opening marks

pocket

indented edge

pants front

pocket (wrong side)

35. Lay the pants front, wrong side down, on a flat surface, and place the indented edge of the pocket, facing side down, over it. Be sure to match the pocket-opening marks on the pocket with those on the pants piece.

36. Pin and baste the pants and the pocket together between the marks; then remove the pins, and machine stitch 5/8 inch from the outside edge. Remove the basting.

37. Make horizontal clips in the seam allowance at the top and bottom of the row of stitching. The clips should come to within 1/8 inch of the stitching line.

38. Trim the seam allowance of the pocket and the facing to 1/4 inch between the clips made in Step 37. Do not trim the pants seam allowance.

39. Remove the pin from the top layer of the pocket and fold the pocket to its original position.

pocket (wrong side)

narrow facing

wide facing

pocket

pants front (wrong side)

crotch stay

40. Turn the pocket right side out, then turn it to the wrong side of the left pants front.

41. Fold back the top layer of the pocket and pin it out of the way.

42. Roll the seam made in Step 36 between your fingers so that the seam turns slightly toward the inside of the pocket. Pin it in place.

43. Baste, and remove the pins, then machine stitch 1/4 inch from the fold. To finish the ends of the row of topstitching, leave about 4 inches of loose thread at the beginning and end of the stitching line.

44. Pull the loose threads to the wrong side of the pocket and tie them off.

45. Remove the pin holding the top layer of the pocket out of the way, and release the wide facing. Repin the pocket out of the way.

continued

PREPARING THE SIDE SEAM

F

46. Turn the left pants front over, wrong side down, and align the raw side edges with the outer edge of the wide facing. Pin at the top and bottom of the pocket opening.

47. Machine baste over the pins from 3/4 inch above the top of the pocket opening to 3/4 inch below the top of the pocket opening, keeping the stitching as close as possible to the pocket-opening fold. Repeat at the bottom of the pocket opening. Remove the pins.

48. Make a 5/8-inch-deep horizontal clip through the pants front and the top layer of the pocket at a point even with the top edges of the facings. Fold in the pocket edge above the clip as far as possible, and pin it out of the way.

49. Make a second 5/8-inch-deep horizontal clip on a line even with the base of the indentation in the top layer of pocketing, cutting through the pants front, the top layer of the pocket and both facings.

50. Measure the distance between the clips made in Steps 48 and 49.

51. Cut a rectangle of pocketing fabric 2 inches wide and 1/4 inch longer than the measurement made in Step 50. This will be used as a pocket stay to attach the side pocket to the side seam.

52. Place the pocket stay on an ironing board wrong side up, and turn up a 1/4-inch hem. Press, then baste the hem.

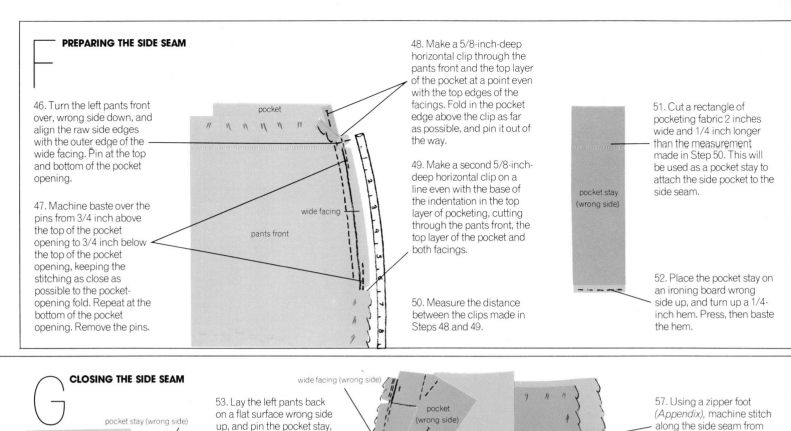

CLOSING THE SIDE SEAM

G

53. Lay the left pants back on a flat surface wrong side up, and pin the pocket stay, wrong side up, to it, aligning their raw side edges. The upper, unhemmed edge of the stay should be 1 1/4 inches below the waistline edge of the pants.

54. Baste and remove the pins.

55. Turn the left pants back wrong side down.

56. Pin the left pants front to it, aligning the side seam edges from the waist to the bottom edge. Baste and remove the pins.

57. Using a zipper foot (*Appendix*), machine stitch along the side seam from the waistline edge to 1 inch below the pocket opening.

58. Without breaking the threads, replace the zipper foot with a conventional presser foot, and continue to stitch the side seam to the bottom of the pants leg.

59. Remove the tailor tacks and basting from the side seam and the pocket stay. Remove the machine basting at the top and bottom of the pocket opening. Press open the seam.

60. At the waistline end of the side seam, tuck the pants-front seam allowance under the side pocket.

61. Tuck the seam allowance below the clip made in Step 49 under the side pocket.

62. Fold the pocket stay over the seam allowance, aligning its raw edge with the seam. Press.

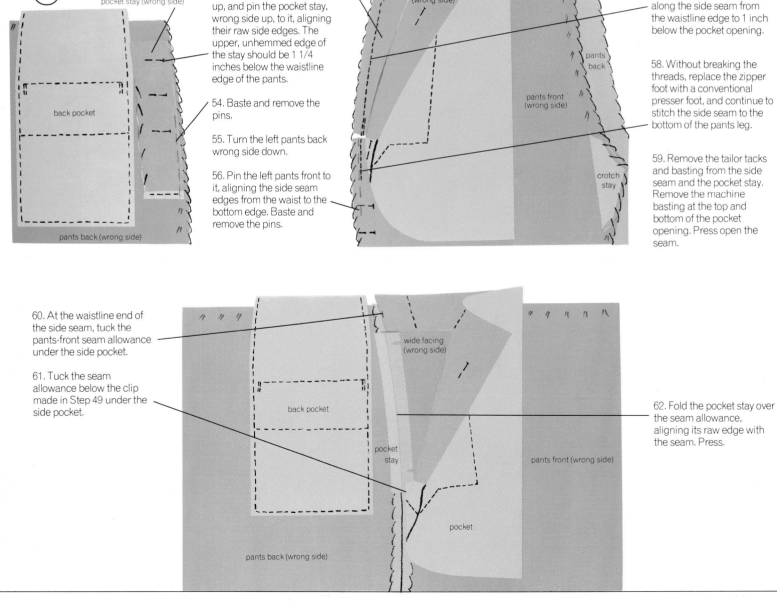

63. Unpin the top layer of the pocket and press flat. Fold the raw edge under so that it extends slightly beyond the fold of the pocket stay. Then pin the folded edge.

64. Baste and remove the pins.

65. Rethread your sewing machine with thread that matches the pocketing fabric, and machine stitch 1/4 inch inside the fold from the center fold of the pocket to the waistline edge, rolling the pocket seam slightly under.

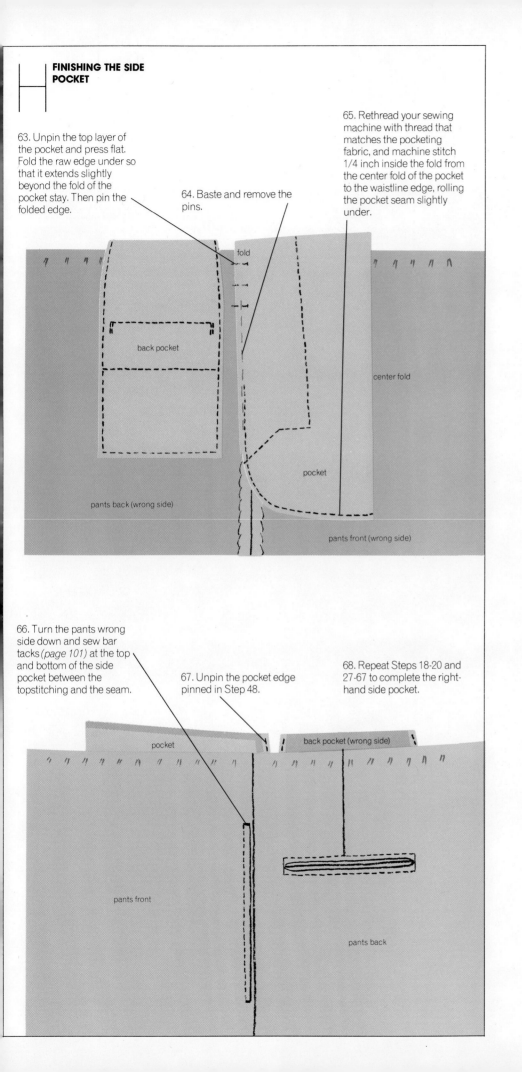

fold

back pocket

center fold

pocket

pants back (wrong side)

pants front (wrong side)

66. Turn the pants wrong side down and sew bar tacks (*page 101*) at the top and bottom of the side pocket between the topstitching and the seam.

67. Unpin the pocket edge pinned in Step 48.

68. Repeat Steps 18-20 and 27-67 to complete the right-hand side pocket.

pocket

back pocket (wrong side)

pants front

pants back

Hidden tricks about the waistline

The fly front and the waistband are fairly sophisticated bits of construction, skillfully designed to appear simple. The well-tailored fly is long enough to make the pants easy to put on and take off. Sewed in with multiple rows of stitches to keep it from ripping out, the zipper is concealed behind a generous fold of neatly pressed fabric. Men's pants traditionally close left side over right as shown here; and the demonstrations on the following pages detail the methods for attaching a zipper in this manner. For women's pants which generally close the other way, simply reverse the directions.

A trim fit at the waist is achieved by making the waistband of a single thickness of trouser material, reinforced with a tough, nonstretching interfacing. This assembly is shielded on the inside with a waistband facing and a trouser curtain, the latter a strip of pocketing fabric that conceals the interior stitchery and smooths it to the body's touch.

The number of belt loops (pattern companies often call them carriers) is to some extent a matter of personal preference. Instructions for attaching eight loops are given in the following pages.

THE RIGHT FLY PIECE

A CUTTING OUT THE FLY PIECES

1. To make the fly pattern piece, begin by placing the pants-front pattern piece on a flat surface, printed side up. Pin a sheet of stiff tracing paper over the fly area.

2. Draw a line 5/8 inch inside of—and parallel to —the center-front fold line, from the waist cutting line to a point 2 inches above the inseam stitching line. Make sure the lower portion of the line follows the curve of the fold line.

3. Starting at a point even with the top of the first line, draw a second line 2 3/4 inches outside of—and parallel to—the first line. End the line at the point where the first line starts to curve.

4. Connect the tops of the two lines by tracing over and extending the waist cutting line.

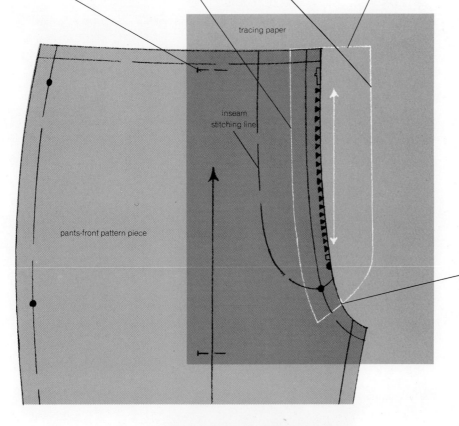

tracing paper

inseam stitching line

pants-front pattern piece

5. Then connect the bottoms of the lines with a gently curved line, as shown. Make a mark on the line at the fly cutting line.

6. Draw a grain-line arrow parallel to the long vertical lines and midway between them.

7. Remove the tracing paper, and cut out the fly pattern piece along the lines.

8. Fold a piece of pants fabric in half, wrong side out, along the lengthwise grain.

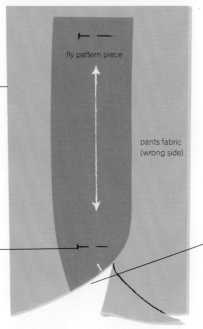

fly pattern piece

pants fabric (wrong side)

9. Place the fly pattern piece, marked side up, on the fabric so that the grain-line arrow is parallel to the fold. Pin.

10. Cut out the fly pieces by trimming around the edges of the pattern piece. The upper fabric piece is for the left fly; the lower piece for the right fly. Set aside the left piece for later use.

continued

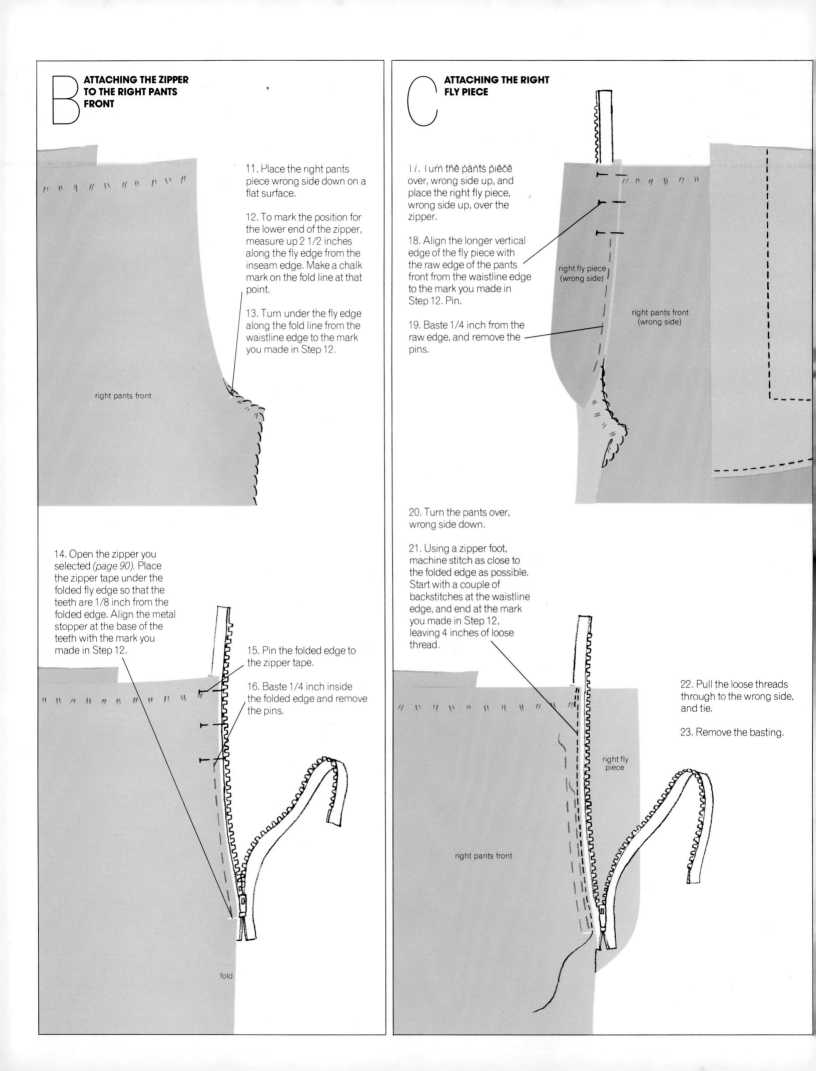

B ATTACHING THE ZIPPER TO THE RIGHT PANTS FRONT

11. Place the right pants piece wrong side down on a flat surface.

12. To mark the position for the lower end of the zipper, measure up 2 1/2 inches along the fly edge from the inseam edge. Make a chalk mark on the fold line at that point.

13. Turn under the fly edge along the fold line from the waistline edge to the mark you made in Step 12.

right pants front

14. Open the zipper you selected (page 90). Place the zipper tape under the folded fly edge so that the teeth are 1/8 inch from the folded edge. Align the metal stopper at the base of the teeth with the mark you made in Step 12.

15. Pin the folded edge to the zipper tape.

16. Baste 1/4 inch inside the folded edge and remove the pins.

fold

C ATTACHING THE RIGHT FLY PIECE

17. Turn the pants piece over, wrong side up, and place the right fly piece, wrong side up, over the zipper.

18. Align the longer vertical edge of the fly piece with the raw edge of the pants front from the waistline edge to the mark you made in Step 12. Pin.

19. Baste 1/4 inch from the raw edge, and remove the pins.

right fly piece (wrong side)

right pants front (wrong side)

20. Turn the pants over, wrong side down.

21. Using a zipper foot, machine stitch as close to the folded edge as possible. Start with a couple of backstitches at the waistline edge, and end at the mark you made in Step 12, leaving 4 inches of loose thread.

22. Pull the loose threads through to the wrong side, and tie.

23. Remove the basting.

right fly piece

right pants front

THE RIGHT WAISTBAND

A MAKING THE BELT LOOPS

1. To determine the width of the strips of fabric needed for the belt loops, decide how wide you want a finished belt loop to be —usually between 3/8 and 3/4 inches. Then multiply by two and add 1/2 inch for seam allowances.

2. To determine the length of the fabric strip, decide how wide you want the finished waistband to be —usually between 1 3/8 and 1 3/4 inches. Add 2 inches for seam allowances and for the loop to extend below the waistband. Then multiply by four for four belt loops.

3. To make belt loops for both sides of the pants—a total of eight belt loops—cut two strips of pants fabric to the dimensions determined in Steps 1 and 2. Make sure the long edges are parallel to the lengthwise grain.

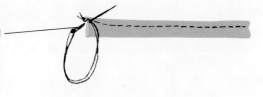

pants fabric (wrong side)

4. Fold one of the strips in half, crosswise, so that the wrong sides are out. Pin. Then baste 3/8 inch inside the long cut edges, and remove the pins.

5. Machine stitch along the cut edges. Begin at one corner and curve in; then sew 1/4-inch from the edges to the other end of the strip. Remove the basting.

6. Trim the seam allowances to 1/8 inch.

7. To turn the closed strip right side out, begin by threading a large-eyed needle with a double strand of sturdy thread knotted at the ends. Take two stitches at the end of the strip over the curved machine stitching.

8. Insert the eye end of the needle into the strip and work it through to the other end.

9. As you pull on the needle with one hand, work the strip right side out with the other hand. Remove the thread.

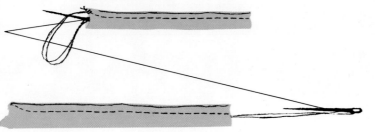

pants fabric

10. Press the strip flat so that the seam is centered between the folded edges.

11. Cut the strip into four belt loops of equal length. Repeat Steps 4-10 on the other strip.

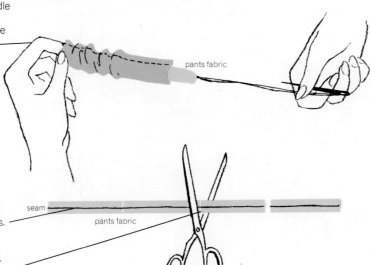

seam

pants fabric

continued

**POSITIONING
THE BELT LOOPS**

12. Place the right pants piece wrong side down. Along the waistline edge, measure in 2 inches from the center-back seam line and make a chalk mark.

13. Measure between the chalk mark and the side seam. Then mark the midpoint.

14. Measure between the side seam and the folded fly edge. Mark the midpoint.

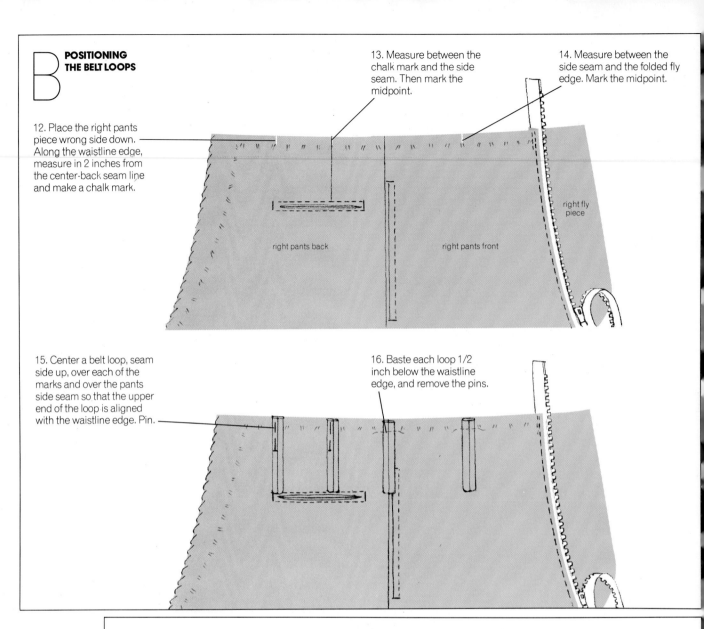

right pants back

right pants front

right fly piece

15. Center a belt loop, seam side up, over each of the marks and over the pants side seam so that the upper end of the loop is aligned with the waistline edge. Pin.

16. Baste each loop 1/2 inch below the waistline edge, and remove the pins.

C **MAKING THE RIGHT WAISTBAND**

17. To determine the width of the fabric piece needed for the waistband, add 1 1/4 inches for seam allowances to the finished waistband width you decided on in Step 2.

18. To determine the length of the waistband piece, measure the waistline edge of the right pants piece from the center-back edge to the outer edge of the attached fly piece.

19. Cut two waistband pieces from pants fabric, using the dimensions you determined in Steps 17 and 18. Make sure the long edges are parallel to the lengthwise grain.

20. Then cut two pieces of interfacing for the waistband. Make the length the same as the waistband pieces, but make the width 5/8 inch less. Again, be sure the long edges are parallel to the lengthwise grain.

21. Place one of the waistband pieces wrong side up. Then, place one of the interfacing pieces on the waistband piece so that the interfacing overlaps the waistband piece by 5/8 inch along one long edge. Pin.

22. Baste the pieces together. Remove the pins.

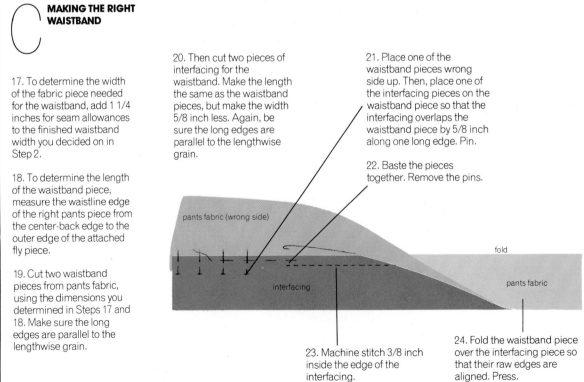

pants fabric (wrong side)

interfacing

fold

pants fabric

23. Machine stitch 3/8 inch inside the edge of the interfacing.

24. Fold the waistband piece over the interfacing piece so that their raw edges are aligned. Press.

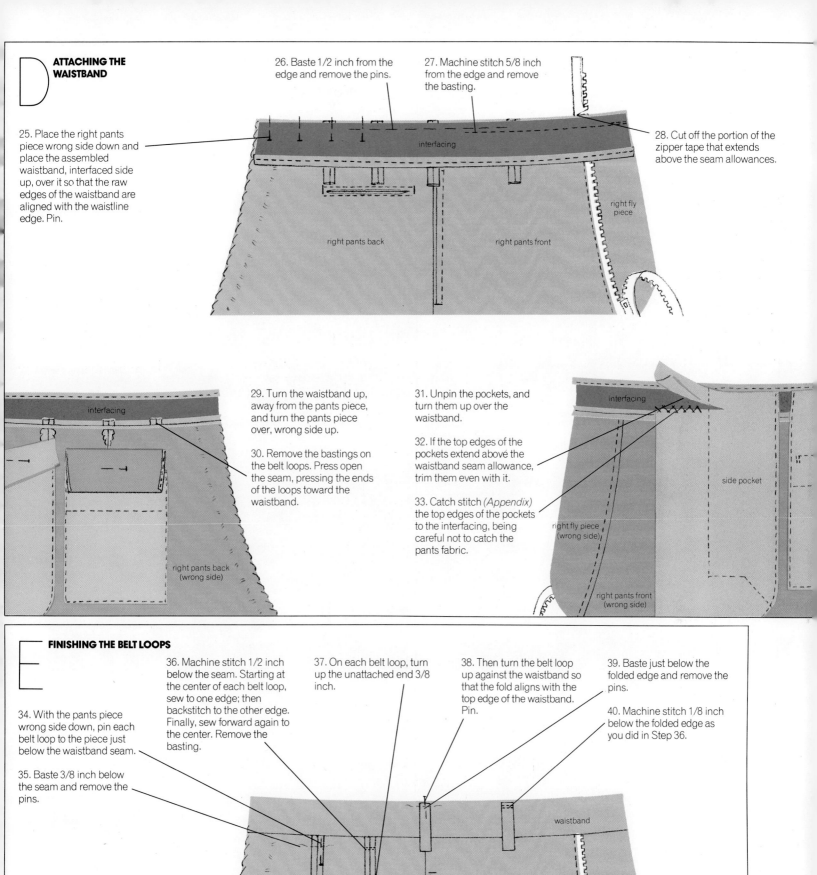

D ATTACHING THE WAISTBAND

26. Baste 1/2 inch from the edge and remove the pins.

27. Machine stitch 5/8 inch from the edge and remove the basting.

25. Place the right pants piece wrong side down and place the assembled waistband, interfaced side up, over it so that the raw edges of the waistband are aligned with the waistline edge. Pin.

28. Cut off the portion of the zipper tape that extends above the seam allowances.

interfacing

right fly piece

right pants back

right pants front

29. Turn the waistband up, away from the pants piece, and turn the pants piece over, wrong side up.

30. Remove the bastings on the belt loops. Press open the seam, pressing the ends of the loops toward the waistband.

31. Unpin the pockets, and turn them up over the waistband.

32. If the top edges of the pockets extend above the waistband seam allowance, trim them even with it.

33. Catch stitch (Appendix) the top edges of the pockets to the interfacing, being careful not to catch the pants fabric.

interfacing

interfacing

side pocket

right pants back (wrong side)

right fly piece (wrong side)

right pants front (wrong side)

E FINISHING THE BELT LOOPS

36. Machine stitch 1/2 inch below the seam. Starting at the center of each belt loop, sew to one edge; then backstitch to the other edge. Finally, sew forward again to the center. Remove the basting.

37. On each belt loop, turn up the unattached end 3/8 inch.

38. Then turn the belt loop up against the waistband so that the fold aligns with the top edge of the waistband. Pin.

39. Baste just below the folded edge and remove the pins.

34. With the pants piece wrong side down, pin each belt loop to the piece just below the waistband seam.

40. Machine stitch 1/8 inch below the folded edge as you did in Step 36.

35. Baste 3/8 inch below the seam and remove the pins.

waistband

right fly piece

right pants back

right pants front

THE RIGHT PANTS FACINGS

A MARKING AND CUTTING THE FLY FACING

1. Take a piece of pocketing fabric at least 16 inches by 16 inches, and place it wrong side up. Place the fly pattern piece, marked side up, on top of it so that the grain-line arrow is on the bias of the fabric *(Appendix)*. Pin.

2. Draw a line parallel to and 5/8 inch outside the straight part of the long vertical edge of the pattern piece. At the top of the pattern, extend the line by a distance equal to the width of the waistband. Then extend the line below the bottom of the pattern piece for about 3 inches.

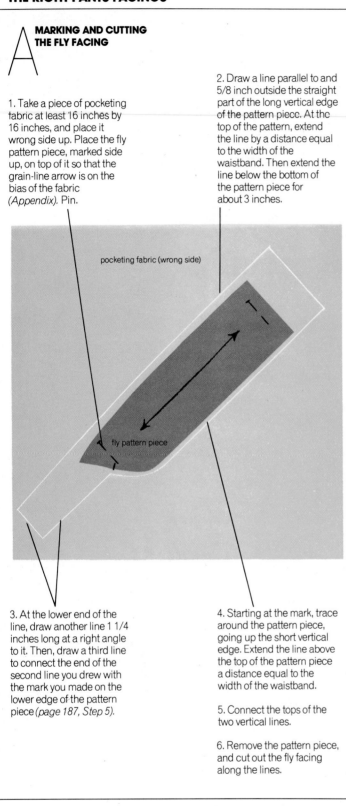

pocketing fabric (wrong side)

fly pattern piece

3. At the lower end of the line, draw another line 1 1/4 inches long at a right angle to it. Then, draw a third line to connect the end of the second line you drew with the mark you made on the lower edge of the pattern piece *(page 187, Step 5)*.

4. Starting at the mark, trace around the pattern piece, going up the short vertical edge. Extend the line above the top of the pattern piece a distance equal to the width of the waistband.

5. Connect the tops of the two vertical lines.

6. Remove the pattern piece, and cut out the fly facing along the lines.

B ATTACHING THE FLY FACING

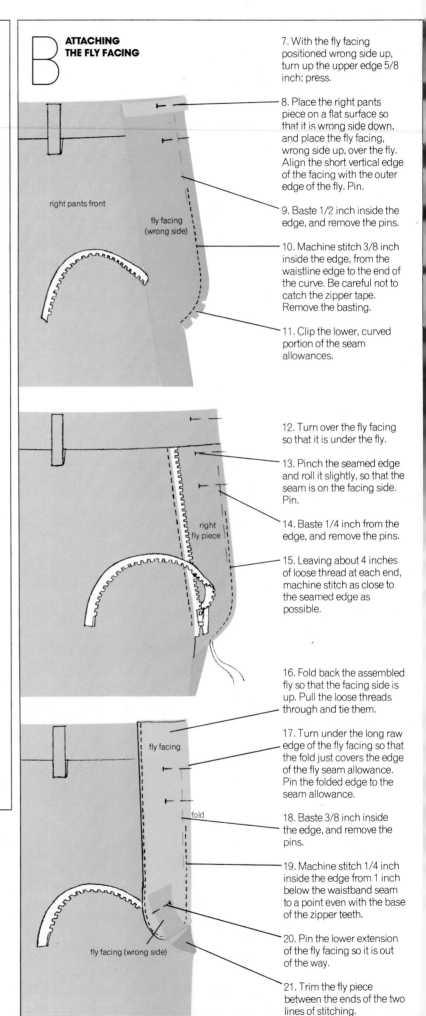

right pants front

fly facing (wrong side)

right fly piece

fly facing

fold

fly facing (wrong side)

7. With the fly facing positioned wrong side up, turn up the upper edge 5/8 inch; press.

8. Place the right pants piece on a flat surface so that it is wrong side down, and place the fly facing, wrong side up, over the fly. Align the short vertical edge of the facing with the outer edge of the fly. Pin.

9. Baste 1/2 inch inside the edge, and remove the pins.

10. Machine stitch 3/8 inch inside the edge, from the waistline edge to the end of the curve. Be careful not to catch the zipper tape. Remove the basting.

11. Clip the lower, curved portion of the seam allowances.

12. Turn over the fly facing so that it is under the fly.

13. Pinch the seamed edge and roll it slightly, so that the seam is on the facing side. Pin.

14. Baste 1/4 inch from the edge, and remove the pins.

15. Leaving about 4 inches of loose thread at each end, machine stitch as close to the seamed edge as possible.

16. Fold back the assembled fly so that the facing side is up. Pull the loose threads through and tie them.

17. Turn under the long raw edge of the fly facing so that the fold just covers the edge of the fly seam allowance. Pin the folded edge to the seam allowance.

18. Baste 3/8 inch inside the edge, and remove the pins.

19. Machine stitch 1/4 inch inside the edge from 1 inch below the waistband seam to a point even with the base of the zipper teeth.

20. Pin the lower extension of the fly facing so it is out of the way.

21. Trim the fly piece between the ends of the two lines of stitching.

C CUTTING AND ASSEMBLING THE WAISTBAND FACING

22. To determine the length of the waistband facing, measure the waistband on the right pants piece from the inner edge of the fly facing to the center-back edge. Then add 1/2 inch.

23. To determine the width of the waistband facing, measure the width of the finished waistband. Then add 1 1/4 inches for hem and seam allowances.

24. Cut two waistband facings from pocketing material, using the dimensions you determined in Steps 22 and 23. Make sure the long edges are parallel to the lengthwise grain.

25. From pocketing material cut two trouser curtains, which will be used to reinforce the lower edge of the facings. Make the length the same as that of the facings, but make the width 3 1/4 inches, so that the finished trouser curtain will measure 1 inch. Again, be sure the long edges are parallel to the lengthwise grain.

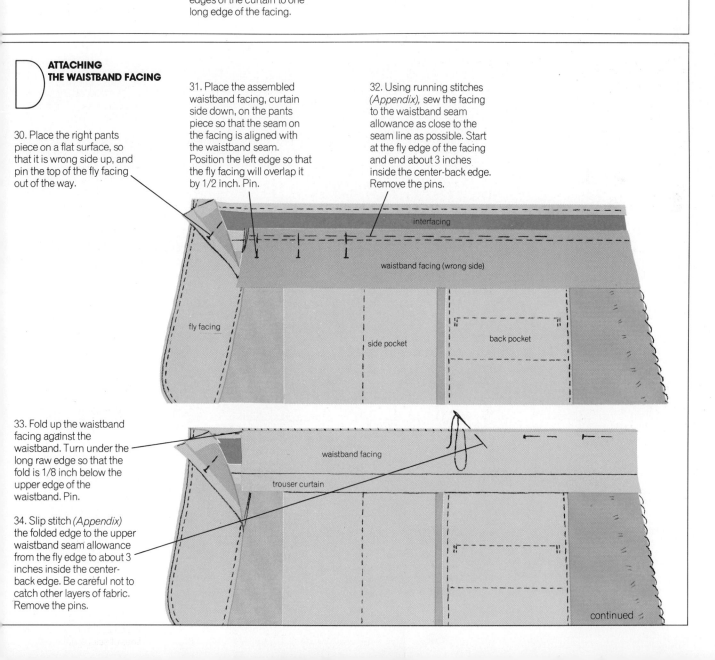

trouser curtain

waistband facing

26. Fold one of the trouser curtains in half lengthwise, wrong sides together, and press.

27. Place a waistband facing wrong side down, and position a trouser curtain over it. Pin the long raw edges of the curtain to one long edge of the facing.

28. Baste 1/2 inch from the edge and remove the pins.

29. Machine stitch 5/8 inch from the edge, and remove the basting.

D ATTACHING THE WAISTBAND FACING

30. Place the right pants piece on a flat surface, so that it is wrong side up, and pin the top of the fly facing out of the way.

31. Place the assembled waistband facing, curtain side down, on the pants piece so that the seam on the facing is aligned with the waistband seam. Position the left edge so that the fly facing will overlap it by 1/2 inch. Pin.

32. Using running stitches (Appendix), sew the facing to the waistband seam allowance as close to the seam line as possible. Start at the fly edge of the facing and end about 3 inches inside the center-back edge. Remove the pins.

interfacing

waistband facing (wrong side)

fly facing

side pocket

back pocket

33. Fold up the waistband facing against the waistband. Turn under the long raw edge so that the fold is 1/8 inch below the upper edge of the waistband. Pin.

waistband facing

trouser curtain

34. Slip stitch (Appendix) the folded edge to the upper waistband seam allowance from the fly edge to about 3 inches inside the center-back edge. Be careful not to catch other layers of fabric. Remove the pins.

continued

193

THE LEFT FLY PIECE AND WAISTBAND

A BACKING FOR THE LEFT FLY PIECE

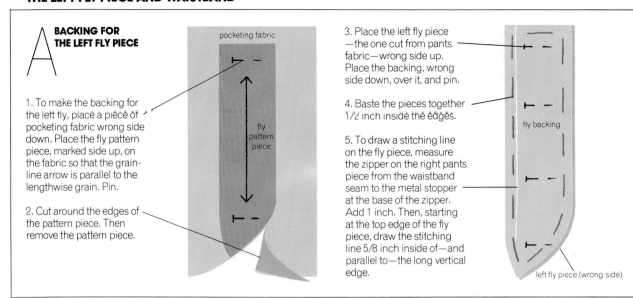

1. To make the backing for the left fly, place a piece of pocketing fabric wrong side down. Place the fly pattern piece, marked side up, on the fabric so that the grain-line arrow is parallel to the lengthwise grain. Pin.

2. Cut around the edges of the pattern piece. Then remove the pattern piece.

3. Place the left fly piece —the one cut from pants fabric—wrong side up. Place the backing, wrong side down, over it, and pin.

4. Baste the pieces together 1/2 inch inside the edges.

5. To draw a stitching line on the fly piece, measure the zipper on the right pants piece from the waistband seam to the metal stopper at the base of the zipper. Add 1 inch. Then, starting at the top edge of the fly piece, draw the stitching line 5/8 inch inside of—and parallel to—the long vertical edge.

B ATTACHING THE FLY PIECE

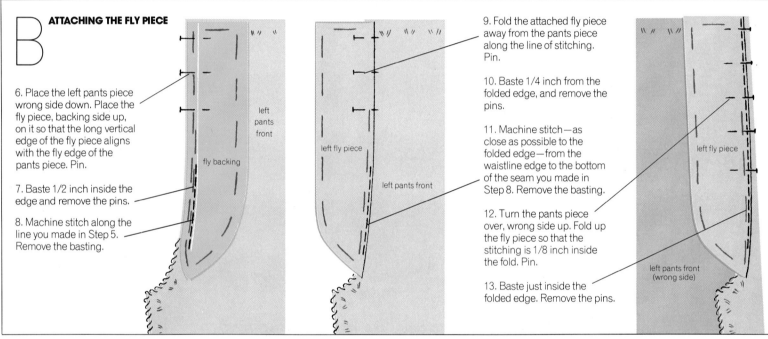

6. Place the left pants piece wrong side down. Place the fly piece, backing side up, on it so that the long vertical edge of the fly piece aligns with the fly edge of the pants piece. Pin.

7. Baste 1/2 inch inside the edge and remove the pins.

8. Machine stitch along the line you made in Step 5. Remove the basting.

9. Fold the attached fly piece away from the pants piece along the line of stitching. Pin.

10. Baste 1/4 inch from the folded edge, and remove the pins.

11. Machine stitch—as close as possible to the folded edge—from the waistline edge to the bottom of the seam you made in Step 8. Remove the basting.

12. Turn the pants piece over, wrong side up. Fold up the fly piece so that the stitching is 1/8 inch inside the fold. Pin.

13. Baste just inside the folded edge. Remove the pins.

C ATTACHING THE ZIPPER

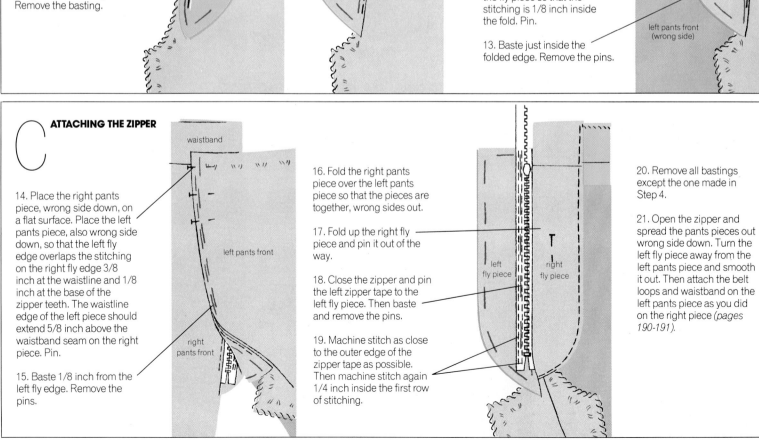

14. Place the right pants piece, wrong side down, on a flat surface. Place the left pants piece, also wrong side down, so that the left fly edge overlaps the stitching on the right fly edge 3/8 inch at the waistline and 1/8 inch at the base of the zipper teeth. The waistline edge of the left piece should extend 5/8 inch above the waistband seam on the right piece. Pin.

15. Baste 1/8 inch from the left fly edge. Remove the pins.

16. Fold the right pants piece over the left pants piece so that the pieces are together, wrong sides out.

17. Fold up the right fly piece and pin it out of the way.

18. Close the zipper and pin the left zipper tape to the left fly piece. Then baste and remove the pins.

19. Machine stitch as close to the outer edge of the zipper tape as possible. Then machine stitch again 1/4 inch inside the first row of stitching.

20. Remove all bastings except the one made in Step 4.

21. Open the zipper and spread the pants pieces out wrong side down. Turn the left fly piece away from the left pants piece and smooth it out. Then attach the belt loops and waistband on the left pants piece as you did on the right piece (pages 190-191).

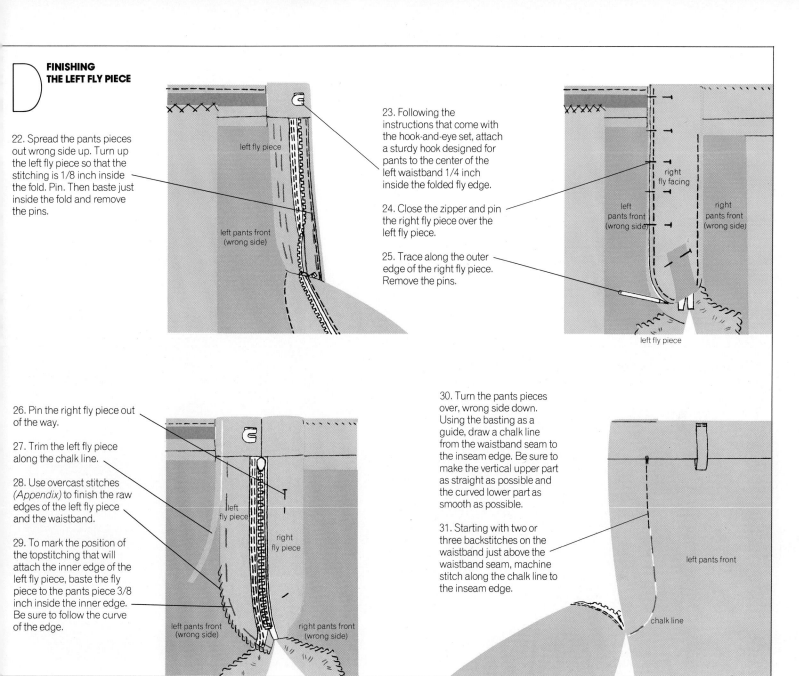

D ▷ FINISHING THE LEFT FLY PIECE

22. Spread the pants pieces out wrong side up. Turn up the left fly piece so that the stitching is 1/8 inch inside the fold. Pin. Then baste just inside the fold and remove the pins.

left fly piece

left pants front (wrong side)

23. Following the instructions that come with the hook-and-eye set, attach a sturdy hook designed for pants to the center of the left waistband 1/4 inch inside the folded fly edge.

24. Close the zipper and pin the right fly piece over the left fly piece.

25. Trace along the outer edge of the right fly piece. Remove the pins.

right fly facing

left pants front (wrong side)

right pants front (wrong side)

left fly piece

26. Pin the right fly piece out of the way.

27. Trim the left fly piece along the chalk line.

28. Use overcast stitches (*Appendix*) to finish the raw edges of the left fly piece and the waistband.

29. To mark the position of the topstitching that will attach the inner edge of the left fly piece, baste the fly piece to the pants piece 3/8 inch inside the inner edge. Be sure to follow the curve of the edge.

left fly piece

right fly piece

left pants front (wrong side)

right pants front (wrong side)

30. Turn the pants pieces over, wrong side down. Using the basting as a guide, draw a chalk line from the waistband seam to the inseam edge. Be sure to make the vertical upper part as straight as possible and the curved lower part as smooth as possible.

31. Starting with two or three backstitches on the waistband just above the waistband seam, machine stitch along the chalk line to the inseam edge.

left pants front

chalk line

E ▷ ATTACHING THE WAISTBAND FACING

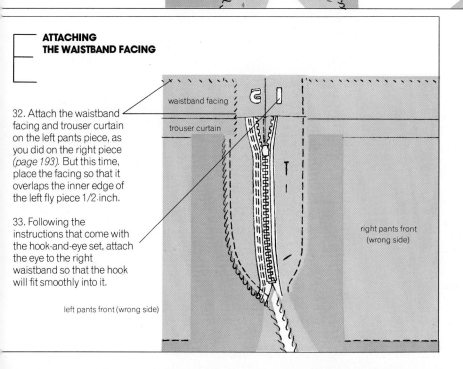

32. Attach the waistband facing and trouser curtain on the left pants piece, as you did on the right piece (*page 193*). But this time, place the facing so that it overlaps the inner edge of the left fly piece 1/2 inch.

33. Following the instructions that come with the hook-and-eye set, attach the eye to the right waistband so that the hook will fit smoothly into it.

waistband facing

trouser curtain

right pants front (wrong side)

left pants front (wrong side)

FINISHING THE PANTS LEGS

A CLOSING THE INSEAMS

1. Fold the left pants piece in half, wrong side out. Align the inseam stitching lines. Pin.

2. Baste just outside the stitching line, and remove the pins.

3. Machine stitch along the stitching line from the hem to the crotch. Remove the basting.

4. Press open the seam.

5. Close the inseam on the right pants piece by repeating Steps 1-4.

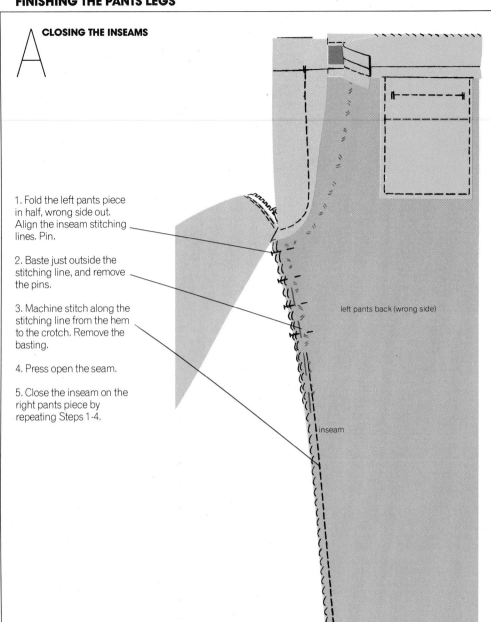

left pants back (wrong side)

inseam

B PRESSING IN THE CREASES

6. Turn the pants right side out.

7. Arrange the pants on an ironing board so the inseam of one of the legs is facing you. Match the inseam with the side seam at the crotch and hem edges.

8. Using a pressing cloth, steam press in the back crease. If you are making men's pants, pull the calf area outward, and press in a slight curve so that the pants will hang gracefully over the calf.

9. Now press in the front crease. On men's pants, shrink the ripples caused by pulling the calf area of the back crease. Repeat on the other leg.

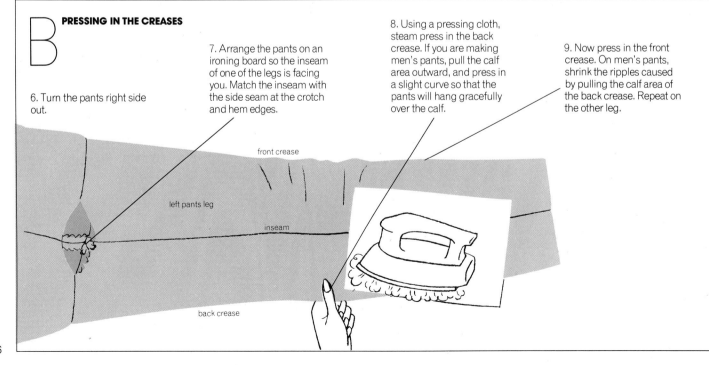

front crease

left pants leg

inseam

back crease

FINISHING THE UPPER PART OF THE PANTS

A CLOSING THE CROTCH SEAM

1. On both the right and left legs, make a 1/2-inch clip in the crotch seam allowance at the base of the fly piece.

2. With the upper part of the pants turned wrong side out as shown, align the curved crotch seam lines. Match and pin at the inseams and at the waistband edge, making sure to turn the waistband facings out of the way. Then finish pinning the crotch seam.

3. Baste just outside the seam line and remove the pins.

4. To check the fit, try on the pants. Make any adjustments required, following the instructions on pages 78-79.

5. Machine stitch along the seam line and remove the basting.

6. Press open the seam.

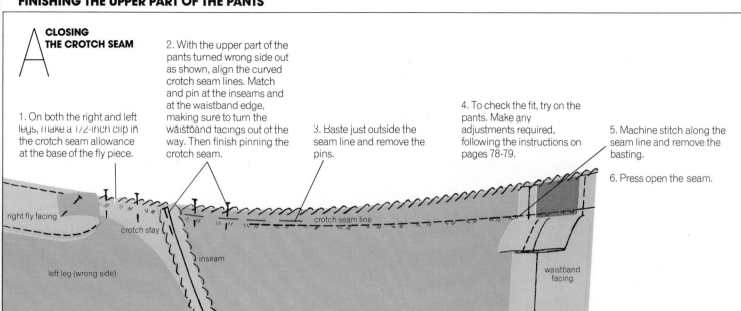

right fly facing

crotch stay

inseam

left leg (wrong side)

crotch seam line

waistband facing

B FINISHING THE FLY AND WAISTBAND

7. Slip stitch (Appendix) the upper and inner edges of the fly facing to the trouser curtain and waistband facing.

8. Unpin the lower extension of the fly facing and smooth it over the crotch seam allowances. If it extends more than 3/4 inch beyond the inseam, trim it.

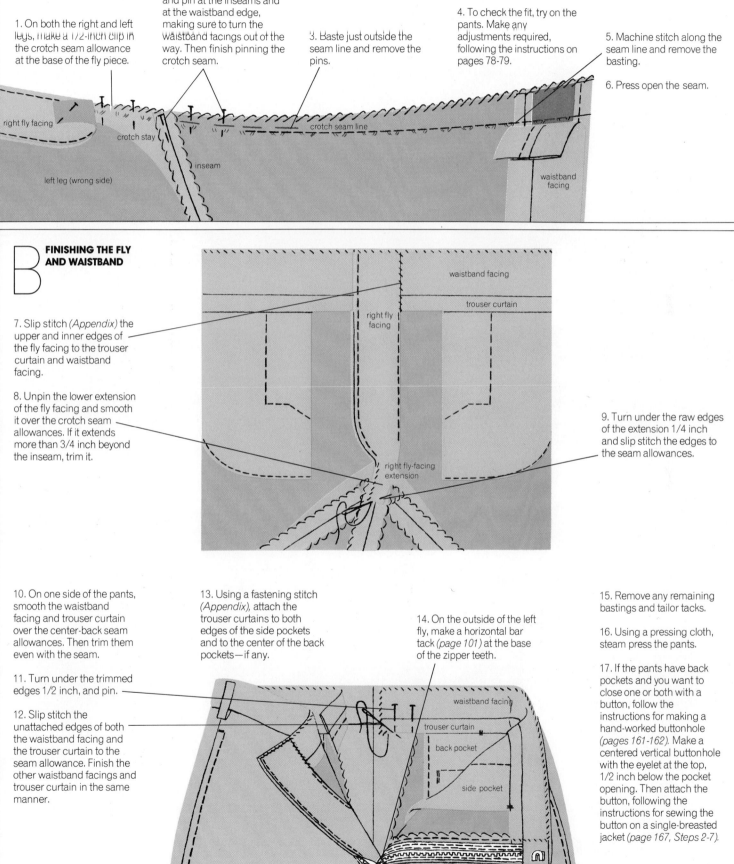

waistband facing

trouser curtain

right fly facing

right fly-facing extension

9. Turn under the raw edges of the extension 1/4 inch and slip stitch the edges to the seam allowances.

10. On one side of the pants, smooth the waistband facing and trouser curtain over the center-back seam allowances. Then trim them even with the seam.

11. Turn under the trimmed edges 1/2 inch, and pin.

12. Slip stitch the unattached edges of both the waistband facing and the trouser curtain to the seam allowance. Finish the other waistband facings and trouser curtain in the same manner.

13. Using a fastening stitch (Appendix), attach the trouser curtains to both edges of the side pockets and to the center of the back pockets—if any.

14. On the outside of the left fly, make a horizontal bar tack (page 101) at the base of the zipper teeth.

15. Remove any remaining bastings and tailor tacks.

16. Using a pressing cloth, steam press the pants.

17. If the pants have back pockets and you want to close one or both with a button, follow the instructions for making a hand-worked buttonhole (pages 161-162). Make a centered vertical buttonhole with the eyelet at the top, 1/2 inch below the pocket opening. Then attach the button, following the instructions for sewing the button on a single-breasted jacket (page 167, Steps 2-7).

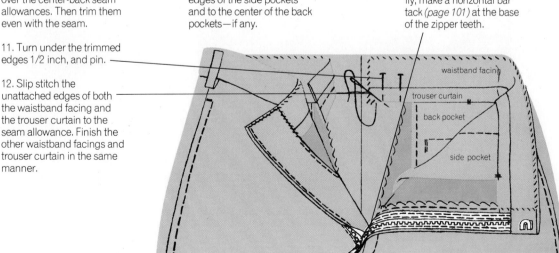

waistband facing

trouser curtain

back pocket

side pocket

The pants maker's bottom line

In pants—as in business—it is the bottom line that counts. Whether that pants line is cuffed or cuffless, it must fall in precisely the right place. If too low, it may get stepped upon; too high, it will expose a gauche ring of sock. At its most stylish length, the front of the pants leg should just touch the shoe's vamp (the upper surface of the toe) and at the rear it should cover the joint where the heel meets the shoe. For normal shoes this means the rear measurement is 1/2 inch longer than the front.

In making cuffs, be sure that the inseam and side seam of the turned-up cuff meet those of the pants leg precisely. And bear in mind that the final tailored touch, applying heel stays, is not intended merely for elegance. They protect the trouser material from abrasion at its most vulnerable spot, thus adding greatly to the life of the pants.

MAKING CUFFS

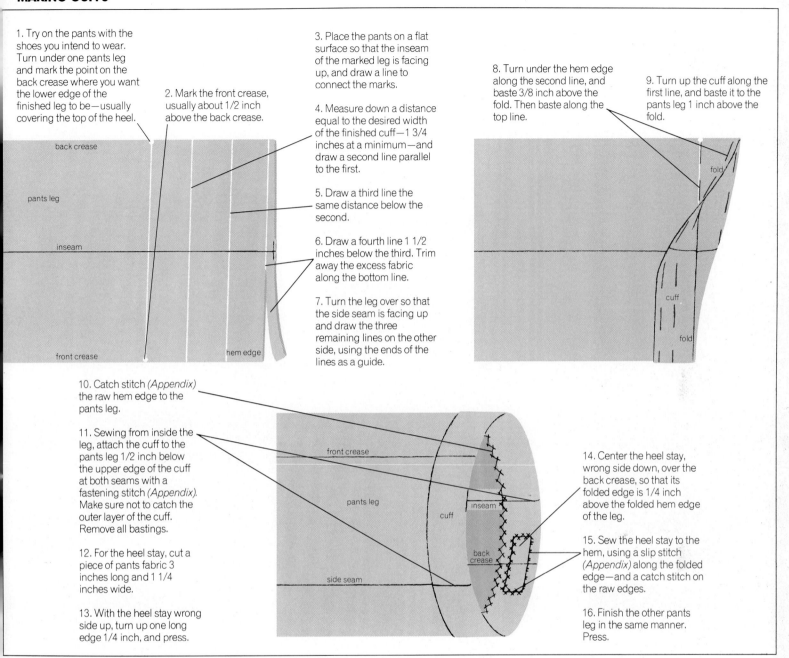

1. Try on the pants with the shoes you intend to wear. Turn under one pants leg and mark the point on the back crease where you want the lower edge of the finished leg to be—usually covering the top of the heel.

2. Mark the front crease, usually about 1/2 inch above the back crease.

3. Place the pants on a flat surface so that the inseam of the marked leg is facing up, and draw a line to connect the marks.

4. Measure down a distance equal to the desired width of the finished cuff—1 3/4 inches at a minimum—and draw a second line parallel to the first.

5. Draw a third line the same distance below the second.

6. Draw a fourth line 1 1/2 inches below the third. Trim away the excess fabric along the bottom line.

7. Turn the leg over so that the side seam is facing up and draw the three remaining lines on the other side, using the ends of the lines as a guide.

8. Turn under the hem edge along the second line, and baste 3/8 inch above the fold. Then baste along the top line.

9. Turn up the cuff along the first line, and baste it to the pants leg 1 inch above the fold.

10. Catch stitch (Appendix) the raw hem edge to the pants leg.

11. Sewing from inside the leg, attach the cuff to the pants leg 1/2 inch below the upper edge of the cuff at both seams with a fastening stitch (Appendix). Make sure not to catch the outer layer of the cuff. Remove all bastings.

12. For the heel stay, cut a piece of pants fabric 3 inches long and 1 1/4 inches wide.

13. With the heel stay wrong side up, turn up one long edge 1/4 inch, and press.

14. Center the heel stay, wrong side down, over the back crease, so that its folded edge is 1/4 inch above the folded hem edge of the leg.

15. Sew the heel stay to the hem, using a slip stitch (Appendix) along the folded edge—and a catch stitch on the raw edges.

16. Finish the other pants leg in the same manner. Press.

HEMMING CUFFLESS PANTS

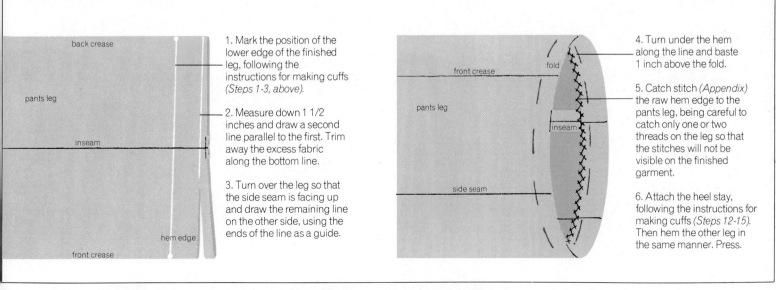

1. Mark the position of the lower edge of the finished leg, following the instructions for making cuffs (Steps 1-3, above).

2. Measure down 1 1/2 inches and draw a second line parallel to the first. Trim away the excess fabric along the bottom line.

3. Turn over the leg so that the side seam is facing up and draw the remaining line on the other side, using the ends of the line as a guide.

4. Turn under the hem along the line and baste 1 inch above the fold.

5. Catch stitch (Appendix) the raw hem edge to the pants leg, being careful to catch only one or two threads on the leg so that the stitches will not be visible on the finished garment.

6. Attach the heel stay, following the instructions for making cuffs (Steps 12-15). Then hem the other leg in the same manner. Press.

GLOSSARY

BASTE: To stitch pieces of fabric together temporarily, or to indicate pattern markings on both sides of a piece of fabric.

BEATER: See TAILOR'S CLAPPER.

BIAS: A line running diagonal to the threads in a woven fabric. A 45° bias is called a true bias.

BODKIN: See TAILOR'S BODKIN.

CANVAS: A tailoring term used to describe a completed interfacing assembly made of several layers of different fabric. See also WOOL INTERFACING.

CLAPPER: See TAILOR'S CLAPPER.

CLEAR FINISH: See HARD FINISH.

CLIP: A small straight cut made into a seam allowance, often up to the line of stitching, to help the seam lie flat around curves and at corners.

COLLAR INTERFACING: Stiff, firmly woven linen fabric that is sewed between the collar surface and the undercollar to help give shape to the collar.

COVER CLOTH: A loosely woven fabric (such as cotton flannel) with a slightly fuzzy surface, sewed over haircloth to prevent the sharp ends of the horsehair from scratching the wearer.

DART: A stitched fabric fold, tapering to a point at one or both ends, used to shape fabric around curves.

DRESSMAKER'S CARBON: A marking paper, available in a range of colors, used to transfer pattern markings to fabric.

DRILL CLOTH: Durable linen or cotton twilled fabric of varying weights, commonly used for work clothes.

EASE: An even distribution of fullness in fabric, created without perceptible gathers or tucks, that enables one section of a garment to be smoothly joined to another slightly smaller section.

FACING: A piece of fabric—usually cut from the same cloth as the garment—that is sewed along the raw edge of an opening such as the neckline and then turned to the inside to give the edge a smooth finish.

FINDINGS: Materials such as padding and interfacings, used to reinforce and structure a garment.

FOUNDATION CANVAS: See WOOL INTERFACING.

FRENCH TACK: A chain of thread that connects the hem of a lining to the garment hem.

GIMP: Heavy cord made of silk, cotton or wool strands with a metal wire core, used to reinforce the edges of hand-worked buttonholes.

GORGE LINE: The line made by a diagonal seam joining the end of the collar to the top of the lapel.

GRADING: The act of trimming each seam allowance within a multilayer seam (one containing the fabric, facing, interfacing, etc.) to a different width so as to reduce bulk and make the seam lie flat.

GRAIN: The direction of threads in a woven fabric. The warp—threads running from one cut end of the material to the other—forms the lengthwise grain. The woof, or weft—threads running across the lengthwise grain from one finished edge to the other—forms the crosswise grain.

HAIR CANVAS: See WOOL INTERFACING.

HAIRCLOTH: A wiry, extraresilient interfacing fabric made from a mixture of strong cotton fibers and tough horsehair. It is sewed over the wool interfacing to reinforce the chest and shoulder areas of a man's jacket.

HAM: See TAILOR'S HAM.

HARD FINISH (also called clear finish): The surface of a fabric that has no nap. The fabric may be naturally smooth and flat, or it may have had a nap that was sheared off. In both cases, the weave of the fabric is clearly visible. Most hard-finished fabrics are woven from worsted yarns.

INTERFACING: A fabric sewed between two layers of garment fabric to stiffen, strengthen and support parts of the garment. See also HAIRCLOTH; WIGAN; WOOL INTERFACING.

LAPELS: The portions of facings—turned to the outside of a garment—that run down the sides of the front opening from the end of the collar to the top button.

LINING: A fabric, usually lightweight, covering the inside of part or all of a garment.

MELTON CLOTH: A durable woolen that is used as undercollar fabric in most men's jackets to give shape to the collar.

MUSLIN: An inexpensive, plain-woven cotton fabric used for making prototypes of garments (called muslins) as an aid to styling and fitting.

NAP: A fabric's short surface fibers that have been drawn out and brushed in one direction—such as on velvet or corduroy.

NOTCH: A V- or diamond-shaped marking made on the edge of a garment piece as an alignment guide; intended to be matched with a similar notch or group of notches on another piece. Also a triangular cut into the seam allowance of a curved seam to help it lie flat. In a jacket, the V-shaped space between the end of the collar and the top of the lapel.

NOTIONS: Items such as buttons, hooks and zippers that are required to finish a garment.

PIPING: In tailoring, a narrowly folded strip of garment fabric, generally used to finish the top and bottom edges of a pocket opening.

PIVOT: A technique of machine sewing for making angular corners. The sewer stops the machine with the needle down at the apex of a corner, raises the presser foot, pivots the fabric and then lowers the presser foot before continuing to stitch again.

PLAIN WEAVE: A weave in which the yarns are interlaced in a simple checkerboard fashion. Plain weave is one of the two basic weaves used in tailored fabrics (the other is twill weave).

POCKETING FABRIC: Tightly woven twilled cotton fabric, usually with a soft, satiny finish. Pocketing fabric is available in different weights and is used also to make facings and reinforcements. See also SILESIA.

POINT PRESSER (also called a seam or tailor's board): A narrow hardwood board mounted on its side and shaped into a fine point at one end; used for pressing open small seams in hard-to-reach places, and for pressing open regular seams on hard fabrics.

POUNDING BLOCK: See TAILOR'S CLAPPER.

PRESHRINK: The process of treating fabric to shrink it to an irreducible size before cutting. Washable fabric can be preshrunk simply by immersing it in water and pressing it when almost dry. Nonwashable fabric should be preshrunk by a dry cleaner.

PRESS MITT: A padded, thumbless mitten used to press small curved areas that do not fit over a tailor's ham or a regular ironing board. One side of the mitt should be covered with cotton drill cloth, the other with soft wool.

PRESSER FOOT: The part of a sewing machine that holds down fabric while it is being advanced under the needle. An all-purpose, or general purpose, foot has two prongs of equal length and is used for most stitching. A straight-stitch foot has one long and one short prong and can be used for straight stitching and stitching over fabrics of varying thicknesses. A zipper foot has only one prong and is used to stitch zippers and cording.

PRESSING CLOTH: A piece of fabric, preferably cotton drill cloth, that is placed between the iron and the garment when pressing.

REINFORCE: To strengthen a seam with additional stitches, or to add an extra layer of fabric to a stress area.

ROLL: To manipulate fabric between the fingers, usually along a seam line, in order to bring the seam out to the edge—or beyond the edge to the wrong side—of the garment.

ROLL LINE: The pattern marking along which the collar and lapel are turned back.

SEAM: The joint between two or more pieces of fabric, or the line of stitching that makes a fold in a single fabric piece, e.g., a dart.

SEAM ALLOWANCE: The extra fabric—usually 5/8 inch—that extends outside a seam line.

SEAM BOARD: See POINT PRESSER.

SELVAGE: The lengthwise finished edge in woven fabric.

SHANK: The link of threads between a button and the fabric to which it is sewed.

SHOULDER PADS: Triangular pads—made of lambswool fleece or cotton batting covered with muslin or cotton wadding—that are used to shape and build up the shoulders of a jacket.

SILESIA: A pure cotton twill fabric used as pocketing material in fine tailored garments.

SLEEVE BOARD: A small ironing board used for pressing garment areas (such as sleeves) that will not fit over a regular ironing board.

SLEEVE HEADS: Strips of cotton wadding or lambswool fleece placed around the tops of sleeves to create a smooth line and to support the roll at the sleeve cap.

SLIDE FASTENER: See ZIPPER.

SOFT FINISH: A fuzzy nap on the surface of a fabric. The nap may be natural, as on woolens such as Harris tweed; or it may be created artificially on a smooth fabric like flannel, by brushing the surface of the fabric with steel combs.

STAY: An extra piece of fabric sewed into a garment to reinforce a point of possible wear, such as a crotch, heel or pants pocket.

STAY STITCH: A line of regular machine stitches, sewed along the seam line of a garment piece before the seam is stitched. Stay stitching prevents curved edges from stretching, and acts as a guide for folding an edge accurately.

STAY TAPE: See TWILL TAPE.

STRIKER: See TAILOR'S CLAPPER.

TACK: Several stitches made in the same place to reinforce a point of strain, hold garment parts permanently in position or finish the ends of pockets, pleats and buttonholes securely. Also a synonym for a quick, temporary "stitch" in certain instances. See FRENCH TACK and TAILOR TACKS.

TAILOR TACKS: Hand stitches used for marking pattern seam lines and symbols on fabrics that cannot be easily marked or that might be damaged by other methods.

TAILOR'S BOARD: See POINT PRESSER.

TAILOR'S BODKIN: A slender, 4-inch-long ivory stick, pointed at one end and rounded at the other, used to pull out basting threads and to round out the eyelets of hand-worked buttonholes.

TAILOR'S CHALK: Flat squares made of wax, stone or clay, used to transfer pattern markings or adjustments onto fabric.

TAILOR'S CLAPPER (also called beater, striker or pounding block): An oblong or rectangular piece of hardwood which is wielded like a paddle to flatten parts of a garment, typically the edges of collars, hems and lapels, trouser creases and pleats or to smooth and reduce the bulk of seams.

TAILOR'S HAM: A firm, ham-shaped cushion with built-in curves that conform to various contours of the body; used for pressing areas that require shaping. One half of a ham is covered with cotton drill cloth for general pressing, the other half with soft wool—which is used when pressing woolen fabric to prevent shine.

TAILOR'S SLEEVE CUSHION: A long, flat pad with a sleevelike silhouette; inserted into a completed sleeve when pressing to prevent wrinkling the underside or forming undesirable creases.

TAILOR'S THIMBLE: An especially sturdy metal thimble that is open at the top.

TOPSTITCHING: A line of machine stitching on the visible side of the garment parallel to a seam.

TRACING WHEEL: A small wheel attached to a handle, used with dressmaker's carbon paper to transfer pattern markings to fabric. Tracing wheels for most fabrics have serrated edges to keep the wheel from slipping off line; a plain-edged wheel should be used for knit fabrics to prevent snagging.

TRIM: To cut away excess fabric in a seam allowance after a seam has been stitched.

TROUSER CURTAIN: A strip of soft, durable fabric that extends below the waistband of trousers to keep the waist area from stretching, hold pleats in place and conceal interior stitching.

TWILL TAPE (also called stay tape): A thin, extra-strong tape of twilled linen or cotton fabric that is sewed along the lapel edges and roll line of a jacket as reinforcement, and to prevent stretching.

TWILL WEAVE: A weave in which the yarns interlace in a steplike formation to create a diagonal rib on the surface of the fabric. The rib may slant to the right or to the left, or it may zigzag in alternating directions, as in herringbone twill (sometimes called chevron or broken twill).

UNDERCOLLAR FABRIC: The fabric that is sewed to the collar interfacing to form the underside of the collar. In women's clothes it is usually cut from the same cloth as the garment. In men's jackets it is generally made from melton cloth. See also MELTON CLOTH.

UNDERLINING: A tightly woven fabric cut in the shapes of the main pieces of a garment and attached to these pieces before the garment is sewed together. Used only for women's garments to stabilize shape in stretchy woven fabrics and to conceal construction details like seam allowances in lightweight woven fabrics.

VENT: A slit in the skirt of a tailored jacket which keeps the hem line from binding when the wearer bends or reaches into a pants pocket.

WAISTBAND INTERFACING: A strip of strong, canvas-like fabric used for reinforcement.

WARP: See GRAIN.

WEFT: See GRAIN.

WELT POCKET: An interior pocket that opens to the outside, finished with a horizontal band of garment fabric that covers the opening.

WIGAN: A loosely woven, durable interfacing fabric, used to reinforce sleeve hems.

WOOF: See GRAIN.

WOOL INTERFACING (also called hair or foundation canvas): A strong, highly resilient fabric made of cotton, wool and/or goat hair. Used on a jacket to help shape and support the fabric.

WOOLEN: Fabric made from short, uncombed fibers of wool that is characteristically soft to the touch and often finished with a nap.

ZIPPER: A mechanical fastener consisting of two tapes holding parallel lines of teeth or coils that can be interlocked by a sliding bracket.

ZIPPER FOOT: See PRESSER FOOT.

BASIC STITCHES

The diagrams below and opposite indicate how to make the elementary hand stitches referred to in this volume.

THE FASTENING STITCH

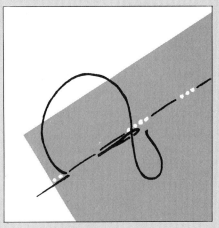

To end a row with a fastening stitch, insert the needle back 1/4 inch and bring it out at the point at which the thread last emerged. Make another stitch through these same points for extra firmness. To begin a row with a fastening stitch, leave a 4 inch loose end and make the initial stitch the same way as an ending stitch.

THE RUNNING STITCH

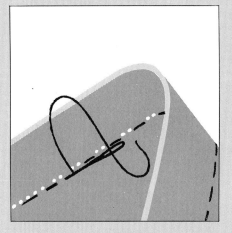

Insert the needle, with knotted thread, from the wrong side of the fabric and weave the needle in and out of the fabric several times in 1/8-inch, evenly spaced stitches. Pull the thread through. Continue across, making several stitches at a time, and end with a fastening stitch. When basting, make longer stitches, evenly spaced.

THE CATCH STITCH

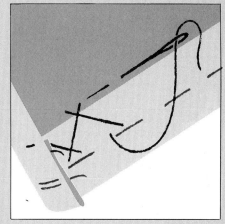

Working from left to right, anchor the first stitch with a knot inside the hem 1/4 inch down from the edge. Point the needle to the left and pick up one or two threads on the garment directly above the hem, then pull the thread through. Take a small stitch in the hem only (not in the garment), 1/4 inch down from the edge and 1/4 inch to the right of the previous stitch. End with a fastening stitch.

THE SLIP STITCH

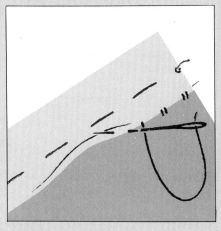

Fold under the hem edge and anchor the first stitch with a knot inside the fold. Point the needle to the left. Pick up one or two threads of the garment fabric close to the hem edge, directly below the first stitch, and slide the needle horizontally through the folded edge of the hem 1/8 inch to the left of the previous stitch. End with a fastening stitch.

THE HEMMING STITCH

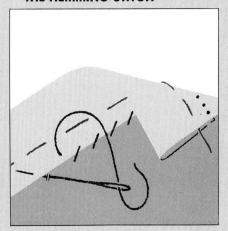

Anchor the first stitch with a knot inside the hem; then pointing the needle up and to the left, pick up one or two threads of the garment fabric close to the hem. Push the needle up through the hem 1/8 inch above the edge; pull the thread through. Continue picking up one or two threads and making 1/8-inch stitches in the hem at intervals of 1/4 inch. End with a fastening stitch.

THE OVERCAST STITCH

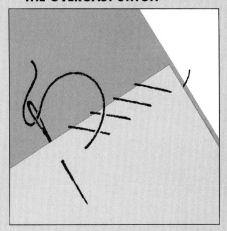

Draw the needle, with knotted thread, through from the wrong side of the fabric 1/8 to 1/4 inch down from the top edge. With the thread to the right, insert the needle under the fabric from the wrong side 1/8 to 1/4 inch to the left of the first stitch. Continue to make evenly spaced stitches over the fabric edge and end with a fastening stitch.

THE BACKSTITCH

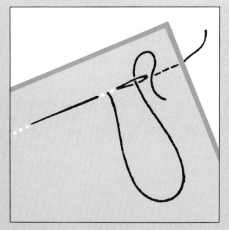

Bring the needle up from the bottom layer of fabric and pull it through, leaving a 1-inch-long loose end. Insert the needle 1/8 inch to the right of where the thread emerged and bring it out 1/8 inch to the left of the thread. Continue inserting the needle 1/8 inch to the right, and bringing it out 1/8 inch to the left of the point where the thread last emerged. End with a fastening stitch on the bottom layer of fabric.

THE DIAGONAL BASTING STITCH

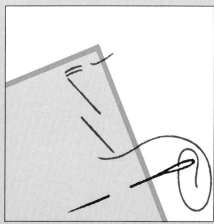

Anchor the basting with a fastening stitch *(opposite)* through all fabric layers. Keeping the thread to the right of the needle, make a 3/8-inch stitch from right to left, 1 inch directly below the fastening stitch. Continue making diagonal stitches, ending with a backstitch if the basting is to be left in, or a 4-inch-long loose end if the basting is to be removed.

THE BLIND HEMMING STITCH

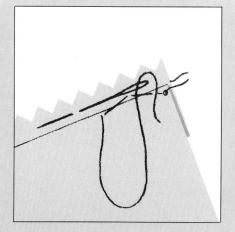

Baste the prepared hem to the garment 1/4 inch from the edge of the hem. Fold the hem along the basting so that the hem lies underneath the garment and the unstitched edge projects above the garment. Using knotted thread, insert the needle through one or two threads of the garment just below the fold and pull the thread through. Then pick up one or two threads just above the fold and 1/2 inch to the left of the previous stitch. Pull the thread through. Continue with similar stitches; end with a fastening stitch on the hem.

THE PRICK STITCH

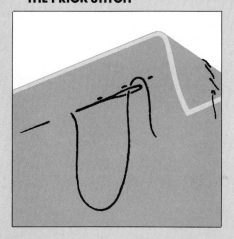

Using a knotted thread, draw the needle up from the bottom layer of fabric and pull it through. Insert the needle to the right three or four threads, and bring it out 1/4 to 3/8 inch to the left of where it last emerged. Continue the process, ending with a fastening stitch on the bottom layer of fabric.

THE BUTTONHOLE STITCH

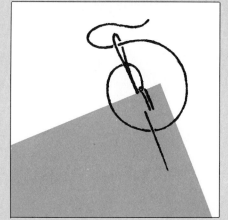

Using a knotted thread, draw the needle up from the wrong side of the fabric 1/8 inch from the top edge. Loop the thread around in a counterclockwise circle and draw the needle up again from the wrong side of the fabric through the point at which it last emerged, keeping the looped thread under the needle. Draw the thread through, pulling it straight up toward the top edge of the fabric. Repeat these steps directly to the left of the first stitch to make close stitches of even length that form a firm ridge along the top. End with a fastening stitch on the wrong side of the fabric.

CREDITS

Sources for the illustrations in this book are shown below. Credits from left to right are separated by semicolons, from top to bottom by dashes.

6,7—Ryszard Horowitz. 10—Paulus Leeser courtesy Costume Institute, The Metropolitan Museum of Art, New York. 11—Picture Collection, Branch Libraries, New York Public Library except center Culver Pictures. 14,15—Ryszard Horowitz, background Marvin E. Newman from Woodfin Camp & Associates. 16,17—Ryszard Horowitz, background Ernst Haas. 18,19—Ryszard Horowitz, background Oscar Buitargo from Black Star. 20,21—Ken Kay. 25—Derek Bayes, from *A Tour in Scotland and Voyage to the Hebrides* by Thomas Pennant, 1776. 26 through 31—Jack Escaloni. 34 —Drawings by Raymond Skibinski. 35 through 47—Drawings by Jane Poliotti. 48,49—Ken Kay. 52,53—Alen MacWeeney, muslin by Bill Blass. 54,55—Tasso Vendikos. 56 through 69—Drawings by Raymond Skibinski. 70 through 79—Drawings by Jane Poliotti. 80,81—Anthony Blake courtesy Colin Hammick. 85—Henry Poole and Co. Ltd. 86 through 89—Anthony Blake courtesy Colin Hammick. 90,91—Reg van Cuÿlenburg. 92 through 95—Tom Jackson. 96 through 101—Drawings by Ted Kliros. 103—Al Freni. Adapted from *The Unfashionable Human Body* by Bernard Rudofsky. 104—Tasso Vendikos. 105 through 111 —Drawings by John Sagan. 112—Tasso Vendikos. 113 through 127—Drawings by John Sagan. 128—Tasso Vendikos. 129 through 133—Drawings by Raymond Skibinski. 134—Tasso Vendikos. 135 through 141—Drawings by Raymond Skibinski. 142 —Tasso Vendikos. 143 through 149 —Drawings by Raymond Skibinski. 150 —Tasso Vendikos. 151 through 159 —Drawings by John Sagan. 160—Tasso Vendikos. 101 through 107—Drawings by John Sagan. 168,169—Tasso Vendikos. 172,173—Drawings from *Evolution of Fashion, 1066-1930 Patterns and Cuts* by Margot Hamilton Hill and Peter Bucknell. Copyright 1967 by Margot Hamilton Hill. Reprinted by permission of Van Nostrand Reinhold Company. 174—Tasso Vendikos. 175—Drawings by Gene Brod and Carmen Mercadal. 176,177—Drawings by Carolyn Mazzello. 178,179—Drawings by Gene Brod and Carmen Mercadal. 180 through 185— Drawings by Carolyn Mazzello. 186— Tasso Vendikos. 187 through 193—Drawings by Raymond Skibinski. 194 through 197—Drawings by John Sagan, 198— Tasso Vendikos. 199 through 203—Drawings by John Sagan.

ACKNOWLEDGMENTS

For their help in preparing this book the editors would like to thank the following individuals: Helen Barer; Giovanni Battistoni; Bill Blass; Leon M. Block, Dunhill Tailors; Karen B. Booth; Roberto Cabrera; K. C. Cole; Audrey C. Foote; Carolyn Mazzello; Isabel B. Wingate.

The editors would also like to thank the following: The Armo Company; Pierre Balmain Boutique; J. Bellini, Inc.; Abe Bloom & Sons; Bloomingdale's; Brooks Brothers; Jerry Brown Imported Fabrics, Inc.; Henri Bendel, Inc.; Butterick Fashion Marketing Co.; David and Dash; T. Jones, Inc.; Lord & Taylor; Maxine Fabrics Co., Inc.; The McCall Pattern Company; William Rose Fabrics; Scalamandré; Morton Sills, Inc.; Southern Worsted Mills, Inc.; Staron-Lafitte; Tiziani of Rome; Weller Fabrics, Inc.; The Wool Bureau.

INDEX

Numerals in italics indicate an illustration of the subject mentioned.

Abdomen, tight, adjusting on muslin, *70*
Acrylic crepe, 32
Adjustment(s), muslin, marking and measuring, *73*
Adjustment(s), to patterns. *See* Pattern(s), adjustments to
Appearance, of fabric(s), *chart 32-33*
Arm length, measurement of, *55*
Armhole(s): adjustment of, *89;* as crucial area of fit, 51, *53;* depth, measurement of, *54,* 55; seam, *154, 156, 157*
Arrowhead tack (tailoring), 96, *100;* instructions for, *100;* left-handed instructions for, *100;* uses of, 96, 100

Back, of man's jacket, adjusting: long, *76;* loose, *75;* narrow, *76;* short, *76*
Back, of woman's jacket, fitting in muslin: long upper, *63;* loose, *64-65;* short upper, *63-64;* tight, *65*
Back length, measurement of, *54-55*
Back pocket, of trousers, *174, 176-179;* with piping, *174, 177;* position of, 174, 176; use of, 174
Back-waist length, measurement of, *55*
Back width, measurement of, *54, 55*
Backstitch (hand sewing), *203*
Bar tack (tailoring), 96, *101;* instructions for, *101;* left-handed instructions for, *101;* uses of, 96, 101, 162, *177, 185, 197*
Basting stitch, diagonal (hand sewing), *203*
Basting stitch, two-handed (tailoring), *96;* instructions for, *96;* left-handed instructions for, *96;* uses of, 96
Batting, cotton, 93
Beater. *See* Tailor's clapper
Belt loops, *186;* constructing, *189, 190, 191;* finishing, *191;* positioning, *190;* turning, *189*
Between(s), *90*
Blass, Bill, 50-53; fitting methods of, *51-53*
Blazer, 102
Blended fabric(s), 32, *chart 32-33,* 93
Blind hemming stitch (hand sewing), *203*
Block, pounding. *See* Tailor's clapper
Bodkin, *90*

Boots, 11, 12, 172, *173*
Breeches, 9, 172, *173*
Brummell, George Bryan (Beau): influence of on fashion, 10-12; style introduced by, *10,* 11
Bust, measurement of, 54, *55*
Bustle, 13
Button(s), 90, *91;* on jacket, *103;* metal, 102; nonfunctional, 102-*103;* outmoded, *103;* on pants pocket, *174,* 197; positioning, *167;* sewing on, 160, *167;* shank for, how to make, *167;* on sleeve, 103; on vest, *103*
Buttonhole(s), 160; bound, *18;* eyelet of, *161;* instructions for, *161-162;* length of, 161; on pants pocket, *174,* 197; placement of, 160, 161, 162; reinforcing with bar tack, 162
Buttonhole stitch (hand sewing), *203*

Canvas, linen, 93
Cape, *18-19*
Carbon paper, dressmaker's, *40*
Carriers. *See* Belt loops
Catch stitch (hand sewing), *202*
Cavalry twill, *chart 32-33*
Chain stitch (tailoring), 96, *99;* instructions for, *99;* left-handed instructions for, *99;* uses of, 96, 99
Chalk, tailor's, 90
Check, hound's-tooth, 24, *27*
Chest circumference, measurement of, *54,* 55
China silk, 32
Clapper, 95; combined with point presser, *94,* 95
Cloth, pressing, *94,* 95
Coat(s): cutaway, 11; in ensemble, 16, *17;* frock, 9; sack, 102-*103*
Coatdress, *16-17*
Collar(s), 142; adjusting, on man's jacket, 54, *74, 75;* construction of, 142, *144-149;* of man's jacket, *142, 144-147;* of woman's jacket, *148-149*
Collar interfacing, *92,* 93
Corner, pulling out, instructions for, *115*
Cotton batting, 93
Cotton fabric(s), 8, 22, *30-31, chart 32-33,* 93
Cotton wadding, 93
Cover cloth, 32, 44, 93, 104
Cravat, 11
Crease(s), trouser; origin of, 171; pressing in, *196*
Crepe: acrylic, 32; wool, *18-19*
Crofter(s), 25
Crotch: fitting, in muslin, *70;* length, measuring, *55;* seam,

closing, 74, *197*
Cuff(s), *169, 198;* with heel stay, *199;* instructions for, 198, *199;* length of, *52;* origin of, 171
Custom tailor(s), *80-89;* introduction to, 82-83, 86; procedure of, for making suit, 84-86; workmanship of, 85-86
Cutaway coat, 11
Cutter, 85, *88*
Cutting, 28, 38, 52

Diagonal basting stitch (hand sewing), *203*
Dinner jacket, 102
Donegal tweed, *chart 32-33*
Double knit fabric(s), *28, chart 32-33*
Doublet(s), 9
Dressmaker's carbon paper, *40*
Dressmaking, 8-9
Dummy, for fitting, *89*
Dunhill Tailors, 83

Easing, 150
Edging, braid, 102
Edinburgh, Duke of, 82
Edward VII, 83, 171
England, production of wool by, 22-24
Ensemble, 16, *17*
Evening clothes, 8, 11, *18-19*
Eyelet, of buttonhole, *161*

Fabric(s), *20-35;* acrylic, *chart 32-33;* appearance of, *chart 32-33;* for blazers, 102; blended, *chart 32-33,* 93; for business suits, *26-27,* 102; camel's hair, 134, 136, 141; canvas, linen, 93; care of, 28; cavalry twill, *chart 32-33;* characteristics of, 27, 28, 30, *chart 32-33;* China silk, *chart 32-33;* choosing, *chart 32-33;* classic, for fine tailoring, 23, *26-29;* for coats, *chart 32-33;* collar interfacing, *92,* 93; cotton, 8, 22, *30-31, chart 32-33;* cotton blends, *chart 32-33,* 93; cotton wadding, 93; cover cloth, *chart 32-33,* 93; crepe, *chart 32-33;* Donegal tweed, *chart 32-33;* double knit, *28, chart 32-33;* for dressmaking, 8; English wool, 22-25; for evening clothes, *18-19,* 102; for facings, 93; finish of, 27, *chart 32-33;* flannel, 28, *29, chart 32-33,* 102; Flemish, 23; folding, *35;* foundation canvas, *92,* 93; gabardine, wool, *16-17, 18,* 24, *26-27, chart 32-33;* glen-plaid, *14-15, 26,* 27;

grain of, *34;* grosgrain, 102; hair canvas, *92,* 93; haircloth interfacing, *chart 32-33, 92,* 93; hand-woven, 24-25; handling of, 28, *chart 32-33;* hard woolen, *27;* Harris tweed, 24-25, *28, chart 32-33;* herringbone, *14,* 15, 24; horsehair cloth, *92,* 93; hound's-tooth check, 24, *27;* interfacing, 8, 23, *chart 32-33, 92,* 93; for jackets, *26-27, chart 32-33;* knit, 28, *chart 32-33,* 34; for lapels, 102; laying out patterns on, *38-39, 41, 42-43;* linen, 22, 30, *31, chart 32-33,* 102; linen canvas, 93; linen interfacing, *92,* 93; lining, *chart 32-33,* 34; make-up of, *chart 32-33;* marking, 38, *40;* melton, wool, 16, *17,* 93; mohair, 102; muslin, 93; map of, 34, 35, 38; novelty weave, *chart 32-33;* novelty tweed, *chart 32-33,* 134, 136, 141; for pants, *chart 32-33;* pinstripe, *14,* 15; plaid, *27,* 28, *35,* 102; plaid, folding, *35;* plaid, laying out patterns on, *41, 42-43;* pocketing, 34, *92,* 93; polyester blends, *chart 32-33;* preparing, *34-35;* preshrinking, 34, *35,* 93; for pressing cloth, 95; for pressing equipment, 95; rayon blends, *chart 32-33;* for sack coats, 102; satin, 102; Saxony, *27, chart 32-33;* Scots tweed, *88;* seersucker, *chart 32-33,* 102; serge, 24, *26, 27, chart 32-33,* 102; Shetland wool, 16, *17;* SiBonne, *chart 32-33;* silesia, 93; silk, 8, 22, *30-31, chart 32-33;* Siri, *chart 32-33;* sizing in, 93, 95; for skirts, *chart 32-33;* for slacks, *chart 32-33;* soft, *28-29;* for sportswear, *28-29, chart 32-33,* 102; stay tape, 93; straightening, *34, 35;* striped, 102; striped, folding, *35;* striped, laying out patterns on, *41, 42-43;* for suits, *26-27, chart 32-33,* 102; for summer wear, 102; surah, *chart 32-33;* taffeta, *chart 32-33;* for tailoring, 8; tartan, 24; texture of, *chart 32-33;* for tropical wear, 102; tropical worsted, *chart 32-33;* for trouser curtain, 93; for trousers, *26-27, chart 32-33;* tweed, 9, 24-25, *28-29, chart 32-33,* 102, 134; twill gabardine, 16, *17;* twill tape, 34, *92,* 93; underlining, *chart 32-33,* 34; undercollar, 93; unfinished worsted, *chart 32-33;* uses of, *chart 32-33;* for variations of sack coat, 102; for vests, *chart 32-33;* wadding, cotton, 93; for waistband interfacing, 93; for warm weather, 30; weave of, 27, 28, *chart* 32-33; wigan, 93; wool, English, 22-25; wool interfacing, *chart* 32-33, 34, 44, *92, 93;* woolen, 22-25, *26-29;* worsted, 8, 24, *26-27, chart* 32-33, 102; woven, 34

Facing(s): fly, *192;* waistband, 93, *193, 195. See also* Lapel(s)

Fasteners, 90, *91*

Fastening stitch (hand sewing), *202*

Findings, *92-93*

Finish, of fabrics, *chart* 32-33

Finished jacket length, measurement of, *54-55*

Fit: crucial areas of, 51-52; importance of, 50-52; introduction of, 10-11; methods of achieving, by Bill Blass, *51-53. See also* Fitting, man's jacket; Fitting, man's trousers; Fitting with muslin

Fitting, man's jacket, *74-77,* 86, *89;* armhole of, *89;* back of, *75, 76;* body of, 77; collar of, *74, 75;* first, *74-77;* neckline of, *74;* second, 77, *126-127;* shoulder of, *75, 89;* sleeve of, 77

Fitting, man's trousers, 74, *78-79*

Fitting, with muslin, *51-53, 56-73;* abdomen, of pants, *70;* adjustments of, marking and measuring, *73;* armhole seam, 51-52, *53;* back of jacket, *63-64, 64-65;* by Bill Blass, *51-53;* crotch, *70;* jacket, *56-65;* marking adjustments in, *73;* measuring adjustments in, *73;* neckline, *57, 58;* pants, *66-72;* around pelvis, 52; seat, 52, *71, 72;* shoulder, 51-52, *53, 59, 60, 61, 62;* side of jacket, *64-65;* side seam of pants, *66, 67, 68;* sleeve, 51-52, *53;* sleeve cap, *61, 62;* upper back of jacket, *63-64;* waist, of pants, 69

Flannel: cotton, 93; wool, 28, *29, chart* 32-33, 102

Flap pocket(s), *112;* instructions for, *118-123*

Fleece, lamb's-wool, 93

Fly front, of trousers, *186;* attaching zipper in, *188, 194;* construction of, 186, *187-188, 192, 194-195, 197;* length of, 186; for man's pants, 186; for woman's pants, 186

Folding: fabric for cutting, 34; solid-colored fabric, *35;* striped or plaid fabric, *35*

Foundation, of jacket:

constructing, *104-111;* for man's jacket, 104, *105-111;* materials for, *92-93,* 102, 104; for woman's jacket, 104, *107-111*

Foundation canvas. *See* Wool interfacing

French tack (tailoring), 96, *101;* instructions for, *101;* use of, 96, 101

Frock coat, 102

Gabardine, *16-17, 18,* 24, *26-27, chart* 32-33

Galligaskins, 172, *173*

George IV, 12, 24

Gimp, 90, *91,* 162

Glen-plaid, *14-15, 26,* 27

Gloss, how to remove, 95

Gorge line, *142, 145*

Grosgrain, 102

Hacking jacket, 102

Hair canvas. *See* Wool interfacing

Haircloth interfacing, 32, 33, 93

Ham, tailor's, *94,* 95

Hammick, Colin, 84, 86, *87*

Hand-woven fabric, 24-25

Handling, of fabric(s), *chart* 32-33

Harris tweed, 24-25, *28-29, chart* 32-33; certification of, *chart* 32-33; characteristics of, 24, 25, *chart* 32-33; as hand-made woolen, 24-25; manufacture of, *24-25*

Hawes & Curtis Ltd., 82

Heel stay, 198; instructions for, *199*

Hem(s): instructions for, *137, 141,* 150, *151, 153;* reinforcing, 134, *136, 141,* 150, *151*

Hemming stitch (hand sewing), *202*

Hemming stitch, blind (hand sewing), *203*

Herringbone, *14,* 15, 24

Hip, measurement of, *54-55*

Horsehair cloth, *92,* 93, 104

Hose, *172-173*

Hound's-tooth check, 24, *27*

Hunting costume, 11, *80-81,* 84

Huntsman, H., & Sons, Ltd., *80-81,* 84, *86, 87,* 88

Inseam, measurement of, *54,* 55

Interfacing(s): amount of needed, 44; collar, *92,* 93, *144;* cotton, *92,* 93; cover-cloth, 44, *45,* cutting, *45, 46, 47;* in foundation of man's jacket, 104; haircloth, 44, *45,* 85; lapel, *126;* linen, *92,* 93; for man's jacket,

32, *44-45,* 74, *105-111, 124-125;* marking, *44, 45, 46, 47;* measuring for, 44; preparation of, 34; shrinking, 34; tips for, 44; types of, 44; waistband, 93, *186;* for woman's jacket, 32, 44, *46-47, 107-111, 124-125;* wool, 32, 24, *44, 45, 46,* 85, *92,* 93, 104

Iron, 95

Jacket(s), man's: armhole seam of, 154, 156; assembling for first fitting, *108-111;* back of, assembling, 134, *135-139;* buttonholes on, 160, *161-162;* buttons on, 160, *167;* collar of, *142, 144-147;* constructing foundation for, 104, *105-107;* dinner, *18-19,* 102; fabrics for, *26-27, chart* 32-33; finishing, 160; first fitting of, *109-111;* fitting, *74-77,* 86, *89, 126-127;* front of, constructing, *112-133;* history of, 102; interfacings of, 44, *105-107;* lapels of, constructing, *125-126,* 128, *129-133;* lining of, 128, *130, 133, 137-139, 152-153, 156, 157,* 160, *161;* making of, by custom tailor, 85, *88-89;* molding, 95; nonfunctional elements of, 102-103; pockets of, constructing, *112, 114-123;* pressing, 95, 160, *163-165;* reinforcing materials for, *92-93, 104;* reinforcement of, *88-89,* 134; second fitting of, 77, *126-127;* Shetland wool, *16-17;* shoulder of, *143-144;* shoulder pads in, 150, *155;* sleeve head of, *157;* sleeves of, *150, 151-157;* tartan, 24; timelessness of, 102-103; underlining of, *41;* variations of, 102; vents in, *134, 135, 151-152. See also* Fitting, man's jacket

Jacket(s), woman's: assembling for first fitting, *108-111;* back of, assembling, 134, *140-141;* by Bill Blass, *52-53;* buttonholes on, 160, *161-162;* buttons on, 160, *167;* collar of, 142, *148-149;* early 20th Century, *11;* fabrics for, *26-27, chart* 32-33; finishing, 160; first fitting of, 111; fitting, *51-53, 56-73;* foundation for, constructing, 104, *107-108;* front of, constructing, *112-133;* glen-plaid, *14-15;* interfacing of, 44, 104, *107-108;* lapels of, *125-126, 128-133;* lining of, 128, *152,* 160, *165-167;* molding, 95; muslin mockup of, *51-53, 56-73;* pockets of, *112, 114-123;*

pressing, 95, 160, *163-165;* reinforcement of, 134; reinforcing materials for, *92-93,* 104; second fitting of, 77, *126-127;* shoulder of, *143,* 158; shoulder pads in, 150, *159;* sleeves of, 150, *151-152, 158;* timelessness of, 102-103; underlining of, *41;* vents in, 134. *See also* Fitting, with muslin

Jacket length, measurement of, *54-55*

Kilt(s), 24

Knit fabric(s): double, *28, chart* 32-33; preparation of, 34; straightening, *34*

Lamb's-wool fleece, 93

Lapel(s), *128-133;* construction of, 128, *129-133;* curve of, shaping, *43;* interfacing of, padding, *126;* notched, *11,* 102; origin of, 102; roll line of, *125,* 128; sewing collar to, 142

Laws, protective, 23-24

Length, of pants, 198

Linen(s): for interfacing, *92,* 93; for tailored clothes, 22, 23, 30, *31, chart* 32-33, 102

Lining(s): fabrics for, preparing, *34;* of man's jacket, 128, *130, 133, 137-139, 152-153, 156, 157,* 160, *161;* of sleeve of man's jacket, 150, *152-153, 156-157;* of woman's jacket, 128, *152,* 160, *165-167*

Loops, belt. *See* Belt loops

Makeup, of fabric(s), *chart* 32-33

Marking(s), pattern, transferring to fabric, 38; tools for, 38, 40-41

Measurement(s): for adjusting pattern, 54, 74; for buying pattern, 54; crucial, for women's garments, 51; by custom tailor, *84-85;* how to take, *54-55;* men's, *54,* 55, 74; women's, 51, 54, 55

Measuring tape, *90-91*

Melton cloth, 16, *17,* 93, 142

Military tunic, 102

Mohair, 102

Morton, Digby, 170

Muslin. *See* Fitting, with muslin

Muslin (fabric), 93

Nap: direction of, 34; layout, 38

Neckline, fitting: loose, *58, 74;* tight, *57*

Needle(s), *90*

Norfolk jacket, 102
Notion(s), 90
Novelty tweed, *chart* 32-33, 134, 136, 141
Novelty weave, *chart* 32-33

Overcast stitch (hand sewing), *202*
Oxford bags, 171

Padding, 8, 102. *See also* Shoulder pad(s)
Padding stitch (tailoring), 96, *98;* instructions for, *98;* left-handed instructions for, *98;* uses of, 96, 98, 155, 159
Pantaloons, *10,* 11
Pants. *See* Fitting, man's trousers; Fitting, with muslin; Trousers
Pantsuit, 13
Pattern(s), adjustment(s) to: at abdomen, *70;* from adjusted muslin, 56, *57-72;* from body measurements, 54, 56, 74; at crotch, *70;* for jacket, from muslin, 56, *57-65;* of jacket back, *63, 64, 65;* of jacket side, *65;* before making muslin, 56; for man's garments, 54, 74; from muslin, 56, *57-72;* at neckline, *57, 58;* for pants, from muslin, *66-72;* at pants side seam, *66, 67, 68;* at seat, *71, 72;* at shoulder, *59, 60, 61, 62;* at sleeve cap, *61, 62;* of upper jacket back, *63, 64;* at waist, *69*
Pattern(s), laying out, 38; jacket, on plaid or striped fabric, *42-43;* jacket, on solid-colored fabric, *39;* on napped fabric, 38; pants, on plaid or striped fabric, *41;* pants, on solid-colored fabric, 38; on solid-colored fabric, 38, *39;* on striped or plaid fabric, 38, *41, 42-43*
Pattern(s), modifying: to add tailoring details, 36; to allow for ease, 36; to correct vent of back-lining piece, 36; to correct vent of sleeve, 37; for cuffs, 36; to eliminate standard sewing features, 36; for pants, *37;* to remove darts, 36, *37;* for striped or plaid fabric, 36, *37;* for style, 36
Pattern marking(s), transferring to fabric, 38; methods of, 38, *40-41;* with tailor tacks, 40; tools for, 38, 40-41; with tracing wheel and carbon, 40
Philip, Prince, 82
Pinks, hunting, 84
Pinstripe, *14,* 15

Piping: on back pants pocket, *174, 177;* on flap pocket, *112, 120-121*
Plaid fabric: folding, *35;* glen, *26, 27;* laying out jacket pattern on, *42-43;* laying out pants pattern on, *41;* Saxony, *27*
Pleats, *18,* 102
Pocket(s) *103, 112, 174;* back trouser, *174, 176-179;* flap, *112, 118-123;* jacket, *112, 114-123;* with piping, *112, 118-123; 174, 177;* position of, 37, 174, 176; side trouser, *174, 180-185;* trouser, *174, 176-185;* uses of, 103, 174; welt, *112, 114-118*
Pocketing fabric, 34, *92,* 93
Polyester blend(s), 32
Point presser, 95; combined with clapper, *94,* 95
Poole, Henry, 83, 84, 85
Pounding block. *See* Tailor's clapper
Preshrinking, 34, *35*
Press mitt, 95
Pressing: equipment for, *94,* 95; final, 160, *163-165;* importance of, 95; purpose of, 95
Pressing cloth, *94,* 95
Prick stitch (hand sewing), *203*
Pulling out corner(s), instructions for, *115*
Pumps, 11

Rayon, 32
Reinforcing materials, *92-93*
Riding jacket, 102
Rise, measurement of, *54,* 55
Ruler, *90*
Running stitch (hand sewing), *202*

Sack coat, 102, 103
Sample model, 51, *52-53*
Sari, 8
Satin, 102
Savile Row, *83-86*
Saxony, *27, chart* 32-33
Scissors, *90*
Scotland: production of woolens by, 24-25; tartans of, 24; tweeds of, 24-25, *88*
Seat: measurement of, *54,* 55; fitting, in muslin, *71, 72*
Seersucker, *chart* 32-33, 102
Serge, 24, *26,* 27, *chart* 32-33, 102
Sharp(s), 90
Shawl collar, 11
Shears, tailor's, *90-91*
Shetland wool, 16, *17*
Shine, how to remove, 95
Shoulder, *143-144;* adjustment of, on man's jacket, *75, 80-81, 89;*

as crucial area of fit, 51, *53;* fitting, in muslin, *59-62;* of man's jacket, *143-144;* of woman's jacket, *143*
Shoulder pad(s), *92,* 93, 102, *111,* 150, *155, 159*
Shoulder width, measurement of, *54,* 55
Side, jacket, fitting in muslin, 64-65
Side pocket, of trousers, *174, 180-185*
Side seam length, measurement of, *55*
Silesia, 93
Silk(s): China, 32; interfacing fabric for, 32; linen-textured, *chart* 32-33; lining fabrics for, 32; surah, 32; taffeta, 32; for tailoring, 8, 22, 23, *30-31, chart* 32-33
Sizing, 93, 95
Skirt(s), fabrics for, *chart* 32-33
Sleeve(s), *150;* armhole seam of, 51, *53;* assembling, *127;* attaching, in man's jacket, 150, *154-155;* attaching, in woman's jacket, 150, *158-159;* construction of, 150, *151-152;* easing of at sleeve cap, 150; fitting, *53,* 74, 77, 155; lining of, in man's jacket, 150, *152-153, 156-157;* shoulder pads with, 150, *155, 159;* sleeve heads with, 150; vents of, 150, *151*
Sleeve board, *94,* 95
Sleeve cap, 61, 62, 93
Sleeve cushion, *94,* 95
Sleeve heads, *92,* 93, 150, *157*
Sleeve length, measurement of, *54,* 55
Slip stitch (hand sewing), *202*
Sponge, *94,* 95
Squaring corner, instructions for, *115*
Stay tape, 93
Stitch(es), hand sewing, *96-101, 202-203;* arrowhead tack, 96, *100;* backstitch, *203;* bar tack, 96, *101;* basting, diagonal, *203;* basting, two-handed, *96;* blind hemming, *203;* buttonhole, *203;* catch, *202;* chain, 96, *99;* in custom tailoring, 85-86; diagonal basting, *203;* fastening, *202;* French tack, 96, *101;* hemming, *202;* hemming, blind, *203;* instructions for, *96-101, 202-203;* overcast, *202;* padding, 96, *98;* permanent, 96, *98-101;* prick, *203;* running, *202;* slip, *202;* tack, arrowhead, 96, *100;* tack, bar, 96, *101;* tack, French, 96, *101;* tack, tailor, 96, *97;* tailor tack, 96, *97;*

temporary, *96-97;* two-handed basting, *96*
Stitch(es), tailoring, *96-101;* arrowhead tack, 96, *100;* bar tack, 96, *101;* basting, two-handed, *96;* chain, 96, *99;* French tack, 96, *101;* instructions for, *96-101;* padding, 96, *98;* permanent, 96, *98-101;* tack, arrowhead, 96, *100;* tack, bar, 96, *101;* tack, French, 96, *101;* tack, tailor, 96, *97;* tailor tack, 96, *97;* temporary, *96-97;* two-handed basting, *96*
Straightening fabric, *34, 35*
Striker. *See* Tailor's clapper
Striker (cutter), 85
Striped fabric: folding, *35;* laying out jacket pattern on, *42-43;* laying out pants pattern on, *41*
Structuring materials, *92-93*
Suit(s), man's: cost of custom-made, 84; double-breasted, *14,* 15; fabrics for, *26-27;* foundations of, *92-93;* French, 1826, *10;* key measurements for, *54-55;* process of making, in Savile Row, 84-86; sculptured style of, *10;* single-breasted, *14,* 15; two-piece, as wardrobe staple, *14-15;* wide-lapelled, *14,* 15. *See also* Jacket(s), man's; trousers
Suit(s), woman's: by Bill Blass, *52-53;* evening, *18;* fabrics for, *26-27;* foundations of, *92-93;* of jacket and trousers, *14-15;* key measurements for, *54-55;* man-tailored, early 20th Century, *11;* muslin mockup of, *52-53. See also* Jacket(s), woman's; trousers
Surah, silk, 32
Synthetics, 22

Tack, arrowhead, 96, *100;* instructions for, *100;* left-handed instructions for, *100;* uses of, 96, 100
Tack, bar, 96, *101;* instructions for, *101;* left-handed instructions for, *101;* uses of, 96, 101, 162, 177, *185*
Tack, French, 96, *101;* instructions for, *101;* uses of, 96, 101
Tack, tailor, *40,* 96, *97;* instructions for, *97;* left-handed instructions for, *97;* uses of, *40,* 97
Taffeta, 32
Tail coat, 102
Tailor tack, *40,* 96, 97; instructions for, *97;* left-handed instructions

for, *97;* uses of, *40,* 97
Tailoring: compared with
  dressmaking, 8-9; emphasis of
  on fit, 10; English leadership in,
  9-10; history of, 9-13; influence
  of Beau Brummell on, 10-12;
  tools for, 85, *90-91;* of women's
  clothes, 12-13
Tailor's bodkin, *90*
Tailor's chalk, 90
Tailor's clapper, 95; combined
  with point presser, *94,* 95
Tailor's ham, *94,* 95
Tailor's shears, *90-91*
Tailor's sleeve cushion, 94, 95
Tailor's thimble, 90, *91*
Tape, measuring, *90-91*
Tape, stay, 93
Tape, twill, *92,* 93
Tape measure, *90-91*
Tartan(s), 24
Texture, of fabrics, *chart 32-33*
Thimble, tailor's, 90, *91*
Thread(s), 90, *91*
Toga, 8
Tracing wheel, *40*
Trews, 24
Tropical worsted, *chart 32-33*
Trouser curtain, 93, 186, *195, 197;*
  attaching, *195;*
  finishing, *197*
Trousers: adjusting length of, *52;*
  assembling, 174, *175;* belt
  loops of, 170, *186, 189-191;*
  creases in, 171, *196;* crucial
  measurement for, 52; cuffless,

hemming, *199;* with cuffs, *198,
  199;* fabrics for, *26-27, chart 32-
  33;* facings of, *192-195, 197;* fly
  front of, *186, 187-188, 194-195,
  197;* heel stays of, *199;* history
  of styles in, 170-171, *172-173;*
  length of, 198; loose-cuffed,
  1826, *10;* man's slacks, 16, *17;*
  pantaloons, 1826, *10;* pockets
  of, *174, 176-183, 185;*
  sculptured style of, 1826, *10;*
  styles of, set by Beau
  Brummell, *10;* tartan, 24; trews,
  24; trouser curtain on, 193, 197;
  waistband of, *186, 189-191,
  194, 197;* woman's, *14-15,* 16,
  17; women's, history of, 13;
  zipper of, *194. See also* Fitting,
  man's trousers; Fitting, with
  muslin; Pants
Tunic, military, 102
Tuxedo, 102
Tweed(s), *28-29;* characteristics
  of, 8, 24, 25, 28; Donegal, *chart
  32-33;* Harris, 24-25, *28-29,
  chart 32-33;* novelty, *chart 32-
  33,* 134, 136, 141; uses of, 8,
  chart 32-33, 102. *See also*
  Harris tweed
Twill, cavalry, *chart 32-33*
Twill, gabardine, 16, *17*
Twill tape, *92,* 93
Two-handed basting (tailoring),
  96; instructions for, *96;* left-
  handed instructions for, *96;*
  uses of, 96

Undercollar: fabrics for, 93, 142;
  of man's jacket, 142; preparing,
  111; of woman's jacket, 142
Underlining, 28, 32, 34, *41*
Unfinished worsted, *chart 32-33*
Uses, of fabrics, *chart 32-33*

Vent(s): in jacket back, 103, *134,
  135, 151-152;* in sleeves, 150,
  151
Vest(s), 84

Wadding, cotton, 93
Waist, measurement of, *54-55*
Waist length, measurement of,
  54-55
Waistband, of trousers, 74, 186;
  construction of, *186, 189-191,
  193-195, 197;* facing of, 93;
  interfacing of, 93
Waistcoat, 11
Walking costume, *11*
Waulking, 25
Weave, of fabric, 27, *chart 32-33*
Welt pocket(s), *112;* instructions
  for, *114-118*
White tie and tails, 102
Wigan, 93
Windsor, Duke of,
  170, 171
Wool, English, 22-25;
  characteristics of, 22-23; as
  classic fabric for tailoring, 23;
  economic importance of, 22,

23, 24; hand-woven, 24-25;
  history of, 22, 23-24; production
  of, 22, 23; protective laws
  concerning, 23-24; quality of,
  22; Scottish, 24-25; tweeds, 24-
  25; tartans, 24; worsteds, 24
Wool interfacing, 32, 34, 44, *92,*
  93, 104
Woolen(s), *26-27;* for business
  suits, 26, *27;* characteristics of,
  27, *chart 32-33;* English, 22; for
  fine tailoring, *26-27;* Flemish,
  23-24; hard, *26-27;* linings for,
  32; for tailored jackets, *26-27;*
  underlinings for, 32; uses of, 27,
  chart 32-33; weave of, 27
Woolsack, 22
Worsted(s), *26-27;* for business
  suits, *26-27;* characteristics of,
  8, 24, 27, *chart 32-33;* for fine
  tailoring, *26-27;* for formal
  jackets, 102; history of, 24;
  types of, 24, *chart 32-33;* uses
  of, 27, *chart 32-33*
Woven fabric, preparing:
  checking alignment of, *34;*
  folding, *35;* preshrinking, 35;
  straightening, *34, 35*

Yardstick, *90*

Zipper(s), 90, 91; attaching, 74,
  186, *188, 194*
Zoot suit, 171